Wilfried Raussert, Matti Steinitz (Eds.)

Black Power in Hemispheric Perspective

Movements and Cultures of Resistance in the Black Americas

INTER-AMERICAN STUDIES
Cultures – Societies – History

ESTUDIOS INTERAMERICANOS
Culturas – Sociedades – Historia

Volume 25

Wilfried Raussert, Matti Steinitz (Eds.)

Black Power in Hemispheric Perspective

Movements and Cultures of Resistance in the Black Americas

Wissenschaftlicher Verlag Trier

Copublished by

UNO University of New Orleans Press

Black Power in Hemispheric Perspective.
Movements and Cultures of Resistance in the Black Americas /
Ed. by Wilfried Raussert, Matti Steinitz. –
(Inter-American Studies | Estudios Interamericanos; 25)
Trier: WVT Wissenschaftlicher Verlag Trier, 2022
ISBN 978-3-86821-959-3
New Orleans, LA: University of New Orleans Press, 2022
ISBN 978-1-60801-229-9

SPONSORED BY THE
Federal Ministry of Education and Research

The project, on which this book is based, has been funded by the German Federal Ministry of Education and Research (Bundesministerium für Bildung und Forschung, BMBF). The responsibility for the content of this publication lies with the authors.

Cover Image: Alina Muñoz

Cover Design: Brigitta Disseldorf

Library of Congress Cataloging-in-Publication Data

Names: Raussert, Wilfried, editor. | Steinitz, Matti, editor.
Title: Black power in hemispheric perspective : movements and cultures of resistance in the black Americas / Wilfried Raussert, Matti Steinitz (eds.).
Description: Trier : Wissenschaftlicher Verlag Trier ; New Orleans : University of New Orleans Press, 2022. | Series: Inter-American studies; 25 | Includes bibliographical references.
Identifiers: LCCN 2022030140 | ISBN 9781608012299 (paperback)
Subjects: LCSH: Black power--America. | Black people--Political activity--America. | Black people--America--History--20th century. | African Americans--Politics and government--20th century. | Black people--Latin America--Politics and government--20th century.
Classification: LCC E29.B53 B55 2022 | DDC 305.89607--dc23/eng/20220812
LC record available at https://lccn.loc.gov/2022030140

Publisher: WVT Wissenschaftlicher Verlag Trier, Postfach 4005, D-54230 Trier, Bergstraße 27, D-54295 Trier, Tel. 0049 651 41503, Fax 41504, www.wvttrier.de, wvt@wvttrier.de

Copublisher: University of New Orleans Press, 2000 Lakeshore Drive, Earl K. Long Library, Room 221, New Orleans, LA 70148, United States, 504-280-7457, unopress.org

Table of Content

Introduction: Black Power in Hemispheric Perspective

WILFRIED RAUSSERT AND MATTI STEINITZ

"1968" was a generation-defining year for millions of young radical activists who took part in a series of simultaneous, and often interrelated, protest movements for social and racial justice, peace, gender equality, and liberation from colonialism, capitalism, patriarchy, and white supremacy around the world. In tune with global events, 1968 was also a watershed year in the African American freedom struggle, which was perceived by many contemporaries as the vanguard of the global 1960s youth rebellion The assassination of Martin Luther King, Jr., on April 4, 1968, a series of urban rebellions across the United States, and the escalation of the Vietnam War accelerated the rise of the Black Power movement and black nationalism as dominant forces among African American youth who had lost faith in the outcome and the prospects of the Civil Rights movement's moderate leadership and their integrationist and non-violent approach to resistance. The release of James Brown's "Say It Loud – I'm Black and I'm Proud" in August of the same year gave voice to a new mood of black pride, militancy, and assertiveness, quickly reaching the status of a Black Power anthem not only between Watts and Harlem, but also among Afrodescendants in Rio de Janeiro, Montreal, Kingston, and Panama. When U.S. fast-track athletes Tommie Smith and John Carlos – a son of Afro-Cuban immigrants from Harlem – raised their black-gloved fists during a medal ceremony at the 1968 Summer Olympics in Mexico City, they reinforced the widespread feeling of connectedness and identification with the black liberation struggle in the United States. As Afro-Colombian writer Manual Zapata Olivella remembers in *¡Levántate Mulato!* (1990), "the shout of the black revolution," thus broadcast worldwide on television, "shook the slumbering minds of blacks" across the diaspora, "each time the human lightning bolts ascended the winner's podium to raise the victorious fist of 'Black Power'" (Zapata Olivella 331, authors' translation).

In October 2018, marking the 50th anniversary of "1968", a group of scholars, activists, musicians, and artists from Brazil, Canada, Colombia, Cuba, Ecuador, Germany, Great Britain, Jamaica, Peru, Puerto Rico, Suriname, and the United States gathered at the Center for InterAmerican Studies (Bielefeld University, Germany) for the conference "Black Power – Movements, Cultures, and Resistance in the Black Americas." The conference provided a platform to discuss the multifaceted meanings and legacies of Black Power which "radically altered America's social, political, and cultural landscape" and constituted "one of the twentieth century's most important, and controversial, movements for social justice" (Joseph, "The Black Power Movement" 27), human rights, and radical democracy. The meeting was hosted by the Black Americas Network,[1] an international network of scholars, artists, and activists who explore and express the development of black movements, cultures, and histories through a hemispheric lens and who share the belief that "the production of knowledge can only be understood comprehensively if its specific historical-political plurilocal context is taken into account" (Kaltmeier, "General Introduction" 2). The essays collected in this volume are intended to deepen some of the transdisciplinary dialogues on the manifold dimensions of "Black Power" in the Western Hemisphere initiated at the 2018 network conference and its forerunner "Entangled Black Americas" (2017). These paired conferences sought to bring into comparative and international perspective manifestations of cultural, social, and political resistance in the Black Americas that are too often studied in isolation. According to Kate Quinn, this has been "a consequence, in part, of regional divisions within the academy that in many cases have separated studies of the United States from those of Africa, the Caribbean, and other diasporic locations where Black Power had resonance" (Quinn, "Introduction"1).

Whereas there is an increased interest in the transnational dimensions of the movement in the ever-growing field of Black Power Studies, it is quite surprising that its broad impact in the Western Hemisphere has not been addressed more specifically. While a growing concern with Afrodescendant cultures can be noted throughout the Americas, an attempt to capture a comprehensive tapestry mapping Black Power and its hemispheric presence is still missing. The present book wishes to fill this gap by highlighting how the slogans, symbols, and sounds provided by Black Power heralded a new era of Afro-diasporic defiance, militancy, and cultural awareness which transcended the U.S. national boundaries and left its footprints throughout the Americas. As we aim to show, the United States, while certainly a very important center of Black Power activities, was not the only national territory in which influential black movements embedded in transnational, translocal, and transcultural dialogues emerged. This volume sheds light on the very diverse ways Black Power encouraged the emergence of musical genres, antiracist movements, and border-crossing networks of solidarity among Afro-descendants in the Caribbean, Latin and North America, which continue to shape the political and cultural expressions of the Black Americas in the twenty-first century.

In a sense, this volume focuses on the transnational, transcultural, and intergenerational impact of Black Power on movements and popular culture in the Americas and the rich traditions of resistance it was built upon, addressing the following ques-

---

1 Black Americas Network is a platform for transnational exchange between activists, artists, musicians, and scholars whose research, artwork, or activism is related to the Afro-diasporic presence in the Americas. The network was launched by the editors of this volume in 2016 as part of the project "Between Spanish Harlem, Black Rio, and Funky Colón" (funded by DFG-German Research Community), whose findings will be published in *Soul Music and the Rise of Black Power in Afro-Latin America* (2022) by Matti Steinitz.

tions: What turned the Trinidadian-born SNCC leader Stokely Carmichael's call for "Black Power" at a 1966 civil rights march in Mississippi into a global rallying cry that mobilized people in geographically, linguistically, and culturally diverse places? How did discourses, slogans, and symbols of Black Power cross ethnic and national boundaries and how did these influences manifest themselves in local movements, popular culture, literature, and music? How did sociocultural particularities and specific historical configurations as related to different histories of colonial domination, racial and imperial regimes, nation-building, class and gender relations influence the ways Black Power was articulated, translated, rejected or suppressed? What do new generations of activists, artists, and musicians learn from the lessons and legacies of Black Power?

Widening the scope: from Haiti to Black Lives Matter

Departing from the assumption that ideologies and practices of "Black Power" have not only transcended space but also time, we propose a flexible and non-orthodox understanding of the term that encompasses the most diverse political and cultural manifestations of what Cedric J. Robinson has defined as the "black radical tradition" (1983). While the Black Power movement is usually understood as the period of African American freedom struggle between the years 1966 and 1975 in the United States, this volume is committed to the conceptualization of an inter-American perspective on Afro-diasporic movements and cultures which situates Black Power within a much broader temporal and geographical scope than the one that has dominated the scholarly established U.S.-centered master narrative. By including forerunners and sources of inspiration as well as successors and heirs of the movement, we intend to approach the topic from a holistic point of view, one which comprises diverse protagonists of black empowerment and resistance against white supremacy in its diverse hemispheric expressions since at least the eighteenth century.

Adopting Michael West and William Martin's broad historical framework of a "Black International," we conceive Black Power as an essential manifestation of a world-historical movement described by the authors as a tradition of "globally connected waves of struggles by African peoples" (West and Martin 3), which can be traced back to hemispheric manifestations of slave resistance as maroon societies, *palenques*, and *quilombos*, and, importantly, the "Black Jacobins" (James) of the Haitian Revolution (1791–1804). In their periodization of black internationalism, West and Martin contextualize the Black Power era, arguing that "the movements and activists that made up the long black Sixties were driven into combat by the unfulfilled dreams and broken promises of abolition, decolonization, and desegregation" (22). In *Black Cosmopolitanism*, Ifeoma Nwankwo holds that discussions among black abolitionists such as Frederick Douglass and David Walker sparked by the Haitian Revolution constituted the beginning of a "transnational idea of Black community" and a crucial point of departure for an understanding of the interactions between Afrodescendants in the Americas and their struggles "to define self and community between multiple local and global affinities" (8). Combining these approaches with our comprehensive use of the term, the Haitian Revolution may be interpreted as the birth of Black Power in the Americas. W.E.B. Du Bois gave this internationalist tradition in black thought a new impetus when, at the First Pan-African Conference, held in London in 1900, he predicted that "[t]he problem of the twentieth century will be the problem of the color-line – the relation of the darker to the lighter races of men in Asia and Africa, in America and the islands of the sea" (10). Like his contemporary and rival Marcus Garvey, he prominently argued for an internationalization of the African American freedom struggle. Proving the transgenerational continuity of Afro-diasporic radicalism, Garvey's and Du Bois's global visions of black liberation and the interconnectedness of struggles in the Americas, Asia, and Africa was taken up decades later by Malcolm X who would become a towering figure for the most diverse currents within the Black Power movement after his assassination in 1965 (Sales; Marable).

In many ways, the rise of hip-hop in the late 1970s and early 1980s represented a temporal and geographical bridge that not only connected younger generations of African Americans and (Afro-)Latin American migrants in the United States with sonic, aesthetic, and political representations of Black Power but also facilitated their hemispheric dissemination in countries like Brazil, Colombia, and Cuba, where the genre has become an important platform for the articulation of anti-racist critique and black assertiveness (Castillo-Garsow and Nichols; Collins, *From Black Power to Hip Hop*; Ogbar, *Hip-Hop Revolution*; Rose; Rabaka; Saunders). Proving the enduring impact of the symbols and slogans of the 1960s and 1970s, the first decades of the twenty-first century have witnessed a full-scale resurgence of Black Power-inspired activism, manifesting itself in the rise of the Black Lives Matter movement, black athletes taking a knee at globally televised sports events, the omnipresence of intersectionality theories rooted in black feminism in academia and social movements, and a wave of black consciousness in popular music as most prominently displayed by Beyoncé's tribute to Malcolm X and the Black Panthers at her 2016 Super Bowl performance (Lebron; Taylor, *From #blacklivesmatter to Black Liberation*). The emergence of hemispheric networks of solidarity as manifested by acts of protest across the Americas, especially after the assassinations of Afro-Brazilian politician Marielle Franco, Breonna Taylor, George Floyd, and many others, reinforced our belief even further that a look at the past might provide valuable insights to understand the interrelatedness of present forms of global black resistance to regimes of white supremacy and its intersections with class- and gender-based forms of oppression (Bowen et al.; Pousadela)

Theorizing the Black Americas: Transnational and hemispheric perspectives

African Diaspora Studies

This volume draws on various strands of scholarship that have been animated by a generalized drive to overcome "methodological nationalisms" (Wimmer and Schiller) in research on movements and cultures in the Americas. The growing number of studies on the multidirectional flows and movements that have connected African American culture and politics with Afro-diasporic experiences from other contexts provides ample resources for an understanding of the transnational roots and routes of Black Power and the centrality of African American influences as a "source of cultural and political raw material" (Gilroy, *There Ain't No Black* 171) in the emancipation struggles of racialized groups beyond the black community in the United States. These developments come at the heels of the realization that African American Studies (the establishment of which was a major achievement of the Black Power movement), very much like other fields in U.S. academia, have also been influenced by the broad vision we know as American exceptionalism. Dominated by Afrocentrist and black cultural nationalist currents and their promotion of unifying narratives, the tendency to universalize the black experience in the United States, and to often ignore the different dynamics of race in other diasporic contexts was a major characteristic of this form of African American exceptionalism in the late twentieth century (Hanchard, "Black Transnationalism"; Carby and Shatz).

Fueled by ongoing debates about "globalization" and "transnationalism" and unleashed in no small measure by Paul Gilroy's *Black Atlantic* (1992) and his proposal to envision black countercultures beyond national boundaries and essentialist ideologies, the emergence of African Diaspora Studies was driven by the desire to develop a global view of blackness in the New and Old Worlds. While criticized heavily, among other things, for his exclusive focus on matters of cultural exchange between the United States and Europe and his blanket de-legitimization of black nationalism as reactionary essentialism without engaging with its ideological diversity as well as the key role it played in the emergence of the Black Atlantic world, Gilroy did spark a very fruitful and ongoing debate on movements and cultures in the African Diaspora (Chivallon; Chrisman; Lipsitz).[2] In the last three decades, research on the black presence in the United States has gone through a remarkable process of transnationalization towards "the study of African-descended populations across spatial, temporal, linguistic, cultural, and historical boundaries that do not always correspond to the borders of nation-

2 In line with a range of U.S.-based critics of Gilroy, George Lipsitz argues: "While devastatingly accurate in his rebuttal of nationalist claims for primordial, trans-cultural, and trans-historical essences uniting diasporic Africans, Gilroy unfortunately defines as 'essentialist' just about any strategy that relies on ethnic solidarity. But people who catch hell just because they are black act logically and reasonably when they use blackness as a means of augmenting group power and solidarity" (Lipsitz 196).

states nor to the borders of academic disciplines," as Michael Hanchard has pointed out ("Black Transnationalism" 139f). For its emphasis on border-crossing, intercultural, and transversal flows, the concept of African Diaspora has been crucial to what has been labelled the "transnational turn" in American Studies (141). Referring to Walter Mignolo, Quito Swan has argued that African Diaspora Studies constitutes "an interdisciplinary project of Black transnational border thinking" ("Transnationalism" 209).

Marxist African Diaspora scholars such as Robin D. G. Kelley, have long criticized the tendency to "think of identities as cultural matters, when in fact some of the most dynamic (transnational) identities are created in the realm of politics, in the way people of African descent sought alliances and political identifications across oceans and national boundaries" (Kelley, "Uses and Limits" 32). In their influential essay "Unfinished Migrations," Kelley and Tiffany Ruby Patterson argue that black transnationalism is by no means limited or necessarily linked to "pan-Africanism or other kinds of black-isms. Indeed, sometimes it lives through or is integrally tied to other kinds of international movements – socialism, communism, feminism, surrealism, and religions such as Islam" (Kelley and Patterson 27). Based on these assumptions, multiple studies have conceptualized the ways in which ideologies and practices of *black internationalism*, *black transnationalism*, and *black cosmopolitanism* have provided different generations of Afro-diasporic activists, artists, musicians, and intellectuals with means to engage with colonialism, imperialism, capitalist modernity, patriarchy, and systems of white supremacy across the constraints of exclusionary national projects. According to Quito Swan, "the Black Power movement arguably was the most visible example of global Black transnationalism since the UNIA" ("Transnationalism" 210).

Problematizing essentialized notions of blackness and emphasizing the frequently neglected role of black women in these international struggles, recent scholarship on the African Diaspora and black transnationalism addresses differences within the experiences of Afrodescendants, highlighting the role of empire, nation, class, and gender in the often contradictory and multifaceted dimensions of the Black Americas (Blain; Boyce-Davis; Edwards; Stephens, "What Is This Black," *Black Empire*; Tomlinson). In their effort to complicate one-dimensional narratives of timeless black unity, these approaches intend to provide answers to critical questions such as the one which move many of the essays brought together in this volume: How have different colonial legacies, nationalist imaginaries, the role of U.S. imperialism, class and gender divisions, and black migrations defined the patterns of racial subordination and Afro-diasporic resistance in diverse New World contexts?

Afro-Latin American Studies

One of the most criticized features of Gilroy's *Black Atlantic* and other mappings of the African Diaspora has been the absence of Latin America in their accounts of transnational blackness. Considering that the roughly 130 million Afrodescendants living in Latin America make up for a much larger share of the African Diaspora in the Americas than the 40 million African Americans with whose achievements in politics, culture, and sports, people across the globe are familiar with, these imbalances seem paradoxical. This has not only been the result of the global dominance of U.S.-centered approaches and the reproduction of existing hierarchies in academic debates on the African Diaspora which tend to favor Anglophone perspectives, but also of long-lasting traditions of invisibilization and folklorization of black expressions in Latin American academia and societies (Fontaine). By downplaying numerous common features of racial stratification in both contexts, dominant nationalist ideologies such as *mestizaje* and *democracia racial* depicted racism as a problem of the United States exclusively, contrasting it with the exemplary Latin American multiracial democracies where race allegedly did not play any relevant role in social relationships (Wade 51; Dzidzienyo and Oboler). Advocates of these discourses also rejected the import of U.S.-based concepts of blackness, race, and diaspora, making an "incredible effort at containing the internationalization of their Afro-populations as a form of pre-emptive deface against threats from the outside to national unity with an unstated implication that Afro groups were best protected, for their own good from outside contagion" (Dulitzky 59).

An ever-growing number of insightful publications and the establishment of institutions such as Afro-Latin American Research Institute (ALARI) at Harvard have signaled the emergence of Afro-Latin American Studies as a striving new field which has been at the center of efforts to overcome the paradoxical underrepresentation of Afro-Latin America in African Diaspora scholarship (Andrews; De La Fuente and Andrews; Gates Jr.). As pioneering scholars Miriam Jiménez Román and Juan Flores have pointed out in their groundbreaking *Afro-Latin@ Reader: History and Culture in the United States* (2010), the experience of Afro-Latin American immigrants in the United States has served to complicate homogenizing demarcations between blacks, whites, and Latinos that have dominated race relations in the U.S. and Latin America, often rendering Afro-Latinos invisible and contributing to the emergence of a "triple consciousness" (Jiménez Román and Flores 14f) – black, Latino, American – among this group. Building on the legacy of Afro-Puerto Rican New Yorkers such as activist and historian Arturo Schomburg, who was involved in Hispanic Caribbean independence movements as well as in the U.S. black freedom struggle, "transbarrio dialogues" (Steinitz, "We Got Latin Soul") between Afro-Latin immigrants and African Americans have been critical in the emergence of *afrolatinidad* as a new concept which challenged essentialist and nationalist notions of blackness and *latinidad* (Jiménez Román and Flores; Laó-Montes, "Afro-Latinidades"; Sparling). In a special issue of *The Black Scholar* on "Post-Soul and Afro-Latinidades" (2022), the guest editors Trent Masiki and Regina Mills addressed "the increasing interest in and need for critical discussions of Afro-Latino and African American interculturalism in the post-segregation era" (1) and called for a bridging of existing demarcations between Latin American and African American Studies by putting concepts from both disciplines into dialogue with each other. In light of the "perpetual movement of people, politics, and culture" (4) that has defined the realities of Afro-Latin Americans, the editors of *Afro-Latin@s in Movement – Critical Approaches to Blackness and Transnationalism in the Americas* (2016) have equally stressed the need for a hemispheric and transnational understanding of *afrolatinidad.*

Inter-American Studies

It is precisely this interest in conceptualizing transnational and translocal dialogues in the Americas that motivates not only the compilation of this volume, but also the field of research from which the editors of this volume come. Inter-American Studies (also referred to as Hemispheric American Studies) departs from the assumption that a hemispheric perspective is crucial to grasp the manifold entanglements between the Caribbean, North and Latin America, shaped by imperial U.S. policies, mass migration, and the continental diffusion of popular cultures. This approach problematizes concepts comprised in the so-called one-way forms of globalization by emphasizing multiple ways and directions in which mobility manifests itself. These developments are sometimes falsely perceived as total 'U.S. Americanization,' a label often employed to homogenize the current accelerated fusion and diffusion of cultural products on a global scale. "If Hemispheric American studies," as Ralph Bauer holds, "cannot 'discover' the cultural essence of a hemispheric America in the tabula rasa of unfamiliar textual terrains, it can study the rich and diverse history of this idea" (243). It is here that inter-American scholarship gains new momentum and prominence. Beyond the idea of "a hemispheric America" and certainly ever since the collapse of Spanish imperial claims in 1898, concrete cultural, political, and economic dynamics, tensions, and processes within the Americas have increasingly created inter-American webs and networks that manifest "mutual entanglements between locations, regions, and nations beyond a North-South divide" (Raussert, "Mobilizing" 62)

In 1974, Immanuel Wallerstein advanced the idea of "the extended Caribbean," a cultural and historical formation that stretches from Brazil to the east coast of the United States (47). Emphasizing commerce, trade, plantation economy, and cultural transmission, Wallerstein gives us an early example of how to envision the Americas as a space of entanglement(s) beyond European claims and postcolonial boundaries.[3] To us, his focus on economic, environmental, and historical affiliations along the coastlines from Brazil to northern Virginia provides a microcosmic lens to perceive the Americas, hemispherically as well as internally, interconnected beyond Old World-

3 From 2013 through 2019, the Center for InterAmerican Studies (Bielefeld University) hosted the project "Entangled Americas," sponsored by the German Federal Ministry of Research and Education. The research Center explored the Americas as a space of entanglement(s) along the lines of geopolitical imaginaries, transnational flows, and the creation of social and natural ambiance, developing new visions of mobile area studies. Among its results are field-mapping publications such as *The Routledge Companion to Inter-American Studies* (2017) and *The Routledge Handbook Series to the Americas* (2019; 2020).

New World dialectics (Graham and Raussert 9). As Raussert and Anatol point out, an "Inter-American framework aspires towards new knowledge production that revises master narratives, canon-making, and genre-making" (19). In this view, "'knowledge' gets infused by the idea of mobile sites of enunciation, and hence, becomes thinkable as contextually framed yet open, historically grown but changing, specific and at the same time interconnected ..." (19).

As a result, this book embraces many voices and critical positionings from different zones to reflect the expansion and interconnectedness of Black Power within the Americas. While hinting at the need to recognize differences, Raussert argues that "narratives may be aesthetic, cultural, historical, or political, but they all point toward the necessity to think the local in its hemispheric relatedness (Raussert, "Introduction" 6). To study black cultures and histories in a hemispheric perspective, the present book also extends the works of critics like Walter Mignolo and José David Saldívar who have introduced new kinds of border thinking that question traditional knowledge and power hierarchies along the North-South axis which have become as troubling as earlier examples of a divide between East-West. Not only do they introduce mobile border concepts, they also favor dialogical approaches to comprehend the interconnectedness of cultures and cultural productions within the Americas and introduce the necessity of optional discourses such as indigenous knowledge production (Mignolo; Saldívar). Following this, to Olaf Kaltmeier, "an inter-American approach involves understanding cultural and political elements not bounded by a closed national space but instead situated in a space of entanglements" (3). That this space needs to be interpreted as mobile and porous is underscored by Rüdiger Kunow who proposes that "mobility must in a systematic fashion become part also of our critical lexicon, especially so in an American studies that defines itself as cross-cultural, comparatist, and transnational" (245). While the "global flow" and the "global phenomena" of which Shelley Fisher Fishkin spoke in her presidential address to the American Studies Association in 2004 have long been researched in American Studies as they pertain to Europe and their transatlantic and transpacific dimension, we wish to advance existing efforts at conceptualizing the African Diaspora from a hemispheric perspective (Fisher Fishkin 24).

Towards Hemispheric Black Studies

Following our belief that an inter-American framework aimed at crossing regional, national, and linguistic demarcations between academic disciplines constitutes a promising approach to the study of Black Power in the Americas, this volume intends to fuse the theoretical approaches roughly outlined above towards the articulation of Hemispheric Black Studies. It draws on the contributions of scholars such as Ifeoma Nwankwo who was among the first to address the "dearth of critical scholarship on the relations between U.S. African Americans and the rest of the Americas" ("Promises and Perils" 188) and Agustín Laó-Montes who has advanced the concept of "nuestra Afroamérica" in his latest publication (*Contrapunteos diaspóricos*). What unites these approaches is the advocacy for a hemispheric perspective in the study of Afro-diasporic communities and cultures in the Americas in order to fill existing gaps in research on the entanglements between Afrodescendants from the Caribbean, North and Latin America. These research gaps can be attributed to an interplay of several factors. American exceptionalism, imperial policies, military interventions, economic dependencies, and the dominance of U.S. academia, on the one hand, and widespread sentiments of anti-U.S.-Americanism and anti-imperialism, on the other, have shaped research on inter-American relations in ways which have left little space for counter-hegemonic North-South dialogues between Afrodescendants. While African American Studies have often reproduced existing power dynamics by privileging the U.S. context over other Afro-diasporic experiences, African Diaspora studies have focused largely on interrelations of Anglophone black communities in the United States and the Caribbean with Europe and Africa (Meehan 23). It has also become apparent that hemispheric approaches have been rejected by many Latin Americanists who saw them as manifestations of the neocolonial patterns of domination and cultural imperialism that have long characterized the relationship between the United States and Latin America (Stam and Schohat). Whereas new fields, such as Afro-Latin American and Caribbean Studies, address many of these shortcomings, the Hemispheric Black Studies we envision is not confined to research on Afro-diasporic communities, movements, and cultures from one specific linguistic, regional, or historical context. Rather, it emphasizes the dialogues and flows between various Afrodescendant communities in the Americas.

An increasing body of studies on the mobility of people, ideas, and cultural products, has contributed to the development of transnational and hemispheric perspectives, allowing for insights on the multidirectional dialogues and interactions that have defined *the Black Americas*. Research on how the convergence of black migrations from the U.S. Deep South, the Caribbean, and Latin America in the urban centers of the North and circum-Caribbean contact zones such as Panama and Costa Rica created a sense of "hemispheric blackness" (Winant) has contributed significantly to the bridging of African American, Afro-Latin American, and Caribbean Studies (Bryce-Laporte; Laó-Montes and Davila; Opie; Putnam). Referring to Afro-Latin Americans of British Caribbean descent in Central America, Nwankwo has advocated for more attention to be paid to those communities that "blur the lines" between distinct ethnic groups, largely because "an "understanding of the hemisphere can truly be advanced only if we are more attentive to the nuances and complexities of interaction (whether collaboration, conflict, or some combination)" (Nwankwo, "Making Sense" 225f).

In his influential essay on "overlapping diasporas," Earl Lewis describes the role of urban spaces of hemispheric transculturation like New York, "where African-descended immigrants encountered American blacks, creating in the encounter what has been called a transgeographical America" (786). Predating the classical Black Power period by several decades, the trajectories of New York-based Caribbean migrants such as Arturo Schomburg and Marcus Garvey embody the often neglected intersections and dialogues between African Americans and Afrodescendants from other New World contexts as manifested in the inter-American dimensions of the Harlem

Renaissance, *New Negro* radicalism, Négritude, Pan-Africanism, and other twentieth-century black movements (Brown, *Waves of Decolonization*; Guridy; Haas, *Harlem Renaissance*, "Un continente de color"; Meehan; Stephens, *Black Empire*; Valdés). The hemispheric "migration of sounds" (Raussert and Habell-Pallán) such as jazz, blues, mambo, calypso, salsa, cumbia, soul, funk, reggae, hip-hop, and reggaeton and the related emergence of "transversal consumer cultures" (Thies and Raab) has been equally important in the forging of transnational networks of solidarity between diverse Afro-diasporic communities across the Americas (Njoroge; Raussert and Kaltmeier; Rivera; Rivera et al.; Saunders; Steinitz, "We Got Latin Soul," "Black Rio"). Serving as a point of departure for this volume, these hemispheric and comparative perspectives on the Black Americas allow us to discern not only the legacies of "divergent racialization" (34) but also "patterns of convergence" between diverse Afro-diasporic movements and cultures as a "significant … feature of inter-American life" (51), as Kevin Meehan has argued in his analysis of African American and Caribbean cultural exchange.

New directions in Black Power Studies

Since it is our aim to overcome one-dimensional narratives and get an understanding of the hemispheric appeal of Black Power, a closer look at the heterogeneity and diversity that shaped the movement in the context of its origin is imperative. While Martin Luther King, Jr. and the Civil Rights movement have become widely accepted as sources for positive identification and are taught regularly in classes on American history, the legacy of the Black Power movement remains much more contested. Peniel Joseph, a trailblazer in the building of Black Power Studies as a new field within African American Studies, has criticized the "declension narrative" in existing scholarship, which he understands as a tendency to portray Black Power as an "evil twin" of the Civil Rights movement, blaming its negative impulses, separatism, and violent rhetoric for the demise of the African American freedom struggle and the triumph of white backlash initiated by the Nixon administration (Joseph, "Black Power Movement" 751f). Arguing for a more nuanced perspective, Joseph holds that the Black Power movement, "in contrast to the struggle for civil rights, privileged a view of black empowerment that was local, national, and international in scope, held political self-determination as sacrosanct, and called for a redefined black identity that connected black Americans to a national and global political project based on racial solidarity and a shared history of racial oppression" (753). It is this embeddedness of Black Power in a long history of resistance and its relationship with international freedom struggles beyond the boundaries of the African American community in the United States that we are interested in.

According to Sylviane A. Diouf and Komozi Woodard, it is precisely because Black Power touched upon the most diverse aspects of U.S. society that it "galvanized millions of people in the broadest movement in African American history" (viii) and "had a tremendous impact on issues of not only race and citizenship in the United States but also identity, politics, criminal justice, culture, art, and education globally" (vi). As a large number of studies on contrasting dimensions of the movement reveal, the diverse politics and contradicting approaches towards black consciousness and liberation which characterized the Black Power era manifested themselves not only in the scandalized advocacy of armed self-defense and revolution but also in struggles for women's liberation, prison reform, tenant rights, community control of schools, the introduction of Black Studies at colleges and universities, free breakfast programs, the articulation of a black aesthetic in music, fashion, style, theater, literature, cinema, and the arts, the revalorization of African roots, "Buy Black"-campaigns, the building of economic and political power through community organizing and electoral politics, and the forging of strategic alliances with other oppressed groups as Latino and Asian American migrants, Native Americans, working-class whites, anti-war activists, and Third World liberation movements. Whereas the quest for liberation was anything but monolithic, the youthful advocates of Black Power did share some basic convictions. From the religious conservatism of the Nation of Islam to the cultural nationalism of the Black Arts Movement to the revolutionary (inter)nationalism of the Black Panther Party inspired by non-U.S. thinkers such as Marx, Fanon, Guevara, and Mao – most ideological currents that made up the spectrum of Black Power organizations adhered to some core tenets of black nationalism such as the belief that African Americans constituted an internal colony, "a nation within a nation" (Woodard) that was bound to fight for its self-determination (Brown, *Fighting for U.S.*; Carmichael and Hamilton; Ogbar, *Black Power*; Joseph, *Rethinking*; Lazerow and Williams; Smethurst).

The Black Power movement was heavily criticized for its alleged promotion of racial essentialism. Questioning the "call for a fixed, iron-clad black aesthetic" (Ashe 615) that shaped the Black Power era, African American critics as Trey Ellis (1989), Greg Tate (1992), and Bertram Ashe (2007) advocated for a "post-soul aesthetic" that corresponded to their conviction that "blackness is constantly in flux" (Ashe). Indicating the flawed nature of simple generalizations, many of the criticisms directed at the homogenizing, essentialist, separatist, and masculinist tendencies of Black Power have been articulated from within the movement itself. Black feminist and Marxist perspectives provide crucial insights on gender and class dimensions that have contributed significantly to overcoming romanticizing and reductionist visions of Black Power. Living up to its self-image as "the vanguard", the Black Panther Party (BPP) became the place where many of these critical perspectives were formulated and discussed. As Jeffrey O.G. Ogbar emphasizes: "Despite myopic approaches that tend to fixate on the BPP as a bastion of sexism, the party made systematic challenges to patriarchy that were rare for its time. The Panther party was the first major black organization to publicly endorse the women's and gay liberation movements" (*Black Power* 105). Responding to widespread expressions of male chauvinism, sexism, heteronormativity, and homophobia within the movement, female activists and thinkers such as Kathleen Cleaver, Angela Davis, Denise Oliver, Toni Cade Bambara, Audre Lorde, and groups such as the Combahee River Collective and the Third World Women's Alliance sowed the seeds for the emergence of black feminism as one of the most consequential legacies of Black Power (Collins, *Black Feminist Thought*; Davis; Gore et al.; Springer; Taylor, *How We Get Free*).

As revolutionary Marxists, the Black Panthers also rejected black separatism and cultural nationalism and argued for the necessity of class-based coalition-building instead of the race-first approach Black Power is commonly associated with: "Since a nationalist revolution would be considered reactionary if concerned only with the problems of blacks, it was incumbent upon participants to recognize the international character of capitalist oppression and act accordingly. There could be no separate peace with the oppressor," as William L. Van Deburg pointed out (153). Accordingly, the Black Panthers and other left-wing organizations within the movement were deeply critical of the essentialist idealization of blackness and a pre-colonial African past that dominated large parts of the Black Power movement and its cultural manifestations. BPP co-founder Bobby Seale explained this critical perspective in his book *Seize the Time*: "… cultural nationalism will not educate people. It makes racists out of them. … power for the people will not grow out of the sleeve of a dashiki" (Seale 256).[4] Black Marxists criticized that the black nationalists' dogmas of "race-first" and "black unity" disguised existing class divisions within the African American community and undermined the building of transformative multiethnic coalitions (Johnson; Reed).

The debate over race or class, nationalism or Marxism, defined the arguments within radical black organizing in the 1970s and caused internal divisions that contributed to the decline of Black Power. The devastating effects of the FBI's Counter-Intelligence Program (COINTELPRO), and the "white backlash" under Richard Nixon were other crucial factors for the demise of Black Power as a movement for emancipation in the United States in the mid-1970s. While these developments weakened the black freedom struggle consistently, the combination of critical approaches on race, class, and, gender as first articulated by left-wing organizations within the Black Power movement survived the dismantling of the movement and laid the foundations for theoretical frameworks such as *intersectionality* that continue to play a key role in today's critical discourses (Crenshaw).

From Bandung to Birmingham: tracing Black Power internationalism

Black Power in Hemispheric Perspective not only focuses on the movement's transnational impact but also aims to shed light on the primordial role of the external influences that shaped the agendas of its protagonists in the United States. The post-World War II era witnessed the parallel rise of two transformative movements, regarded by many as twin struggles: decolonization and the Civil Rights movement. Against the

---

4 *Dashiki* is an African garment that enjoyed great popularity among the African American population at the height of the Black Power movement.

backdrop of the Cold War, the engagement with global affairs had brought many African American radicals to the conclusion that black liberation in the Americas was intertwined with anti-colonial struggles in Africa and Asia (Dudziak; Munro; Plummer, *Rising Wind* and *In Search of Power*; Von Eschen). The emergence of internationalism at the left wing of the African American freedom movement was intrinsically linked to historical events such as the Afro-Asian Conference in Bandung (1955), the independence of Ghana (1957), the Cuban Revolution (1959), the Sharpeville massacre in South Africa (1960), and the assassination of Congolese prime minister Patrice Lumumba (1961). The "spirit of Bandung," tirelessly invoked by Malcolm X in the last years of his life, encouraged Black Power internationalists in their critique of the Cold War liberalism and anticommunism that characterized the Civil Rights movement's moderate leadership, reinforcing their search for allies beyond the borders of the United States (X). The encounters of Malcolm X with anti-colonial leaders such as Kwame Nkrumah and Sekou Touré during his travels to Africa, the participation of Stokely Carmichael and other African American leaders in Third World alliances as the *Tricontinental*, the granting of exile to African American activists as Robert F. Williams, Eldridge Cleaver, and Assata Shakur by revolutionary Cuba, the opening of an international section of the Black Panther Party in Algiers in 1970, and the global "Free Angela Davis" campaign (1971/1972) reinforced the sense of connectedness between the U.S. black liberation movement and struggles outside the United States. In their wake, the forging of networks of solidarity between African American leaders and left-wing revolutionaries from Algeria, Cuba, Ghana, or Vietnam became a distinct feature of Black Power radicalism, turning its protagonists into serious threats to U.S. national security and, thus, targets of intense state repression (Bush; Beegan and Gustafson; Kelley, *Freedom Dreams*; Mahler; Wilkins; Williams).

The conflicting prioritizations of race, class, culture, and nation are essential for an understanding of the many overlaps and crucial points of contention between black nationalism and black internationalism as the defining currents of Black Power. Whereas ideologies of black nationalism are widely referred to as the common denominators of the Black Power movement, the term might be somewhat misleading because it was precisely the internationalist outlook that distinguished the imaginaries of Black Power from the domestic agenda of the Civil Rights movement. These intersections, fittingly described by Roderick Bush as the "Peculiar Internationalism of Black Nationalism" (35), are related to the fact that African Americans, unlike the anti-colonial movements in Africa and Asia with which they felt connected, had no national territory that they could liberate from white rule in their quest for freedom. Lara Putnam has argued that black nationalism and black internationalism should be understood as different but potentially complementary approaches to black liberation:

> Black nationalism holds that within a racist society, black people's primary political allegiance should reflect racial solidarity. … Meanwhile, black internationalism analyzes racial subordination as a part of systems that function on a supranational scale. … which usually requires communication and alliance across political boundaries, be they national or imperial. (Bush 6)

Interpreting the black freedom struggle as one of both race and class, radical left-wing internationalists such as the Black Panthers propagated a worldwide socialist revolution, arguing that there could be no prospect of freedom and justice for those affected by racism and colonialism within the framework of the capitalist system. Rather than the identitarian ideologies of cultural nationalism, Afrocentrism and the religious separatism espoused by the NOI, many black internationalists advocated for a political Pan-Africanism based not on the invocation of shared African traditions or specific characteristics of all black people but on the shared experience of colonialism, racism, and capitalism. Along with Pan-Africanism, the ideology of Third World Marxism enjoyed the greatest influence among revolutionary black internationalists, as Max Elbaum holds in his essay on the radical internationalism of 1968:

> Third World Marxism saw national liberation in the global South as the cutting edge of the worldwide progressive movement, … it riveted attention on the intersection of economic exploitation and racial oppression, … it embraced the revolutionary nationalist impulses that then held tremendous initiative in communities of color, where Marxism, socialism, and nationalism intermingled and overlapped. … Third World Marxism seemed to many the best framework for taking the most radical themes articulated by Malcolm X and Martin Luther King and transforming them into a comprehensive revolutionary ideology. (Elbaum 41)

Groups influenced by Third World Marxism, such as the Black Panthers, moved even further away from the separatist tendencies of black nationalism toward black internationalism. Against great opposition from sections of the Black Power movement, they advocated for interethnic alliances with non-black communities and movements in the United States and abroad that would be based not on allegiance to a particular racial group but on the common goal of overcoming colonialism, racism, and capitalism and an uncompromising commitment to universal human rights (Young).

Transcending borders: The global appeal of Black Power

The U.S. Black Power movement not only drew extensively from external influences, it also had a tremendous impact on movements, cultures, and communities abroad. Indeed, as Plummer contends, Black Power was a "global phenomenon" which "cannot be situated within a single country but emerged across the diaspora of Africa-descended peoples" ("International dimensions" 103). In the view of many activists across the globe, African Americans, constituted the vanguard of a worldwide movement to overcome imperialism and white supremacy – waging a heroic struggle "in the belly of the beast" (Jeffries). As Steinitz puts it, "the U.S. black liberation movement and its cultural manifestations were global in their appeal, providing marginalized communities in the U.S. as well as abroad with powerful symbols of resistance and self-affirmation in the face of oppression and exclusion" ("Calling Out Around the World" 88). Troubling accounts of Black Power as a manifestation of black separatism, the popularity of Black Power in the United States was by no means confined to people of African descent. Its strategies and rhetoric were adopted and translated by Native Americans, migrant communities, feminists, radical white students, anti-war, and gay liberation activists. Arguing that "ultimately Black Power was not racial but rather a movement against racism," Diouf and Woodard hold that wherever "youth were denied full citizenship or where governments questioned their very humanity, activists claimed the language of Black Power in the fight for their human rights" (x). Countering reductionist U.S.-centered narratives, Nico Slate stresses that "Black Power was interpreted and reinterpreted to suit local causes and changing conditions throughout the world" (5). According to him, there was not one Black Power movement but rather a variety of "global Black Powers" (6). The Black Panthers' urban militant "radical chic" and performative actions, deftly analyzed by Amy Abugo Ongiri in *Spectacular Blackness* (2010) as distinct features of Black Power culture, were key factors in their emergence as global icons of resistance. The emergence of organizations such as the Dalit Panthers in India, the Polynesian Panthers in New Zealand, the Black Panthers of Israel, the Aborigine-led Australian Black Panther Party, and the British Black Panther Movement exposed the ocean-crossing appeal of the Black Panthers and their confrontational approach to the politics of liberation (Plummer, "International Dimensions"; Slate; Smith; Swan, *Pasifika Black*).

What is more, African American popular culture, fashion, and sports played a critical role in the global dissemination of symbols, slogans, and aesthetic representations of Black Power assertiveness. When Muhammad Ali refused to be drafted for the Vietnam War in 1966, stating "I ain't got no quarrel with them Vietcong" (Marqusee 162), he gave voice to the growing anti-war movement in the United States and positioned himself as a defiant spokesperson for the building of international alliances between African Americans and people of color abroad, conquering not only opponents in the ring but also hearts and minds of transnational audiences to whom he represented the dawning of a new day in Black America and across the globe (Marqusee). The impact of global icons like Ali, James Brown, and Angela Davis was also a key factor in the dissemination of Black Power-inspired aesthetics. Popularized by a Harlem-based Garveyite modeling agency named Grandassa Models, "Black is Beautiful" became a defining slogan of the Black Power era to which Afrodescendants in the United States and abroad showed allegiance by sporting natural hair and "soul style" (Ford). Defying Eurocentric beauty standards that were dominant in different colonial and post-colonial contexts, the Afro was, according to Jeffrey Ogbar, a bold "statement of black pride, a metaphorical exclamation point, affirming the beauty of black people and their hair" ("The Looks" 128).

Soul music, a genre that, according to Emily Lordi, embodied black resilience, solidarity, and "virtuosic survivorship" (5), constituted arguably the most consequential conduit of Black Power mobility through which cross-border identification with the African American freedom struggle was expressed, often serving as a medium to express dissent with the repressive status quo in different local contexts (Gaines; Steinitz, "Calling Out Around the World"). In her analysis of Nina Simone's "To Be

Young, Gifted, and Black" (1969) and other Afro-diasporic anthems, Shana Redmond argues that the collective consumption of music functions as a method of participation within the border-crossing liberation projects which are characteristic of the African diaspora, pointing at the relation between the global diffusion of black music and the translation of black radical thought from one diasporic context to another (Redmond 2f). Preceding the emergence of reggae and hip-hop as global youth cultures in the late twentieth century, the translation and creative appropriation of African American soul and funk influences in the 1960s and 1970s constitutes a key chapter in what Livio Sansone has labeled the "globalization of blackness" (1): an ongoing process of cultural transfer between Afro-diasporic communities in which black popular culture from the United States occupied a prominent position as a major focus of identification.

Black Power in hemispheric perspectives

This book is guided by the conviction that an increased attention to specific regional, national, and local contexts beyond the U.S. African American community will usefully expand the scope and depth of our understanding of how different hemispheric notions of blackness, colonial histories, class, and gender hierarchies shape the meanings of Black Power. In keeping with his role as a heir to Marcus Garvey and visionary of Black Power, Malcolm X was among the few African American activists who articulated a concept of black liberation that was inter-American in scope when he emphasized that it was his purpose "to unite everyone in the Western Hemisphere of African descent into one united force" (X 60) at the founding rally of the Organization of Afro-American Unity (OAAU) in May 1964. In the late 1960s, the emergence of militant organizations such as the Brown Berets, the Young Lords, the Red Guard, the American Indian Movement, and the Young Patriots who joined so-called "rainbow coalitions" with the Black Panther Party also demonstrated the interethnic appeal of Black Power among Chicano, Puerto Rican, and Asian American immigrants, Native Americans, and poor whites (Fernández; Ho and Mullen; Muñoz; Ogbar, "Rainbow Radicalism"; Smith and Warrior; Pulido). Referring to the importance of black-brown solidarity and the strong identification with the African American freedom struggle and its cultural manifestations among Puerto Rican immigrants, Juan Flores has hinted at the "guiding, exemplary role of African-American culture and politics" in the emergence of Nuyorican and Afro-Latino identity discourses in the 1960s (*Bomba to Hip-Hop* 82).[5] The translation and appropriation of Black Power symbols and slogans to Latin American and Caribbean idioms as practiced by immigrants in the United States also resonated in their countries of origin where they were met with skepticism and outright

5 The influence of the Black Power/Black Arts movements as defining features of Nuyorican culture manifested itself in Piri Thomas's novel *Down These Mean Streets* (1967), the participation of Young Lords co-founder Felipe Luciano in the black nationalist spoken-word group The Last Poets, and the emergence of Latin Soul/Boogaloo (Flores, "Boogaloo"; Steinitz, "Latin Soul").

hostility. Accounts of the popularization of the Afro hairstyle in Puerto Rico and the role of singers Toni Tornado and Tim Maia in the dissemination of soul music in Brazil after returning from New York speak to the many ways in which manifestations of Black Power travelled across the hemisphere (Rivero; Steinitz, "Black Rio").

The few existing studies of Black Power in hemispheric contexts focus on the Anglophone Caribbean as one of the major strongholds of the movement beyond U.S. borders. In *Black Power in the Caribbean*, Kate Quinn argues convincingly against "the tendency to view the movement from the perspective of a North American center" instead of "exploring parallel or even related mobilizations elsewhere" (*Black Power* 8). According to her, "analysis of Black Power in the Caribbean can broaden our understanding of racial mobilization in multiethnic and nonwhite majority contexts" (18). Studies on Guyanese Black Power leader Walter Rodney and the so-called "Rodney Riots" that broke out in Jamaica after he was banned from entering the country in 1968, the 1970 "Black Power Revolution" in Trinidad and Tobago, the meaning of Black Power in the decolonization of Bermuda, the emergence of Rastafarianism and reggae music as manifestations of a Pan-African consciousness, and antiracist activism of West Indian migrants in Canada have shown that Caribbean Black Power was not just an import of U.S. influences. Rather, it was both the product of intense dialogues with the African American freedom struggle and a movement to be analyzed on its own terms. (Austin; Lewis, *Walter Rodney*; Meehan; Meeks; Quinn, *Black Power in the Caribbean*; Swan, *Black Power in Bermuda*; Tomlinson, *African-Jamaican Aesthetic* and her essay in this volume).

The study of manifestations of Black Power in Latin America is of particular interest. According to widely held perceptions, there was no such thing as "poder negro" [*Black Power*] in Latin American contexts because different colonial pasts and dynamics of race relations have resulted in homogenizing identity discourses that privilege "nation" above "race" (Quinn, "Introduction" 19). Hegemonic ideologies of *mestizaje* and *democracia racial* implied that there was no legitimacy or justification for militant antiracism and the assertion of black identity in societies where racism allegedly did not exist – a stance which is reflected in the scarcity of research on the subject matter. The influence of Black Power on Afrodescendant communities in Latin America was fiercely rejected and vilified as a divisive expression of U.S. racism from an unlikely alliance between different sides of the political spectrum: while nationalist elites and repressive right-wing regimes treated Black Power as a matter of national security fearing the incendiary and subversive effects of U.S. black radicalism on local Afro-Latin communities, left-wing intellectuals denounced the popularization of Black Power-related attitudes and musical styles such as soul music as an expression of U.S. cultural imperialism that contaminated authentic local folk traditions (Alberto). In socialist Cuba and throughout the Latin American left, the militant antiracism of the Black Power movement was rejected as a threat to working-class unity in the anti-imperialist class struggle (see the essay of Alberto Abreu Arcia in this volume).

Despite this hostile environment, Black Power and its cultural manifestations left significant traces all over Afro-Latin America (Steinitz, *Black Power in Lateinamerika*). In the 1970s, the Black Arts Movement became an important source of inspiration to Afro-Latin American writers, poets, and artists such as Nancy Morejón and Nicolás Guillén (Cuba), Nicomedes and Victoria Santa Cruz (Peru), Carlos Guillermo Wilson and Gerardo Maloney (Panama), Quince Duncan (Costa Rica), and Manuel Zapata Olivella (Colombia) in whose works African Americans were "shown as martyrs and as symbols of resistance, model figures in the fight against racism in the hemisphere," as Richard Jackson has pointed out (116). Reaching much wider audiences than literary discourses, the collective mass consumption of U.S. soul music facilitated the popularization of Black Power-inspired symbols and styles among Afro-Latin American working-class youth in such localities as Panama and Rio de Janeiro (Carlos Alberto Medeiros's essay in this volume; Steinitz, "Soulful Sancocho," "Black Rio"). Building on a long tradition of exchange with the United States, 1970s Brazil witnessed the most explicit expressions of Black Power sentiment, manifested not only in the Black Rio movement but also in the emergence of *blocos afros* in Salvador de Bahia – Afro-Brazilian percussion ensembles dedicated to the advocacy of black consciousness among which the most influential was Ilê Aiyê, an Afrocentric cultural group which provoked outrage at the 1974 carnival with a song that included the catchphrase "Temos cabelo duro, somos Black Pau [*We got kinky hair, we are Black Power*]" (Alberti and Pereira; Alberto; Hanchard, *Orpheus and Power*; Pereira; Pinho).

While the impact of Black Power on Afro-Latin American communities remains a largely underexplored field of inquiry, these studies suggest the emancipatory and empowering potential of transnational black influences in contexts where Afro-diasporic communities have been economically and socially marginalized while their cultural expressions are coopted as symbols of national unity by the state. Hinting at the porosity of "boundaries between US and Latin American blackness," Frank A. Guridy and Juliet Hooker stress the "impact of transnational encounters and connections on the work of black intellectuals throughout the hemisphere" and "the centrality of diasporic dialogues and cross-national linkages in the making of Afro-Latin American thought" (185). Next to African decolonization and the struggle against apartheid in South Africa, Civil Rights and Black Power were major influences in the "blackening" (Andrews 182) of Afro-Latin American identity politics as manifested in the rise of black social, cultural, and political movements across the continent that have become transformative forces in many Latin American societies in the last decades (Guridy and Hooker; Laó-Montes, "Cartografía"; Paschel, *Becoming Black Political Subjects*; Dixon). As Tianna Paschel has argued in her account of the rise of urban black movements throughout Latin America in the 1970s, the "upsurge in black mobilization was also directly linked to the emergence of a black cultural scene that borrowed heavily from soul music and black power aesthetics from the United States" ("Rethinking Black Mobilizations" 233).

An inter-American perspective allows for insights into the entanglements of black mobilizations in the Americas, which appear to have shifted their focus of action from North to South in the mid-1970s when the demise of the U.S. Black Power movement coincided with the emergence of Afro-Latin America as a major hub of hemispheric black transnationalism. Starting with three *Congresos de la Cultura Negra de las Américas* held in Colombia (1977), Panama (1980), and Brazil (1982) and continuing with the foundation of hemispheric networks such as *Red de Mujeres Afrolatinoamericanas, Afrocaribeñas y de la Diáspora (*1992) and *Alianza Estratégica Afrodescendiente en América Latina y el Caribe* (2000), Afro-Latin American and Caribbean activists have kept alive the impulse of counter-hegemonic border-crossing between different locations of the African Diaspora that characterized the Black Power era and that we want to put front stage with this volume (Davis et al.; Ratcliffe). Consistently, Afro-Latin American feminists as Beatriz Nascimento, Lélia Gonzalez, Delia Zapata, and Ochy Curiel have been at the forefront of these articulations and organizing processes beyond the nation (Curiel; González; Perry). In the face of new waves of murderous anti-black racism in Brazil, Colombia, and the United States, increased attacks on migrant, women's, and LGBTQ rights, and deepening social inequalities (fueled by the electoral victories of Donald Trump and Jair Bolsonaro and the resurgence of interconnected ultraconservative, right-wing nationalist, and white supremacist movements across the Americas), building emancipatory, hemispheric, and interethnic alliances in the spirit of "1968" seems a logical, if not compelling, strategy. Our book is intended to serve as a source of information and inspiration for the new generations of activists who are following in the footsteps of the Black Power internationalists of the 1960s and 1970s in their quest for freedom and equality.

The essays

Following the approach of the conferences held by the Black Americas Network in 2017 and 2018, this volume is conceived as a transdisciplinary platform of dialogue between black movement activists and scholars from academic disciplines as diverse as history, political science, sociology, anthropology, musicology, literary, and cultural studies. We are deeply grateful to the authors for sharing their personal experiences and insights from their fields of expertise, which have allowed us to take a closer look at the still little-tapped hemispheric dimensions of Black Power. We would especially like to thank George Reid Andrews and Jeffrey O.G. Ogbar, whose advice and guidance throughout the editing process was invaluable. We would also like to express our gratitude to Alexa Kenter and Mahshid Mayar for their tireless support in editing the book.

While the essays brought together here cover a wide range of geographical regions (North America, Central America, South America, and the Caribbean) and historical contexts (from eighteenth-century Canada to twenty-first century Brazil), they relate to each other in the ways they contribute to ongoing efforts at filling gaps in the mapping of the diverse expressions of "Black Power" in the Western Hemisphere. Although it is in the nature of the subject matter that the texts overlap in various ways and although a sharp division into different topics is neither possible nor desirable, for reasons of clarity, we have opted to arrange them roughly along temporal, spatial, and thematic lines which correspond to their relatedness with the U.S. Black Power movement.

The first section deals with different expressions of hemispheric black activism and thought before the advent of the Civil Rights/Black Power era (1955–1975), hinting at the indebtedness of the movement to influential precursors and its transgenerational character. Afua Cooper explores the transnational activism of Thomas Peters – fugitive slave, freedom fighter, and black loyalist soldier in the Revolutionary War – between pre-independence Canada, England, and Sierra Leone in the eighteenth century, arguing that his relentless campaign for black freedom and civil rights made him a forefather of the Black Power movement. Emphasizing the hemispheric dimensions of "Black Power before Black Power," Wilfried Raussert examines how the Pan-Africanist movement of Marcus Garvey, the founder of modern black nationalism, used public space and performance culture in its mass mobilizations of Afro-descendants between Jamaica, Harlem, and Cuba in the era of the Harlem Renaissance and New Negro radicalism (1920s–1940s). While Garvey managed to forge the first Afro-diasporic mass movement with his Universal Negro Improvement Association (UNIA), which gained the support of millions of working-class blacks across the circum-Caribbean migratory sphere, the significance of W.E.B. Du Bois as one of his main critics is to be found in his theoretical contributions to the study of black life in the United States and his critical role in the forging of internationalist alliances between circles of Afro-diasporic and African activists and intellectuals in Europe and the Americas. In his essay on the significance of Du Bois's opus magnum *Black Reconstruction* (1935) in the making of "1968," John Munro argues that the book constitutes one of the most influential contributions to the black radical tradition and that, although published three decades earlier, grappling with its insights is necessary for fully understanding the 1960s Black Power revolution.

Focusing on transnational and interethnic alliances and dialogues, essays in the second section address the ways in which the U.S. Black Power movement was shaped by the participation of immigrants and the engagement with liberation movements and ideas from other hemispheric contexts. The essay by Matti Steinitz on the involvement of Afro-Panamanian immigrant Carlos Russell in the U.S. black freedom struggle and his interventions in the antiracist struggles of his home country deals with the emergence of *Pan-Afro-Americanism* as a defining feature of Black Power internationalism. Next, Portia Owusu examines how the theories of French-Martiniquais intellectual Frantz Fanon on the use of violence as expressed in his influential book *The Wretched of the Earth* (1961) have informed the advocacy of militancy and armed self-defense by the Black Panther Party and other Black Power radicals, emphasizing how Fanonist thought converged with the teachings of Malcolm X although they never met personally. As the vanguard of left-wing revolutionary internationalism, the Black Panthers also were the driving force behind the forging of "rainbow coalitions" with Chicano,

Puerto Rican, Native American, Asian American, and white activists that Jeffrey O.G. Ogbar analyzes in his essay on the profound impact of the Black Power movement on radical activism outside of the African American community. Valeria Carbone's essay on the participation of Stokely Carmichael in the 1967 OLAS conference held in Havana not only analyzes the rapprochement between Black Power and revolutionary Cuba but also the key role of anti-imperialist alliances with liberation movements from Asia, Africa, Latin America, and the Caribbean in the radicalization of the African American freedom struggle.

Shifting the focus from the external influences on Black Power in the United States to its impact abroad, the third section of our volume is dedicated to Afro-Latin American movements which were inspired by antiracist and anticolonial struggles in the United States and Africa and emerged out of local experiences of organization, as George Reid Andrews argues in his introductory overview on black mobilizations in Latin America between 1970 and 2000. In Alberto Abreu Arcia's text on the formation of a group of Afro-Cuban intellectuals by the name of *Black Power Cubano*, and the contested dimensions of solidarity between African American and Afro-Cuban movements from the 1960s to the recent wave of protests on the island, the author touches on the often-neglected persistence of racial inequalities and the repression of anti-racist black activists after the victorious Cuban Revolution. In his essay on the social and cultural influences of Black Power in Colombia, Bogotá-based cultural critic and DJ Ángel Perea Escobar strikes a personal note as he elaborates on how he became affiliated with what he calls "the African-American school of thought," which, according to him, is informed by a sense of connectedness with the music, culture, and politics that emerged in the Black Power era, impacting the collective imagination of his generation's Afro-Colombian youth movements dramatically. Focusing on the Brazilian context, Carla Guerrón Montero explores how the *Quilombo* movement, building on the legacy of ancient maroon societies, has come to constitute an important Afro-Brazilian resistance movement that stresses its linkages with the African diaspora in its quest to overcome invisibility.

The final section of this book addresses the critical role of black popular music in articulations of social critique and the hemispheric mobility of Black Power-related discourses. In her article on sisterhood and soul music as expressions of Black Power, Kensedeobong Blessed Okosun engages with black feminist critiques of black nationalist masculinity discourses, arguing that singers such as Nina Simone and Aretha Franklin have used soul music as a tool of female empowerment. Next, hinting at the significance of soul music for the hemispheric popularization of Black Power, Carlos Alberto Medeiros shares the recollections of his participation in the 1970s Black Rio movement, when sound systems organized so-called *bailes black* on which Afro-Brazilian youth not only danced to the sounds of U.S. soul music but also started to appropriate the styles and symbols of black pride, and, as in the case of the author, began articulating a critique of the disguised forms of anti-black racism that are still operative in Brazil. While *salsa* is often regarded as a "pure" Latin and apolitical form of dance music, Ángel Quintero Rivera explores the impact of interrelated black and Puerto Rican sounds and struggles in the context of New York in his analysis of Eddie Palmieri's LP *Justicia,* which he interprets as a musical expression of "Afro-knowledge" and black-brown solidarity as manifested in the emergence of the Young Lords Party in the late 1960s. Situating her analysis in the context of Caribbean Black Power movements, Lisa Tomlinson concludes this volume with her essay on Jamaican dancehall music as one of the many cultural expressions that has served as a vehicle to assert a form of black nationalism. While critical of its materialist and homophobic tendencies, Tomlinson holds that, dancehall culture offered an alternative vision for black Jamaican working-class social reality, black consciousness, and political protest that speaks to the emancipation of black people globally.

Works cited

Alberti, Verena, and Amilcar Araújo Pereira. *Histórias do movimento negro no Brasil.* Rio de Janeiro: Pallas, 2007. Print.

Alberto, Paulina. "When Rio Was *Black*: Soul Music, National Culture, and the Politics of Racial Comparison in 1970s Brazil." *Hispanic American Historical Review* 89.1 (2009): 3–39. Print.

Andrews, George Reid. *Afro-Latin America, 1800–2000.* Oxford: Oxford UP, 2004. Print.

Ashe, Bertram D. "Theorizing the Post-Soul Aesthetic: An Introduction." *African American Review* 41.4 (2007): 609–623. Print.

Austin, David. *Fear of a Black Nation – Race, Sex, and Security in Sixties Montreal.* Toronto: Between the Lines, 2013. Print.

Bauer, Ralph. "Hemispheric Studies." *PMLA* 124.1 (2009): 234–250. Print.

Beegan, Gerry, and Donna Gustafson, eds. *Angela Davis – Seize the Time.* Munich: Hirmer, 2021. Print.

Blain, Keisha. *Set the World on Fire: Black Nationalist Women and the Global Struggle for Freedom.* Philadelphia: U of Pennsylvania P, 2018. Print.

Bowen, Larnies A., Ayanna Legros, Tianna Paschel, Geísa Mattos, Kleaver Cruz, and Juliet Hooker. "A Hemispheric Approach to Contemporary Black Activism." *NACLA Report on the Americas* 49.1 (2017): 25–35. Print.

Boyce-Davis, Carole. *Left of Karl Marx: The Political Life of Black Communist Claudia Jones.* Durham: Duke UP, 2008. Print.

Brown, David-Luis. *Waves of Decolonization – Discourses of Race and Hemispheric Citizenship in Cuba, Mexico, and the United States.* Durham / London: Duke UP, 2008. Print.

Brown, Scot. *Fighting for U.S.: Maulana Karenga, the U.S. Organization, and Black Cultural Nationalism.* New York: NYU Press, 2003. Print.

Bryce-Laporte, Roy. "Voluntary Immigration and Continuing Encounters between Blacks: The Post-Quincentenary Challenge." *The Annals of the American Academy of Political and Social Science* Vol. 530 (1993): 28–41. Print.

Bush, Roderick D. *The End of White World Supremacy – Black Internationalism and the Problem of the Color Line.* Philadelphia: Temple UP, 2009. Print.

Carby, Hazel V., and Adam Shatz. "The Colour Line in the Americas." *LRB Podcast*. 12 Jan. 2021. Web. https://www.lrb.co.uk/podcasts-and-videos/podcasts/the-lrb-podcast/the-colour-line-in-the-americas.

Carmichael, Stokely, and Charles Hamilton. *Black Power: The Politics of Liberation*. New York: Random House, 1967. Print.

Castillo-Garsow, Melissa, and Jason Nichols, eds. *La Verdad: An International Dialogue on Hip Hop Latinidades*. Columbus: Ohio State UP, 2016. Print.

Chivallon, Christine. "Beyond Gilroy's Black Atlantic: The Experience of the Black Atlantic." *Diaspora* 11.3 (2002): 359–382. Print.

Chrisman, Laura. "Journeying to 'Death: Gilroy's Black Atlantic." *Race and Class* 39.2 (1997): 51–64. Print.

Collins, Patricia Hill. *Black Feminist Thought: Knowledge, Consciousness, and the Politics of Empowerment*. New York: Routledge, 1991. Print.

———. *From Black Power to Hip Hop: Racism, Nationalism, and Feminism*. Philadelphia: Temple UP, 2006. Print

Crenshaw, Kimberle. "Demarginalizing the Intersection of Race and Sex: A Black Feminist Critique of Antidiscrimination Doctrine, Feminist Theory and Antiracist Politics." *University of Chicago Legal Forum* 1 (1989): 139–167. Print.

Curiel, Ochy. "Critica poscolonial desde las practicas politicas del feminismo antirracista." *Nómadas* 26 (2007): 92–101. Print.

Davis, Angela. *Women, Race, and Class*. New York: Random House, 1983. Print.

Davis, Darién J., Tianna S. Paschel, and Judith A. Morrison. "Pan-Afro-Latin African Americanism Revisited: Legacies and Lessons for Transnational Alliances in the New Millennium." *Afrodescendants, Identity, and the Struggle for Development in the Americas*. Ed. Bernd Reiter and Kimberly Eison Simmons. East Lansing: Michigan State UP, 2012. 19-48. Print.

De la Fuente, Alejandro, and George Reid Andrews, eds. *Afro-Latin American Studies – An Introduction*. Cambridge: Cambridge UP, 2018. Print.

Diouf, Sylviane A., and Komozi Woodard, eds. "Introduction." *Black Power 50*. Ed. Sylviane A. Diouf and Komozi Woodard. New York: The New Press, 2016. vii–xiii. Print.

Dixon, Kwame, ed. *Comparative Perspectives on Afro-Latin America*. Gainesville: U of Florida P, 2012. Print.

Du Bois, W.E.B. *The Souls of Black Folk*. New York: New American Library, 1903. Print.

Dudziak, Mary. *Cold War Civil Rights: Race and the Image of American Democracy*. Princeton: Princeton UP, 2011. Print.

Dulitzky, Ariel. "A Region in Denial: Racial Discrimination and Racism in Latin America." *Neither Enemies nor Friends: Latinos, Blacks, Afro-Latinos*. Ed. Anani Dzidzienyo and Suzanne Oboler. London: Palgrave, 2005. 39–59. Print.

Dzidzienyo, Anani, and Suzanne Oboler, eds. "Flows and Counterflows: Latinas/os, Blackness, and Racialization in Hemispheric Perspective." *Neither Enemies nor Friends: Latinos, Blacks, Afro-Latinos*. New York: Palgrave, 2005. 3–35. Print.

Edwards, Brent Hayes. *The Practice of Diaspora: Literature, Translation, and the Rise of Black Internationalism*. Cambridge: Harvard UP, 2003. Print.

Elbaum, Max. "What Legacy from the Radical Internationalism of 1968?" *Radical History Review* 82 (2002): 37–64. Print.

Ellis, Trey. "The New Black Aesthetic." *Callaloo* 38 (1989): 233–243. Print.

Fanon, Frantz. *The Wretched of the Earth.* New York: Penguin, 1965. Print.

Fernández, Johana. *The Young Lords: A Radical History.* Chapel Hill: The U of North Carolina P, 2020. Print.

Fishkin, Shelley Fisher. "Crossroads of Cultures: The Transnational Turn in American Studies: Presidential Address to the American Studies Association, November 12, 2004." *American Quarterly* 51.1 (2005): 17–57. Print.

Flores, Juan. *From Bomba to Hip-Hop: Puerto Rican Culture and Latino Identity.* New York: Columbia UP, 2000. Print.

———. "Boogaloo and Latin Soul." *The Afro-Latin@ Reader: History and Culture in the United States.* Ed. Miriam Jiménez Román and Juan Flores. Durham: Duke UP, 2010. 199–206. Print.

Fontaine, Pierre-Michel. "Research in the Political Economy of Afro-Latin America." *Latin American Research Review* 15.2 (1980): 111–141. Print.

Ford, Tanisha. *Liberated Threads: Black Women, Style, and the Global Politics of Soul.* Chapel Hill: The U of North Carolina P, 2015. Print.

Gaines, Kevin. "Music is a World: Stevie Wonder and the Sound of Black Power." *Black Power Beyond Borders: The Global Dimensions of the Black Power Movement.* Ed. Nico Slate. New York: Palgrave Macmillan, 2012. 191-211. Print.

Gates Jr., Henry Louis. *Black in Latin America.* New York: New York UP, 2011. Print.

Gilroy, Paul. *There Ain't No Black in the Union Jack: The Cultural Politics of Race and Nation.* London: Hutchinson, 1987. Print.

———. *The Black Atlantic: Modernity and Double-Consciousness.* Cambridge: Harvard UP, 1992. Print.

Gonzalez, Lélia. *Por um feminismo afro-latino-americano.* Rio de Janeiro: Zahar, 2020. Print.

Gore, Dayo F., Jeanne Theoharis, and Komozi Woodard, eds. *Want to Start a Revolution? Radical Women in the Black Freedom Struggle.* New York: New York UP, 2009. Print.

Graham, Maryemma, and Wilfried Raussert, eds. "Literary and Cultural Mobilities." *Mobile and Entangled Americas.* London / New York: Routledge, 2016. 9–12. Print.

Guridy, Frank André. *Forging Diaspora – Afro-Cubans and African Americans in a World of Empire and Jim Crow.* Chapel Hill: The U of North Carolina P, 2010. Print.

Guridy, Frank André, and Juliet Hooker. "Currents in Afro-Latin American Political and Social Thought." *Afro-Latin American Studies – An Introduction.* Ed. Alejandro de la Fuente and George Reid Andrews. Cambridge: Cambridge UP, 2018. 179–221. Print.

Haas, Astrid, ed. *The Harlem Renaissance in an Inter-American Perspective.* Special Issue, *FIAR: Forum for Inter-American Research* 7.2 (2014). Print.

———. "Un continente 'de color': Langston Hughes y América Latina." *The Harlem Renaissance in an Inter-American Perspective.* Ed. Astrid Haas. *FIAR: Forum for Inter-American Research* 7.2 (2014): 36–54. Print.

Hanchard, Michael. *Orpheus and Power – The Movimento Negro of Rio de Janeiro and São Paulo, Brazil, 1945–1988.* Princeton: Princeton UP, 1994. Print.

———. "Black Transnationalism, Africana Studies, and the 21st Century." *Journal of Black Studies* 35.2 (2004): 139–153. Print.

Ho, Fred, and Bill V. Mullen, eds. *Afro Asia: Revolutionary Political and Cultural Connections between African Americans and Asian Americans.* Durham: Duke UP, 2008. Print.

Jackson, Richard. *Black Writers and Latin America – Cross-Cultural Affinities*. Washington: Howard UP, 1998. Print.

James, C.L.R. *The Black Jacobins: Toussaint L'Ouverture and the San Domingo Revolution.* London: Secker & Warburg, 1938. Print.

Jeffries, Judson. *Black Power in the Belly of the Beast*. Champaign: U of Illinois P, 2006. Print.

Jiménez Román, Miriam, and Juan Flores, eds. "Introduction." *The Afro-Latin@ Reader: History and Culture in the United States*. Durham: Duke UP, 2010. 1–15. Print.

Johnson, Cedric. *Revolutionaries to Race Leaders: Black Power and the Making of African American Politics*. Minneapolis: U of Minnesota P, 2007. Print.

Joseph, Peniel E. "The Black Power Movement: A State of the Field." *The Journal of American History* 96.3 (2009): 751–776. Print.

———. *Waiting 'til the Midnight Hour: A Narrative History of Black Power*. New York: Henry Holt, 2006. Print.

———, ed. *Black Power Movement: Rethinking the Civil Rights-Black Power Era*. New York: Routledge, 2006. Print.

Kaltmeier, Olaf. "Transnational Americas: Envisioning Inter-American Area Studies in Globalization Processes." *Transnational Americas: Envisioning Inter-American Area Studies in Globalization Processes*. Ed. Olaf Kaltmeier. Trier: WVT / Tempe, AZ: Bilingual, 2013. 1–14. Print.

———. "General Introduction to the Routledge Handbook of the History and Society of the Americas." *The Routledge Handbook of the History and Society of the Americas*. Ed. Olaf Kaltmeier, Josef Raab, Michael Stewart Foley, Alice Nash, Stefan Rinke, and Mario Rufer. London, New York: Routledge, 2019. 1–12. Print.

Kelley, Robin D. G. "How the West was One: On the Uses and Limits of Diaspora." *The Black Scholar* 30.3/4 (2000): 31–35. Print.

———. *Freedom Dreams – The Black Radical Imagination*. Boston: Beacon Press, 2002. Print.

———. "Stormy Weather: Reconstructing Black (Inter)Nationalism in the Cold War Era." *Is it Nation Time? Contemporary Essays on Black Power and Black Nationalism.* Ed. Eddie S. Glaude Jr. Chicago: The U of Chicago P, 2002. 67–90. Print.

Kelley, Robin D. G., and Tiffany Ruby Patterson. "Unfinished Migrations: Reflections on the African Diaspora and the Making of the Modern World." *African Studies Review* 43.1 (2000): 11–45. Print.

Kunow, Rüdiger. "American Studies as Mobility Studies: Some Terms and Constellations." *Re-Framing the Transnational Turn in American Studies*. Ed. Winfried Fluck, Donald E. Pease, and John Carlos Rowe. Hanover: Dartmouth UP, 2011. 245–264. Print.

Laó-Montes, Agustín. "Afro-Latinidades and the Diasporic Imaginary." *Iberoamericana* 5.17 (2005): 117–130. Print.

———. "Cartografía del campo político afrodescendiente en América Latina." *Debates sobre ciudadanía y políticas raciales en las Américas Negras*. Ed. Claudia Mosquera Rosero-Labbé, Agustín Laó-Montes, César Rodriguez Garavito. Bogotá: Universidad Nacional de Colombia, 2010. 279–316. Print.

———. *Contrapunteos diaspóricos. Cartografías políticas de nuestra Afroamérica*. Bogotá: Universidad Externado De Colombia, 2020. Print.

Laó-Montes, Agustín, and Arlene Davila, eds. *Mambo Montage – The Latinization of New York*. New York: Columbia UP, 2001. Print.

Lazerow, Jama, and Yohuru Williams, eds. *In Search of the Black Panther Party: New Perspectives on a Revolutionary Movement.* Durham: Duke UP, 2006. Print.

Lebron, Christopher J. *The Making of Black Lives Matter.* New York: Oxford UP, 2018.

Lewis, Earl. "To Turn as on a Pivot: Writing African American History into a History of Overlapping Diasporas." *The American Historical Review* 100.3 (1995): 765–787. Print.

Lewis, Rupert. *Walter Rodney's Intellectual and Political Thought.* Kingston: U of the West Indies P, 1998. Print.

Lipsitz, George. "Review of *The Black Atlantic.*" *Social Identities* 1.1 (1995): 193–201. Print.

Lordi, Emily J. *The Meaning of Soul – Black Music and Resilience since the 1960s.* Durham: Duke UP, 2020. Print.

Mahler, Anne Garland. *From the Tricontinental to the Global South: Race, Radicalism, and Transnational Solidarity.* Durham: Duke UP, 2018. Print.

Marable, Manning. *Malcolm X: A Life of Reinvention.* New York: Viking, 2011. Print.

Marqusee, Mike. *Redemption Song – Muhammad Ali and the Spirit of the Sixties.* London / New York: Verso, 1999. Print.

Masiki, Trent, and Regina Marie Mills. "Introduction: Bridging African American and Latina/o/x Studies." *The Black Scholar* 52.1 (2022): 1–4. Print.

Meehan, Kevin. *People Get Ready: African American and Caribbean Cultural Exchange.* Jackson: UP of Mississippi, 2010. Print.

Meeks, Brian. *Radical Caribbean: From Black Power to Abu Bakr.* Kingston: U of the West Indies P, 1996. Print.

Mignolo, Walter. *The Darker Side of Western Modernity: Global Futures, Decolonial Options.* Durham: Duke University Press, 2011. Print.

Muñoz, Jr, Carlos. *Youth, Identity, Power: The Chicano Movement.* London / New York: Verso, 2007. Print.

Munro, John. *The Anticolonial Front: The African American Freedom Struggle and Global Decolonisation, 1945–1960.* Cambridge: Cambridge UP, 2017. Print.

Njoroge, Njoroge. *Chocolate Surrealism – Music, Movement, Memory, and History in the Circum-Caribbean.* Jackson: UP of Mississippi, 2017. Print.

Nwankwo, Ifeoma Kiddoe. "The Promises and Perils of U.S. African-American Hemispherism: Latin America in Martin Delany's *Blake* and Gayl Jones's *Mosquito.*" *Hemispheric American Studies: Essays Beyond the Nation.* Ed. Caroline Levander and Robert Levine. New Brunswick: Rutgers UP, 2008. 187–204. Print.

———. "Introduction: Making Sense, Making Selves. Afro-Latin Americans of British Caribbean Descent." *Latin American and Caribbean Ethnic Studies* 4.3 (2009): 221–230. Print.

———. *Black Cosmopolitanism: Racial Consciousness and Transnational Identity in the Nineteenth-Century Americas.* Philadelphia: U of Pennsylvania P, 2014. Print.

Ogbar, Jeffrey O.G. *Black Power: Radical Politics and African American Identity.* Baltimore: Johns Hopkins UP, 2004. Print.

———. "Rainbow Radicalism: The Rise of the Radical Ethnic Nationalism." *Black Power Movement: Rethinking the Civil Rights-Black Power Era.* Ed. Peniel Joseph. New York: Routledge, 2006. 193–228. Print.

———. *Hip-Hop Revolution: The Culture and Politics of Rap.* Lawrence: UP of Kansas, 2007. Print.

———. "The Looks." *Black Power 50.* Ed. Sylviane A. Diouf and Komozi Woodard. New York: The New Press, 2016. 125–136. Print.

Ongiri, Amy Abugo. *Spectacular Blackness: The Cultural Politics of the Black Power Movement and the Search for a Black Aesthetic.* Charlottesville: U of Virginia P, 2010. Print.

Opie, Frederick. *Upsetting the Apple Cart: Black-Latino Coalitions in New York City from Protest to Public Office*. New York: Columbia UP, 2014. Print.

Paschel, Tianna. *Becoming Black Political Subjects: Movements and Ethno-Racial Rights in Colombia and Brazil.* Princeton: Princeton UP, 2018. Print.

———. "Rethinking Black Mobilizations in Latin America." *Afro-Latin American Studies – An Introduction.* Ed. Alejandro de la Fuente and George Reid Andrews. Cambridge: Cambridge UP, 2018. 222–263. Print.

Pereira, Amílcar Araújo. *O Mundo Negro: relações raciais e a constituição do movimento negro contemporâneo no Brasil.* Rio de Janeiro: Pallas, 2013. Print.

Perry, Keisha-Khan Y. "The Groundings with my Sisters: Toward a Black Diasporic Feminist Agenda in the Americas." *The Scholar and Feminist Online.* 2009. Web. https://sfonline.barnard.edu/africana/perry_01.htm.

Pinho, Osmundo Santos de Araujo. *O Mundo Negro – Hermenêutica Crítica da Reafricanização em Salvador*. Salvador: UNIAFRO, 2010. Print.

Plummer, Brenda Gayle. *Rising Wind: Black Americans and U.S. Foreign Affairs, 1935–1960.* Chapel Hill: U of North Carolina P, 1996. Print.

———. *In Search of Power. African Americans in the Era of Decolonization, 1956-1974*. New York: Cambridge UP, 2013. Print.

———. "International Dimensions of the Black Power Movement." *Black Power 50.* Ed. Sylviane A. Diouf and Komozi Woodard. New York: The New Press, 2016. 103–123. Print.

Pousadela, Inés. "#BLM beyond the U.S.: Anti-racist struggles in Latin America." *Open Democracy.* 26 May 2021. Web. https://www.opendemocracy.net/en/democraciaabierta/blm-beyond-the-us-anti-racist-struggles-in-latin-america/.

Pulido, Laura. *Black, Brown, Yellow, and Left: Radical Activism in Los Angeles.* Oakland: U of California P, 2006. Print.

Putnam, Lara. *Radical Moves: Caribbean Migrants and the Politics of Race in the Jazz Age.* Chapel Hill: The U of North Carolina P, 2013. Print.

Quinn, Kate, ed. *Black Power in the Caribbean.* Florida: U of Florida P, 2014. Print.

———. "Introduction: New Perspectives on Black Power in the Caribbean." *Black Power in the Caribbean.* Florida: U of Florida P, 2014. 1–24. Print.

Rabaka, Reiland. *Hip Hop's Amnesia: From Blues and the Black Women's Club Movement to Rap and the Hip Hop Movement.* Lanham: Lexington Books, 2012. Print.

Ratcliff, Anthony. "Black Writers of the World, Unite!" *The Black Scholar* 37.4 (2008): 27–38. Print.

Raussert, Wilfried, and Michelle Habell-Pallán, eds. *Cornbread and Cuchifritos: Ethnic Identity Politics, Transnationalization, and Transculturation in American Urban Popular Music*. Trier: WVT / Tempe, AZ: Bilingual, 2011. Print.

Raussert, Wilfried, and Giselle Anatol. "Introduction: Literature and Music in the Americas." *The Routledge Handbook to the Culture and Media of the Americas*. Ed. Wilfried Raussert, Giselle L. Anatol, Sebastian Thies, Sarah Corona Berkin, and José Carlos Lozano. London / New York: Routledge, 2020. 15–21. Print.

Raussert, Wilfried. "Mobilizing America/América: Toward Entangled Americas and a Blueprint for Inter-American 'Area Studies.'" *FIAR: Forum for Inter-American Research* 7.3 (2014): 59–97. Print.

Raussert, Wilfried, ed. "Introduction." *The Companion to Inter-American Studies*. London / New York: Routledge, 2017. 1-12. Print.

Raussert, Wilfried, and Olaf Kaltmeier, eds. *Sonic Politics. Music and Social Movements in the Americas from the 1960s to the Present*. London / New York: Routledge, 2019. Print.

Redmond, Shana L. *Anthem – Social Movements and the Sound of Solidarity in the African Diaspora*. New York: New York UP, 2014. Print.

Reed Jr., Adolph. "Black Particularity Reconsidered." *Is it Nation Time? Contemporary Essays on Black Power and Black Nationalism*. Ed. Eddie S. Glaude Jr. Chicago: U of Chicago P, 2001. Print.

Rivera, Raquel Z. *New York Ricans from the Hip Hop Zone*. New York: Palgrave, 2003. Print.

Rivera, Raquel Z., Wayne Marshall, and Deborah Pacini Hernandez, eds. *Reggaeton*. Durham: Duke UP, 2009. Print.

Rivera-Rideau, Petra R., Jennifer A. Jones, and Tianna S. Paschel, eds. *Afro-Latin@s in Movement: Critical Approaches to Blackness and Transnationalism in the Americas*. New York: Palgrave Macmillan, 2016. Print.

Rivero, Yeidy: "Bringing the Soul: Afros, Black Empowerment, and Lucecita." *The Afro-Latin@ Reader: History and Culture in the United States*. Ed. Miriam Jiménez Román and Juan Flores. Durham: Duke UP, 2009. 343-357. Print.

Robinson, Cedric J. *Black Marxism: The Making of the Black Radical Tradition*. Chapel Hill: U of North Carolina P, 1983. Print.

Rose, Tricia. *Black Noise: Rap Music and Black Culture in Contemporary America*. Lebanon: UP of New England, 1994. Print.

Saldívar, José David. *Trans-Americanity – Subaltern Modernities, Global Coloniality, and the Cultures of Greater Mexico*. Durham: Duke UP, 2011. Print.

Sales, William. *From Civil Rights to Black Liberation: Malcolm X and the Organization of Afro-American Unity*. Boston: South End Press, 1994. Print.

Sansone, Livio. *Blackness without Ethnicity: Constructing Race in Brazil*. New York: Palgrave Macmillan, 2003. Print.

Saunders, Tanya. *Cuban Underground Hip Hop: Black Thoughts, Black Revolution, Black Modernity*. Austin: U of Texas P, 2015. Print.

Seale, Bobby. *Seize the Time – The Story of the Black Panther Party and Huey P. Newton*. Baltimore: Black Classic Press, 1991. Print.

Slate, Nico, ed. *Black Power Beyond Borders: The Global Dimensions of the Black Power Movement*. New York: Palgrave Macmillan, 2012. Print.

Smethurst, James. *The Black Arts Movement: Literary Nationalism in the 1960s and 1970s*. Chapel Hill: U of North Carolina P, 2005. Print.

Smith, Jennifer B. *An International Story of the Black Panther Party*. New York: Garland, 1999. Print.

Smith, Paul Chaat, and Robert Allen Warrior. *Like a Hurricane: The Indian Movement from Alcatraz to Wounded Knee*. New York: New Press, 1996. Print.

Sparling, Nicole L. "Mothers of *Afrolatinidad*: Dislocating New World Identities in Latino/a Studies and African American Studies." *Expanding Latinidad: An Inter-American Perspective.* Ed. Luz Angélica Kirschner. Trier: WVT / Tempe, AZ: Bilingual, 2012. Print.

Springer, Kimberley. *Living for the Revolution: Black Feminist Organizations, 1968–1980.* Durham: Duke UP, 2005. Print.

Stam, Robert, and Ella Shohat. *Race in Translation – Culture Wars Around the Postcolonial Atlantic*. New York: New York UP, 2012. Print.

Steinitz, Matti. *Black Power in Lateinamerika: Nord-Süd-Dialoge in der afroatlantischen Diaspora*. Berlin: WeltTrends, 2014. Print.

———. "Black Power in a paraíso racial? The Black Rio Movement, U.S. Soul Music, and Afro-Brazilian Mobilizations under Military Rule (1970–1976)." *Politics of Entanglement in the Americas: Connecting Transnational Flows and Local Perspectives.* Ed. Lukas Rehm, Jochen Kemner, and Olaf Kaltmeier. Trier: WVT / Tempe, AZ: Bilingual, 2017. 13–30. Print.

———. "'Calling out around the world': How Soul Music Transnationalized the African American Freedom Struggle in the Black Power Era (1965–75)." *Sonic Politics: Music and Social Movements in the Americas.* Ed. Olaf Kaltmeier and Wilfried Raussert. London / New York: Routledge, 2019. 88–106. Print.

———. "We got Latin Soul! Transbarrio Dialogues and Afro-Latin Identity Formation in New York's Puerto Rican Community during the Age of Black Power (1966–1972)." *Human Rights in the Americas*. Ed. Luz Kirschner, Maria Herrera Sobek, and Francisco Lomeli. New York / London: Routledge, 2021. 243–262. Print.

———. "Soulful Sancocho – Soul Music and Practices of Hemispheric Black Transnationalism in 1960s and 1970s Panama." *The Black Scholar* 52.1 (2022): 15–26. Print.

Stephens, Michelle. "What Is This Black in Black Diaspora?" *Small Axe* 13.2 (2009): 26–38. Print.

———. *Black Empire: the Masculine Global Imaginary of Caribbean Intellectuals in the United States, 1914–1962*. Durham: Duke UP, 2005. Print.

Swan, Quito. *Black Power in Bermuda: The Struggle for Decolonization.* New York: Palgrave Macmillan, 2009. Print.

———. "Transnationalism." *Keywords for African American Studies*. Ed. Erica R. Edwards, Roderick A. Ferguson, and Jeffrey O. G. Ogbar. New York: New York UP, 2018. 209–213. Print.

———. *Pasifika Black – Oceania, Anti-colonialism, and the African World.* New York: New York UP, 2022. Print.

Tate, Greg. "Cult Nats Meet Freaky Deke." *Flyboy in the Buttermilk: Essays on Contemporary America*. New York: Simon & Schuster, 1992. 198–210. Print.

Taylor, Keeanga-Yamahtta. *From #blacklivesmatter to Black Liberation.* Chicago: Haymarket Books, 2016. Print.

———. *How We Get Free: Black Feminism and the Combahee River Collective*. Chicago: Haymarket Books, 2017. Print.

Thies, Sebastian, and Josef Raab, eds. *E Pluribus Unum? National and Transnational Identities in the Americas*. Berlin: Lit Verlag, 2009. Print.

Thomas, Piri. *Down These Mean Streets.* New York: Vintage Books, 1967. Print.

Tomlinson, Lisa. *Una Marson.* Kingston: U of the West Indies P, 2019. Print.

Valdés, Vanessa. *Diasporic Blackness: The Life and Times of Arturo Alfonso Schomburg.* New York: SUNY Press, 2017. Print.

Van Deburg, W. *New Day in Babylon: The Black Power Movement and American Culture, 1965–1975.* Chicago: U of Chicago P, 1992. Print.

Von Eschen, Penny. *Race against Empire: Black Americans and Anticolonialism, 1937–1957.* Ithaca: Cornell UP, 1997. Print.

Wade, Peter. *Race and Ethnicity in Latin America.* London: Pluto Press, 1997. Print.

Wallerstein, Immanuel. *The Modern World-System: Capitalist Agriculture and the Origins of the European World-Economy in the Sixteenth Century.* New York: Academic Press, 1974. Print.

West, Michael O., and William G. Martin. "Introduction: Contours of the Black International From Toussaint to Tupac." *From Toussaint to Tupac: The Black International since the Age of Revolution.* Ed. Michael O. West, William G. Martin, and Fanon Che Wilkins. Chapel Hill: U of North Carolina P, 2009. 1–44. Print.

Wilkins, Fanon Che. "The Making of Black Internationalists: SNCC and Africa before the Launching of Black Power, 1960–1965." *The Journal of African American History* 92.4 (2007): 467–490. Print.

Williams, Yohuru. "'They've Lynched our Savior, Lumumba in the Old Fashion Southern Style': The Conscious Internationalism of American Black Nationalism." *Black Power Beyond Borders: The Global Dimensions of the Black Power Movement.* Ed. Nico Slate. New York: Palgrave Macmillan, 2012. 246–281. Print.

Wimmer, Andreas, and Nina Glick Schiller. "Methodological Nationalism and Beyond: Nation-State Building, Migration, and the Social Sciences." *Global Networks* 2.4 (2002): 301–334. Print.

Winant, Howard. "Foreword – A New Hemispheric Blackness." *Comparative Perspectives on Afro-Latin America.* Ed. Kwame Dixon and John Burdick. Gainesville: U of Florida P, 2012. Ix–xiv. Print.

Woodard, Komozi. *A Nation within a Nation: Amiri Baraka (LeRoi Jones) and Black Power.* Chapel Hill: U of North Carolina P, 1999. Print.

X, Malcolm. *By Any Means Necessary.* New York: Pathfinder Press, 1998. Print.

Young, Cynthia. *Soul Power: Culture, Radicalism, and the Making of a U.S. Third World Left.* Durham: Duke UP, 2006. Print.

Zapata Olivella, Manuel. *¡Levántate Mulato! Por mi raza hablará el espíritu.* Bogotá: Rei Andes, 1990. Print.

The Roots of Canadian Black Power: Thomas Peters and the Struggle for Black Freedom in the Eighteenth Century

AFUA COOPER

This essay sheds light on the roots of Black Power in Canada. It does so by noting the importance of the movement in Canada and its marginalization in global discourses on Black Power. It reveals that there was a home-grown movement in Canada, with global influences that, like most Black Power movements, came of age during the 1960s and 1970s, echoing throughout the 1980s and beyond. However, the main contribution of this paper lies in the argument that there is a genealogy of Black Power in Canada that goes back to the eighteenth century. It explores this phenomenon by looking at the life and work of Thomas Peters, a former slave turned Black leader. Peters articulated a Black Power philosophy that placed Black empowerment at the center of his praxis. Though Peters was truly a transnational leader whose activism spanned the Atlantic world, his contributions to Black Power in Canada were legion. Therefore, as this chapter argues, Peters deserves to be better known.

Black Power as a concept and certainly as a practice goes all the way back to the landing of the first collective of kidnapped African captives whom Whites took to the Americas to work as slaves. Over the centuries, these captives engaged in acts of resistance against enslavement, colonization, and White supremacy. Their actions were manifested in organized slave revolts, rebellions, and revolutions like Tacky's War in Jamaica (1760/61), the Haitian Revolution (1791–1804), and Nat Turner's Revolt in the United States (1831). Captives also fled slavery and created maroon communities, palenques, and quilombos such as the Palenque of Yanga in Mexico, Palmares in Brazil, and Accompong Town in Jamaica. During the post-slavery era, the agitations of Henry McNeal Turner through his emigrationist movement and Marcus Garvey's Universal Negro Improvement Association (UNIA) were some of the most visible manifestations of Black Power *avant la lettre*.

Outside the Americas, too, the twentieth-century decolonization movements throughout Africa were an expression of Black Power. In fact, some of the names associated with this movement – Amilcar Cabral, Kwame Nkrumah, Patrice Lumumba, Walter Sisulu, Frantz Fanon, Sekou Touré, and Nelson Mandela – inspired the Black Power movement in the United States and at the same were influenced by it themselves.

But how is Black Power defined, and what are some of its core components? To answer this question, I turn to the iconic moment in the Civil Rights era when the term Black Power was popularized. This is attributed to Willie Ricks and Stokely Carmichael, who were activists and organizers of the Student Nonviolent Coordinating Committee (SNCC). In June 1966, in Greenwood, Mississippi, at a SNCC rally, Willie Ricks primed Carmichael to use the term Black Power, which he did. Carmichael called for "Black Power" and led the marchers into chanting the slogan.[1]

Stokely himself defines what he meant by Black Power. In an interview with sociologist Joyce Ladner, Carmichael defined the term as "the ability of black people to politically get together and organize themselves so they can speak from a position of strength rather than a position of weakness" (Ladner 8). In *Black Power: Politics of Liberation in America* (1967), Carmichael and Hamilton explain this more deeply, discussing the core components of Black Power: its anti-racist nature, its commitment to struggle against White supremacy and colonialism, and even more crucially, the ability of Blacks to be fully empowered in order to have sovereignty in and over their own communities, their lives, their bodies, and their brains. In other words, Black Power calls for Black people having the power to organize and create their own societies in which they exercise spiritual, material, cultural, economic, and emotional sovereignty outside the confines of a debilitating and oppressive social structure.

Black Power in Canada

Black Power then was a global phenomenon. But as a Black intellectual who lives, works, and teaches Black Studies epistemologies in Canada, I have come to the painful realization that Canada is often missing from North American and global discussions about Black power, even though similar racial currents that led to Black power practices and manifestations in the United States were also present in Canada.[2] The sidelining of Canada in Black Power discourse is strange given that some of the main leaders of the movement, like Stokely Carmichael (Kwame Turé) and Walter Rodney, spent time in Canada, and events like the Congress of Black Writers, the Sir George Williams University Affairs in Montreal, and the activities of the Black Panthers in Halifax, Nova Scotia had international resonance.[3] One reason for the lack of discussion about Black Power in Canada is the belief that Canada was free from racism, a country where Black people enjoyed equal rights with Whites. The two-hundred-year presence of slavery in Canada is often dismissed while the segregation and racial violence that

1 "Stokely Carmichael on his black power speech." https://www.youtube.com/watch?v=4A9SKoMfzek.

2 Nico Slate's edited volume *Black Power Beyond Borders* is just one example of the exclusion of Canada from scholarship and discussions about Black Power.

3 David Austin teases out the diminishment of the Black Power movement in Canada and provides a discussion of some of the critical activities that took place in the 1960s in Montreal. See his "'All Roads Led to Montreal': Black Power, the Caribbean, and the Black Radical Tradition in Canada."

Canadian Black people were subjected to has remained relatively unknown in global epistemologies about Black life.[4]

Despite the lack of knowledge about Black Power practices in Canada, Marcus Garvey's UNIA, which was headquartered in Harlem, New York, created for all intents and purposes a "national network of Black Power" by establishing dozens of chapters in various Canadian provinces. In fact, three of the earliest UNIA chapters established in North America during 1918 and 1919 were established in Cape Breton, Montreal and Toronto respectively. Eventually, 32 chapters were established across Canada from Nova Scotia in the east to British Columbia in the west. Each chapter owned or rented a "Liberty Hall" which became its organizing sites of resistance and community development. The Canadian UNIA branches were also linked globally to other UNIA networks in the United States, Latin America and the Caribbean, Europe, and West Africa. When Garvey was deported from the United States in 1927, Canada gained prominence as the site from which Garvey directed UNIA operations. He himself toured Canada in the 1930s and in 1937 gave a stirring speech in Sydney, Cape Breton, with the rallying cry "we must emancipate ourselves from mental slavery." Decades later, Bob Marley would put those words to verse in "Redemption Song."[5] In the 1940s, Hugh Burnett with the National Unity Association in Ontario, and Viola Desmond in Nova Scotia challenged White Supremacy.

As some scholars of the Canadian Black experience have shown, in the 30 years from 1950 to 1980, national and global events gave a new urgency to the creation of a modern Black Power movement within Canada. Some of these currents include the formation of the Black Panther Party in the U.S., the Black Power and independence movement in the Caribbean, and the decolonization movements in Africa, including various revolutions across the continent and the struggle to end apartheid in South Africa. This urgency was manifested in the Congress of Black Writers in Montreal in 1968, the Sir George Williams University Computer Affair in 1969 (also in Montreal), the formation of the Afro-Canadian Liberation Movement (ACLM), the Black United Front (BUF) in Nova Scotia, and the creation of such groups as League of Revolutionary Black Workers, the Black Workers Alliance, (BWA), and the African Liberation Support Committee (ALSC).[6] These groups had decidedly left-wing positions ranging

4 For a discussion on how the Canadian settler state renders Black people and their history invisible, cf. George Elliot Clarke. On the subject of Canada's two-hundred-year enslavement of Africans, cf. Afua Cooper (*The Hanging of Angelique*).

5 See the "Marcus Garvey and UNIA Papers Project" at the UCLA African Studies Center, https://www.international.ucla.edu/africa/mgpp/. Cf. Carla Marano, "We All Used to Meet at the Hall."

6 Chris Harris goes into details about some of the various Black Power groups that coalesced in Toronto in "Canadian Black Power, Organic Intellectuals, and the War of Position in Toronto, 1967–1975." In *Revolutionary*, Burnley "Rocky" Jones, provides a discussion on his involvement in the movement, his hosting the Black Panthers in Halifax, and information on the Afro-Canadian Liberation Movement, and the Black United Front. Agnes Calliste enriches our knowledge of Canadian Black Power with "The In-

from Black Nationalism, Pan-Africanism, Marxism-Leninism, and Maoism. People who provided intellectual heft include Rosie Douglas, Ann Cools, Rocky Jones, and Valerie Belgrave, with contributions from transnational Caribbean intellectuals and activists, such as C.L.R. James, Walter Rodney, and Carmichael, who spent time in Canada.

Yet, there is an even longer history to Canadian Black Power, even before the UNIA, the struggles in Montreal, and the BUF in Nova Scotia which goes back to militant Black protest, activism, and organizing in the eighteenth-century world of slavery and freedom. The idea and practice of Black people having the ability to organize themselves and communities for uplift and independence were at the heart of the activism of eighteenth-century fugitive slave, Revolutionary War soldier, and freedom-fighter Thomas Peters (1738–1792). Peters espoused a Black Power ethos in the middle and latter decades of the eighteenth century in Canada, and later in Sierra Leone, West Africa. He protested the mistreatment of his fellow Blacks and campaigned relentlessly for Black freedom and civil rights and the empowerment of Black people. Thus, I view Thomas Peters as a forefather of the Canadian Black Power Movement.

Thomas Peters is known in various roles and by several identities. A Yoruba prince from the Egba sub-clan, an enslaved man in Louisiana and North Carolina, a runaway slave, a soldier in the Black Pioneers military unit that fought on the side of the British during the American Revolutionary War, a Black Loyalist in Nova Scotia, a Black power leader and civil rights activist in Nova Scotia and New Brunswick, a husband and father, a proponent of African emigration, an emigrant on one of the 15 ships that left Nova Scotia for Sierra Leone in January 1792, an advocate for Black rights in Sierra Leone, and finally one of the founding fathers of Sierra Leone.[7] In the 54 years that Peters lived, he did so on three continents. He spent at least half of his life in slavery.[8] Peters made up to four transatlantic crossings, the last three in service to Black freedom, and died fighting a White power structure in Sierra Leone that was bent on denying Black people liberation and power.

The purpose of this essay is to examine what I call Thomas Peters's Black Power activism and agency. The paper seeks to contextualize this inquiry within the history of the Black Loyalist experience in North America and West Africa. In what follows, I focus on the years Peters spent in Nova Scotia, New Brunswick, and Sierra Leone,

---

fluence of the Civil Rights and Black Power Movement in Canada." More light is shed by Austin on the formation of Black Power groups in Montreal.

7 Though information about Thomas Peters has appeared in several publications, there is no dedicated biography about him. Historian Gary B. Nash notes that memory about Peters "has been lost in the fog of our historical amnesia …". See Nash's "Thomas Peters: Millwright and Deliverer." Poet Valerie Mason-John has also immortalized Thomas Peters in her poem "The Ghost of Thomas Peters," https://www.youtube.com/watch?v=FCtvIrr_CJA.

8 In the 1783 military register named the "Book of Negroes," in which the name of Peters is recorded, his age is given as 45 years.

especially because this era is the best documented of his life – a period during which he was most active in the quest for Black freedom and Black power.[9]

The American Revolution and the emergence of the Black Loyalists

The Black Loyalist identity was created within and after the American Revolution. By the end of 1775, the 13 American colonies were in revolt against the Mother Country, Great Britain. Feeling that they were under the 'yoke of slavery,' the colonies clamored for independence. At this time the royal governor of Virginia, Lord Dunmore issued a proclamation promising "liberty to the slaves," provided that they ran away from slavery to join the British during the ensuing war. It must be noted that Dunmore committed himself to freeing only those runaway slaves who were owned by rebel masters (that is, those who supported the colonists' side). Ironically, those Blacks enslaved by masters who were loyal to Britain were not offered freedom. As a consequence, hundreds of enslaved men, held in bondage by rebel owners, soon found their way to the British line. Dunmore quickly formed them into the "Ethiopian Regiment" and had "liberty to slaves" inscribed across their jackets. These runaways fought for the British against the American side.

Most American military officials only desired Blacks to work in servile positions or menial labor. As Ellen Gibson Wilson notes, Dunmore was the first colonial commander, British or American, who was "committed to using Blacks in combat." On their side of the war, Americans only began deploying Blacks into combat several years into the Revolution, and only as a deliberate necessity (Quarles). This emancipatory move by Dunmore, not only strengthened the British forces but it also was an effective war strategy that robbed American plantations of slaves' much needed labor, thus destabilizing the economy (Gibson Wilson 26).

Approximately a year later, in 1776, British general Henry Clinton, appeared off the coast of North Carolina with his war ships. Soon enough, acting upon Dunmore's Proclamation, 71 runaway slaves approached Clinton's ships. Peters was among them. He had fled from his White owner, one Duncan Campbell, in Wilmington, North Carolina. Peters was quickly enlisted in the Black Pioneers, a provincial corps formed by Clinton (Black Loyalists Digital Collections.). In 1779, Clinton further expanded Dunmore's proclamation in what became known as the Phillipsburg Proclamation (Walker, *Black Loyalists* 2–3). Over the course of the war, Black Pioneers fought with Clinton in North Carolina, Rhode Island, Philadelphia, and New York City. Like Peters, with the promise of freedom ringing in their ears, thousands of slaves eventually joined and fought for the British cause. Those Americans who served and remained loyal to the British were simply called Loyalists, those who were enslaved and Black were thus called Black Loyalists. This was an identity forged in and through war. It

9 James Walker in his work on the Black Loyalists has written extensively on Peters in Nova Scotia and Sierra Leone.

must be noted that it was not Dunmore, Clinton, or any other British general who freed these enslaved Blacks. They were the ones who freed themselves.[10]

It took courage, determination, and a strong desire for freedom to convince them to run away, because, if caught, the runaway could be resold, brutally punished, or killed by their owner. Indeed, to even conceive of the idea of running away required a breaking of the chains of mental slavery. The act of running away was the first step for many in forging an antislavery consciousness, accompanied by internalizing the idea that freedom was worth fighting for. Runaways like Thomas Peters and Harry Washington were part of a military corps like the Black Pioneers or the Ethiopian Regiment. They engaged in battle. They killed and were killed. In fact, Peters was wounded twice during the war. They were taken prisoners. Some like Richard Pierpont and Colonel Tye joined and led guerilla units (Gibson Wilson 27; Meyler and Meyler). Others like Boston King worked as spies. King was captured by the Americans, jailed, made prisoner, escaped again to the British side, and served out the rest of the war in New York. Black women Loyalists like Violet King met her husband Boston in New York. She worked as a cook there for British forces. The Kings like the other Black Loyalists held on to the promise of freedom made to them by the British (Robertson and Holmes Whitehead).

After seven years of fighting, the war ended with the British as the losers and the Americans as the victors of the war. One article in the ensuing treaty of Paris insisted upon by slave trader, plantation owner, and founding father, Henry Laurens was that the British return to the American rebel masters (including George Washington) all the enslaved Africans who had fled to British side during the war. Richard Oswald who negotiated for the British agreed and signed the treaty. Oswald himself was also a slave trader and founder of the notorious slave-trading emporium in Sierra Leone known as Bunce Island. He and Laurens were also close friends and business partners. But it was the generals on the ground who were going to eventually decide if that particular article was to be honored. Some generals, unfortunately, did return runaway slaves to their American owners.[11] But others like Guy Carleton and Clinton came up with the idea of issuing certificates of freedom for some of the enslaved who had enlisted with the British before a certain date in 1782. When George Washington came to New York at the end of the war to meet with Carleton on the issue of returning runaway slaves, Carleton told Washington he was not going to hand over all the enslaved who had escaped to British lines (Hochschild 99–103). Carleton commanded General

---

10 The literature on Black Loyalism and the American Revolution is extensive. I have already mentioned Walker's work. Other publications include Ellen Gibson Wilson, *The Loyal Blacks*; Alan Gilbert, *Black Patriots and Loyalists*; Maya Jasanoff, *Liberty's Exiles*; Graham Russell Hodges, ed. *The Black Loyalist Directory*. On Dunmore's emancipatory proclamation, cf. Walker (*Black Loyalists* 1); Wilson (25); on Clinton's proclamation, cf. Walker (*Black Loyalists* 2).

11 On the Peace Treaty between the victorious Americans and the defeated British, cf. Jasanoff (78–81).

Birch to register and give certificates of freedom to some of the enslaved who had gathered in New York. Birch and his subordinates registered over 3000 Black men and women in a list that came to be called the *Book of Negroes*. Certificates of freedom were issued to them.[12] Peters received his certificate signed by Colonel Stewart under the command of General Birch. These 3000 Black Loyalists would eventually leave New York City for Nova Scotia and New Brunswick.

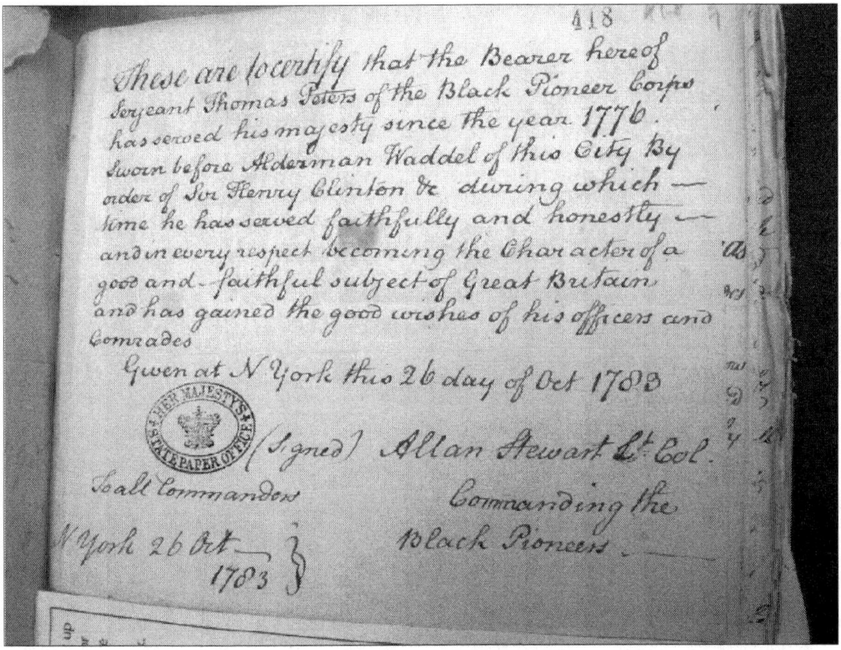
418
These are to certify that the Bearer hereof
Sergeant Thomas Peters of the Black Pioneer Corps
has served his majesty since the year 1776.
Sworn before Alderman Waddel of this City By
order of Sir Henry Clinton &c during which —
time he has served faithfully and honestly —
and in every respect becoming the Character of a
good and faithful subject of Great Britain
and has gained the good wishes of his officers and
Comrades
Given at N York this 26 day of Oct 1783
(Signed) Allan Stewart Lt Col.
To all Commanders
Commanding the
Black Pioneers
N York 26 Oct 1783

Thomas Peters's certificate of freedom

The sum of the story is: these Black Loyalists had endured American slavery, fled their slavemasters, fought for the Crown, many had already lost families, and embarked, with grim determination, upon the high seas in pursuit of that elusive freedom. Here were a people whose consciousness had been wrought in the oppression of slavery, resistance to it, and a bloody war. The British had fought a colonial war; the Americans a war for their independence, but the Black people had fought a war for their freedom. By 1776, the war had ended for the Americans and the British. But for Blacks, the quest for liberty, happiness, and independence had only entered a new phase. Given the circumstances, many of them had no choice but to leave the newly-founded United States.

12 On the issue of the Certificates of Freedom, cf. Walker (*Black Loyalists* 11).

Evacuation of both White and Black Loyalists took place from such port cities as Charleston, Savannah, Saint Augustine, and New York City. It was from New York that Thomas Peters, his wife Sally (also called Sarah), their two children Clarry (Clara) and John, and Murphy Steele, a fellow Black Pioneer, boarded a ship heading for Annapolis Royal, Nova Scotia in 1783. All the above-mentioned had their names and status recorded in General Birch's *Book of Negroes*. Thomas is described condescendingly as an "ordinary fellow." But even by the time Peters and his family left New York, he had accomplished extraordinary things. He would go on to Canada, later England, and then Sierra Leone to do even more.

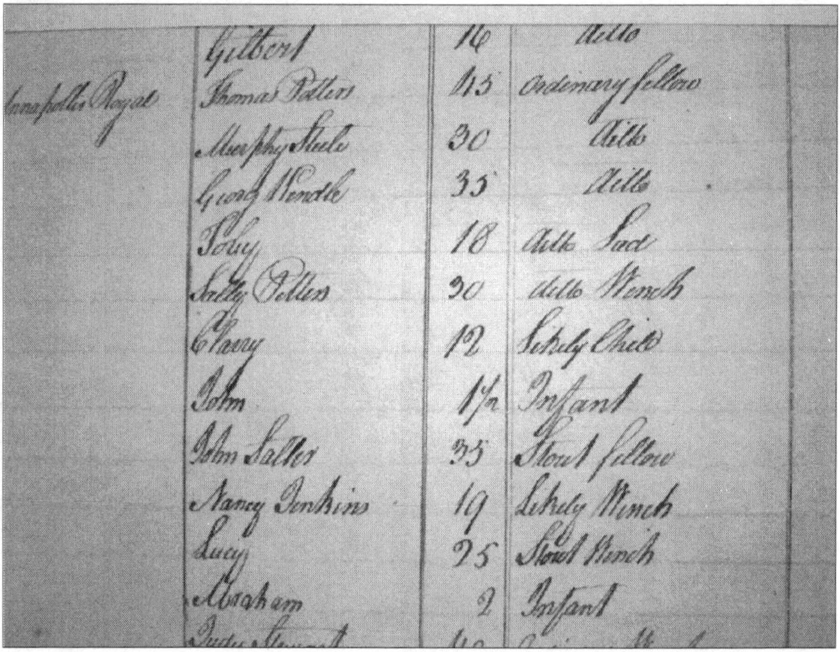

	Gilbert	16	ditto
Annapolis Royal	Thomas Petters	45	Ordinary fellow
	Murphy Steele	30	ditto
	George [illegible]	35	ditto
	Tolly	18	ditto [illegible]
	Sally Petters	30	ditto Wench
	Clarry	12	Likely Child
	John	1½	Infant
	John Salter	35	Stout fellow
	Nancy Jenkins	19	Likely Wench
	Lucy	25	Stout Wench
	Abraham	2	Infant

Thomas Peters's name, 2nd from the top, in *Book of Negroes*

In November 1783, the Peters and Steele families, as well as other Black Loyalists, left New York for Nova Scotia on board the *Joseph*. But this was not going to be a direct journey. It was the end of the Atlantic hurricane season, and two weeks out to sea, the *Joseph* encountered a hurricane, suffering severe damage. It was blown off course and ended up in Bermuda. Peters, his family, and their shipmates were grateful to be alive. They spent the rest of the winter in Bermuda. In the spring of 1784, the *Joseph* set sail for Nova Scotia and by May of the same year it had reached the town of Annapolis Royal on the Bay of Fundy. Finally, Peters had arrived in Canada where he hoped he and the rest of the 3000 free Black Loyalists would find real freedom and a genuine refuge.

Before they sailed from New York, they had been promised by the British that in their new home they would get land on which to establish themselves. They were further promised to be provided with tools and provisions for three years and to get to serve on juries. Their understanding of the 'contract' with the British was that in Nova Scotia and Eastern Canada they would enter society as free and equal persons with Whites, enjoying all the available civil rights and opportunities that Whites themselves enjoyed.

As Adam Hochschild notes, this was "the first mass emancipation" of enslaved Africans held by the British and the first free mass migration of Africans anywhere in the Atlantic world. Hence, these Black Loyalists would constitute one of the most significant diasporas of the modern world (Hochschild 98).

Broken promises in Eastern Canada

We know the story of what happened to the Black Loyalists when they arrived and settled in Nova Scotia and New Brunswick. Those who received land were given plots much smaller than those of their White neighbors. In fact, most Blacks received no land at all. Likewise, many did not even receive the rations, tools, and other supplies that were promised to them. On an immediate level, the rations were critical. Rations were needed to stave off hunger and starvation. The Crown had promised up to three years of rationing. White settlers received the promised amount of provisions, but most of the Blacks, including those who settled at Annapolis Royal and Digby received only three-months' worth of supplies. As a result, arriving in winter, and not having sufficient food, many of the Black Loyalists starved. Black laborers were also paid lower wages than Whites. Given the land and wage inequalities, many Black Loyalists resorted to sharecropping and indentureship to survive. There were also cases of free Blacks being kidnapped and sold back into slavery in the United States and the Caribbean. Racial discrimination also pervaded the area of civil rights. Black persons did not get the right to vote and could not serve on juries.

With the arrival of both the White and Black Loyalists and the enslaved Africans owned by White Loyalists, a new social and racial order began to evolve in Nova Scotia and New Brunswick. This order was founded on a familiar binary: Black inferiority and subordination vis-à-vis White superiority and hegemony. At the same time, the Maritime provinces and the Canadian colonies were being constructed as a 'White man's country,' in which Whites preside over every sector of society and Black marginalization was the norm.[13]

13 Gibson Wilson and Walker (*Black Loyalists*), have written extensively on the experience of the Black Loyalists in Nova Scotia and New Brunswick and the hardships they faced. An excellent website that tells the story of the Black Loyalists in the Canadian

This idea was implemented in racist laws that were put in place by the White power structure. Some of these laws impinged directly on Black social spaces and led to the increased marginalization of the Black Loyalist community. In 1785, for example, White authority in Shelburne made it an offence for Blacks to keep 'dances or loiter,' to engage in what they called "Negro frolicks."[14] To top off the discrimination and oppression that were meted out to these Black Loyalists by Whites, in July 1784, White laborers and disbanded soldiers accused the Black Loyalists of working for lower wages and attacked the Black community in Shelburne and Birchtown. They tore down the houses of the Black Loyalists, beat them up and drove them out of town. This incident has been dubbed by historians as Canada's first race riot (Kimber 167–194). Contemporary diarist Simeon Perkins also recorded the events that took place in this anti-Black riot: "They report that an extraordinary mob or riot has happened at Shelburn. Some thousands of people assembled with clubs and drove the Negroes out of the town, and threatened some people" (Gibson Wilson 93).

The social structure that Whites re-inscribed in the Canadian colonies was reminiscent of that of the 13 Colonies. In the minds of Whites, Blacks were to continue in subordination and servitude. In other words, it was believed that if Blacks stepped out of that designated place, they had to be disciplined through such measures as a race riot. To ensure that salient features of the *status quo ante* continued, colonial Whites in the Maritimes commandeered the political, economic, and financial resources for their own benefit. And that was why they were able to get state officials to attend to their needs and interests. In the minds of Whites, Blacks could gain their freedom but only as the poorest and most disenfranchised members of the new society.

Yet, for no other issue did the Black Loyalists feel more bitter, disappointed, betrayed, and abused than that of land allotment. Further, the land distribution question revealed colonial duplicity, underscoring the precarious nature of Black existence in the maritime colonies. On fleeing the 13 Colonies and arriving in Eastern Canada, Blacks expected to be treated as Whites in receiving similar allotments of land (and provisions); but this was not to be: The land claims of the Black Loyalists were usually the last to be attended to; theirs was last on the list to be surveyed; and when they did get land it was given at a later date than Whites, in much smaller allotments, and on rocky and infertile soil. For example, in the Preston area, Blacks who received land got 50 acres or less compared with the 100 acres or more that Whites received. In Shelburne, a similar pattern was at work. Across the province, Whites got upward of 100 to 1000 acres. Black got 50 acres or less (sometimes in fact only one acre). As mentioned, the majority of Black Loyalists received no land at all. It had been determined earlier by the authorities that one needed at least 200 acres as the basis for a viable farm (Gibson Wilson 100–114; Walker, *Black Loyalists* 18–32).

Maritime colonies is the *Black Loyalists Digital Collection*: https://blackloyalist.com/cdc/index.htm.

14 The White population of Shelburne made Black entertainment such as "frolicking" a crime. https://blackloyalist.com/cdc/story/prejudice/frolick.htm.

Historian Ellen Gibson Wilson argues that denying the newly freed Blacks the land that they had been promised served the purpose of turning them into a rootless servant class. Whites' policy and actions toward Blacks ensured that these Black people would not be given the essential basis for self-support (100-114). The British Crown had used the Black Loyalists in its war effort as a strategy to destabilize the American economy and felt that, at the war's end, the freedom given to the Black Loyalists was compensation enough. The Black Loyalists were left to fend for themselves in the Maritime colonies under the rule of an uncaring and deceitful government and in a spiteful community of Whites, some of whom had been slaveowners in the 13 Colonies and continued to hold slaves in the Maritimes.

But these New World Africans fought back. Black Loyalists organized themselves in church congregations and military units. Many Black veterans like Peters and Murphy Steele who had fought together in the Black Pioneers embarked on the same ship to Nova Scotia and settled together with their families in the same communities. Thus, they shared a common bond, which had its roots in the Revolutionary War and which they used as a platform in Nova Scotia and New Brunswick in order to protest their conditions and the way they were treated. They wrote letters, sent petitions to the colonial and imperial governments, and demanded that promises made to them by the British during the war be fulfilled.

In the face of British betrayal, Thomas Peters emerged as a leader and a spokesperson for the Black community. Historian Simon Schama calls him "the very first leader of African Americans" (Schama 254). Peters had attained the rank of sergeant in the Black Pioneers and had commanded fellow Blacks during the war; he therefore held a natural leadership position. After departing from New York harbor in 1783, Peters first settled with his family, and members of the Black Pioneers in Annapolis Royal. When he stepped ashore at in May 1784, he must have felt relieved that the long sea journey was over and was filled with anticipation for the new life he was ready to build with his family and community in Annapolis Royal. This settlement lay in a beautiful, protected harbor nestled on the Bay of Fundy. Annapolis Royal was the site of one of the earliest European inhabitants in Canada and the capital of the French colony of Acadia. Canadian and Nova Scotia Black history began at this site, especially because it was here, then named Port Royal, that the French colonial government in 1604, had an un-named Black man in its employ. Later evidence reveals that in 1608 Mathieu Da Costa, the first documented Black individual, had entered into a contract with the French at Port Royal for translation services between the French and the Mi'kmaq nation.

But it was at this picturesque village on the Fundy, three months after he arrived in Nova Scotia, that Peters along with Murphy Steele fired the first volley at the colonial government of Nova Scotia, protesting the disenfranchisement and marginalization of the Black Loyalists in land and provisions. In a petition sent to John Parr, governor of the province, Peters and Steele first declared their bona fides as Black Pioneer veterans who served in his Majesty's Army during the "American Rebellion" and attained the rank of sergeant. "We would be very much obliged to your excellency if you would be so good as to grant the articles allowed by the government to us as the rest of the disbanded soldiers of his Majesty's army … land and provisions the same as the rest of the disbanded soldiers which we have not yet received" (Peters and Steele).

Peters and Steele called for full equality with the White soldiers and White people in general. These constituencies had been provided for with land and provisions, but after a whole year, the Blacks of Annapolis Royal had not been so fortunate.[15] The letter to Parr was described as being written and sent on "behalf of the Black Pioneers," an observation meant that indicates that Peters and Steeles were not acting solely for themselves but for the entire collective of Black Pioneers who had emigrated together from New York to settle as a community in Annapolis Royal and the surrounding areas. The petition seemed to have borne fruit because in 1785 the Black Pioneers including Peters were awarded one-acre lots in Brindley Town, a small community just outside the town of Digby, located about 30 kilometers from Annapolis Royal. Some of them were also given some farm lots.

Henceforth, Peters moved to Brindley Town. But several problems arose. One was that as the Blacks tried to occupy and farm the farm lots, Whites claimed these lots as their own. Therefore, the Black people were denied these acres. Also, the one-acre town lots were patently insufficient for the needs of the Black Loyalists. Another vexing issue was that in Brindley Town, the Black people were given rations for only three months, while the Whites were given their allotted yearly rations. And for the Blacks to even get the rations they had to perform the work of building and maintaining roads. Betrayed once more, Peters kept campaigning in the Digby/Annapolis area for land, provisions, Black rights, and racial equality. Consequently, however, he was disappointed at the colonial authorities in the province for their refusal to honor the promises made by the British, their insistence on upholding White supremacy, and their lack of concern for the needs of Black people.

Learning that things might be better for Blacks in New Brunswick, Peters eventually left the Digby area with his family and some other Black Pioneers and crossed the Bay of Fundy to St. John in what is now New Brunswick. He also did a short stint in Fredericton.[16] In each of these communities, Peters served as a leader and advocate

---

15 Thomas Peters and Murphy Steele signed the petition. It is not clear if Peters or Steele could read or write, or if the petition was written by a professional scribe. "Petition on Behalf of the Black Pioneers," 20 August 1784, Commissioner of Public Records, Nova Scotia Archives, RG1, Vol. 359, #65, Microfilm 15428. In an "Untold Lives" blogpost from the British Library, a letter from Peters to the Sierra Leone Company officials, Peters marked an X beside his name. In this case, the letter had clearly been written by a scribe. See The British Library, 3 Nov. 2020, "Tracing the Lives and Letters of the Black Loyalists-Part 2, Thomas Peters." https://blogs.bl.uk/untoldlives/2020/11/-tracing-the-lives-and-letters-of-the-black-loyalists-part-2-thomas-peters.html.

16 In 1784, New Brunswick was carved out of Nova Scotia. Thus, when the Black Loyalists arrived the entire territory was called Nova Scotia. With the creation of New Brunswick, those Blacks who were domiciled there now came under a new colonial government.

for the community. The impetus behind Peters's nomadic journey was his search for land on which Blacks would establish themselves and build lives of freedom and empowerment. The quest for justice was also interwoven with the search for land. As a result, Thomas Peters kept petitioning the local legislatures in New Brunswick and Nova Scotia to make good on the promise made to the Black Loyalists when they served the Crown during the Revolutionary War.[17]

Peters found out that the land situation for Blacks in New Brunswick mirrored the Nova Scotia situation. He therefore tried securing farmland close to Fredericton, but his application was denied. Peters and the New Brunswick Black Loyalists assuaged their frustration by petitioning several times the lieutenant- Governor Thomas Carleton. In April 1790, after years of landlessness, and government apathy, and a pernicious racism Peters sent off the following petition:

> To His Excellency Thomas Carleton, Esquire, Governor and Commander in Chief of the Province of New Brunswick, Petition of Thomas PETERS a Black Man Serjt. of the Late Black Prs.who Serv'd his Majesty 7 years
>
> Most Humbly Sheweth,
>
> That your Petitioner and Numbers of other Blacks are unprovided with Lands, he humbly implores in the name of the whole that something May be done for them as he and many others are now Suffering. Their present Situation is Such that they are incapable of paying the poor tax –
>
> Your Petitioner
> As in duty bound will
> Ever Pray
> Thos. PETERS[18]

The petition was sent to Carleton in 1790. This is six years after the arrival of Peters and his cohort in the Maritimes. For those arriving in 1783, it would be seven years. This certainly was a long time to wait for the land promised to the Black Loyalists. In this petition, Peters pointed out the suffering his community was enduring because of the neglect by the colonial government. Their lack of economic opportunity prevented them from paying what was the bane of colonial governance – the poor tax. One can imagine the frustration of the Black Loyalist community as they watched promises made to them broken time and time again, both in Nova Scotia and in the newly created province of New Brunswick. Their bitterness must have increased as they realized that most if not all White Loyalists had received their land allotments within a few years of their arrival in British North America. Black people watched in dismay as government surveyors took years to survey land for them in contract to the speed with which they pursued surveying land for Whites.

---

17 Stephen Davidson writes about the itineracy of Peters and his quest for Justice in "Thomas Peters: A Passion for Justice."

18 New Brunswick Land Petitions, 1790. Public Archives of New Brunswick, RS 108, Reel F 1037. http://www.royalprovincial.com/military/black/blkpet1.htm.

Peters knew that land was the foundation of independence. Fleeing from slavery where they owned no land, and in which their talents and labor were used to enrich others, Black Loyalists arrived in the Maritime Colonies trusting the British promise of landownership. For them, land was intimately linked to freedom, and the promise of equality with Whites. This was how they would become a community, free from constant dependence on Whites. Peters knew that acquiring and working land would translate into both individual and communal power for Black people.

The pleas of these Black Loyalists generally fell on deaf ears. Finally, when it appeared to these Loyalists that those in power in Nova Scotia and New Brunswick were not listening to their pleas, they took matters into their own hands. In 1791, 102 individuals in the Annapolis Royal area of Nova Scotia and 200 Black families from New Brunswick chose Peters as their representative to cross the ocean to Britain to present their grievances and plead their cause to the king.

Clearly, the Black Loyalist community felt that if they sent a representative to England to complain, it would make a difference. They were now going above the colonial governments whom they did not trust and whom they rightly felt were not interested in their cause. They were to place their trust in an authority above the colonial governments who did nothing but further their subordination and marginalization in society. This hands-on politicking was an example of self-determination and agency displayed by the Black Loyalists in the 13 Colonies and in Canada.

Thomas Peters in London

With a 'memorial' addressed to the British government, in late 1790, Peters crossed the Atlantic Ocean once again, and made his own way to London, where he remained for about 10 months. We do know that he met his former commander Sir Henry Clinton, who most likely presented him to the Home Secretary, William Grenville to whom he eventually presented two petitions. In this first petition to Grenville, Peters presented himself with confidence:

> The humble memorial and Petition of Thomas Peters a
> free Negro and late a serj [sergeant] in the Regiment of Guides
> and Pioneers serving in North America under the command of
> Genl. Sir Henry Clinton on behalf of himself and others, the
> Black Pioneers and loyal Black Refugees …. (Peters, "Humble Memorial")

Peters states his status: he was free, not enslaved. He served the British during the American Revolutionary War and attained the rank of sergeant. His regiment was that of the Black Pioneers, which was formed by Clinton, under whose command he served. Peters boldly states that he is presenting the petition to Grenville, not only on behalf of himself, but also on behalf of the Black Loyalist community of two provinces. Listing his qualifications as a free Black, Thomas Peters revealed himself to be a man of purpose and stature.

After stating his identity, Peter then launched into the issue that brought him to London – that of land and the landlessness of the Black community. He spoke specifically of the Black Pioneers and their families: "That notwithstanding they have made repeated applications to all persons in that country in possession of their due allotments, the said Pioneers with their wives and children amounting to 102 people, now remain at Annapolis Royal have not yet obtained their allotments of land, except one single acre each for a town lot" (Peters, "Humble Memorial"). He also noted that 100 families in New Brunswick who also sent him to London were also, in effect, landless ("Humble Memorial").

Historian James Walker notes that what happened in the Maritimes to the Black Loyalists and the Black Pioneers in particular ran counter to the directives issued by Guy Carleton at New York as the Black Loyalists prepared to leave that city in 1783. Carleton "sent orders that the Black Pioneers embarking for Nova Scotia in October 1783 were to receive town lots and, if they were to be farmers, a 100-acre country lot, the same as white Loyalists of similar rank" (Walker, "Myth, History, and Revisionism" 90). Seven years after the Black Loyalists arrived in the Maritimes, Peters was in London telling the story of Black Loyalists abuse and betrayal. It is important to note that Peters revealed that he was empowered by his community in the Maritimes to go to London to plead their cause:

> That the said two descriptions of people have authorized and empowered your memorialist to act for them as their attorney, he was at much trouble and made his way into this country in the hope that he should be able to procure for himself and his fellow sufferers some establishment where they may attain competent settlement for themselves .... (Peters, "Humble Memorial")

This petition was a stinging rebuke against the Nova Scotian and New Brunswick governments with respect to their treatment of the Black community. Governors of both these provinces would later deny, when pressed by the secretary of state, that they had mistreated Black people.

In London, Peters also met with the pioneering White abolitionist activist Granville Sharp. With Sharp's assistance, he drafted a new petition and presented it to Grenville. This petition was even more damning than the first with respect to the experience of Blacks in the Maritimes. In this petition, Peters protested the "degrading and unjust prejudice against people of colour" such that they were "refused the common rights and privileges of the other inhabitants, not being permitted to vote at elections nor to serve on juries" (Whitfield 79–80).[19] He also expresses his frustration, dismay, and outrage at the lack of protection for Black Loyalists in Canada, all this compounded with their general landlessness. What galled Peters most was that some Whites were kidnapping Black people and selling them into West Indian slavery or tricking them into such indentureship contracts that amounted to enslavement. To add insult to inju-

19 This second petition is similarly titled as the first. "The Humble Petition of Thomas Peters, a Negro" FO 4/1 C308757. The National Archives, London, England. Reprinted in Whitfield (79–80).

ry, Blacks in Nova Scotia could not even get justice from the courts. As Peters wrote, "even the king's courts in Nova Scotia have publicly decided in favour of slavery and refused the protection of the laws for the poor Negroes." As he made clear, "the free people of colour … cannot conceive that it is really the intention of the British government to favour injustice, or to tolerate slavery in Nova Scotia" (79–80).

From Peters's perspective, what made the situation worse was that these Blacks had loyally and dutifully served the British during the late war. The petition asserted that English liberties should also exist in the colonies. These two petitions that Peters presented in London laid out the case of the Black Loyalists to the British government. After appealing to the two colonial governments (Nova Scotia and New Brunswick) for their rights and freedoms, and not attaining much success, Peters hoped that the imperial government would turn an open ear to the Black plight and act justly.

Other than Lord Grenville and Granville Sharp, Peters also met with many celebrated individuals in the abolitionist circles, including Thomas Clarkson who was a co-founder of the Society for the Abolition of the Slave Trade and a key figure in the passage of the Slave Trade Act 1807, which ended British participation in the slave trade. Given that Peters spent ten months in London, it is likely that he also could have met with Black abolitionist and civil rights advocate Gustavas Vassa, otherwise known as Olaudah Equiano, and other Black abolitionists. For certain, Peters met with ordinary members of London's Black community.

The Sierra Leone project

In Peters's discussion with Granville Sharp, the subject of Sierra Leone came up. Sharp was involved with the St. George's Bay Company, renamed in 1792 as the Sierra Leone Company, an overgrowth of White English entrepreneurs, abolitionists, and investors, who were establishing a colony in Sierra Leone with Blacks from England. Some of these persons of colour were Loyalists who had fought in the late war on the side of the British. At the end of the war, they journeyed to the United Kingdom instead of Canada or the West Indies. Experiencing great distress in England, many of these Black Loyalists were sent to Sierra Leone as part of Britain's colonial endeavor in the West African territory.

By Peters's account, the Sierra Leone project was well-known in North America. Peters asked Sharp if the Black Loyalists might go to Sierra Leone. Later, he met with the directors of the Sierra Leone Company, which was to become the *de facto* government of Sierra Leone. Peters wanted land and equal participation in the proposed government of Sierra Leone for his people. He discussed with Sharp certain safeguards for the rights of the Loyalists should they move to Sierra Leone. Eventually, the other members of the board of the Sierra Leone Company made the promise that the Black Loyalists would get full rights as British subjects in the West African colony.

Satisfied with his discussion with Sharp, Peters decided that the answer to the Black Loyalists problem lay in removing themselves completely from North America, where slavery and its vestiges still haunted their lives. Sierra Leone was to be the panacea. Thus, while in London, Peters was able to receive full support from the Sierra Leone Company for the emigration of the Black Loyalists to Sierra Leone, "the Province of Freedom." But that was not all. The British Government agreed to launch an investigation into Peters's claims of maltreatment by the governments of Nova Scotia and New Brunswick. The imperial officials also agreed to pay the full cost for the removal of the emigrants. Later, they informed the two colonial governors that the Loyalists had free pass to migrate to Sierra Leone and that these governments should cooperate with the Loyalists.

Peters had been empowered by his community to travel to the United Kingdom to protest the treatment of the Black Loyalist communities and to present their grievances. He wanted some speedy, satisfactory solution from the imperial government. Peters's campaigns for Black rights in Canada, the UK, and subsequently Sierra Leone (as we shall find out) were manifestations of Black Power. Like Stokely Carmichael almost two centuries later, Peters knew that for Blacks to lift themselves out of their marginalization and to gain power, they had to act politically and organize themselves, in order to speak from a position of strength rather than a position of weakness (Carmichael and Hamilton). And, most importantly, neither in Canada nor in England did Peters act in a servile or subordinate manner vis-a-vis Whites.

However, instead of letting Thomas Peters lead the exodus from Canada to Sierra Leone, given his standing in the Black community there, the Sierra Leone Company and Granville Sharp chose the younger brother of Thomas Clarkson, the 27-year-old John Clarkson, a naval officer, to organize and lead the emigration of the Black Loyalists from Canada to Freetown. The choice of Clarkson, a White British man, over Peters, a Black man, who was the champion of the Black Loyalist cause in Canada, to lead the exodus, reveal the racist views of the Company officials toward Black leadership. For the Company officials, Blacks themselves were patently incapable of leading themselves and needed to be led by the White.

The imperial government also responded to Peters's petitions in another fashion. The new Home Secretary, Henry Dundas, sent copies of the petitions to the governors of New Brunswick and Nova Scotia. In a letter to Thomas Carleton, lieutenant-governor of New Brunswick, Dundas noted that if what Peters said was true, then "the Blacks have certainly strong grounds for complaints."

> I transmit to you herewith a
> Memorial of Thomas Peters, a Black, who
> served with The King's Troops in America
> during the late War and afterwards removed
> into the Province of Nova Scotia, complaining
> that he and his Associates have not
> obtained the allotments of Land promised
> to be granted to them and that others in
> the Province of New Brunswick continue
> in the like unprovided state:- If what
> the Petitioner represents be true, they have

> certainly strong grounds for Complaint: I
> am therefore to desire that You will imme-
> diately after the receipt of this Letter,
> give Orders that the several Circumstances
> stated in the Memorial so far as regards
> the Situation of the Petitioner and his
> Associates in the Province under Your
> Government, may be enquired into …. (Dundas)

What a feat this was for Peters. He had taken his cause to the seat of power and London and had eventually also won. Not only had he been successful in getting one of the King's most important ministers to look into his case, but the said minister was now chastising the colonial governor, under whose watch the Black people had suffered so much grief.

In the letter to Carleton, Dundas advised the governor to start an inquiry into the landlessness of the Black Loyalists. He also introduced Carleton to the developments in Sierra Leone, informing Carleton about the desire of Peters and his community to migrate to that place. The shock to Carleton must have been compounded when Dundas informed him that the imperial government was prepared to give them free passage to Sierra Leone and that the governors were to dispatch "a discreet officer" to various parts of the provinces where Black s now lived to advertise the terms of settlement.[20] Carleton was instructed to assist the Blacks of New Brunswick who desired to travel to Sierra Leone. They were to travel from New Brunswick to Annapolis Royal in Nova Scotia, where the governor Parr of Nova Scotia was to assist them to travel to Halifax to board ships for Sierra Leone:

> that any of them who may
> be desirous of becoming Settlers in
> Sierra Leona, may be conveyed thither
> with their Families free of Expence,
> and as soon as the numbers desirous of
> embarking in this Undertaking can
> be sufficiently ascertained, You will
> order sufficient Craft to be taken up for
> sending them over to Annapolis, where
> Governor Parr as you will see by an Extract
> of my Letter to him, will have provided
> Shipping for their reception and –
> conveyance to the place of their destination. (Dundas)[21]

---

20 The terms of settlement were given to Peters and Clarkson and noted in the "Advertisement for the settlement of black Nova Scotians in Sierra Leone."

21 It is to be noted that Dundas sent similar information and directives to Gov. Parr of Nova Scotia.

Campaigning for emigration to Africa

And so, the exodus to Africa by Maritime Blacks was planned. John Clarkson left London for Nova Scotia. Likewise, Thomas Peters sailed back to Canada to lay the grounds for the departure of those Black Loyalists who wished to leave Nova Scotia and New Brunswick for Africa.

Arriving in the Maritime colonies, Peters travelled through the two provinces, trying to spread the news in various Black communities, of the British government's offer to go to Sierra Leone and establish a free colony. He wanted them to know that they were going to be given land, have the chance to serve in the government and attain the independence they desired and deserved. Clarkson himself also travelled through Nova Scotia spreading the news about the Sierra Leone opportunity and the impending departure. Both men were armed with a poster-type document issued by the directors of the Sierra Leone Company. Copies of the document were given to members of the Black community across New Brunswick and Nova Scotia. Copies were also placed on church doors and other public places. At the top of the document, and in bold headline, it read: "FREE SETTLEMENT OF THE COAST OF AFRICA." It promised "that every free Black … shall have a grant of not less than twenty acres of land for himself, ten for his wife, and five for every child …." It also promised that, once in Sierra Leone, Blacks were going to enjoy the same "civil, military, personal, and commercial rights and duties" in the same manner as Whites. The document was signed by the 13 directors of the Sierra Leone Company (SLC). These men included such abolitionist luminaries as William Wilberforce, Thomas Clarkson, Granville Sharpe, and the Company chair Henry Thornton. The document also noted that the SLC was incorporated by an act of Parliament.[22] The land issue with respect to the potential Black settlers seems to have been taken care of by the directors of the Company. Nodding to patriarchy, men were acknowledged as heads of families, with them getting the lion's share of land.

The response by the Black Maritime community to the news of Sierra Leone was tremendous. In some places, entire communities and church congregations decided to leave Canada. At least half of the 800 Blacks in the Birchtown-Shelburne area decided to emigrate. 180 members of the Black communities of Brindley Town/Digby/Annapolis Royal and surrounding areas left for Sierra Leone. Likewise, 220 persons from the Preston area joined the exodus. 200 individuals from New Brunswick region also emigrated (Gibson Wilson 219). It seems that eventually a total of 1,190 Black Loyalist men, women, and children departed for Sierra Leone. This was at least two-fifth of the original 3000 who left New York City in 1783 for Nova Scotia.

Thomas Peters himself led about 94 persons from the Annapolis Royal area to be part of the exodus. Peters, along with his family members and 94 Black Loyalists ar-

22 "Advertisement for the settlement of black Nova Scotians in Sierra Leone," Nova Scotia Archives, RG1, vol. 419 #1, microfilm 15460. https://archives.novascotia.ca/africanns/archives/?ID=44; https://blackloyalist.com/cdc/documents/official/free_settlement_coast_of_africa.htm.

rived in Halifax at the end of November 1791 to join with hundreds of others who were about to embark on ships bound for Sierra Leone in January 1792 (Gibson Wilson 212–213). In the meantime, many Blacks who lived in isolated communities did not know that such a departure was planned and only learnt of it after the ships sailed. Other Blacks who did not go to West Africa had family members in slavery or serving out indentureships and did not want to leave them behind.

Arguably, more would have joined the exodus if there had not been such a strong White opposition to Black departure. Whites had come to see and use the Blacks as a reservoir of cheap labor and were now horrified that they were going to lose this labor force. Who would till their soil, cook their food, mind their children? Work for them for little or no pay if the Blacks left? White people therefore placed obstacles in the path of Black emigration by claiming falsely in many instances that Blacks owed them money. It was against the Sierra Leone Company policy that debtors be allowed to travel to Africa. Peters himself suffered abuse from Whites and was physically attacked as he journeyed throughout Nova Scotia and New Brunswick, informing fellow Blacks about the Sierra Leone opportunity. Even the lieutenant-governor of New Brunswick, Thomas Carleton stood against Peters. Carleton was incensed that Peters had gone to London and complained to the higher authorities about the state of life for Blacks in New Brunswick under Carleton's regime (Gibson Wilson 212).

The words of Black Loyalist preacher and emigrant David George summed up the behavior of many Whites who did not want the Black Loyalists to leave Nova Scotia and who put obstacles in the paths of would-be emigrants: "The White people … were very unwilling that we should go, though they had been very cruel to us, and treated many of us as bad as though we had been slaves" (Gibson Wilson 209).

Despite all this hardship, a large group of people chose to go to Sierra Leone. Many of the important Black Loyalist leaders also followed Peters's call for emigration. Among these were known preachers like Boston King, David George, Moses Wilkinson as well as prominent, non-religious figures like Catherine Abernathy, Nathaniel Snowball, and Harry Washington.

Fruit of his labor: the exodus to Sierra Leone

Eventually, 15 ships carrying over one thousand Black Loyalists left Canada for Sierra Leone on January 15 of 1792. As Ellen Gibson Wilson notes, "Their fleet was unique in history. Nowhere else on the Atlantic was there another vessel laden with Blacks who were also free" (Gibson Wilson 228). The usual traffic on the Atlantic consisted of slavers sailing *from* Africa, and with chained Africans bound for New World slavery. Therefore, this was to be the largest free Black migrations during the eighteenth century anywhere in the Atlantic world, made possible by the extraordinary vision of Thomas Peters.[23]

23 The departure of the Black Loyalists from Nova Scotia and from Canada in 15 ships is memorialized in the poem "15 Ships" by Afua Cooper. https://www.youtube.com/watch?v=4UD99JDbm4w.

These Blacks who were simultaneously Africans, Nova Scotians, British subjects, and Black Loyalists, pulled out roots once again and embarked upon the high seas yet another time. They had been in Canada for nine years and had reached the limits of their endurance. They protested the impunity and disrespect with which they had been treated, by leaving as a free people. Rather than going to another Canadian colony, they crossed the Atlantic Ocean in pursuit of freedom and dignity. The vast majority had made oceanic voyages before. Some among them had even crossed the dreaded Middle Passage leg of the Atlantic Ocean as captives of chattel slavery. Yet, here they were, traversing this ocean once more, not as bonded persons but as free persons in search of a home.

In March 1792, after a two-month sea voyage, the 15 ships sailed into Freetown harbor. The return to Africa was indeed a voyage home for over half the Nova Scotians, including Peters and others, such as Isaac Anderson, who were going to play such a prominent role in Sierra Leone. One can only wonder at what those who had once left Africa in such traumatic circumstances felt about their return and what they told their children and other first-time travelers about their experiences of the continent. We know for example, that at least one-third of the emigrants to Sierra Leone were indeed born in Africa and had earlier crossed the Atlantic in slave ships (Gibson Wilson 221). There was certainly age and youth making the voyage. One of the returnees was 104 years old and three settlers were born during the voyage itself. Several of those who returned from Nova Scotia had unexpected reunions in Africa. Martha Webb who had been sold into slavery as a teenager in Sierra Leone spotted her mother, who was living in the village of a local ruler, King Tom, near Freetown. Frank Peters who had been abducted as a child from Sierra Leone had joined the British Army in North America in 1779 and the became a Birchtown woodcutter. Two weeks after his arrival, he was found by his mother who instantly recognized him.

Soon upon arrival, however, Thomas Peters discovered that the SLC had lied. The newly arrived were not given the land they had been promised. In fact, no land had been surveyed for them. And they could only get the promised rations (from the Company stores) on credit. Moreover, Black people were not free to organize under their own religious denominations. They would not have social and racial equality with the Whites who were already in the colony. The "civil, military, personal and commercial rights" promised by the Company were thus denied. To add insult to injury, none of the Black Loyalists, now called Nova Scotians, were to be integrated into the government. Likewise, Peters was denied any position of leadership in the power structure. The government was an all-White council led by Clarkson himself who was made governor by the SLC. It was White power, not Black power, that was to rule over the new colony of Sierra Leone. This led to Peters's protest against this situation to Clarkson. Fully empowered by the SLC, Clarkson responded in a peevish, vindictive, and autocratic manner. He threatened to hang any settlers who disobeyed him and began to have Thomas Peters surveilled. It is evident that Clarkson feared and was jealous of Peters's influence over the Nova Scotians. He wrote in his journal that Peters wished to sideline him and be the leader of the Nova Scotians. But surely Clarkson must have already realized that indeed Peters was held in high esteem by his people and that many of them wanted him to be their leader in Sierra Leone.

Even before arriving in Canada, Peters was a man of influence in his community. And later, in Nova Scotia and New Brunswick, it was Peters who led the charge against anti-Black racism, wrote petition after petition to various colonial governments, went back and forth through two provinces, spoke on behalf of the Black people, and encouraged them in their struggle. And when governments turned a deaf ear, it was Peters whom the Black Loyalists elected to go to England to present their grievances to the imperial authorities and seek a solution. It was Peters who accepted the Sierra Leone solution and convinced his community in Canada to migrate. It is therefore hard to understand why Clarkson could not understand that Peters was a natural leader of the Black community, or that the Blacks themselves would desire to have Peters as their governor or, at least, share power with Clarkson.

Interestingly, both Peters and Clarkson had worked together to bring news of the exodus to Blacks in Nova Scotia and New Brunswick, and, at one point, could even have been considered friends. All that changed in Sierra Leone when the SLC's true colors were revealed and Clarkson stood as their henchman. An open conflict ensued between Peters and Clarkson. The governor wrote that the Nova Scotians had "imbibed strange notions from Thomas Peters as to their civil rights" (Hart). Peters maintained that the promises made in London were not kept. In response, Clarkson warned the Nova Scotians against "improper notions of liberty" (Hart). Implicit in Clarkson's paternalistic comment was the idea that Blacks were too independent minded and should wait patiently for full freedom. It was not the first time that, when Blacks pressed for their rights as British subjects, a White official had suggested that they were too independent. None other than William Wilberforce, the most well-known of the British abolitionists and a director of the Sierra Leone Company, learning of the agitation of the Blacks in Sierra Leone for their rights, had called them "Jacobins." Wilberforce also noted that the Blacks were acting "as if they had been trained & educated in Paris" (Gibson Wilson 388). Wilberforce's back-handed paternalism draws our attention to the militancy of the Black Loyalists and their rejection of White power and rule, but also to the fact that Wilberforce and his colleagues were very much aware that the Black Loyalists were infused with the spirit of revolution much, like their brethren and sistrens in Haiti and the revolutionaries in France had been (Gibson Wilson 388).

Visionary of Black Freedom in the age of slavery and colonialism

Thomas Peters and the Black Loyalists found themselves in a world that was not prepared to grant free Black people full equality. Slavery was the defining feature of Black life in the late eighteenth century and most Whites, even well-meaning ones like John Clarkson, still saw free Blacks as a population fit only to perform servile task. In their view, Blacks were inferior beings bound to be subordinated and guided by the

White hand toward a hard-to-reach state of freedom some time in the future. Contrary to this view, free Black people saw themselves as worthy of equal citizenship. They had enlisted in the Crown's armies on a higher proportion than Whites had. What is more, they had valiantly fought for their freedom. In their minds, they were free and, therefore, autonomous. It is these two world views that clashed in Maritime Canada, London, and Freetown.

The fact that Peters had been born free and that he lived as a free person in West Africa as an adult undoubtedly had an impact on his attitude toward slavery. He arrived in the Americas already armed with African conceptions of freedom. Though he endured enslavement, like many Black Loyalists who risked their lives to gain their freedom, Peters had long shaken off the shackles of mental slavery. His freedom was enhanced in the crucible of the American War for Independence. No doubt, his memory of his life as a free person in Africa shaped Peters's political consciousness. His life in the colonies as slave and soldier and his subsequent career as a Black Loyalist show that Peters had well-developed ideas about justice, liberty, community building, and Black capacity.

For nine years, he campaigned tirelessly for human and civil rights for the Black communities in Nova Scotia and New Brunswick. When his pleas and petitions fell on deaf ears, he travelled to London on behalf of a beleaguered Black community that was devastated by landlessness, sharecropping, hunger, severe racial discrimination, and the legacy of slavery. Through his efforts, the imperial government agreed to pay for the transportation and resettlement of Nova Scotian Blacks in Sierra Leone and to investigate his charges of anti-Black racism carried out by the governments of New Brunswick and Nova Scotia. This was a major concession on the part of the British government, and a big success for the resolute Peters and the Black Loyalists.

Upon arrival in Freetown, Sierra Leone, Peters quickly discovered that the British had once again lied about giving land and rights to the Black Loyalists. John Clarkson who had positioned himself as a "friend of the Blacks" began acting like an autocrat. This betrayal stung Thomas Peters. He quickly organized a challenge to Clarkson and to the Sierra Leone Company. Race and status played out a prominent role in Freetown. The Sierra Leone Company was composed of White British men who ruled a colony made up mainly of Black people, most of whom had been enslaved within the Americas. But these former slaves had a strong sense of who they were as a Black collective. They had earned their own freedom in the bloody American Revolution and had defended freedom when rampant racism in Canada had threatened to push them once again into misery. What became clear was that Thomas Peters was not afraid of the White men who had established colonial rule in Sierra Leone. He and the rest of the Nova Scotians knew well that there was going to be no colony without their efforts and participation.

But Peters's time as a Black activist, visionary, and leader was soon to end. On 26 June 1792, three months after his arrival in Sierra Leone, he caught malaria and died soon after. However, his work continued and his spirit of resistance was carried on by other Nova Scotians, like Henry Beverhout, who on the very day Peters passed away presented a petition to John Clarkson. The Beverhout petition demanded mixed juries and Black people in the governing structure of the colony. Part of the petition reads:

> We are all willing to be governed by the laws of England in full, but we do not consent to give it to your honour without having any of our Colour in it … we take it that we have a right to chose men that we think proper to act for us in a reasonable manner …. We do not want anything but what is fair honest and just … what was concluded upon in Halifax that we should assist you in public matters and we are willing to take the trouble off your honour's hands by taking of small matters upon ourselves. (Fyfe 25–26)

Beverhout and his colleagues, against the backdrop of Peters's death, or perhaps because of it, used the petition to protest the lack of Black representation and participation in the colonial government, racial discrimination, and the unfulfilled promises made by the Company regarding land, taxes, and religious freedom. These were the same promises made to them when they fled Nova Scotia two years prior to Sierra Leone in search of full freedom and independence.

But the response of Clarkson and the SLC was to ignore, dismiss, and deride Black aspirations and to continue to treat them in an autocratic manner. While the Sierra Leonean dream had become a nightmare for the Black Loyalists, they continued to rebel and resist. In 1794, colleagues of Peters – Isaac Anderson, Nathaniel Snowball, Harry Washington, and others – acted against imperial treachery by rioting against the Sierra Leone Company. In 1800, these men led an armed rebellion against the said Company. One result of this uprising was that the Sierra Leone Company was shorn of its powers by London and the territory became a Crown colony, directly administered from London. Finally, the Black Loyalists were given some modicum of civil and human rights. Though he died shortly upon arriving in Sierra Leone, it was Peters who had laid the groundwork for this armed uprising.

As Agnes Calliste in her influential article on Civil Rights and Black Power in Canada notes, "[s]ince racism was as much an issue of identity and culture as it was an issue of access to state institutions [I would also add, state resources], or discrimination in employment and social relations, the Black Power Movement questioned the legitimacy of the entire social order" (126). Two hundred years before the modern Black Power movement exploded, Thomas Peters had questioned the "legitimacy of the entire social order" and challenged this system, built upon racism and White supremacy, in the 13 Colonies, Canada, and Sierra Leone. Thus, Peters was the one who had begun writing a shaping chapter of the story of Black self-actualization and power in North America. Today, Thomas Peters is remembered and honored as a founding father of Sierra Leone. The struggle that that country endured to rid itself of colonial rule and establish a form of independence in which a Black majority was at its helm is traceable back to the activism and vision of Peters who dreamed of power for the Black Loyalists.[24]

---

24 Sierra Leone singer Shabaka pays tribute to Peters in his song and YouTube video "Black Loyalist." https://www.youtube.com/watch?v=SAB5nKP3mbM.

Works cited

Austin, David. "All Roads Led to Montreal: Black Power, the Caribbean, the Black Radical Tradition in Canada." *Journal of African American History* 92.4 (2007): 516–539. Print.

Black Loyalists Digital Collections. "Thomas Peters." N.d. Web. http://blackloyalist.com/cdc/people/secular/peters.htm.

Calliste, Agnes. "The Influence of the Civil Rights and Black Power Movement in Canada." *Race, Gender & Class* 2.3 (1995): 123–139. Print.

Carmichael, Stokely, and Charles V. Hamilton. *Black Power: The Politics of Liberation in America*. New York: Vintage Books, 1967. Print.

Cooper, Afua. *The Hanging of Angelique: The Untold Story of Slavery in Canada and the Burning of Old Montreal*. Toronto: HarperCollins, 2006. Print.

———. "15 Ships." Poem. 7 Mar. 2015 Web. https://www.youtube.com/watch?v=4UD99JDbm4w.

Davidson, Stephen. "Thomas Peters: A Passion for Justice." *Black Loyalists in New Brunswick. The lives of eight African Americans in colonial New Brunswick 1783-1834*. Halifax: Formac Publishing, 2020. 99–101. Print.

Dundas, Henry. "Letter from Henry Dundas to Thomas Carleton, 6 August 1791." *Black Loyalists in New Brunswick, 1783–1854. Atlantic Canada Virtual Archives*. Provincial Archives of New Brunswick, Fredericton, New Brunswick.

Fyfe, Christopher, ed. *Our Children Free & Happy*: *Letters from Black Settlers in Africa in the 1790s*. Edinburgh: Edinburgh UP, 1992. Print.

Gibson Wilson, Ellen. *The Loyal Blacks*. New York: Capricorn Books, 1976. Print.

Gilbert, Alan. *Black Patriots and Loyalists: Fighting for Emancipation in the War for Independence*. Chicago: U of Chicago P, 2012. Print.

Harris, Chris. "Canadian Black Power, Organic Intellectuals, and the War of Position in Toronto, 1967–1975." *The CLR James Journal* 20.1–2 (2014): 139–158. Print.

Hart, J. de, ed. "Diary of Lieutenant J. Clarkson, R.N." *Sierra Leone Studies* 8.16 (1927): 1–114. Print.

Hochschild, Adam. *Bury the Chains: Prophets and Rebels in the Fight to Free an Empire's Slaves*. Boston: Houghton Mifflin, 2005. Print.

Hodges, Graham Russell, ed. *The Black Loyalist Directory, African Americans in Exile after the American Revolution*. New York: Garland Publishing, 1996. Print.

Jasanoff, Maya. *Liberty's Exiles: American Loyalists in the Revolutionary World*. New York: Alfred A. Knopf, 2012. Print.

Jones, Burnley "Rocky." *Revolutionary*. Halifax: Fernwood, 2016. Print.

Kimber, Stephen. *Loyalists and Layabouts: The Rapid Rise and Faster Fall of Shelburne, Nova Scotia, 1783–1792*. Toronto: Doubleday Canada, 2008. Print.

Ladner, Joyce. "What 'Black Power' Means to Negroes in Mississippi." *Trans-Action* (Nov. 1976): 8. Print.

Marano, Carla. "'We All Used to Meet at the Hall': Assessing the Significance of the Universal Improvement Association in Toronto, 1900–1950." *Journal of the Canadian Historical Association* 25.1 (2014): 143–175. Print.

Mason-John, Valerie. "The Ghost of Thomas Peters." Poem. 2015. Web. https://www.youtube.com/watch?v=FCtvIrr_CJA.

Meyler, David, and Peter Meyler. *A Stolen Life: Searching for Richard Pierpont*. Toronto: Natural Heritage, 1999. Print.

Nash, Gary B. "Thomas Peters: Millwright and Deliverer: Struggle and Survival in Colonial America." *Struggle and Survival in Colonial America*. Ed. David G. Sweet and Gary B. Nash. Berkeley: U of California P, 2020. 69–85. Print.

Peters, Thomas, and Murphy Steele. "Petition on Behalf of the Black Pioneers." 20 Aug. 1784, *Commissioner of Public Records*, Nova Scotia Archives, RG1, Vol. 359, #65, Microfilm 15428.

Peters, Thomas. "The Humble Memorial and Petition of Thomas Peters, a Free Negro." Original at the National Archives, London, 217/63. Print.

Peters, Thomas. "The Humble Petition of Thomas Peters, a Negro" FO 4/1 C308757. The National Archives, London, England. Reprinted in Whitfield (79–80). Print.

Quarles, Benjamin. *The Negro in the American Revolution*. Williamsburg, Virginia: Omohundro Institute of Early American History and Culture, 1996. Print.

Robertson, Carmelita, and Ruth Holmes Whitehead, eds. *The Life of Boston King*. Halifax: Nimbus, 2003. Print.

Schama, Simon. *Rough Crossings: Britain, The Slaves, and The American Revolution*. Toronto: Vikings Canada, 2005. Print.

Slate, Nico, ed. *Black Power Beyond Borders: The Global Dimensions of the Black Power Movement*. New York: Palgrave MacMillan, 2012. Print.

Walker, James. *The Black Loyalists: The Search for a Promised Land in Nova Scotia and Sierra Leone, 1783–1870*. Toronto: U of Toronto P, 1992. Print.

———. "Myth, History, and Revisionism: The Black Loyalists Revisited." *Acadiensis* (Autumn 1999): 90. Print.

Whitfield, Harvey Amani, ed. *Black Slavery in the Maritimes: A History in Documents*. Peterborough, Ontario: Broadview Press, 2018. Print.

Before 'Black Power' there was Black Power: Garveyism and Public Performance Culture in the American Hemisphere

WILFRIED RAUSSERT

A long history of black struggle and resistance precedes the iconic 'Black Power' movement also in terms of hemispheric outreach. From the maroon communities of Jamaica, Suriname, and Brazil to black independence movements starting with the Haitian Revolution, black movements across the Americas have long expressed a demand that black history, culture, and politics be recognized and respected. The intellectual leader who most effectively embedded the idea of black resistance and self-assertion in a hemispheric and pan-African narrative was certainly Marcus Garvey. He made use of a new *zeitgeist* at the beginning of the twentieth century, which not only manifested an increased interest in Africa and black cultures, but also gave rise to Afro-descendant and indigenous movements that radically challenged the Western paradigms of modernity and society.

Garvey's movement shaped the process of diasporization among diverse Afro-descended peoples in the Americas and beyond. The outcome of these changes was a mass movement that created a transcultural understanding of the African diaspora. "If the history of nations in the Americas is a history of 'intermeshed transculturations,' so too is the history of the distinct yet interconnected populations that comprise the African diaspora" (Guridy 63). For example, the Garvey movement played a pivotal role in the making of Afro-diasporic linkages between Cubans and Anglophone African descendants during the 1920s (62). As Guridy convincingly illustrates, the movements of Garveyites throughout the Eastern seaboard, the Caribbean, and Central America revealed the emergence of a densely interlinked U.S.-Caribbean world, linked together by translocal networks of capital, labor, and ideas.

Particularly striking in Garvey's movement is the longing to think black community hemispherically and to implement the necessity to make black solidarity visible and audible in public action. For this reason, Garvey and the Garveyites from Afro-Caribbean and African American cultures developed a politically charged performance culture in order to design and provoke a hemispheric panorama of black coherence and resistance. And the idea of performing black pride and community in the streets and parks was essential for what I call a hemispheric Black Power movement in the early decades of the twentieth century. The article explores the hemispheric dimension of performing Black Power in public space by looking at Garvey's performance culture and its flows and links between Jamaica, Harlem, and Cuba.

At the turn of the twentieth century, a call for a gathering of intellectuals in London in order to explore the conditions under which peoples of African ancestry lived in

Africa, North and Latin America, and the Caribbean captured the attention of black activists, artists, and intellectuals. In 1900, Henry Sylvester-Williams coordinated the first Pan-African meeting in collaboration with a number of black intellectuals representing the rich spectrum of African Diasporic experiences. Consequently, 'Pan-African' became a key term for black intellectuals in the struggle against colonialism. Among the thirty delegates of the first gathering, the majority of participants came from England and the West Indies. Few African and African American intellectuals joined the first meeting, including W.E.B. Du Bois who would become the propelling force for future Pan-African congresses of an elite character, as John Munro points out in his essay of this collection (Adejumobi).

Along with the hope for overcoming allegations of "Negro inferiority" in scientific circles, this ensuing Pan-African movement emerged to confront global issues of colonial discrimination against peoples of African descent. Participating thinkers from different peoples of African ancestry shared the belief that historical experience, cultural values, social anxieties, and strong hope united many black cultures around the globe. London's Pan-African conference of 1900 further echoed the impact of the "American Negro Exhibit" that had taken place a few months prior at the *Rue des Nations* in Paris. This exhibit combined books, photography, and visual, industrial, and fine art products that celebrated black cultural and industrial production of the post-slavery period of the U.S., and to document black presence in the public sphere in the Western world. The common tenor among black intellectuals celebrated the evidence of black equality and productivity "once the veil of slavery had been lifted" (Powell 24). Pan-African ideas gained momentum and were met with a new exoticizing fascination with the black continent and its diasporic offspring in the so-called "African craze." This opened venues for black cultural and artistic practices to enter public space and, during the 1920s, the channels through which blues and jazz reached the public multiplied rapidly. The phonograph, the radio, and talking pictures took the market by storm and helped spread various forms of black music from the Americas (Raussert 29; cf. Ogren, *The Jazz Revolution*). As a result, a somewhat ambiguous enthusiasm and clichéd representation of African cultural expression pushed artistic expression in music, cabaret, visual arts, and literature to new horizons. Thus, a reinvention of modernity, nourished by the desire for a truly "American" aesthetic and vernacular began to flourish in the United States, and particularly in Harlem, NY.

Harlem: mecca for black art, culture, and thinking

Various social factors influenced and shaped Harlem's unique role in the development of African American art, music, and literature during the first black arts movement in the 1920s, a movement that is better known as the Harlem Renaissance. After a short period of postwar decline, the American economy had soared because of the tremendous profits earned from World War I and African Americans in the Northern cities had begun to profit from this economic boom. In years of general national prosperity,

African American artists found their way into the nation's cultural industry. Wealthy patrons sponsored black artists, inviting the latter to regular salon gatherings of artists and patrons. Indeed, Harlem was an economically prospering area of New York City and a place where optimism developed in the black community. James De Jongh points out that Harlem provided the matrix for the growth of new ideas and new concepts of race, through which "new ways of thinking could flourish" (9). Overall, the early decades of the twentieth century marked a period of tremendous social and geographical change within the black communities. The large migration from the South to the North between 1914 and 1918 and the emergence of World War I had great significance for black people in the United States (Drake and Cayton 55–64).

The outbreak of World War I launched a reversal of European migration. At the beginning of the war, immigration had actually reached a standstill. Many a foreign-born, white citizen returned to his home country in Europe to join the troops in combat. Consequently, while U.S. American industry experienced increasing production during the war years, it had to confront a lack of labor force, too. Many recruiting agents travelled South to attract black people to the urban centers up North. Cotton farming had repeatedly been set back through flood, famine, and the boll weevil epidemic (Raussert 19). As a result, due to harsh social and economic conditions – not to mention the local racial problems – many African Americans moved to the big cities up North.

While industrial centers up North faced a steadily increasing wave of black migrants from the South, Harlem witnessed the arrival of many black artists and intellectuals of varied national descent. They arrived from the Caribbean, Latin America, and Africa. Despite individual differences in politics and ethics, most of the black intellectuals at the time pursued the goal of establishing an alternative aesthetic to the modernist forms of Euro-American art. This aesthetic was "tied to a sense of myth, geography, history, and culture that was truly indigenous to the countries, rather than merely reflective of European trends, whether conservative or avant-garde" (Rampersad 67). As the international makeup of the artistic and literary Harlem scene suggests, multiple approaches to aesthetics, politics, and history gained access to the cultural discourse and production. At a time when ritual lynchings in the South and race riots against African Americans in the North were still popular, Harlem was taken to be an enclave of change. Whereas colonial policy continued the world-wide suppression of black people, Harlem profited from the African craze that accompanied the modernist period and generated a space for a tremendous intellectual and artistic exchange between various black cultural traditions. Arguably, the strongest interAmerican connection during the early decades of the twentieth century developed at this point between writers and intellectuals from Jamaica and their black counterparts from Harlem. This link is especially significant because it enhanced an artistic re-appropriation of public space by black literary, musical, and artistic agents. Performance arts like jazz, public poetry readings, street performances, parades, and cabaret shows fed the literary and artistic imagination (Ogren, "Controversial Sounds") and developed along an interAmerican exchange between actors and sites in Harlem and in Kingston, Jamaica. As it is further examined below, these artistic practices continue to highlight the significance of the connection between performance and public space for rethinking modernist aesthetics and politics from Afro-descendent perspectives.

As a frequent traveler between Jamaica and the U.S., Marcus Garvey embraced ideas of Pan-Africanism, ideas that had been inflected by his extensive knowledge of Jamaican and Southern U.S. cultural traditions. Garvey's experience as a labor migrant in Costa Rica and Panama prior to his arrival in New York City would add an important dimension to his work as trailblazer of a hemispheric black consciousness and an alternative voice to Du Bois's elitism (Burnett 39–40). The experience as labor migrant in Costa Rica and Panama explains the former's solidarity with the workers and why his influence helped push the Universal Negro Improvement Association's (UNIA) massive input in Central America (Harpelle 46–48). Garvey is therefore rightly understood as the intellectual figure among black radical thinkers who placed strong emphasis on the importance of public space and visibility in public space for the advancement of black people. Performance in public space was crucial to his politics and aesthetics of change. In parades, public theatre performances, and variety shows, Garvey demonstrated his performative style of excess and his knack for "exploiting the subversive potential of multiple sites of cultural production" (Ford-Smith 20).

Garvey's Universal Negro Improvement Association and public parades

Garvey's Universal Negro Improvement Association (UNIA) was arguably the most influential anticolonial organization in Jamaica in the first decades of the twentieth century. His legacy includes his mastery of heterogeneous performance languages. He integrated spectacular parades, elocution competitions, variety concerts, pageants, ceremonial rites, choirs, dance, plays, public debates, and speeches in his programs to mobilize, educate, inform, and transform his followers. As Ford-Smith points out, "UNIA performances were as crucial to the making of Jamaican identity as they were to anticolonial resistance" (18; cf. Hill 18–19). Garvey employed performance to create an imagined anticolonial nation (McClintock). Through performance in public space, he could reach a huge audience, including those who had not had the resources to acquire literacy. Performance skills enabled Garvey and his followers to share with the public forms of knowledge commonly unauthorized by dominant systems of knowledge. He used performances in streets and public sites to envision communities of resistance by unleashing memory and alternative ways of knowing that had been encoded in body, movement, dress, and voice (cf. Hamilton; Gaines, *Uplifting the Race*). With thousands of people participating in his parades and many thousands more witnessing them, Garvey established public space as a black domain for spectacle and cultural and political affirmation.

Garvey's spectacular UNIA parades came out of a tradition of parade culture that had developed in Harlem in the early twentieth century. James Weldon Johnson describes Harlem's parade culture in *Black Manhattan*:

> Harlem is also a parade ground. During the warmer months of the year no Sunday passes without several parades. There are brass bands, marchers in resplendent regalia, and high dignitaries with gorgeous insignia riding in automobiles. Almost any excuse for parading is sufficient – the funeral of a member of the lodge, the laying of a corner stone, the annual sermon to the order, or just a general desire to turn out …. [G]enerally these parades are lively and add greatly to the movement, colour and gaiety of Harlem. (Johnson168)

Parades brought music, religion, performance, and protest into the streets. Arguably, the first massive African American public protest took place on July 28, 1917 in New York City. Among the demonstrators were many children who participated in the Silent Protest Parade against the East St. Louis Riots. According to press releases, between 8,000 and 10,000 African Americans marched in silence against lynching and anti-black violence. The march followed the East St. Louis Riots of May and July of that year, which were an outbreak of labor-, class-, and race-related violence.[1]

But it was another parade that announced the beginning of a new era for African Americans in the aftermath of World War I: the return of the 369th Regiment in 1919. That parade literally marched through Harlem, starting at 61st Street, proceeding up 5th Avenue, across 110th Street, and up Lenox Avenue. When a later UNIA parade for the 1922 convention transgressed into the area occupied by whites, according to a report in the *New York World*, banners appeared reading, "White man rules America, black man shall rule Africa," "We want a black civilization," and "God and Negro Shall Triumph" (Robertson n. pag.). As noted before, thousands of blacks, from the West Indies and the American South, were migrating to New York between 1910 and 1920, particularly during the labor shortages of the war, so Marcus Garvey's and the UNIA's message of black unity, pride, and economic independence was quick to take root and flourish among a disaffected people.[2]

For the African American community, which had repeatedly faced segregation, exclusion, violence, and lynching in public spaces, the occupation of public sites meant an act of cultural and political empowerment. Responding also to the housing situation in Harlem, a large part of African American communal life took to the streets, stoops, and sidewalks (figure 1).

---

1 https://blackthen.com/first-massive-african-american-protest-in-u-s-history-was-led-by-children-marching-against-lynching-in-the-silent-protest-parade/.

2 https://www.nydailynews.com/new-york/marcus-garvey-powerful-man-harlem-article-1.796006.

Figure 1: Children playing on sidewalk, 1940s (© Schomburg Center)[3]

In sum, singing in groups, preaching in public, delivering soap-box political speeches, and enjoying verbal games like "playing the dozens" formed a crucial part of social life and community-building during the spring and summer months in Harlem. Partly an escape from the confines of crowded apartment buildings, these gatherings offered an environment for sharing ideas, developing community, and practicing art in public (cf. Compton 60). With the arrival of migrants from the Caribbean, Latin America, and Africa, further creolization of black cultural and political life in streets, marketplaces, and shopping zones took shape.

The spaces in Harlem that served to educate and strengthen the community were "the play street, the speaker's corner, the parade route" (Reid 7). They "provided a precarious safety and doubled as the crucible in which resistance movements were fomented" (7). In a way, these public sites turned into "homeplaces," which were often shaped by women and fostered the growth of community from home to the larger Harlem public (hooks 72). As Reid reminds us, Harlem was rich in small public spaces "to empower community enrichment through performance and expression of culture" (7). The development of Harlem as an urban enclave for the black population brought

3 Source: Sid Grossman, Photographs and Prints Division, Schomburg Center for Research in Black Culture. The New York Public Library, Astor, Lenox and Tilden Foundations.

about a production and re-shaping of space: external social and economic conditions, cultural and political strategies of power, and social confinement by way of exclusion led to the emergence of a wide number of these homeplaces, even if they were only of a tenuous nature. In turn, these homeplaces led to an intense epoch of social organization and cultural production in Harlem. Amidst the abundance of artistry in music clubs, theaters (e.g., the National Black Theater, the Harlem Suitcase Theater, and the American Negro Theater), and poetry readings in literary salons, the venues for social and cultural performance ranged "from sidewalk to ballroom to backroom rent party" (44–45). It was Harlem's sidewalk and community art practices in particular that built a sense of black pride and community. Harlem's development illustrated that grassroots creative expression in public space could make a significant difference in the living conditions of disenfranchised communities. Grassroots rituals and public art practices situated in community spaces during the Harlem Renaissance further fostered dialogic and communal forms of cultural expression that tremendously shaped the social life in Harlem.

For a population facing constant oppression, public sites in the enclave of Harlem provided venues for free artistic expression and individual as well as communal empowerment. A striking performance of self was represented by the "soapbox or street corner" speaking practice (Reid 56). This expression of oral culture included poetry, history lessons, exchanges about culture, and promotion of new concepts of blackness, all of which took place in parks, streets, and on sidewalks – spaces that were accessible to all who took the time to listen. Above all, black agency took its fullest force in the act of public assembly and parades. As concerns the latter, the preparation of the pageantry was just as important as the practice of parading itself. Both were acts of self-empowerment that created a spirit of group solidarity to give voice to what had been labelled the "New Negro" consciousness. The pageantry provided a space for reinventing the self through costuming and puffery. While it was playful, it contained the power to subvert and resist colonial practices of domination. No simple mimicry and mockery, it included a deep sense of reflexivity about self-positioning, social conditioning, and historical change. Reid sums it up nicely:

> In Harlem, urbanity was evidenced by parades, which utilized space as a forum for peacocking and pageantry and provided a release for artistry; play streets as safe containers for creative play; community art spaces as sites to educate and nourish the body to prepare for political action; and speakers' corners as public spheres spaces serving as incubators for nascent resistance movements which ultimately advanced civil rights. (66)

This rich tapestry of performing self, culture, and politics is inconceivable without the tremendous exchange that took place between different black cultures in Harlem. In practice, Garveyism was a series of early performances of Black Power. As in most Caribbean anticolonial settings, in Jamaica performances played a key role in carving narratives of identity and community. Garvey's spectacular parades drew on long established Caribbean traditions and represented an exemplary educational tool to teach black history to the public. While the parades recreated narratives of black colonial history, they also provided a venue for contemporary protest and militancy. Garvey's plays such as "Slavery from Hut to Mansion," frequently performed in theaters as well as open public sites, carried out cultural memory work that unraveled the pain and grief of enslavement. At the same time, they served as effective provocations to social and political action.

Most powerful, though, were Garvey's UNIA parades for the propagation of black nationalism both in Jamaica and Harlem (Ford-Smith 20) – events that enabled a Pan-African vision of communal bonding. Participants could be identified by their African liberation colors and, at ceremonials, by their elegant military uniforms. Participants carried banners and flags with symbolic images borrowed from Egyptian history. They also integrated swords, weaponry, and other regalia into "a complete *mise en scène*" (Ford-Smith 24). In sum, large numbers of black people occupied public space, conveying the UNIA's message of black pride and nationalism through the parades. In addition, these practices were extended, for UNIA members, through intense exercises in controlled public speaking and effective rhetoric. Rituals and regal displays, too, were deepened in organizational practice. Garvey's mastery of performance shines through in the most impressive UNIA parades in August 1920 and August 1922 in New York, the latter of which launched the Third International Convention of the Negro Peoples of the World. As part of a spectacular *mise en scène*, hundreds of people marched the streets of New York City in full regalia. As Ford-Smith points out, these parades were "at once a fiction and a threat" and they opened performative spaces that "allowed for multiple maneuvers among the movement's subjects" (25).

Figure 2: UNIA parade, organized in Harlem, 1920s (© Schomburg Center)[4]

4 Schomburg Center for Research in Black Culture, Photographs and Prints Division, The New York Public Library.

Performances in Jamaica and Cuba

A mix of entertainment and politics in public space also characterized Garvey's cultural practices in Jamaica. Inspired by the rich black entertainment scene of the Harlem Renaissance, he founded the Edelweiss Park Amusement Company at 57 Slipe Road in Kingston in 1931. InterAmerican flows brought Harlem-style variety shows to the Caribbean island. Performance practices, styles of variety, and names such as that of the nightclub Dreamland were borrowings from Harlem nightlife. Indeed, Garvey's concept of black agency fully embraced cultural production as an important political tool. The mission of the Amusement Company was to propel black cultural production on the island. The Company's task included the management of the facilities and cultural sections of the UNIA, which included presenting artistic work and seek out local talent (Hamilton 92). In effect, Edelweiss Park was the site where much of the cultural work took place in Kingston. It consisted of a two-story house, a number of outbuildings, an attached spacious yard, and, most importantly, an outdoor amphitheater that could hold an audience of several thousands, refurbished for the 1929 UNIA convention in Jamaica.

What is more, the Amusement Company project was truly transcultural, combining amusement park with variety shows. American popular cultural industries, often in the style of Harlem Renaissance performances, set the variety shows apart from established theater traditions in the Caribbean. Black-face minstrel shows which had emerged in the northern U.S. in the antebellum years, vaudeville practices, and elegantly staged chorus lines in the style of black musical cabaret from Harlem found their way into Jamaican entertainment and were re-appropriated for the struggle against colonialism (Reid 37–38).

As Reid points out: "Relying on glamour and spectacle on the one hand, and social satire, comedy, exaggeration, and repetition on the other, variety performers drew in and transformed multiple influences from both 'high' and 'low' culture" (37–38). The acts comprised a wide range of cultural and artistic practices – including recitations, dances (acrobatic, classical, and jazz), musical revues, minstrel shows, comedy shows, carnivals, plays, garden parties, choral concerts of spirituals, religious services, classical recitations, and orchestral concerts. The idea behind all these was to reach a large public and thus shape the public sphere through cultural practices in open air space. For further transmission of variety programs, amplified "radio broadcasts" were installed to reach those who could not attend the events. A panorama of largely but not exclusively afro-descendent musical genres and styles shaped a variety show program that syncretized jazz, mento, and glamorous song and dance routines. The charleston, the black bottom, the rumba, and tap were all part of the regular program (33–34).

In parades and variety shows, the UNIA offered performers a set of modes of production and distribution. It arranged opportunities to occupy and redefine public space through cultural practice and to communicate with a large audience to advance the anticolonial struggle. The skillful and performative use of paraphernalia and symbolism allowed Garveyites to do more than simply stage an Afro-diasporic imagination for the public. As embodied practices, they were also essential to the ways the UNIA engaged in politics. In Cuba, UNIA performances in Camagüey were designed by African American, West Indian, and Cuban leaders to transmit the organization's legitimacy to the wider Cuban public, and in all this, music always played a central role. As Guridy reminds us, "*De Heladas Cordilleras*" [From (Greenland's) icy mountains] was played at the beginning of every session, while the "Himno Etiópico Nacional" (Ethiopian national anthem) was performed at the end of meetings" (98). And while the parades in Kingston, Harlem, and Camagüey generally followed a more rigidly gendered, military pattern, with men wearing military uniforms and women donning nurse dresses, the performers of variety shows added diversity in terms of gender and class consciousness to the anti-colonial struggle. Many performances undermined colonial cultural tastes to create others based on new class and gender evaluations.

Through often contradictory interAmerican processes of borrowing and transforming influences from Caribbean festival tradition and American popular culture, black and black-identified performers reappropriated public space to create a rich spectrum of popular narratives and new spectacles with social visions beyond the control of white coloniality, and even outside the orthodoxies of the UNIA's mainly patriarchal black nationalism. Performances opened spaces for women in real world politics. To this end, different women took center stage in the UNIA movement such as Amy Jacques Garvey, Garvey's second wife, who was involved in the international and national UNIA leadership. She helped build and expand the movement at the same time as she took a strong stand against male domination of the movement. Louise Little, a working-class Grenadian immigrant and the wife of a U.S.-born black minister and UNIA member, Earl Little, joined and created UNIA chapters throughout the Midwest. Louise and Early Little would become the parents of Malcolm X, trailblazer of Black Power in the United States in the1960s. Louise Little played an active role in the UNIA as a grassroots organizer and leader who wrote reports of meetings and organizational activities for *The Negro World* (Walton 8).

To conclude, it is worth noting that the performances in the UNIA movement were characterized by remarkable degrees of flexibility, parody, and excess. Exploring and employing the effervescence of performance in public space, Garvey and his followers succeeded in expanding the subversive power of cultural production. Beyond doubt, a multitude of performance styles in the parades, but even more so in the variety shows, created a sense of possibility (cf. Burton). At the same time, the combination of critique, parody, acculturation, and assimilation was constantly in flux and bound to change from context to context. Regardless of context, however, the movement's high visibility in public space provided cultural agency for "plural projects of resistance across a range of sites and subject positions" (Reid 41). Hence, arguably for the first time in American history, it was through the work of UNIA members such as Garvey and the Littles that a truly hemispheric network of Black Power manifested its presence and agency.

Works cited

Adejumobi, Saheed. "Pan-African Congresses, 1900–1945." *Black Past.* N. pag. 2008. Web. https://www.blackpast.org/global-african-history/pan-african-congresses-1900-1945/.

Burnett, Carla. "'Unity is Strength': Labor, Race, Garveyism, and the 1920 Panama Canal Strike." *The Global South* 6.2 (2012): 39–64. Print.

Burton, Richard. *Afro-Creole: Power, Opposition, and Play in the Caribbean.* Ithaca, NY, London: Cornell UP, 1997. Print.

Compton, Allyson. *The Breath Seekers: Race, Riots, and Public Space in Harlem, 1900–1935.* New York Hunter College. Thesis, 2017. Print.

De Jongh, James. *Vicious Modernism: Black Harlem and the Literary Imagination.* New York: Cambridge UP, 1990. Print.

Drake, St. Clair, and Horace R. Cayton. *Black Metropolis: A Study of Negro Life in a Modern Community.* New York: Harcourt, Brace & World, 1945. Print.

Ford-Smith, Honor. "Unruly Virtues of the Spectacular: Performing Engendered Nationalisms in the UNIA in Jamaica." *Interventions: International Journal of Postcolonial Studies* 6.1 (2004): 18–44. Print.

Gaines, Kevin K. *Uplifting the Race: Black Leadership, Politics, and Culture in the Twentieth Century.* Chapel Hill / London: U of North Carolina P, 1996. Print.

Guridy, Frank A. *Forging Diaspora: Afro-Cubans and African Americans in a World of Empire and Jim Crow.* Chapel Hill: U of North Carolina P, 2010. Print.

Hamilton, Beverley. "Marcus Garvey: Cultural Activist." *Jamaica Journal: Quarterly of the Institute of Jamaica* 20.3 (Aug.–Oct. 1987): 21–30. Print.

Harpelle, Ronald. "Crosscurrents in the Western Caribbean: Marcus Garvey and the UNIA in Central America." *Caribbean Studies* 31.1 (2003): 35–73. Print.

Hill, Errol. *The Jamaican Stage, 1655–1900: Profile of a Colonial Theater.* Amherst, MA: U of Massachusetts P, 1992. Print.

hooks, bell. *Yearning: Race, Gender, and Cultural Politics.* London: Turnaround, 1991. Print.

Johnson, James Weldon. *Black Manhattan.* University of Virginia: Perseus Books Group, 1930. Print.

McClintock, Anne. *Imperial Leather: Race, Gender, and Sexuality in the Colonial Contest.* London / New York: Routledge, 1995. Print.

Ogren, Kathy J. *The Jazz Revolution: Twenties America & the Meaning of Jazz.* New York: Oxford UP, 1989a. Print.

———. "Controversial Sounds: Jazz Performance as Theme and Language in the Harlem Renaissance." *The Harlem Renaissance: Reevaluations.* Ed. Amritjit Singh, William S. Shiver, and Stanley Brodwin. New York: Garland, 1989b. 159–184. Print.

Powell, Richard J. *Black Art: A Cultural History.* London: Thames & Hudson, 2002. Print.

Rampersad, Arnold. "Langston Hughes and Approaches to Modernism in the Harlem Renaissance." *The Harlem Renaissance: Reevaluations.* Ed. Amritjit Singh, William S. Shiver, and Stanley Brodwin. New York: Garland, 1989. 49–72. Print.

Raussert, Wilfried. *Negotiating Different Temporalities: Blues, Jazz, and Narrativity in African American Culture.* Heidelberg: Winter, 2000. Print.

Reid, Marsha. *1917–2017 Public Space: Culture of Exclusion, Exclusion of Culture.* Middleton: Wesleyan University. Thesis, 2018. Print.

Robertson, Stephen. "Parades in 1920s Harlem." *Digital Harlem: Everyday Life 1915–30.* 2011. Web. https://digitalharlemblog.wordpress.com/2011/02/01/parades-in-1920s-harlem/.

Walton, David M. aka Kalonji A. Butholenkosi. "A Re-Introduction to the New Negro Movement and Pioneers of Modern Black Radical Thought." 2008. Unpublished paper. Print.

Black Reconstruction and Black Power: W.E.B. Du Bois and the Radical Roots of 1968

JOHN MUNRO[1]

Black Reconstruction is a book for our times. W.E.B. Du Bois's 1935 blockbuster presented a multi-layered argument which placed the African American working class center stage in what was, as the book's opening line has it, "easily the most dramatic episode in American history" (Du Bois, *Black Reconstruction* 3). How the U.S. might be organized absent the foundational structure of racial slavery, and what the country might look like without white supremacy, were questions posed and answered in Du Bois's account by the enslaved and the "Freedmen" themselves. Their call to dismantle a system in which "the capitalist owns not only the nation's raw material, not only the land, but also the laborer himself" (29) and their response of building an abolition democracy to succeed it were matters of political theory as well as political praxis. What followed Confederate surrender at Appomattox was not the inappropriate imposition of misrule upon a subjugated South that so much professional scholarship and popular culture had claimed it was, but rather represented a Black-led experiment in conceptualizing and actualizing substantive democracy. *Black Reconstruction* – with its emphasis on abolition, social movement, and Black Power – spoke to the past, as it did to its Depression-era present and, as I want to argue here, to its future.

Black Reconstruction's insights were kept in conversation by the Black radical tradition it exemplified. I will attempt to chart something of that conversation here by remarking on the book's contemporary influence before considering the political landscape of the decades preceding its publication, its arrival amid the Great Depression, and its future through the Black freedom struggle after World War II. By foregrounding the internationalism which emerges unmistakable in Wilfried Raussert's analysis of Garveyism and in other chapters in this collection, I will signal that 1968 and its radicalisms had many origins. At the same time, I will contend that there is much to be gained by seeing 1968 as, exactly, a century in the making. Why? Because Du Bois was born in 1868, and because *Black Reconstruction* played a noteworthy role in giving shape to the politics of the year that this volume takes up. Even if at first glance it might seem that Du Bois's opus was too distant in topic and publication date to have

1 A big thank you to Afua Cooper, Wilfried Raussert, and Matti Steinitz for inviting me to the "Black Power: Movements, Cultures, and Resistance in the Black Americas" conference, and for including my paper in this volume. Thanks also to Sarah Dunstan, Nick Grant, Lydia Plath, Nick Witham, and Jenny Woodley for helpful feedback on an earlier draft.

much connection to 1968, my contention is that grappling with the insights of *Black Reconstruction* is necessary for fully understanding the year in question, as it is a prerequisite for fully understanding our own times.

Black Reconstruction today

Over a century and a half after Du Bois's birth and the experiment in abolition democracy that Reconstruction represented, and over 50 years after the many radical articulations of 1968, evidence for *Black Reconstruction*'s contemporary relevance is not difficult to find. In 2008, for example, historian Keeanga-Yamahtta Taylor referred to *Black Reconstruction* as "the story of the rise of the modern American state, the political and economic consolidation of its bourgeoisie, and the means by which that class came to power – through war, exploitation, oppression, terrorism, and racism; and on the backs of all of the workers that created its fabulous wealth" (Taylor n. pag.). In 2014, theorist and literary critic Gayatri Spivak argued that "the entire purpose of the establishment of capitalist democracy was at the expense of the failure of black reconstruction" (Rafaty n. pag.). The following year, in her account of the transnational and imperial groundings of Western liberalism, American studies scholar Lisa Lowe gave a prominent place in her argument to Du Bois's book, calling it, along with C.L.R. James's *Black Jacobins*, "an unparalleled history of the struggles for freedom by the enslaved people of African descent, originating a new critical ontology that challenges the coloniality of the European philosophy of history" (Lowe 140). In 2017, when asked what one book he wished everyone in the United States would read right now, commentator Chris Hayes's answer was simply "*Black Reconstruction* by Du Bois" (Hayes n. pag.). That same year, the Center for Political Education put on a six-session *Black Reconstruction* study group led by organizers Isaac Ontiveros, Rachel Herzing, Phil Hutchings, Sayinka Bryant, and Linda Burnham, and historians Paula Austin and Robin D.G. Kelley (Center for Political Education). In March of 2018, Kevin Gaines highlighted Reconstruction and Du Bois's interpretation of it in order to come to terms with the open racism that has become the Republican Party's mainstream: "At this moment of right-wing populism and white racism animating the rise of Donald Trump, the Reconstruction Era remains a crucial starting point for understanding continuing struggles for citizenship, civil and political rights, and racial and economic justice" (Gaines 114). A month after Gaines's article was published, historian Eric Foner gave a public lecture in which he pointed out that "Du Bois, in *Black Reconstruction* … set the agenda in the 1930s for the scholarship that would flourish 30 years later and continues to do so" (Foner, "Du Bois" n. pag.).

Even more recently, *Black Reconstruction* figured prominently in the influential "1619 Project," as it has in *New York Times* columnist Jamelle Bouie's public writing.[2] When prominent authors were asked in late 2020 what books they thought the incom-

2 Cf., for example, Baradaran; Bouie.

ing U.S. President should put at the top of his reading list, historian Annette Gordon-Reed recommended that Joe Biden take lessons from Du Bois's argument "that the successes of interracial government were deliberately sabotaged by white supremacists who preferred to maintain a racial hierarchy rather than move into a future grounded in equal citizenship among all Americans" (Qasim n. pag.). In an insight-packed 2021 roundtable discussion of the book, historians Adam McNeil, Hilary N. Green, Robert Greene II, and Ashleigh Lawrence-Sanders turned to *Black Reconstruction* as an essential source of insight into the coup attempt of 6 January in Washington, DC. In explaining the wave of worker unrest and mass quitting that spread across the United States in the autumn of 2021, Nelson Lichtenstein, probably the most influential historian of labor and capitalism, pulled Du Bois's "epochal study" down from the shelf for its innovative treatment of general strikes (Lichtenstein n. pag.). And for up-to-the-minute updates on the book's continuing influence, there's the Twitter hashtag #DYRBRY, or "Did you read *Black Reconstruction* yet?" Clearly, this is no forgotten classic. *Black Reconstruction* remains relevant because the transnational structure of racial capitalism it critiques remains intact; because *Black Reconstruction* came into existence in a political landscape fashioned by critiques of that structure; and because the Black radicals and their allies engaged with *Black Reconstruction* and its ideas in the decades after its publication.

Born in a time of revolution

W.E.B. Du Bois was born a couple of months before Karl Marx celebrated his fiftieth birthday. The timeline of Du Bois and Karl Marx's lives overlapped until Marx's death in 1883, a few weeks after Du Bois turned fifteen. More than mere biographical trivia, there is considerable substance to the connection between Du Bois, Marx, and the era of the Civil War. Marx and Friedrich Engels championed abolition and closely followed the events of the U.S. Civil War and its aftermath, and indeed the struggle against slavery influenced their own views about class struggle in Europe (cf. Marx and Engels). Du Bois's interpretation of the Civil War and Reconstruction was, in turn, influenced by Marx. Born on 23 February 1868, Du Bois's early life and times might be summarized in any number of ways, but there is really no better account than his own. In his 1940 autobiography, *Dusk of Dawn*, Du Bois accounted for his beginnings thus:

> Less than a month after my birth Andrew Johnson passed from the scene and Ulysses Grant became President of the United States. The Fifteenth Amendment enfranchising the Negro as a race became law and the work of abolishing slavery and making Negroes men was accomplished, so far as law could do it. Meanwhile elsewhere in the world there were stirring and change which were to mean much in my life: in Japan the Meiji Emperors rose to power the year I was born; in China the intrepid Empress Dowager was fighting strangulation by England and France; Prussia had fought with Austria and France, and the German Empire arose in 1871. In England, Victoria opened her eighth parliament; the duel of Disraeli and Gladstone began; while in Africa came the Abyssin-

> ian expedition and opening of the Suez Canal, so fateful for all my people. (Du Bois, *Dusk of Dawn* 8–9)

As was his bent, Du Bois not only offered lyrical historical stage-setting for the circumstances of his birth, but also provided transnational context for that history. Within the U.S., compared to the degradations of slavery just a few years earlier, Reconstruction indeed represented a racial revolution, and its example might have upset the global structure of white supremacy, which took the form of segregation in the United States and colonialism around the world. But it was not to be. After 1877, without the protection of the nation's armed forces, the African American community was left in a very vulnerable situation, though many Black families and individuals resisted the white supremacist order by whatever means were available to them. By the 1890s, the Jim Crow laws became enshrined at federal level, and racial segregation, itself common enough in the North, was imposed throughout the South (Foner, *Reconstruction*).

It was during this nadir in U.S. race relations that W.E.B. Du Bois became the first African American to earn a PhD from Harvard University (in 1895), and published what came to be his best-known work, *The Souls of Black Folk* (in 1903). Meanwhile, if the struggle for freedom in the Reconstruction era had, for the time, been decided in favor of those who opposed democracy, the conflict over how it was to be remembered was just getting started. In the culture wars over Reconstruction's representation, the forces of white supremacy had the advantages of money and power which let them set the tone for dominant depictions of that era. As the twentieth century began and the movie industry took off, white film makers, D. W. Griffith of 1915's *Birth of a Nation* fame most prominent among them, presented the history of the United States as a white history, which portrayed whites as the true subject of world history and its civilizations. This white supremacist mass culture was not limited to film. Cereal boxes, household ceramics, children's literature, games and toys, magazines, postcards, newspaper comics, playing cards, history books, museums, schools and colleges, country, state, and world's fairs: everywhere vicious stereotypes of Black inferiority were on display. African American performers, artists, intellectuals, activists, and film makers did challenge these absurd images at every turn, but they were up against a considerable set of cultural apparatuses backed by substantial wealth (Robinson, *Forgeries* 82–126).

Du Bois embodied this spirit of challenge. Amid the collection of writing selections that were published together in 1920 as *Darkwater*, he affirmed that people of European descent were not the only contributors to world historical "ability or ideas." He further argued that the continued denial of the African American "voice in their government and of the right to self-development" would undermine all notions of democracy (Du Bois, *Darkwater* 89). These words were in many ways a continuation of the attack on the hypocrisy that enabled the existence of white supremacy within a supposed democracy that Du Bois put forward in *The Souls of Black Folk* in 1903, but intervening historical events gave *Darkwater* a resonance that would have been unthinkable at the beginning of the century (Du Bois, *The Souls*). In the years following the First World War, new expressions of Black radical critique appeared in the form of the Pan-African Congresses, the Universal Negro Improvement Association (UNIA), and the Communist Party of the United States of America (CPUSA).

From 19th to 21st of February 1919, fifty-seven influential Black delegates met at the Grand Hotel in Paris for the convening of the first Pan-African Congress (following the first Pan-African Conference of 1900 in London). The majority of the delegates were from the United States, but representatives from Britain, France, Portugal, Spain, and Belgium also participated (Toll 208–209). In reformist tones, the Congress called for an international code for the protection of Africans, which was to include the abolition of forced labor, limited participation in governing, and access to education (Esedebe 66–67). The next Pan-African Congress was held in London in August of 1921, with further sessions in Brussels and Paris. Du Bois penned the manifesto for the 1921 congress, and its uncompromising tone exhibited a willingness to confront the colonial rulers. Du Bois's phrasing in places betrayed a patronizing tone in such statements as "It is the duty of the world to assist in every way the advance of the backward and suppressed groups of mankind" (Du Bois, "To the World" 43) but when it came to calling the imperialist powers on the nature of their rule, he did not mince words: "It is shameful, unreligious, unscientific and undemocratic that the estimate, which half the peoples of earth put on the other half, depends mainly on their ability to squeeze profit out of them" (43). Pan-African Congresses also took place in Lisbon and London in 1923 and in New York in 1927, with their attendant speeches and resolutions. In concrete terms, these Congresses achieved little, but Du Bois encapsulated why they nonetheless mattered: "we have kept an idea alive; we have held to a great ideal, we have established a continuity, and some day when unity and co-operation come, the importance of these early steps will be recognized" (Du Bois qtd. in Geiss 262). Yet, the elite character of the Congresses placed distance between their high-minded resolutions and the aspirations of African Americans who preferred to express their diasporic solidarity through Marcus Garvey's Universal Negro Improvement Association (UNIA).

Marcus Garvey rose to the fore of Black politics in the aftermath of the East St. Louis massacre of 1917, the Red Summer of 1919's white mob attacks on Black communities, and the resulting instances of resistance across the country. In this context, African Americans enthusiastically received Garvey's call for a mass mobilization of the peoples of Africa and the diaspora. He dispensed with the intellectual's exclusionary diction, he espoused pride in Blackness while white supremacist ideology belittled the cultures of Africa and the diaspora, and he did not hesitate to criticize traditional African American leadership. The UNIA was a vast and complex movement, one component of which was its international focus, particularly on Africa (Martin; Stein; Ewing; James, *Holding*). When Garvey exhorted "Up you mighty race!" his words were not meant to apply to African Americans alone (Fujino 113).

The UNIA reached its zenith in the early 1920s, after which internal and external problems brought about the rapid decline of the movement and the downfall of Garvey himself. A. Philip Randolph, Chandler Owen, and W.A. Domingo organized the "Garvey Must Go" campaign, while Du Bois and the NAACP as well as Robert Abbott's *Chicago Defender* publicly criticized (James, *Holding*, 270–271, 282–283). This hostility, combined with organizational and financial mismanagement, plus Federal Bureau of Investigation surveillance and an eventual court case against Garvey for mail fraud sealed the UNIA's, and particularly its leader's, fate. Garvey lost his case, was imprisoned in 1925, and deported two years later. The organization would never recover. It had to share the stage in capturing and maintaining the attention of African Americans in the years following Garvey's deportation with a rising American organization: the Communist Party of the United States. As Patricia Sullivan concludes, the CP was uniquely positioned to gain adherents or at least sympathetic audiences in the South as a whole: "As a Marxist organization in the South, the Communist Party had a special appeal as an action-oriented organization, as demonstrated by its efforts on behalf of the unemployed and disfranchised workers and its bold defense of nine young black men in the widely publicized Scottsboro trials" (Sullivan, *Days of Hope* 73).[3] Beyond legal proceedings, the Party organized hunger marches, contested racism within the labor movement, organized Unemployed Councils, and fought tenant evictions. The Pan-African Congresses, the UNIA, and the CPUSA were all distinct and easily distinguishable from one another, yet, there was also much overlap between the three. For instance, Du Bois's brand of Pan-Africanism shared a "race first" approach with the UNIA, while the UNIA shared a working-class constituency with the CP, and all three groups were staunchly opposed to imperialism as well as white supremacy within the United States.

Black Reconstruction and the Great Depression

Against this historical backdrop, the publication of *Black Reconstruction in America* in June of 1935 marked a watershed in history writing about the United States. Du Bois's analysis of Reconstruction had noteworthy political implications for the era in which it was published. Reconstruction and its overthrow were more than just early chapters in a tale of Gilded Age and late Victorian imperialism. By intensifying colonial competition and transnational cycles of capital accumulation, the post-Reconstruction order led to the conflagrations of World War I and the Great Depression. Coming to terms with the history of the nineteenth century, in other words, was a prerequisite to comprehending the global politics of the twentieth. An obvious corollary followed: anyone serious about opposing the Jim Crow order in the United States would sooner or later need to address racism's international, imperial, and economic dimensions. As Du Bois explained, "The emancipation of man is the emancipation of labor and the emancipation of labor is the freeing of that basic majority of workers who are yellow, brown, and black" (*Black Reconstruction* 16).

3 Cf. Kelley (*Hammer*); Naison; Solomon.

Du Bois had written about the international relationship between race and class before, including within his iconic formulation in *The Souls of Black Folk* about the color line constituting the twentieth century's central problematic. His thinking was also influenced by the Mexican Revolution as a challenge, like Reconstruction, to the global system of racial capitalism (Luis-Brown 104). With the advent of World War I and the Bolshevik revolution, he had turned to Marx. In the late 1920s, he visited the Soviet Union. Consequently, by the mid-1930s, Du Bois's thinking about race and empire became more structural. "Abruptly," he later described his immersion in Marxism, "I had a beam of new light" (Du Bois, *The Autobiography* 289). His willingness to shine this new light on his subject of inquiry is evident in his characterization of the enslaved's support for the Union as a "general strike" against the Confederate rebellion, or of the Reconstruction order as a "dictatorship of the proletariat" protected by the arms of the state. At one point in the book, Du Bois goes so far as to call Reconstruction "one of the most extraordinary experiments of Marxism that the world, before the Russian Revolution, had seen" (*Black Reconstruction* 55–83, 635, 358). Indeed, as political theorist Charisse Burden-Stelly has pointed out, among *Black Reconstruction*'s contributions to radical scholarship was the theme it provided for its author's own subsequent life course: Du Bois's "original insights offered an epistemologically revolutionary narrative that animated his own politics and activism for years to come: that ordinary black toilers were in fact the agents of freedom and progress" (Burden-Stelly, "W.E.B. Du Bois" 190). Those insights would persist, they would help shape 1968, and as we have already seen, they would only grow in influence in more recent decades.

Du Bois and the postwar Black freedom struggle

Within a decade, the political situation in and beyond the United States was much changed. The immediate postwar moment in the U.S. was an uncertain one, imbued as it was with recent popular memories of new relationships between state and citizen, gains for organized labor and losses for white supremacy, revised gender relations, and wartime co-operation with the state that headquartered world Communism. In the face of such developments, domestic ideological rollback complemented the expanded imperial reach of a U.S. foreign policy designed to contain Soviet directed or inspired contestations. The U.S.S.R. obstructed the United States in ways no other single imperial or national entity could, but U.S. empire building continued apace after the Second World War. The core capitalist nations of Europe needed restructuring, U.S. wartime capital surpluses needed new spaces for investment, products needed markets, production needed raw materials, and all of this needed a global military network that was capable of containing Communism.

These circumstances, removed as they were from the radical possibilities of the 1930s, diminished the political space open to substantive critique. But if anything, Du Bois's internationalism intensified (Blain). He not only continued to believe that white supremacy could only be overcome with the dismantlement of international capitalism, but also felt increasingly that the Soviet Union and later the People's Republic of China were the inspirational leaders of global liberation. The political price of his ideas was a steep one. Arrested, harassed, and barred from leaving the country, Du Bois was undeniably persecuted under anticommunism. In what was probably the most high-profile example of the McCarthyite attacks against him, Du Bois was indicted in 1951 for failing to register the Peace Information Center (PIC), which he chaired, as an agent of the Soviet Union. The PIC advocated, in keeping with the foreign policy goals of the Soviet Union, nuclear disarmament in the United States. The group circulated and publicized the Stockholm Peace Appeal, which the PIC claimed had garnered 1.5 million signatures from 40 states by July of 1950. Secretary of State Dean Acheson called the appeal Soviet propaganda, the PIC was required to register as a foreign agent, and Du Bois was ultimately subject to an infamous and degrading search and handcuffing when he appeared in Washington as a defendant in *U.S. v. Peace Information Center*. The case against Du Bois, lacking any evidence, was dismissed in 1951, he put his ordeal in the context of a power that had "rushed … madly at the spoils left by European empire," and he did receive support from friends, but was nonetheless shaken by the experience.[4]

This type of very real persecution has led some historians to conclude that what we call the Cold War led to the demise of the expansive visions of liberation represented by intellectuals and activists like Du Bois, in favor of liberal integration in which opposition to white supremacy's gendered, economic, and international dimensions would remain off the freedom agenda. This thesis, though, conceals as much as it reveals. Yes, McCarthyism made life difficult for Du Bois and thousands of others on the postwar left. But there is good evidence to show that Du Bois's radical ideas, including the specific arguments put forward in *Black Reconstruction*, were kept alive during the Civil Rights movement, itself also known as the Second Reconstruction (Marable). Consider, briefly, three postwar examples.

For one, at the Southern Youth Legislature of the Southern Negro Youth Congress (or SNYC, or sometimes "the first SNCC"), which was held in Columbia, SC, in 1946, Du Bois delivered "Behold the Land," which became one of his most reprinted speeches. The speech featured some of the arguments from *Black Reconstruction*. Esther Cooper Jackson gave the opening address at this event, and in concluding her remarks drew the audience's attention to the rear of the hall, where portraits of the Black members of Congress during Reconstruction were on prominent display, thus directly dramatizing the lessons of Du Bois's book and connecting them to the struggle ahead (Munro 75–77).

Secondly, Howard Fast, whose popular historical fiction comprises another stream that conveyed Du Bois's ideas for a broader audience, also spoke at the SNYC event. Although he became most famous for his 1951 novel *Spartacus*, his 1944 novel

4 Cf. Intondi (32–40); Burden-Stelly ("W.E.B. Du Bois" 195–196); Du Bois (*I Take My Stand* 10).

Freedom Road, based on the interpretation of *Black Reconstruction*, was far from obscure. *Freedom Road* was about the past, but centered themes of large-scale resistance and the intricacies of antiracist alliance across the color line that would feature prominently in the 1960s (Wald). By the end of the twentieth century, the novel had been translated into 82 languages and had sold over 30 million copies. It was even produced as a made-for-TV movie in 1979, starring Kris Kristofferson and Muhammad Ali (Sorin; Bland). By such means, radical views about what took place after the Civil War reached audiences who might never have heard of W.E.B. Du Bois.

A third example of the proliferation of the lessons of *Black Reconstruction* comes by way of Jack O'Dell, a movement intellectual in the Black radical tradition whose weighty contributions to human liberation began during World War II and continued into the twenty-first century. A left-wing organizer in the South during the McCarthy period, he went on to become one of Martin Luther King's, and later Jesse Jackson's, most important advisors.[5] O'Dell was in the audience at the Southern Youth Legislature in Columbia in 1946, where Reconstruction portraits engendered in him a deep connection between the tasks of the present (in 1946 or thereafter) and those of previous generations. When speaking in 2004 about the SNYC, Mr. O'Dell emphasized this point:

> I saw [the importance of these pictures], and … when I taught in the citizenship schools of SCLC [Southern Christian Leadership Conference] in 1962, I taught people that had never heard of this. And that's what I taught. When they'd go out and recruit, I'd look at what the roster of states represented, and I would teach that part of *Black Reconstruction*.[6]

Clearly, McCarthyism abolished neither Du Bois's interpretation of post-Civil War history nor its enduring lessons for the Second Reconstruction. Du Bois lived long enough to see the Supreme Court decide, in 1958's *Kent v. Dulles*, that the right to travel is a part of the "liberty" of which the citizen cannot be deprived on the basis of their political beliefs. He and Shirley Graham Du Bois got on a plane for Europe the following month, where, among other things, the Doctor was able to pay a visit to Karl Marx's gravesite in London. Black radical feminist Claudia Jones, who was influenced by Du Bois and, like him, had been persecuted by Cold War anticommunism, would be buried to Marx's left a few years later (Burden-Stelly, "In Battle"; Davies).

When Du Bois arrived in Ghana in 1960, he and Shirley Graham were received by full military guard, a band, various officials, and crowds gathered behind a barricade. By this time, the Du Boises were growing accustomed to state-level delegations, as they had been shielded – during trips to China and the Soviet Union – from the deprivation and oppression faced by the people of most of the Communist world (Frazier 48–51). The trip to Ghana had special meaning, not least because in 1961 it would lead

5 The best introduction to Jack O'Dell's life and work remains Nikhil Pal Singh, ed., *Climbin' Jacob's Ladder* (2010).

6 Author's interview with Jack O'Dell, 14 August 2004, Vancouver, BC.

to Du Bois's vacating the United States, where he had fought for racial equality for so long, to become a Ghanian citizen. As a parting shot to the U.S., he made a formal application for membership in the Communist Party of the United States (Lewis 567). He died in Accra on the 27th of August, 1963, on the eve of the March on Washington for Jobs and Justice. With Du Bois's death, an era had come to an end. But, does this mean that passing away half a decade before 1968, it is perhaps a stretch to say that Du Bois had much of a role to play in ushering that fateful year into existence?

It does not. Following historian Van Gosse's convincing argument that the central figure for the entire sixties New Left was Martin Luther King Jr., further, meaningful continuities of Du Bois's influence beyond his death come into view (Gosse 35–37). The fact that Du Bois passed away the day before King delivered a speech about having a dream that became one of the most cited in the history of American oratory might itself suggest something of a continuity-of-influence by way of timing. More important, though, is the way that the response of the Federal Bureau of Investigation (FBI) to King's words placed him in a political lineage in which Du Bois occupied a significant place. The day after King related a dream in which "one day on the red hills of Georgia, the sons of former slaves and the sons of former slave owners will be able to sit down together at the table of brotherhood," William Sullivan, the head of the FBI's Domestic Intelligence Division, issued his memorandum on what had taken place in Washington:

> In the light of King's powerful demagogic speech yesterday he stands head and shoulders over all other Negro leaders put together when it comes to influencing great masses of Negroes. We must mark him now, if we have not done so before, as the most dangerous Negro of the future in this Nation from the standpoint of communism, the Negro and national security. (Sullivan to A.H. Belmont n. pag.)

This letter sparked off a further campaign by the Bureau to discredit King, which included efforts to compel him to commit suicide (Capaccio; Gage).

Du Bois, of course, had been described in similar terms for many years, as had the Black Power radicals of the 1960s. C.L.R. James, speaking in 1967, placed Du Bois within an explicitly Black Power lineage:

> There is no noteworthy American historian writing today and during the last fifty years who does not owe a tremendous debt to Du Bois's work in history. So that in all these respects he was far more than "a leader of our people." In fundamental respects he was a generation in advance of most American thinking of his time and he is one of the great citizens of the United States in the twentieth century. We must bear that mistake in mind and not make it again as we are on the way to doing in regard to the advocates of Black Power. (James, "Black Power" n. pag.)

In 1968 itself, Du Bois's ideas and influence helped make it a year that was truly a century in the making. On 23 February 1968, 100 years to the day after Du Bois was born, the journal *Freedomways* put on a centennial tribute at New York's Carnegie Hall. Jack O'Dell, by this time *Freedomways*' Associate Editor, opened the proceedings, actor Ossie Davis served as MC, fellow actor Cynthia Belgrave read poetry, James Baldwin spoke, and Pete Seeger played some music. All this led up to the evening's main event, the Centennial Address by Dr. King. King took time out from an SCLC conference to attend the New York event and to praise Du Bois, whose statement of application to the Communist Party King kept a copy of in his own desk drawer. "King," as historian Robert Greene II explains in reference to this event, "knew the importance of historical narrative in giving people something to believe in" (Greene n. pag.). And to convey such a narrative, King's Carnegie Hall address drew at length upon *Black Reconstruction*. The book, King noted, "restored to light the most luminous achievement of ... Reconstruction – [that] it brought free education into existence not only for the benefit of the Negro, but it opened school doors to the poor whites. [Du Bois] revealed," King went on,

> that, far from being the tragic era white historians described, it was the only period in which democracy existed in the South. This stunning fact was the reason why the history books had to lie because to tell the truth would have acknowledged the Negro's capacity to govern and fitness to build a finer nation in a creative relationship with poor whites." (King, "Honoring" n. pag.)

By the time of the Du Bois Centennial, King himself had less than two months to live. What we might call the Du Boisian strain in King's thinking wasn't new; but it went back at least to his being deeply impressed by the achievement of Ghanaian independence in 1957. In 1965, King contrasted the apparent advances of decolonization to the lack of substantive change in the U.S. racial order, while he felt that "Africans should use the influence of their governments to make it clear that the struggle of their brothers in the U.S. is part of a worldwide struggle" (King, "Playboy Interview" 364). Two years after that, King's internationalism motivated his public opposition to the U.S. war against Vietnam, and although he saw the linked antiracist and anticolonial movements of the period as beacons of what he called "revolutionary times," like Du Bois before him had, King saw new dangers arising from recent victories, particularly given white supremacy's entanglement with capitalism. "The postcolonial period," King said, "is more difficult and precarious than the colonial struggle itself" (King, *Conscience for Change* 19).[7] Dr. Du Bois would undoubtedly have agreed.

"Sixties liberation movements," as Andrew Hartman has pointed out, "lobbed the first shots in the culture wars that would come to define late-twentieth-century American political culture" (Hartman 37). As that decade's most symbolic year, 1968 set the terms for much that has followed in the United States and elsewhere. A century after his birth, Du Bois helped shape the politics of a watershed year, a year that continues to influence politics today. In the half-century in between, the Black radical tradition and its allies kept *Black Reconstruction* and its insights in view. The most notable example, and the one most influential on my argument here, is Cedric Robinson's 1983 *Black Marxism: The Making of the Black Radical Tradition*, a work that critiques Marxism, reconceptualises the history of capitalism, and reveals the significance of the Black radical tradition. *Black Marxism* is directly in dialogue with *Black Reconstruc-*

7 Cf. Singh (*Black is a Country* 1–4).

tion, and the history of *Black Marxism* even parallels that of *Black Reconstruction*, for two reasons: both are monumental in their contributions, and both are themselves subjects of renewed contemporary interest but also sources of ongoing Black and allied radical engagement. In addition to Cedric Robinson, activists and intellectuals such as Angela Davis, David Roediger, Ruth Wilson Gilmore, George Lipsitz, Robin D.G. Kelley, and Derecka Purnell, among others, have over the past few decades insisted on the ongoing relevance of *Black Reconstruction*, often in reference to its conception of "abolition democracy."[8] "Abolition democracy," Du Bois wrote, "demands for Negroes physical freedom, civil rights, economic opportunity and education and the right to vote, as a matter of sheer human justice and right" (*Black Reconstruction* 325). In the United States, across the Americas, and beyond, this vision indicts the twenty-first century for falling short while inspiring present and future struggles toward achieving it. *Black Reconstruction* is a book for our times indeed.

Works cited

Baradaran, Mehrsa. "Fabric of Modernity: How Southern Cotton Became the Cornerstone of a New Global Commodities Trade." *New York Times Magazine* (20 Aug. 2019): 36–40. Print.

Blain, Keisha N. "I Lifted Up Mine Eyes to Ghana." *Jacobin.* 27 Aug. 2018. Web. https://www.jacobinmag.com/2018/08/w-e-b-du-bois-colonialism-pan-african-congress.

Bland, Robert. "Muhammad Ali, Freedom Road, and the Legacy of Reconstruction." *Black Perspectives.* 24 Jun. 2016. Web. https://www.aaihs.org/muhammad-ali-freedom-road-and-the-legacy-of-reconstruction/.

Bouie, Jamelle. "Beyond 'White Fragility': If You Want to Let Freedom Ring, Hammer on Economic Justice." *New York Times.* 26 Jun. 2020. Web. https://www.nytimes.com/2020/06/26/opinion/black-lives-matter-injustice.html.

Burden-Stelly, Charisse. "W.E.B. Du Bois in the Tradition of Radical Blackness: Radicalism, Repression, and Mutual Comradeship, 1930–1960." *Socialism and Democracy* 32.3 (2018): 181–206. Print.

———. "In Battle for Peace During 'Scoundrel Time': W.E.B. Du Bois and United States Repression of Radical Black Peace Activism." *Du Bois Review* 16.2 (Fall 2019): 555–574. Print.

Capaccio, Tony. "MLK's Speech Attracted FBI's Intense Attention." *Washington Post.* 27 Aug. 2013. Web. https://www.washingtonpost.com/politics/mlks-speech-attracted-fbis-intense-attention/2013/08/27/31c8ebd4-0f60-11e3-8cdd-bcdc09410972_story.html.

Center for Political Education. "Reading Black Reconstruction." 2017. Web. https://politicaleducation.org/program/2017-2/reading-black-reconstruction-session-materials/.

Davies, Carole Boyce. *Left of Karl Marx: The Political Life of Black Communist Claudia Jones*. Durham: Duke UP, 2008.

8 Davis; Roediger; Petitjean; Lipsitz; Kelley ("'But a Local'"); Purnell.

Davis, Angela Y. *Abolition Democracy: Beyond Prison, Torture, and Empire.* New York: Seven Stories Press, 2005. Print.

Du Bois, W.E.B. *The Souls of Black Folk.* 1903. New York: Dover, 1994. Print.

———. "To the World (Manifesto of the Second Pan-African Congress)." *Modern Black Nationalism: From Marcus Garvey to Louis Farrakhan.* Ed. William L. Van Deburg. New York: New York UP, 1997. 41–46. Print.

———. *Darkwater: Voices Within the Veil.* Reprint. 1920. New York: Dover, 1999. Print.

———. *Black Reconstruction in America: An Essay Toward a History of the Part Which Black Folk Played in the Attempt to Reconstruct Democracy in America, 1860–1880.* 1935. New York: Atheneum, 1962. Print.

———. *Dusk of Dawn: An Essay Toward An Autobiography of a Race Concept.* 1940. London: Transaction Publishers, 1984. Print.

———. *I Take My Stand for Peace.* New York: Masses & Mainstream, 1951. Print.

———. *The Autobiography of W.E.B. Du Bois: A Soliloquy on Viewing on My Life from the Last Decade of its First Century.* New York: International Publishers, 1968. Print.

Esedebe, Peter Olisanwuche. *Pan-Africanism: The Idea and Movement, 1776–1991.* Washington, DC: Howard UP, 1994. Print.

Ewing, Adam. *The Age of Garvey: How a Jamaican Activist Created a Mass Movement and Changed Global Black Politics.* Princeton: Princeton UP, 2014. Print.

Fanon, Frantz. *The Wretched of the Earth.* 1961. New York: Grove Press, 2004. Print.

Foner, Eric. *Reconstruction: America's Unfinished Revolution, 1863–1877.* New York: Harper & Row, 1988. Print.

———. "Du Bois, 'Black Reconstruction,' and the Significance of Reconstruction in American History." Lecture at Bard College at Simon's Rock. 12 Apr. 2018. Web. https://www.youtube.com/watch?v=a3Yg2fjuIbk.

Frazier, Robeson Taj. *The East Is Black: Cold War China in the Black Radical Imagination.* Durham: Duke UP, 2015. Print.

Fujino, Diane C. *Heartbeat of Struggle: The Revolutionary Life of Yuri Kochiyama.* Minneapolis: U of Minnesota P, 2005. Print.

Gage, Beverly. "What an Uncensored Letter to M.L.K. Reveals." *New York Times.* 11 Nov. 2014. Web. https://www.nytimes.com/2014/11/16/magazine/what-an-uncensored-letter-to-mlk-reveals.html?_r=1&referrer=.

Gaines, Kevin K. "The End of the Second Reconstruction." *Modern American History* 1.1 (Mar. 2018): 113–119. Print.

Geiss, Immanuel. *The Pan-African Movement: A History of Pan-Africanism in America, Europe, and Africa.* London: Methuen, 1974. Print.

Gosse, Van. *Rethinking the New Left: An Interpretative History.* New York: Palgrave Macmillan, 2005. Print.

Greene, Robert II. "The Legacy of Black Reconstruction." *Jacobin.* 27 Aug. 2018. Web. https://www.jacobinmag.com/2018/08/web-du-bois-black-reconstruction-civil-rights.

Hartman, Andrew. *A War for the Soul of America: A History of the Culture Wars.* 2015. Chicago: U of Chicago P, 2019. Print.

Hayes, Chris. "By the Book." *New York Times.* 16 Mar. 2017. Web. https://www.nytimes.com/2017/03/16/books/review/chris-hayes-by-the-book.html?smid=fb-nytbooks&smtyp=cur.

Intondi, Vincent J. *African Americans against the Bomb: Nuclear Weapons, Colonialism, and the Black Freedom Movement*. Stanford: Stanford UP, 2015. Print.

James, C.L.R. "Black Power." 1967. Web. https://www.marxists.org/archive/james-clr/works/1967/black-power.htm.

James, Winston. *Holding Aloft the Banner of Ethiopia: Caribbean Radicalism in Early Twentieth-Century America*. New York: Verso, 1998. Print.

Kelley, Robin D.G. *Hammer and Hoe: Alabama Communists During the Great Depression*. Chapel Hill: U of North Carolina P, 1990. Print.

———. "'But a Local Phase of a World Problem': Black History's Global Vision." *Journal of American History* 86.3 (Dec. 1999): 1045–1077. Print.

King Jr., Martin Luther. "Playboy Interview: Martin Luther King, Jr." *A Testament of Hope: The Essential Writings and Speeches of Martin Luther King, Jr.* Ed. James Melvin. Washington / San Francisco: Harper & Row, 1986. 340–377. Print.

———. *Conscience for Change: Massey Lectures 1967*. Toronto: Canadian Broadcasting Corporation, 1967. Print.

———. "Honoring Dr. Du Bois." 23 Feb. 1968. *W.E.B. Du Bois Papers*. Special Collections and University Archives, University of Massachusetts Amherst Libraries. N.d. Web. http://credo.library.umass.edu/view/full/mums312-b287-i008.

Lewis, David Levering. *W.E.B Du Bois: The Fight for Equality and the American Century, 1919–1963*. New York: Henry Holt and Co., 2000. Print.

Lichtenstein, Nelson. "Are We Witnessing a 'General Strike' in Our Own Time?" *Washington Post*. 18 Nov. 2021. Web. https://www.washingtonpost.com/outlook/2021/11/18/are-we-witnessing-general-strike-our-own-time/.

Lipsitz, George. "Abolition Democracy and Global Justice." *Comparative American Studies* 2.3 (2004): 271–286. Print.

Lowe, Lisa. *The Intimacies of Four Continents*. Durham: Duke UP, 2015. Print.

Luis-Brown, David. *Waves of Decolonization: Discourses of Race and Hemispheric Citizenship in Cuba, Mexico, and the United States*. Durham: Duke UP, 2008. Print.

Marable, Manning. *Race, Reform, and Rebellion: The Second Reconstruction and Beyond in Black America, 1945–2006*. 1984. Jackson: UP of Mississippi, 2007. Print.

Martin, Tony. *Race First: The Ideological and Organizational Struggles of Marcus Garvey and the Universal Negro Improvement Association*. Dover, MA: Majority Press, 1976. Print.

Marx, Karl, and Friedrich Engels. *The Civil War in the United States*. 1937. Ed. Andrew Zimmerman. New York: International Publishers, 2016. Print.

McNeil, Adam, Hilary N. Green, Robert Greene II, and Ashleigh Lawrence-Sanders. "Roundtable on W.E.B. Du Bois' *Black Reconstruction in America* (1935)." *New Books Network*. 1 Feb. 2021. Web. https://newbooksnetwork.com/roundtable-on-w-e-b-du-bois-black-reconstruction-in-america-1935.

Munro, John. *The Anticolonial Front: The African American Freedom Struggle and Global Decolonization, 1945–1960*. Cambridge: Cambridge UP, 2017. Print.

Naison, Mark. *Communists in Harlem during the Depression*. New York: Grove Press, 1983. Print.

Petitjean, Clément. "Prisons and Class Warfare: An Interview with Ruth Wilson Gilmore." *Verso Blog.* 2 Aug. 2018. Web. https://www.versobooks.com/blogs/3954-prisons-and-class-warfare-an-interview-with-ruth-wilson-gilmore.

Purnell, Derecka. "How I Became a Police Abolitionist." *The Atlantic.* 6 Jul. 2020. Web. https://www.theatlantic.com/ideas/archive/2020/07/how-i-became-police-abolitionist/613540/.

Qasim, Noor. "What Books Should Biden Read?" *New York Times.* 20 Dec. 2020. Web. https://www.nytimes.com/2020/12/20/books/joe-biden-book-recommendations.html.

Rafaty, Ryan. "Who Will Educate the Educators? An Interview with Gayatri Spivak." *King's Review.* 24 Apr. 2014. Web. http://kingsreview.co.uk/articles/who-will-educate-the-educators-an-interview-with-gayatri-spivak/.

Robinson, Cedric J. *Black Marxism: The Making of the Black Radical Tradition.* 1983. Chapel Hill: U of North Carolina P, 2000. Print.

———. *Forgeries of Memory and Meaning: Blacks and the Regimes of Race in American Theater and Film before World War II.* Chapel Hill: U of North Carolina P, 2007. Print.

———. ed. *Climbin' Jacob's Ladder: The Black Freedom Movement Writings of Jack O'Dell.* Berkeley: U of California P, 2010. Print.

Roediger, David R. *The Wages of Whiteness: Race and the Making of the American Working Class.* London: Verso, 1991. Print.

Singh, Nikhil Pal. *Black is a Country: Race and the Unfinished Struggle for Democracy.* Cambridge, MA: Harvard UP, 2004. Print.

———, ed. *Climbin' Jacob's Ladder: The Black Freedom Movement Writings of Jack O'Dell.* Berkeley: U of California P, 2010. Print.

Solomon, Mark. *The Cry Was Unity: Communists and African Americans, 1917–1936.* Jackson: UP of Mississippi, 1998. Print.

Sorin, Gerald. "The Long, Unfinished Journey of Howard Fast's *Freedom Road.*" *Indiana UP Newsblog.* 11 Nov. 2014. Web. https://iupress.typepad.com/blog/2014/11/guest-post-the-long-unfinished-journey-of-howard-fasts-freedom-road.html.

Stein, Judith. *The World of Marcus Garvey: Race and Class in Modern Society.* Baton Rouge: Louisiana State UP, 1986. Print.

Sullivan, Patricia. *Days of Hope: Race and Democracy in the New Deal Era.* Chapel Hill: U of North Carolina P, 1996. Print.

Sullivan, W.C., to A.H. Belmont. *APM Reports.* 30 Aug. 1963. Web. https://features.apmreports.org/arw/king/images/fbifiles/other/full/10.jpg.

Taylor, Keeanga-Yamahtta. "Classics of Marxism: W.E.B. Du Bois, *Black Reconstruction in America, 1860–1880.*" *Internationalist Socialist Review* 57. Jan.–Feb. 2008. Web. http://www.isreview.org/issues/57/feat-reconstruction.shtml.

Toll, William. *The Resurgence of Race: Black Social Theory from Reconstruction to the Pan-African Conferences.* Philadelphia: Temple UP, 1979. Print.

Wald, Alan M. "Back to the Future in Howard Fast's *Freedom Road.*" *Reading the Postwar Future: Textual Turning Points from 1944.* Ed. Kirrily Freeman and John Munro. New York: Bloomsbury Academic, 2020. 199–214. Print.

Hemispheric Ambassador of Black Power: Carlos E. Russell and the Practice of *Pan-Afro-Americanism* between New York and Panama[1]

MATTI STEINITZ

It was on a sunny afternoon in late September of 2018 when a group of about 100 people gathered at Brown Memorial Baptist Church in Washington Avenue, Brooklyn, New York. Most of them were members of the Crown Heights and Flatbush Afro-Caribbean and African American communities. They had come together for a memorial celebration to pay respect to the life and legacy of Carlos E. Russell, a leader of the Afro-Panamanian diaspora in Brooklyn who had passed away at the age of 84. The church was decorated with a Panamanian flag and balloons in red, black, and green – the colors which had been established as the symbols of black liberation in the U.S. and globally by Marcus Garvey and his Universal Negro Improvement Association in the 1920s (see the article by Wilfried Raussert in this volume).

Among the speakers who talked about Russell's contributions to social and racial justice struggles in New York, Panama, and beyond, was Felipe Luciano, a New Yorker with Afro-Puerto Rican background and one of the founding members of the Young Lords. Honoring the role of Carlos Russell as a mentor of the group of radical students during their time at Old Westbury College, Luciano told the audience that

> Carlos never let us forget that we weren't just Puerto Rican, we were black. You know how difficult it is, to be a black Latino in a Latino community? The Panamanians in this city were the first migrants from a Latin American country to say that they were black, which was revolutionary in those days. The Young Lords would have never existed without him." (Luciano, "Young Lords" n. pag.)

Charles Barron, a former member of the Black Panther Party who had become a long-term representative of Brooklyn in the New York City Council and a member of the New York State Assembly, concluded his speech by calling on the audience to "rise up for Carlos Russell. Pledge yourself to be radical and revolutionary in the 21st century and say with me: Power to the people! Revolution now! Get in trouble with me, say:

---

1 I would like to thank Carlos E. Russell for taking the time to share his memories with me, even though his health was already deteriorating, and Luis Pulido Ritter for putting us in touch and driving me to his massive Caribbean-style home on the outskirts of Panama City, where we conducted the interview on March 28, 2017, on which this article is based. I am also grateful to Carlos T. Russell and Khari Russell for inviting me to participate in their father's memorial service held on September 29, 2018, in Brooklyn.

Black Power!" (Barron n. pag.) to which the service attendees responded by standing up, raising their fists and exclaiming: "Black Power!"

Pioneer of Hemispheric Black Transnationalism and *Pan-Afro-Americanism*

Who was the man who inspired such a celebration of Black Power in the twenty-first century? Under which circumstances did a Panamanian immigrant become acquainted with African American leaders such as Malcolm X, Martin Luther King, Angela Davis, Jesse Jackson, and the Young Lords? What was it that made this scholar-activist, poet, and playwright such an inspiring voice to black activists across national borders, be they from the United States, Puerto Rico, or Panama? And how did he become what I call *a hemispheric ambassador of Black Power*? Besides his outstanding intellect, knowledge, and curiosity, and his charismatic and often provocative personality, one of the explanations for Russell's transnational and transgenerational impact is to be found in his biography, a journey decisively shaped by migration and constant crossings of national, cultural, and ethnic boundaries. What distinguished Russell were his first-hand experiences and his deep knowledge of the many guises that racism and white supremacy assumed in the diverse hemispheric contexts he and his ancestors had lived in. Following Michael West and William Martin who define black internationalism as "globally connected waves of struggles by African peoples" (West and Martin 3), which were "a product of consciousness, that is, the conscious interconnection and interlocution of black struggles across man-made and natural boundaries" (1), Russell was a black internationalist *par excellence*. In *The Practice of Diaspora* (2003), Brent Hayes Edwards describes black internationalism as the imagination of a black international community that resulted from the experiences of Afro-diasporic intellectuals like Russell who became increasingly skeptical of nation-states as they were forced to cross spatial and linguistic boundaries "by the pressure of the times." According to Edwards, "black radicalism necessarily emerges through boundary crossing – black radicalism is an internationalization" (243).

Brought up as the grandson of Anglo-Caribbean labor migrants who had to navigate between the rigid Jim Crow segregation in the U.S.-controlled Panama Canal Zone and the anti-West Indian sentiment in the surrounding Republic of Panama, Russell had developed a global vision of the African Diaspora. His trajectory as a transnational activist was informed by the ideologies of black liberation that he learned about when he fully immersed himself in the African American freedom struggle after having moved from Panama to the United States in 1955. In many ways, Russell's life closely resonates with Boyce-Davis and Nixon's observation that "the Caribbean is produced by and produces a series of global transformative movements that both receive and propel distinct social, cultural, economic and political changes" (Boyce-Davis and Nixon 1). Although his name is conspicuously absent from existing scholarship on black internationalism, Carlos Russell is firmly rooted in the black radical tradition and stands in a line with other intellectuals and activists of Caribbean descent such as Henry Sylvester Williams, Arturo Schomburg, Hubert Harrison, Uma Marson, C.L.R. James, Amy Jacques, and Marcus Garvey, Claudia Jones, Aimé Cesaire, Frantz Fanon, Walter Rodney, Stokely Carmichael, Harry Belafonte, Malcolm X, and his mother Louise Little, many of whom emerged as leaders of the global black freedom struggle during the time they spent in New York. Like Carlos Russell, their practical and theoretical impulses played a crucial role in the revolutionary, internationalist orientation that distinguished the late 1960s and early 1970s discourses and practices of the U.S. Black Power movement from the more domestically oriented agenda of the moderate Civil Rights leadership (Bush, *The End*; Plummer; West and Martin; Young, *Soul Power*).

I argue that Carlos Russell's life and the ways he challenged established notions of *blackness*, *caribbeanness*, and *latinidad* allow for insights into the interplay of Afro-diasporic mobility and the emergence of hemispheric black transnationalism as a driving force of change that I propose to define as *Pan-Afro-Americanism*. Russell's trajectory demonstrates that Black Power was not exclusively attached to the black experience in the U.S. national context. Asserting the pivotal role that Panamanians of Afro-Caribbean descent played in the history and politics of the young Republic, Russell contributed to the deconstruction of the myth of Panama as a purely Hispanic nation. Importantly, his activism was part of a multi-layered challenge to Latin America's mostly white elites' efforts at preventing black communities from developing international ties, which, in their view, could imperil national unity (Dulitzky 59). The flowering of black social and cultural movements throughout Latin America in the 1970s and 1980s, analyzed by George Reid Andrews in this volume, was not an autochthonous development but rather the result of an interplay between internal developments and external influences from world events and black liberation movements in the United States, the Caribbean, and Africa. As Rivera-Rideau, Jones, and Paschel argue in *Afro-Latin@s in Movement*, there is a need for a hemispheric and transnational understanding of *afrolatinidad* which is intrinsically linked to the continual circulation of people, cultural representations, and politics that has defined the realities of Afro-descendants in the Americas (3).

***Between a rock and a hard place*: West Indian community formation in Panama**

Carlos Enrique Russell was born in 1934 to Anna Codrington and Alberto Russell. He spent the first years of his life in La Boca, "a mostly all-Black town" (Corinealdi, "Dr. Carlos E. Russell" n. pag.) at the Pacific end of the Panama Canal Zone, which had been established by the U.S. government when construction work on the imperial megaproject began in 1904. His grandparents were from Jamaica and Barbados and had settled in Panama as participants in "the most important modern migration of African descendants within Spanish America and the Caribbean" (Duke 75), a migration during which about 200.000 contract workers from the Caribbean had been recruited as cheap labor force to work in a series of U.S. projects such as the Panama Railroad, the banana plantations established by the United Fruit Company throughout Central America, and, most importantly, the construction of the Panama Canal between 1904 and 1914 (Guerrón Montero 29).

The large-scale settlement of Caribbean labor migrants in Panama during the construction of the Canal in the early twentieth century constituted the peak phase of a much wider phenomenon that had its roots in the demise of the Caribbean sugar industry, which had caused circular migration waves from the Caribbean to the United States and Latin American countries such as Venezuela, Nicaragua, Belize, Guatemala, Honduras, Colombia, Cuba, Costa Rica, and Panama since the mid-nineteenth century. In *Radical Moves: Caribbean Migrants and the Politics of Race in the Jazz Age* (2013), Lara Putnam demonstrates how the mass migration of black sojourners from the Caribbean had contributed to the emergence of a circum-Caribbean migratory sphere that stretched from Harlem to Colón, the Caribbean gate to the Panama Canal. Marginalized and excluded by the British Empire, the United States, and the republics in the Spanish-speaking circum-Caribbean, border-crossing awareness of political developments related to matters of racial discrimination and black protest in the different locations of this trans-Caribbean sphere was part and parcel of these processes (Putnam).

The construction of the Panama Canal had not only sealed the replacement of Spanish and British empires as the ruling powers in the Caribbean by the United States; it had also begun to define the character of the new Panamanian republic as a catalyst for inter-American relations in the first half of the twentieth century. Functioning as a bridge between Afro-Caribbean, Afro-Latin American, and U.S. African American experiences, the presence of the mostly Anglophone community that Carlos Russell grew up in played a decisive role in the emergence of Panama as a hub of *black cosmopolitanism* (Nwankwo): a hemispheric crossroads where peoples, ideas, and cultural products from the Black Americas and beyond constantly passed through and came into contact with each other. Following the parallel, and related, establishment of the U.S. Canal Zone and the foundation of the Republic of Panama, the Isthmus also became a place where different racial paradigms from the United States and Latin America coexisted (Priestley 51). In the Canal Zone, U.S. authorities had established a Jim Crow regime in which the segregation between black West Indian and white "Zonians" and a racialized "gold roll" and "silver roll" wage system shaped all spheres of public life (Bryce-Laporte). When the parents of a very young Carlos Russell left the Canal Zone in the mid-to-late 1930s, they hoped for a new life in the supposedly less racist, "color-blind" Republic of Panama. The Russells moved to Rio Abajo, a neighborhood in Panama City, which was becoming a stronghold of the Afro-Caribbean community when West Indians started to move out of the Canal Zone. Shortly after relocating, the Russell family experienced what it meant lo live *between a rock and a hard place*: in the early 1940s, when the conservative President Arnulfo Arias launched a racist and xenophobic campaign against West Indian immigrants and accused them of anti-nationalism and collusion with the imperialist United States, their hopes for freedom from discrimination in the Panamanian republic began to shatter (Stephenson Watson).

To understand the internationalist drive that shaped Carlos Russell's trajectory as an activist, it is imperative to take into account his community's traumatic experience of parallel race- and nationality-based exclusion and marginalization in the U.S.-administered Canal Zone and the Panamanian republic – dual forces that reinforced existing drives to seek for allies beyond the Isthmus, in the broader African Diaspora and, more specifically, among African Americans whose experiences of racialization resembled that of their own. Exposure to different manifestations of unvarnished racism and white supremacy made the Afro-Caribbean community in Panama susceptible to ideologies of global black liberation such as Pan-Africanism.[2] Importantly, the experience of living in a Deep South-like U.S.-administered "Canal Zone neocolony" (Corinealdi, "Envisioning") gave rise to a deep sense of connectedness and solidarity with the African American freedom struggle among Afro-Caribbean migrants in Panama.

These international alliances were further nurtured by West Indian schools in which children were encouraged to see themselves as "world citizens" (Corinealdi, "Envisioning" 91) and a constant flow of ships, peoples, ideas, and cultural products between New York and Panama, two major destinations of Afro-Caribbean migration. Many African Americans came to Panama as sailors or as GIs who were stationed at one of the different U.S. military posts in the Canal Zone. Reinforcing relations with black U.S. Americans even further, civil rights organizations like the NAACP and African American leaders such as W.E.B. DuBois and Paul Robeson supported anti-segregation campaigns such as the "Citizen's Committee to End Silver-Gold Jim Crow in Panama" in the post-war period (Zien). As a consequence of these dialogues, the familiarity, and often identification, with African American affairs significantly shaped Afro-Panamanian culture and politics in the decades since the completion of the Canal – a connection that was to manifest itself with particular intensity in the Black Power era of the late 1960s and early 1970s (Steinitz, "Soulful Sancocho").

1950s: From Panama to the trenches of the Civil Rights movement

Against this backdrop, ideas of black internationalism and black cosmopolitanism became distinct features of Afro-Caribbean thought in Panama that left an imprint on a young Russell who recalls "rampant" racism on both sides of the demarcation line be-

2 In the 1910s and 1920s, Marcus Garvey gained a significant followership among Panama's black immigrants: local UNIA chapters were founded in the Canal Zone and Colón; people read the organization's newspaper *Negro World*; and in 1920, a mass strike of the West Indian canal workers organized by Garveyites demonstrated his influence in Panama. In 1927, and upon his deportation from New York, around 50.000 West Indians welcomed Marcus Garvey at the port of Colón (Burnett).

tween the Canal Zone and the republic (Russell, *Personal Interview*). An excellent student and an eloquent writer not only in English but also in Spanish, Russell remembers that once he was told by one of his Panamanian teachers that a short story he had submitted could not have been written by him, because she did not believe *antillanos* were able to write so well in Spanish (*Personal Interview*). Despite of widespread racial prejudices and anti-immigrant resentment in Panamanian schools and colleges, Carlos Russell's outstanding talent enabled him to become one of the first black students at the prestigious *Instituto Nacional* (Pulido Ritter, "Carlos E. Russell"). When he realized that, as a black man, he was the only one who could not get a job after graduating from Panama's most important educational institution, he decided to leave the country (Russell, *Personal Interview*).

In 1955, the detrimental effects of the Remón-Eisenhower Treaty between the then-presidents of the United States and Panama for West Indian Zone residents and the overall lack of economic opportunities and political participation for blacks in Panama caused a north-ward exodus of a generation of highly ambitious Anglophone Afro-Panamanian youngsters in the late 1950s and early 1960s (Priestley 53). Russell was part of this cohort when he left Panama for Chicago on a student visa in 1955. He recalls his first experience upon arrival: "When I arrived in the U.S., the first thing I saw in the newspaper was a picture of Emmett Till, all messed up … that was when I knew I had to get involved in the black movement" (Russell, *Personal Interview*).

The lynching of Emmett Till by a white mob in Mississippi in August 1955 and the subsequent outrage all over Black America when his disfigured body was displayed in a Chicago church is considered to be one of the trigger moments of the modern Civil Rights movement. It would also be the beginning of Carlos Russell's lifelong involvement in the African American freedom struggle. Although "the irony of leaving Panama because of racism only to come to the mother load of racism at that time" (*Personal Interview*) did not escape Russell, the United States still held a great attraction for him, as he remembers: "In the U.S., blacks were much more focused on opposing racism and white supremacy, which is what turned me on to the black movement there" (*Personal Interview*). As Russell's account illustrates, the confrontational direct-action approach of the U.S. black movement resonated heavily among second and third generation Afro-Caribbean Panamanians who harbored a growing sense of assertiveness and militancy in the face of the persistent racial exclusion that their community was confronted with in Panama and the Canal Zone (Donoghue 107).

After spending a couple of years in Chicago, Russell settled in Brooklyn where the emerging Afro-Caribbean neighborhoods of Crown Heights and Flatbush had become a focal point of Afro-Panamanian migration to New York, the area around Franklin Avenue eventually gaining a reputation as "Little Panama" for its role as the center of this vocal, mobile, hybrid, and transnational migrant community. As the biography of Russell suggests, their multilingual, cross-cultural, and cosmopolitan backgrounds enabled Afro-Caribbean Panamanians, "'pre-sensitized to African American culture'" (Opie 11) through their encounters with black GIs in the Canal Zone, to become important interlocutors between other immigrant groups from Latin America and the Caribbean and African Americans. Driven by day-to-day interactions with a highly mobilized African American community and exposure to events related to ongoing black liberation struggles in the United States and abroad, Russell became deeply involved in the political and cultural affairs of Black America. Somewhat following in the footsteps of pioneering Afro-Panamanian migrants such as Harlem Renaissance writer Eric Walrond (Pulido Ritter, "Notas") and Louis Armstrong's bandleader Luis Russell (Pérez Price), Russell became an influential bridge-builder between African American and Afro-Panamanian politics and culture.

"The Spirit of Bandung": Black Internationalism in 1960s New York

By the time Carlos Russell arrived on the New York scene, some critical developments that changed the course of the black liberation movement were already under way. Infused by the "spirit of Bandung" (X, *The Final Speeches* 163),[3] two events heralded the rise of the radical wing of the African American freedom movement with its increasingly left-wing revolutionary internationalist agenda which challenged the restrictions and moderations McCarthyism and Cold War anti-communism had imposed on the established Civil Rights leadership. In September 1960, the leader of the Cuban revolution Fidel Castro, who had come to New York to talk before the UN General Assembly, endeared himself to many African Americans when he decided to leave an expensive midtown Manhattan hotel and stay at the black-owned Hotel Theresa in Harlem where he was welcomed by Malcolm X (Young, "Havana Up in Harlem"). Five months later, on February 15, 1961, a group of black radicals, including Amiri Baraka (then Leroi Jones), jazz singer Abbey Lincoln, writers Maya Angelou and Trinidad-born Rosa Guy, disrupted a session of the UN Security Council protesting against the complicity of the United States and the United Nations in the assassination of Congolese prime minister Patrice Lumumba in front and inside of the UN headquarters (Plummer 116). Most of the New York-based activists behind these activities identified as black nationalists although their ideological orientation might be described more accurately as black internationalism: inspired by the teachings of Malcolm X and militant NAACP leader Robert F. Williams, the Cuban revolution, and the rise of anti-colonialism in Africa, Latin America, and Asia they fused Marxism and pan-Africanism and came to see black liberation in the United States as part of a global struggle to end white supremacy, capitalism, and imperialism (Joseph, *Waiting* 35–42). As Cynthia Young observes, the "new black American identity was not forged in isolation. It did not emerge solely within the U.S. political context; rather, it was always the result of a transnational consciousness, one that drew upon anticolonial critiques for its political analysis and international legitimacy" ("Havana up in Harlem" 33).

3 In 1955, the first Afro-Asian Conference conference was held in Bandung, Indonesia which gathered leaders from newly independent nations and anti-colonial leaders and a delegation of African Americans, heralding "the rise of the dark world" as manifested in the twin struggles against racism and colonialism that would shape the decades to come (Bush 15).

Upon arrival in New York, Carlos Russell joined these black internationalist intellectual circles in which the seeds for the emergence of the Black Power and Black Arts movements later in the decade were sown. He became a member of the Brooklyn branch of the prestigious Harlem Writers Guild (founded in 1950 by John Oliver Killens, Rosa Guy, and others) and started to work as an editor for the *Liberator*. Members of both organizations had acted as driving forces behind the forging of alliances with revolutionary Cuba, African leaders, and the UN protest rally. As an internationalist magazine with emphasis on the connectedness of black liberation struggles in the United States and abroad, *Liberator* became "an incubator of radical Black Nationalist thought" (Tinson 3) and a key platform for the articulation of ideas that shaped the revolutionary left wing of the burgeoning Black Power movement.[4] At *Liberator*, Russell became a colleague of protagonists of 1960s black radical thought such as Black Arts Movement founder Larry Neal and Harold Cruse, whose book *The Crisis of the Negro Intellectual* (1967) was a major theoretical contribution to the emerging Black Power movement. Working as an editor for the self-proclaimed "Voice of the Protest Movement" (Tinson 6), in which some of the most influential African American thinkers, writers, and activists of the era such as Sonia Sanchez, Toni Cade Bambara, Amiri Baraka, Julian Mayfield, John Henrik Clarke, and James Baldwin published regularly, left a life-long imprint on Russell's political thought.

1964: Meeting "Brother Malcolm X"

Carlos Russell recalls one of his most memorable assignments as an editor and writer for the *Liberator* in May 1964: "I was so damn' arrogant when they sent me to do an interview with Malcolm X. I asked 'Why the hell am I going to the Hotel Theresa? Who is this man?'" (*Personal Interview*). Carlos Russell's "Exclusive Interview with Brother Malcolm," published in the May 1964 edition of the *Liberator*, was the first time Malcolm X spoke to the press after he had left the Nation of Islam (NOI) and founded the Organization for Afro-American Unity (OAAU). Resonating with Russell's *Pan-Afro-Americanist* perspective, the OAAU was, according to Malcolm X, committed to bringing about freedom for "people of African descent here in the Western Hemisphere … by any means necessary" (X, *By Any Means Necessary* 59).

With his new-found independence from the NOI, Malcolm X was in the process of leaving behind the conservative black religious separatism that had kept him from getting directly involved in the struggle as Elijah Muhammad's minister. To the great delight of his admirers in left-wing black radical circles, in the year before his assassination in February 1965, Malcolm X was embracing a revolutionary internationalist agenda which was inspired by his encounters with socialist anti-colonial leaders from

4 In early 1965, Askia Touré (then Rolland Snellings), who would become a leading figure of the militant Revolutionary Action Movement and the Black Arts Movement, published "Afro-American Youth and the Bandung World," a programmatic text of Black Power internationalism, in the *Liberator*.

Africa and directed towards building a united front against racism, regardless of religious beliefs (Sales). Against this backdrop, Carlos Russell urged Malcolm in his interview to provide an answer to the question that was on the mind of many activists at that time: "How come neither you nor any of the other leaders ever use the term Socialism as an alternative?" In his answer, Malcolm X left enough room for interpretation to fuel the hopes of many left-wing activists that he was on his way to their camp: "Why speak of it! If you want someone to drink from a bottle, you never put the skull and crossbones on the label, for they won't drink" (Russell, "Exclusive Interview" 13).

In the interview, which is more of a dialogue between two mutually sympathetic radical minds, Russell doesn't shame away from pointing out some of the contradictions in Malcolm X's arguments. As Russell critically remarks, while struggling to liberate himself from the constraints of the NOI's black supremacism, Malcolm X still resorted to some of their anti-white slogans from time to time: "Strange, on one hand we were all brothers (of course, he spoke of the black man); on the other hand the white man is the devil" (Russell, "Exclusive Interview" 16). In the personal comment that concluded his interview, Russell gave voice to the belief of many left-wing black radicals that the departure of Malcolm X from the NOI and the rapid reconceptualization of his political thought would allow him to become the conscious leader of black liberation they envisioned:

> He knew the problem, but I felt that he was struggling with the solution. One thing is sure – Malcolm X is indeed a charismatic leader; if he were able to fully integrate all of those loose ends which, at the moment, seem to escape him, in terms of economics and politics, he would indeed become the most formidable leader black people have ever known. (16)

From cultural nationalists to revolutionary internationalists, all who became part of the emerging Black Power generation would probably have confirmed that Russell was correct in his prediction. The importance of Malcolm X as the voice of urban Black America would only increase after he was assassinated on February 21, 1965, less than ten months after his encounter with Russell.

Carlos Russell interviews Malcolm X for *The Liberator*, May 1964 (© The Russell family).

1967: "You will be our chairman!"

In the mid-to-late 1960s, Russell evolved from critical observer and commentator to active participant and protagonist of the struggles that reached a new dynamic when the parallel movements for black liberation and against the Vietnam War intensified dramatically. With the goal of forging a coalition between Civil Rights, Black Power, and New Left movements to launch a third party with Dr. Benjamin Spock and Martin Luther King as presidential candidates, the National Conference on New Politics (NCNP) of 1967 gathered an impressive range of radical activists, including Tom Hayden, Cesar Chávez, Angela Davis, and H. Rap Brown. African American participants in the conference created a black caucus in which all the significant leaders and organizations of the black movement at the time were represented. When it came to voting a chairman, intense debates sparked between the ideologically opposed fractions. Russell recalls: "After I gave a short speech, a woman from Mississippi suddenly said: 'You will be our chairman!' This is how I, the Panamanian immigrant, accidentally became the national chairman of the NCNP's black caucus" (Russell, *Personal Interview*).

Due to his freshly gained "aura of leadership" (Russell, *Personal Interview*) and his reputation as a person who had also established close ties to the black nationalist wing of the movement in New York and at the first National Conference on Black Power in Newark (1967), Russell was recruited to join Martin Luther King's team of advisors in his Poor People's Campaign in late 1967. Responding to the increased radicalization and militancy of young African Americans, manifested in a series of urban rebellions in Watts, Detroit, and other major cities, the Poor People's Campaign became an essential element of King's shift to the left, which had already begun to take place after he positioned himself as a fierce critic of the Vietnam War (West, *The Radical King*). The idea of the Poor People's March was to unite poor whites, African Americans, Native Americans, and Latino migrants in a massive protest demonstration to Washington, D.C. to address the social and economic dimensions of inequality in the United States. Preparations for the demonstration and the gradual convergence between the ideas of Martin Luther King and Malcolm X at the end of their lives, that has been emphasized in recent scholarship, were brutally halted when King too was assassinated in April 1968 (Joseph, *The Sword*). Along with Cirilo McSween from Chicago, Russell was one of the two Afro-Panamanian pallbearers at King's funeral (Russell, *Personal Interview*). Concerned that he might leave the impression that he was exaggerating the level of his involvement, Russell suggested to take a look at the documentary *Eyes On The Prize* (1990): "You will see me there discussing strategies with King's men, Ralph Abernathy, Andrew Young, Hosea Williams, all of them" (*Personal Interview*). And indeed, at minute 16:35 of Part 10 of the famous PBS documentary on the Civil Rights movement, he makes his appearance arguing and gesticulating in the midst of an intense debate (Shearer and Stekler).

1968: "Un-American activities" in Chicago and beyond

With disruptive events spilling over in the United States and around the world, 1968 became the year of global revolt, and Carlos Russell – "… a lot of things in my life happened accidentally but when they happened I was prepared" (*Personal Interview*) – was always where the action was. The assassination of King and that of Bobby Kennedy only two months later, followed by an intensification of the Vietnam War by the Lyndon B. Johnson administration, resulted in a radicalization of both the anti-war and the black movement. The overall mood of insurgency fully manifested itself during the massive riots that unfolded in Chicago at the Democratic National Convention (DNC) in August of that same fateful year.

In October 1968, U.S. representative and chair of the notorious House Committee on Un-American Activities Richard Ichord from Missouri conducted congressional hearings to find out more about the alleged communist involvements in the *National Mobilization Committee to End the War in Vietnam*, which was behind the violent demonstrations in Chicago. As transcripts of the hearings reveal, Carlos Russell was a leading figure in the preparations for the protest activities and the so-called "Subversive Unit" of the Chicago Police Department was fully aware of his role (United States Congress). Questioned by the zealous anti-communist Ichord, Chicago police sergeant of the intelligence division Joseph Grubisic reported on a meeting, held in February 1968 in Chicago, at which a large number of high-profile representatives of radical left-wing, anti-war, student, black, and Latino organizations including Denver-based Chicano leader Corky Gonzales[5] and peace activist Tom Hayden gathered to discuss how to disrupt the coming DNC. As witness Grubisic pointed out, the so-called "Convention Committee" was chaired by Rennie Davis, a Students for a Democratic Society leader from Chicago, and Carlos Russell who represented the black caucus (United States Congress 2292).

The minutes of the meeting were presented to the House Committee as evidence, with Grubisic quoting Russell's assessment that "radical whites today are basically occupied with anti-war activity," whereas "blacks are focusing on black liberation" (United States Congress 2293). Accordingly, Russell proposed a "parallel structure of anti-war and black liberation organizations" to prepare the Convention challenge (United States Congress 2293). A New York Times article reported on how the activists tried to combine Black Power politics with multiethnic coalition-building: "In keeping with current black separatist philosophy, Negroes met separately … 'with the goal of creating a parallel organizational structure in which white and black people operate from a basis of separate and equal strength.' Carlos Russell, black power advocate from New York organized that meeting" (Janson 1968).

5 Corky Gonzales, who first introduced the term "Chicano" for Mexican-American migrants in the U.S. was a protagonist of the "revolutionary alliances" between the Black Power movement and other ethnic communities Jeffrey Ogbar writes about in this volume.

According to the minutes, Corky Gonzales gave an insight into the debates surrounding the emerging issue of black-brown solidarity when he voiced his concerns about the division in black and white caucuses, as proposed by chairman Russell: "I am wondering what relation the Mexican-American community will have to any possible structure. I must remind the blacks, who sometimes overlook us, about the oppression of their brown brothers and sisters. If the structure were divided into black and white, where would the browns fit in?" To which Carlos Russell replied: "The black caucus assumed that the Mexican-American community would be a part of the black coalition" (United States Congress 2295). As the transcripts of the meetings show, Russell's proposal was ultimately implemented: Latino members joined the black caucus. Apparently, the fact that Russell, like Gonzales, was an immigrant from a Latin American country did not play a major role in these discussions. As Russell recalls: "At that time in the movement, a black was a black, no matter where you came from" (Russell, *Personal Interview*).

After discussing the minutes, the Committee's general counsel Chester Smith continued to present the House representatives with a summary of Carlos Russell's alleged communist ties:

> Carlos Russell has been a supporter of the W.E.B. Du Bois Clubs of America, youth front of the Communist Party, U.S.A. … Russell has been affiliated with the Fort Hood Three Defense Committee, a Communist-supported organization. He has served as an activist in the National Conference for New Politics, a New Left-oriented organization which is heavily infiltrated by Communist elements. (United States Congress 2304)

It was not mentioned that Russell did in fact develop a close relationship to then CPUSA member Angela Davis with whom he was on a delegation to Cuba in 1968 where he "taught her to cut sugar cane" (Russell, *Personal Interview*). These multiple interactions with Communists notwithstanding, however, he never affirmed to have become one himself: "I went with a Communist, and I was not one, but they knew they could trust me because I was honest" (*Personal Interview*).

As another piece of evidence, a letter was presented to the Committee in which all major African American organizations that had gathered for the first Black Power conference in Newark in 1967 were asked for their support in "exposing the racist, corrupt, imperialist character of the Democratic Party" at the planned challenge to the DNC in Chicago (United States Congress 2337). Recipients were asked to send in ideas and comments to 486 Brooklyn Avenue, New York – Carlos Russell's home address (2337). In the end, the efforts of Russell and like-minded black activists to close ranks with the mostly white anti-war movement did not succeed, likely also due to declining support for alliances with whites in black activist circles after King's assassination. As sergeant Grubisic confirmed (2336), black participation in the disruption of the 1968 Democratic National Convention was very limited, despite of the participation of Bobby Seale who represented the Black Panther Party and their reinforced push to build an interethnic "rainbow coalition" despite of heavy criticism from black cultural nationalists. But perhaps the failure to enlist broader black support was what saved Russell from being charged with conspiracy and incitement of riot as had happened to the original "Chicago Eight," among whom were Bobby Seale, and Russell's white "co-conspirators" Rennie Davis and Tom Hayden (Seale).

1969: Black Solidarity Day

Carlos Russell's organizational skills and the extensive network of local and national black activists that he had forged from the most diverse ideological currents since his arrival in New York at the beginning of the decade became crucial assets when he initiated Black Solidarity Day in 1969. Inspired by *Day of Absence* (1965), a theater play by Harlem Writers Guild member Douglas Turner Ward in which black people boycott a fictional southern U.S. town, the guiding idea behind it was a call to all black New Yorkers to "make their presence felt by their absence" on the first Monday of each November, which in election years would be the day before ballots were cast (Russell, *Personal Interview*). By refraining from going to work and to school, using public transport and spending money in businesses, this yearly boycott was meant to demonstrate "what would happen if all the black people disappeared?" (*Personal Interview*). In the run-up to the first Black Solidarity Day in 1969, Russell explained that he and his collaborators intended to "make November 3, a Black Monday, a demonstration of Black solidarity, a general protest against the intensifying repression that threatens the very existence of Black people in America" (Corinealdi, "Dr. Carlos E. Russell" n. pag.).

For his Black Solidarity Day Committee, Russell managed to gain support from a broad coalition of New York-based civil rights and Black Power organizations, unions, religious congregations, educational institutions, politicians, artists, and activists, which, among many others, included Lincoln Lynch, a Jamaican-born Royal Air Force WWII veteran and Long Island leader of the Congress of Racial Equality (CORE). Activities around Black Solidarity Day featured the public display of the colors red, black, and green on buttons and flags, clearly hinting at its embeddedness in the ongoing black liberation struggle. Ultimately, Black Solidarity Day solidified Russell's status as a leading political figure of Black New York. To the day, Black Solidarity Day remains a fixed date in the calendars of local black activist circles (Barron).

Carlos Russell leading the Black Solidarity Day march to the United Nations headquarter, November 1979 (© The Russell family).

Mentoring the Young Lords at Old Westbury

At the same time that Carlos Russell made himself a name as a skilled organizer at the intersection of Civil Rights, Black Power, and New Left movements, he also became involved in education. In the late 1960s, he started to teach courses in African American Literature, Latin American and African Culture and Politics at Brooklyn College, eventually becoming the dean of Contemporary Studies.[6] As director of SEEK, a forerunner to Affirmative Action programs, created by the New York State Assembly to assist black and Latino students, and one of the first black professors at Old Westbury College, he lived up to his vision of becoming a "scholar-activist" helping to organize some of his students who would become leading members of the Young Lords' New York chapter (Russell, *Personal Interview*). In his autobiography, Young Lords organizer Mickey Melendez emphasizes Russell's influence on the ideological formation of his group: "Carlos had interviewed Malcolm X …. It was the closest we got to Malcolm. … We liked Carlos because he was smart and had answers. He told us where to find the truth. Carlos left a mark on our political consciousness forever" (Melendez 78). Denise Oliver, the only African American woman in the Young Lords leadership,

6 One of the alumni of Brooklyn College was Barbadian-born Shirley Chisholm, the first black congresswoman who was advised by Carlos Russell in her 1972 campaign to become the first black woman to run for president for the Democratic Party. Her life is featured in the movie *Shirley* (2022).

recalls how Russell introduced this young group of radical-minded black and Latino students to the world of the broader African Diaspora in the Americas:

> In those days, there was no such thing as Latin American Studies. And we certainly didn't learn anything about Afro-Latinos, black struggles in Latin America, at all. Nothing. He opened the doors to a much broader understanding of blackness that was not limited to the United States, but included blackness in Mexico, blackness in Central America, blackness in Latin America as well as the Caribbean. Carlos was expanding our perspectives. He had a global knowledge that was very important for us. He was a mentor for all of us. (Oliver, *Personal Interview*)

According to Felipe Luciano, it was Russell's Afro-Panamanian background which enabled him to teach them about the transnational dimensions of racism and anti-racism in the Americas:

> He was the first to use the term systemic racism, as far as I know. … Panamanians were the first Latino migrants who identified with African Americans. … They identified as black and weren't ashamed of it. They came from a country that was also raped by the US, so they knew how that worked …. Carlos Russell was told consistently to 'not help those guys, they're socialists.' But he did. … Personally, I owe so much to him because he deepened my sense of *afro-latinidad*, of a Latino negritude. (Luciano, *Personal Interview*)

Melendez, Oliver, and Luciano, who would all become members of the New York Young Lords Central Committee upon its foundation in 1969, confirm the critical role of Russell in the emergence of the Young Lords as a revolutionary multiethnic vanguard organization that connected Black Power ideologies with the liberation struggles of immigrants from Latin America and the Caribbean, as analyzed by Jeffrey O.G. Ogbar in this volume. Johanna Fernández hints at the fact that despite its self-conception as "Puerto Rican revolutionary nationalists, approximately 25 percent of its members were black Americans" (5), providing a guiding example for the "making of a U.S. Third World Left" (Young, *Soul Power*) that built on the work of such translocutors between movements as Carlos Russell.

Carlos Russell with Shirley Chisholm during her 1972 campaign to become the first black woman to run for president (© The Russell family).

1970s: Omar Torrijos, the Brooklyn Diaspora, and the re-nationalization of the Panama Canal

Just like it did for the United States and many other places around the world, 1968 proved to be a consequential year for Panama. On October 11, president-elect Arnulfo Arias, who had played a key role in stirring up anti-West Indian nationalism in the 1940s, was toppled by a military coup. Although the seizure of power by military regimes was very common in 1960s and 1970s Latin America, the political developments in Panama took a completely different course when General Omar Torrijos took control of the junta in 1969. The *proceso revolucionario* initiated by Torrijos implicated a populist-progressive and nationalist agenda, which challenged the country's conservative and wealthy *mestizo* elites. It further proclaimed the recuperation of the Canal from the United States as its main goal (Priestley). In search of allies for his ambitious program, Torrijos embraced formerly excluded and marginalized sectors of the society, most prominently West Indian and Afro-Hispanic Panamanians. As part of his efforts to enlist Afro-Caribbean Panamanians for his platform of social justice, inclusion, and national sovereignty, Torrijos condemned racial discrimination and segregation in the Canal Zone, promising equality for blacks in a country free of U.S. occupation. While embarrassing to the United States, it gained him considerable support among Afro-Caribbean Panamanians who had developed deep mistrust of the U.S. authorities, many of them aligning themselves with the Panamanian nationalist struggle against U.S. rule over the Canal. Torrijos's strategical alliance with Afro-Panamanian anti-racist struggles became a powerful propagandistic tool for discrediting the U.S. Canal Zone and heralded an era of new opportunities and inclusion for Panama's West Indian community (Conniff 147). In the 1970s, Torrijos's regime supported the creation of several civic organizations as ARENEP (*Acción Reivindicadora del Negro Panameño*) and APODAN (*Asociación de Profesionales, Obreros y Dirigentes de Ascendencia Negra*) which were formed to combat racial discrimination and used by Torrijos to mobilize support for his efforts to recover the Canal among Panama's Afro-Caribbean community (168).

Radical transformations in Panama also had an energizing effect on the Afro-Panamanian diaspora, turning Brooklyn into a center of transnational activism and networks of solidarity between Panama and the United States. True to the motto "Panama at home and Panama abroad" (*Personal Interview*), Russell and other representatives of the Afro-Panamanian community in the United States, such as George Priestley (with whom he had launched *Bayano*, the first Panamanian newspaper in the U.S.), and Cirilo McSween, became important allies in Torrijos's strategy to make use of this network of Afro-Panamanian migrants living in the United States as an effective pressure group for Panama's demands in the negotiations that ultimately lead to the Torrijos-Carter Treaties in 1977. Against this backdrop, Russell was eventually assigned as the Panamanian ambassador to the United Nations and the Organization of American States by the Torrijos government. Furthermore, in 1974, Russell was a key figure in organizing the National Conference of Panamanians in the Poconos, Pennsylvania, which was designed as an umbrella organization of Afro-Panamanians in the United States and, according to Priestley, "provided an opportunity for many to assume Torrijos's nationalist project and position themselves as patriots" (Priestley 56). Underlining the importance of this group for Torrijos's "de-colonization project," the gathering featured Panama's then foreign minister Juan Antonio Tack as a keynote speaker (56). In the wake of the meeting, Russell and his companions used their embeddedness in the African American community as a platform for a sustained lobbying campaign to gain the support of the U.S. Congressional Black Caucus and influential leaders, such as Jesse Jackson (who visited Panama in 1977 after the plebiscite on the Canal treaties had been ratified) for the ultimately successful quest to secure renationalization of the Canal (Conniff 168; Priestley 55). Hinting at the increased identification with Panamanian nationalism among Afro-Caribbean intellectuals and activists in the United States, Carlos Russell noted:

> Ironically, during this same period of Panamanianization, Panamanians of Caribbean ancestry living in the United States, perhaps because of their distance from Panama and their presence in the United States during the throes of the civil rights and social revolution taking place, rediscovered their Africanness while accentuating their Panamanian nationality and Caribbean origin. It seemed as if all across the U.S. Panamanians sought to collectively reenter the bosom of the Panamanian nation not as wards but as full participants. (Russell, *The Last Buffalo* 42)

Brooklyn's representative to the New York State Assembly Al Vann (left) and Carlos Russell (middle) with Jesse Jackson during his first presidential campaign in 1984 (© The Russell family).

Black Power in Panama?

Against the backdrop of Third World decolonization, the radicalization of the African American freedom struggle in the U.S., and the seizure of power by Omar Torrijos in 1969, the emergence of black militancy sent shockwaves through the Canal Zone and

Afro-Caribbean neighborhoods in Colón and Panamá City. Constant exposure to African American influences, widespread frustration with white supremacy as experienced in the Canal Zone and the passivity of their parents and grandparents, had significant impacts on younger, more radical generations of Afro-Panamanians, as Michael Conniff describes: "Young persons of West Indian descent picked up the language and style of American blacks, including techniques of confrontation virtually unknown in Panama. The U.S. imports probably came with black servicemen stationed in army and navy bases. Canal youth wore Afro hairdos and Swahili robes and adopted other symbols of the black power movement" (165). Black popular culture from the United States, specifically soul music, became an important source of inspiration for Afro-Caribbean youth in Panama and the Canal Zone, as was manifested in the rise of the *combos nacionales* (Steinitz, "Soulful Sancocho"). Despite of heavy restrictions on political activities in the Canal Zone, local organizer Alberto Smith Fernández founded *Asociación Afro-Panameña* in the late 1960s, modeled after black movements in the United States. According to Michael Donoghue, the local adherents of U.S.-style Black Power, who were regarded as "rebels," "boat-rockers," and "trouble-makers" by older West Indians and Zone officials, "gave another Black Power salutes and high-fives, and refused to defer automatically to whites in the manner of their fathers" (Donoghue 122f).

While a large portion of Afro-Caribbean Panamanian activists and intellectuals at home and abroad had become strongly involved in the nationalist and anti-imperialist struggle to recover the Canal, they were still confronted with racism, anti-West Indian sentiment and hostility regarding manifestations of black pride in late 1960s and 1970s Panama. *Mestizo* elites, nationalists, and communists alike rejected influences from the Black Power movement among Afro-Panamanians as manifestations of U.S. cultural imperialism or as imported racialized discourse, allegedly totally out of place in the proclaimed Panamanian *crisol de razas*. Black activism was encouraged, but only as long as it was in line with Torrijos's nationalist agenda (Conniff 167). In the mid-1970s, Torrijos's minister of Justice Juan Materno Vásquez gave voice to persistent anti-West Indian sentiment when he engaged in a public attack on Afro-Caribbean Panamanians, questioning their contributions and loyalty to the nation, urging them to assimilate and conform to Hispanic culture and national identity, based on Spanish language, Catholicism, and the struggle against the U.S. According to Materno Vásquez, "black power and negritude had no place in Panama" (167). The ambivalence of Torrijos's race politics manifested itself in hostility against expressions of black pride in times of new opportunities for Afro-Panamanians, epitomized by a brutal campaign against blacks with an Afro hairdo. In 1970, an executive decree directed at Canal Zone residents, prohibited "the entrance into Panama of men wearing extra-long hair" (*The Panama Canal Spill Way* 1), a clear message to black Canal youth among which the Afro had become an extremely popular symbol of black pride and identification with the African American freedom struggle. What followed was a campaign that implicated a daily assault on blacks with Afro in the streets of Panama City and Colón, who were forcedly shaved by members of the military and the National Guard. When the Dinámicos Exciters, a Panamanian soul band that was among the most successful of the Afro-Caribbean dominated *combos nacionales* initiated the Miss Soul Queen beauty pageants (*La Reina Soul*) in the same year, this constituted an act of antiracist defiance. According to influential community organizer Alberto Barrow, the Miss Soul Queen parades, which featured Afro-Panamanian women with Afro hairdos, represented "a rebellion against the persistence of racism in Panama and the Canal Zone" (Steinitz, "Soulful Sancocho" 22f).

After spending most of the time since his migration to the United States quite detached from the realities in Panama, Carlos Russell became increasingly involved in debates about the anti-racist struggle in his home country from the 1970s onwards. His involvement in the African American freedom struggle and his intense contacts with icons of black resistance in the United States had already made him an influential source of information and inspiration for Afro-Caribbean activists in Panama. Russell represented the transnational community of Afro-Panamanians in the United States which gained new visibility in Panama due to their crucial role in the Canal negotiations, creating a highly frequented channel of communication through which Black Power-inspired ideas and symbols infused Panama's emerging black movement.

While not returning permanently, as many other migrants from the United States did during the Torrijos era, Russell would travel back and forth between New York and Panama City, engaging in lively debates on the appropriate strategies for anti-racist activism with Afro-Panamanian activists, leaders, and intellectuals such as Melva Lowe de Goodin, Tito Chandler, Alberto Smith, Leroy Gittens, Leroy Husband, Gerardo Maloney, Alberto Barrow, and many others. While many of these individuals admired his experience and acknowledged that his radical impulses would "raise the levels of consciousness among local leaders significantly," as influential Afro-Panamanian scholar and activist Gerardo Maloney put it (*Personal Interview*, translation mine), others were deeply skeptical of Russell's drive to forge a Panamanian Black Power movement. Reflecting on these experiences, Russell writes:

> I remember returning to Panama in the early seventies and finding that many of my friends, black and Caribbean like myself, arguing and accusing me of 'bringing U.S. racism into Panama.' They said, "here in Panama it is not about race it is about class." … Still, I believe that their 'awakening' was, in great measure, due to the 'Civil Rights Movement' that took place in the United States, which forced them to rethink the existing conditions of Panama. (*Last Buffalo* 25)

Russell's harsh and provocative style, tested and perhaps even necessary to make his voice heard during his involvement in the conflict-ridden U.S. black movement, did not help to further his cause in Panama. His sometimes-condescending attitude manifested itself in his assessment that "the question of Black Power never centered here because they [Afro-Panamanian leadership] are accommodationist, not transformationist" (Russell, *Personal Interview*). When asked about the role Russell played in Black Panama, Melva Lowe de Goodin, leading Afro-Panamanian scholar and founder of *Sociedad de Amigos del Museo Afro-Antillano de Panamá* (SAMAAP) in 1980, suggests that "when you're a leader you can't impose unless you're a dictator. If you want to lead, sometimes you can't move at the pace that you would want. You have to probably slow down and adapt your pace" (*Personal Interview*).

Activist Alberto Barrow, who in the early 1970s was one of the founders of *Guaycucho*, an Afro-Caribbean-led left-wing student organization, points out that, just like Russell,

> we also wanted radical changes to happen here. But Panama is not the United States. Carlos came from the experience of the U.S. black movement which at that time was much more advanced than we were here. Carlos was impatient and called for immediate changes but sociopolitical conditions, not your wishes, will always determine what is possible, and what not. (Barrow, *Personal Interview*, translation mine)

In his book *The Last Buffalo: Are Panamanians of Caribbean Ancestry an Endangered Species* (2003), Russell introduces himself as "a 'chombo'[7] a proud one … conscious of my African and Caribbean heritage … one who clearly comprehends the implications of being Black in the Americas, and in this case Panama" (62f). Throughout the collection of texts, which are clearly shaped by his experiences in the U.S. Black Power movement, Russell articulates a sharp critique of the persistent legacies of white supremacy and anti-West Indian sentiment in Panama which, in his eyes, "is and was a racist country" (64). He reflects in the book on his conflictive relationship with local Afro-Panamanian leadership and gives voice to his concern that the politics of assimilation and the loss of the English language among younger generations of *afro-antillanos* would ultimately lead to the distinction of the Afro-Caribbean community in Panama.

In her analysis of West Indian and Caribbean consciousness in Carlos Russell's poems, many of which have been published in the anthology *Miss Anna's Son Remembers* (1976), Sonja Stephenson Watson interprets the affirmation of his Caribbean heritage and blackness as "black Panamanian West Indian nationalism" (121), stemming from rage against the Panamanian nation-state for its refusal to acknowledge the Caribbean immigrants' primordial role in building the country and for not including them in their national project. Luis Pulido Ritter has pointed out the contradictions between Russell's radical critique of the exclusionary character of a romantic, Hispanic, and Eurocentric Panamanian nationality and his own embrace of a cultural essentialism that manifests itself in tying the survival of the Afro-Caribbean community in Panama to the preservation of the English language. Through his U.S. black nationalist lens, Russell did not acknowledge Panama's intrinsic hybridity and fluidity of race relations, while at the same time he represented the transnational and diasporic character of the nation like few others ever did (Pulido Ritter, "Carlos E. Russell").

---

7 Historically, "chombo" has been used as a derogatory term for Panamanians of Afro-Caribbean descent. It has also been re-appropriated as a self-descriptive term of ethnic pride as in Carlos Wilson's novel *Chombo* (1981).

Carlos Russell, 1934–2018 (© The Russell family).

Conclusion

Carlos Russell's intervention in Panamanian race relations and their ambiguous reception by Afro-Panamanian activists reveal the potential and the pitfalls of hemispheric Black Power politics: While the radical anti-racist critique, as articulated by Russell and inspired by the lessons of historical African American struggles against one of the most sophisticated and brutal systems of global white supremacy, has proven to be a useful tool in uncovering the veiled manifestations of racism operative in Panama and other Latin American contexts, a mere export of U.S. methods and strategies becomes problematic when the strongly differing racial dynamics and specific sociopolitical contexts are not taken into account.

The stunning rise of Carlos Russell, a descendant of poor, exploited, and multiply excluded Caribbean labor migrants in Panama, to a highly influential figure in the African American freedom struggle and at the service of transnational Panamanian politics provides an insight into the hemispheric dimensions of the Black Power movement. In the 1960s, cross-cultural dialogues between Afrodescendants from the United States, the Caribbean, and Latin America in cosmopolitan urban settings such as New York and Panama, facilitated by increased movements of peoples, ideas, and cultural products, gained an unprecedented momentum. In this context, Russell, articulate in English as well as in Spanish, became a trailblazing translocal actor, translator of ideas, interlocutor between movements, and operator of border-crossing networks between predominantly black neighborhoods in the United States and Panama. He not only introduced New York-based African Americans and Puerto Ricans to the often-ignored realities of Afrodescendants beyond U.S. borders and the struggle to end U.S. neocolonialism in Panama, but also urged Afro-Panamanian activists in the Canal Zone, Colón, and Rio Abajo to adopt the disruptive strategies of the U.S. Black Power movement, of whose efficiency he had convinced himself personally as an active participant in the African American freedom struggle. In his manifold interactions with leading representatives of the most diverse currents of Civil Rights, Black Power, New Left, and Afro-Panamanian activism, Russell benefitted from his experiences growing up in a diasporic, transnational, and cosmopolitan environment where he learned to adapt to constantly changing circumstances and to connect multiple perspectives. As he himself recalls, "they used to call me 'the Eclectic' because you could not pin me down to any particular ideology" (*Personal Interview*).

Studying the trajectory of Carlos Russell is an invitation to put the fields of African American, Afro-Latin American, Caribbean, and African Diaspora Studies in fruitful dialogues which will contribute to the advancement of Hemispheric Black Studies as a new and promising field. As we can learn from his teachings and speeches, Russell's experiences allowed him to develop a *Pan-Afro-Americanist* perspective on the black presence in the Western Hemisphere. His legacy is carried on by transnational activists such as Yvette Modestin who grew up in Panama and is now living in Boston, where she has founded *Encuentro Diaspora Afro*, an organization dedicated to the forging of alliances between black communities from the Caribbean, North, and Latin America. Displaying the emancipatory potential of identifications and solidarities beyond the nation, the experiences of Carlos Russell and Yvette Modestin as translocal actors between diverse hemispheric contexts speak to the crucial role migrants play in the emergence of border-crossing networks of solidarity in the Black Americas.

A close friend of Carlos Russell, Yvette Modestin commemorates him in such words:

> Carlos came into my life in the way he moved in the world, firm and unapologetically Black. He was a validation of the fearlessness I knew and saw and I was growing into that came from Panama. He had it. That is why he moved the way he did. He understood the depth and pride of being a Panamanian that he would not give up. His point of entry was that Pan-African mindset that we both grew up with. As I moved in the US and saw the denial and the disconnect within the Black Latino community, Carlos's historical work in the Black Power movement was a must to understand. He understood our connection beyond borders and he challenged us to do the same. He centered Blackness. He saw and felt the connection. He had global eyes. He saw the importance of the Afro-Panamanian experience as a way to educate on building a movement from a Pan-African lens. (*Personal Communication*)

Works cited

Barron, Charles. "Black Empowerment." Speech given at *Memorial Celebration for Dr. Carlos E. Russell.* Brown Memorial Baptist Church, New York. 29 Sep. 2018.

Barrow, Alberto. *Personal Interview*. Panama City. 3 Apr. 2017.

Boyce-Davis, Carole, and Angelique V. Nixon. "Caribbean Global Movements: An Introduction." *The Black Scholar* 51.2 (2021): 1–7. Print.

Bryce-Laporte, Roy. "Crisis, Contraculture, and Religion among West Indians in the Canal Zone." *Blackness in Latin America and the Caribbean – Social Dynamics and Cultural Tansformations.* Vol 1. *Central America and Northern and Western South America*. Ed. Norman E. Whitten and Arlene Torres. Indianapolis: Indiana UP, 1998. 100–118. Print.

Burnett, Carla. "'Unity Is Strength': Labor, Race, Garveyism, and the 1920 Panama Canal Strike." *The Global South* 6.2 (2013): 39–64. Print.

Bush, Roderick. *The End of White World Supremacy: Black Internationalism and the Problem of the Color Line*. Philadelphia: Temple University, 2009. Print.

Conniff, Michael. *Black Labor on a White Canal: Panama, 1904–1981.* Pittsburgh: U of Pittsburgh P, 1985. Print.

Corinealdi, Kaysha. "Envisioning Multiple Citizenships: West Indian Panamanians and Creating Community in the Canal Zone Neocolony." *The Global South* 6.2 (2013): 87–106. Print.

———. "Dr. Carlos E. Russell and the Origins of Black Solidarity Day." *Black Perspectives*. 14 Sep. 2021. Web. https://www.aaihs.org/dr-carlos-e-russell-and-the-origins-of-black-solidarity-day/.

Donoghue, Michael. *American Encounters/Global Encounters: Borderland on the Isthmus: Race, Culture, and the Struggle for the Canal Zone.* Durham: Duke UP, 2014. Print.

Duke, Dawn. "Black Movement Militancy in Panama: SAMAAP's Reliance on an Identity of West Indianness." *Latin American and Caribbean Ethnic Studies* 5:1 (2010): 75–83. Print.

Dulitzky, Ariel. "A Region in Denial: Racial Discrimination and Racism in Latin America." *Neither Enemies nor Friends: Latinos, Blacks, Afro-Latinos*. Ed. Anani Dzidzienyo and Suzanne Oboler. London: Palgrave, 2005. 39–59. Print.

Edwards, Brent Hayes. *The Practice of Diaspora: Literature, Translation, and the Rise of Black Internationalism*. Cambridge: Harvard UP, 2003. Print.

Fernández, Johanna. *The Young Lords: A Radical History*. Chapel Hill: The U of North Carolina P, 2020. Print.

Guerrón Montero, Carla. "Afro-Antillean Presence in the Latin America Melting Pot." *African Diaspora in the Cultures of Latin America, the Caribbean, and the United States*. Ed. Persephone Braham. Wilmington: University of Delaware/Rowman & Littlefield, 2014. 29–45. Print.

Janson, Donald. "Leftists Plan Democratic Convention Disruption: Convene with Black Power Leaders on Coordination of Anti War Campaign." *New York Times.* 24 Mar. 1968. N. pag. Print.

Joseph, Peniel. *Waiting 'Til The Midnight Hour: A Narrative History of Black Power in America*. New York: Henry Holt and Company, 2006. Print.

———. *The Sword and the Shield: The Revolutionary Lives of Malcolm X and Martin Luther King Jr.* New York: Basic Books, 2020. Print.

Lowe de Goodin, Melva. *Personal Interview*. Panama City, 3 Mar. 2017.

Luciano, Felipe. "Young Lords." Speech given at Memorial Celebration for Dr. Carlos E. Russell. Brown Memorial Baptist Church, New York, 3 Sep. 2018.

———. *Personal Interview.* Phone Call. 30 Oct. 2021.

Maloney, Gerardo. *Personal Interview*. Panama City, 30 Mar. 2017.

Melendez, Mickey. *We Took the Streets: Fighting for Latino Rights with the Young Lords.* New York: Rutgers UP, 2005. Print.

Modestin, Yvette. *Personal Communication.* 2 Nov. 2021.

Nwankwo, Ifeoma. *Black Cosmopolitanism: Racial Consciousness and Transnational Identity in the Nineteenth-Century Americas*. Philadelphia: U of Pennsylvania P, 2014. Print.

Oliver, Denise. *Personal Interview.* New York City, 20 Sep. 2018.

Opie, Frederick. *Upsetting the Apple Cart: Black-Latino Coalitions in New York City from Protest to Public Office*. New York: Columbia UP, 2014. Print.

Pérez Price, Ariel René. *Pionero: La historia de Luis Russell*. Panama: Miss Hilda Press, 2021. Print.

Plummer, Brenda Gayle. *In Search of Power: African Americans in the Era of Decolonization, 1956–1974*. New York: Cambridge UP, 2013. Print.

Priestley, George. "Antillean Panamanians or Afro-Panamanians? Political Participation and the Politics of Identity during the Carter-Torrijos Treaty Negotiations." *Transforming Anthropology* 12.1/2 (2004): 50–67. Print.

Pulido Ritter, Luis. "Notas sobre Eric Walrond La inmigración caribeña y la transnacionalidad literaria en Panamá: una excursión por las calles de la memoria, la reflexión y los espacios en movimiento." *inter.c.a.mbio* 5.6 (2008): 175–180. Print.

———. "Carlos E. Russell: Memoria diaspórica nacional y crítica de la nación panameña." *Diasporische Bewegungen im Transatlantischen Raum*. Ed. Stefanie Kron, Birgit zur Nieden, Stephanie Schütze, and Martha Zapata. Berlin: Edición Tranvía, 2010. Print.

Putnam, Lara. *Radical Moves: Caribbean Migrants and the Politics of Race in the Jazz Age.* Chapel Hill: The U of North Carolina P, 2013. Print.

Rivera-Rideau, Petra R., Jennifer A. Jones, and Tianna S. Paschel, eds. *Afro-Latin@s in Movement: Critical Approaches to Blackness and Transnationalism in the Americas.* New York: Palgrave Macmillan, 2016. Print.

Russell, Carlos E. "Exclusive Interview with Brother Malcolm." *Liberator* 4.5 (May 1964): 12–16. Print.

———. *Miss Anna's Son Remembers.* New York: Bayano Publications, 1976. Print.

———, ed. *The Last Buffalo: "Are Panamanians of Caribbean Ancestry an Endangered Species?"* Charlotte: Conquering Books, 2003. Print.

———. *Personal Interview*. Panama City, 28 Mar. 2017. Print.

Sales, William. *From Civil Rights to Black Liberation: Malcolm X and the Organization of Afro-America Unity.* Boston: South End Press, 1994. Print.

Seale, Bobby. *Seize the Time: The Story of the Black Panther Party and Huey P. Newton.* New York: Random House and Vintage Books, 1970. Print.

Shearer, Jacqueline, and Paul Stekler. "The Promised Land (1967–68)." Episode 10 of *Eyes on the Prize: America's Civil Rights Movement*. Public Broadcasting Service. 1990. Web. https://www.youtube.com/watch?v=wQJP0Yj5GO0&list=PLbSXEa23OUG3TvYA95o2tmuNOIThdW0zK.

Steinitz, Matti. "Soulful Sancocho: Soul Music and Practices of Hemispheric Black Transnationalism in 1960s and 1970s Panama." *The Black Scholar* 52.1 (2022): 15–26. Print.

———. *Soul Music and the Rise of Black Power in Afro-Latin America: Hemispheric Movements and Sounds Between Spanish Harlem, Rio, and Panama.* Berlin: DeGruyter, 2022. Print.

Stephenson Watson, Sonja. *Politics of Race in Panama: Afro-Hispanic and West Indian Literary Discourses of Contention.* Gainesville: UP of Florida, 2017. Print.

The Panama Canal Spillway. "R. of P. Decrees Ban on Long Hair." 10 Apr. 1970.

Tinson, Christopher. "'The Voice of the Black Protest Movement': Notes on the 'Liberator' Magazine and Black Radicalism in the Early 1960s." *The Black Scholar* 37.4 (2008): 3–15. Print.

United States Congress. *Subversive Involvement in Disruption of 1968 Democratic Party National Convention: Hearings before the Committee On Un-American Activities*. House of Representatives, Washington, D.C. 1968.

West, Cornel, ed. *The Radical King*. Boston: Beacon Press, 2016. Print.

West, Michael O., and William G. Martin. "Introduction: Contours of the Black International From Toussaint to Tupac." *From Toussaint to Tupac: The Black International since the Age of Revolution*. Ed. Michael O. West, William G. Martin, and Fanon Che Wilkins. Chapel Hill: U of North Carolina P, 2009. 1–44. Print.

Wilson, Carlos. *Chombo*. Miami: Ediciones Universal, 1981. Print.

X, Malcolm. *By Any Means Necessary*. New York: Pathfinder Press, 1970. Print.

———. *The Final Speeches*. New York: Pathfinder Press, 2003. Print.

Young, Cynthia. "Havana up in Harlem: LeRoi Jones, Harold Cruse, and the Making of a Cultural Revolution." *Science & Society* 65.1 (2001): 12–38. Print.

———. *Soul Power: Culture, Radicalism, and the Making of a U.S. Third World Left*. Durham: Duke UP, 2006. Print.

Zien, Katherine. "Race and Politics in Concert: Paul Robeson and William Warfield in Panama, 1947–1953." *The Global South* 6.2 (2013): 107–129. Print.

"The Goose and the Gander": Frantz Fanon and the Rhetoric of Violence in the Black Power Movement

PORTIA OWUSU

> I was born in the Antilles, my observations and my conclusions are valid only for the Antilles – at least concerning the black man at home. Another book could be dedicated to explaining the differences that separate the Negro of the Antilles from the Negro elsewhere. Perhaps one day I will write it. Perhaps too it will no longer be necessary – a fact for which we could only congratulate ourselves.
> (Fanon, *Black Skin* 14)

> We read the work of Frantz Fanon, particularly *The Wretched of the Earth* … we believed it was necessary to know how they gained their freedom in order to go about getting ours. However, we did not want merely to import ideas and strategies; we had to transform what we learned into principles and methods acceptable to the brothers on the block [sic]. (Newton, *Revolutionary Suicide* 116)

> This is what is meant by equality. What's good for the goose is good for the gander. (X 123)

The Black Power movement is often marginalized in twentieth-century American history. When it is represented, the emphasis is on the group's advocation of violence, with speeches, texts, and admonitions by activists sensationalized to make the movement, and those who supported it, appear violent. However, Black Power ideologies, specifically on violence, actually recall – and root itself – in the histories and politics of the United States and Third World Internationalism. This chapter examines these ideas. It looks at how global events and movements, like decolonization, and the work of Afro-diasporic intellectuals, particularly Frantz Fanon, were crucial to the formation and development of the movement and its philosophies, especially pertaining to violence, in the United States during the 1960s and 1970s.

1.

In a speech given in 1967, the Black Power activist, H. Rap Brown, later known as Jamil Abdullah Al-Amin, alluded to the violence of the American Revolution when he said "violence is part of America's culture; it is as American as cherry pie" (Brown 44). Similarly, in interviews given in 1971 and 1972, Huey P. Newton, co-founder of the Black Panther Party, and Angela Davis, a scholar and an activist, explained their explicit support for armed revolution by making references to American Independence and the lived realities of Black Americans. Referring to the actions of George Washington in 1776, Newton, in a television interview with the conservative journalist William F. Buckley, argued that "revolutions always contradict the law" but in the final analysis, they are worth fighting for if "in fact, or objectively, people are … dealt with in a fair way and given more freedom" (Newton, "Firing Line" n. pag.). Similarly, speaking from the San Rafael County Prison, Davis reflected on her memories living in the South. She tells Bo Holmström in a filmed interview: "I remember from the time I was very small … the sounds of bombs exploding across the streets, our house shaking; I remember my father having to have guns disposable at all times because of the fact that at any moment, we might expect to be attacked" (Davis). Consequently, she tells Holmström that when someone criticizes her views on violence, "what it means is the person who's asking that question has absolutely no idea … what Black people have experienced in this country since the time the first Black person was kidnapped from the shores of Africa" (Davis). American history and the lived realities of Black Americans had thus framed Black Power ideologies and strategies for achieving civil rights.

Particularly, Black Power advocates studied the rights afforded to American citizens which are enshrined in the Constitution. They attended to the Second Amendment, the right to keep and bear arms, in order to reinforce the possibilities of violence in the course of achieving freedom. The founders of the Black Power movement and their supporters, many of whom were highly educated, recalled that the Second Amendment was drafted into the Constitution in 1768 when the British Redcoats occupied Boston, Massachusetts. Fearing that they would be attacked when most vulnerable, eight of the original thirteen colonies adopted arms-rights legislations. Massachusetts allowed "the people [to] have a right to keep and to bear arms for the common defence" (Commonwealth of Massachusetts n. pag.). With slight differences in wording, other states followed and provided constitutional rights to individuals and to groups to bear arms in self-defense. In 1788, this right was extended to the entire United States with the Second Amendment of the Constitution, which read: "A well regulated Militia, being necessary to the security of a free State, the right of the people to keep and bear Arms, shall not be infringed [sic]" (United States Constitution n. pag.).

This constitutional right did not, however, extend to men and women of African descent, even those emancipated from slavery. Nonetheless, Black people persisted. They inserted themselves into the narrative of "We the People" by insisting on the right to be armed because it was their constitutional right as citizens. The Second Amendment also held significance for Black people because the gun both promised and threatened Black freedom: it was the primary instrument used by the slave-holders to enforce slavery and by the slaves to resist it. For enslaved persons, the right to be armed was particularly important in the face of the Fugitive Slave Acts, passed into law by Congress in 1850. The legislation empowered slave-holders to violently pursue runaway slaves for re-enslavement, even in free states in the North. The impact of the Fugitive Slave Act on enslaved people was enormous: family separations, kidnappings of freed individuals,[1] deaths but also greater racial and political consciousness among Black people.

---

1 An example of this is the case of Solomon Northup (1807–1857), who was born free in New York, but was kidnapped and enslaved.

In the North, Black individuals and groups armed themselves with weapons to fight against the law and for their freedom. Abolitionists, even those who propagated the ideology of nonviolence and built their image on Black respectability, considered violence as necessary for self-defense; among these, Harriet Tubman, who was frequently pictured with a revolver in hand, and Frederick Douglass, who wrote in an editorial:

> the true remedy for the Fugitive Slave Act is a good revolver, a steady hand, and a determination to shoot down any man attempting to kidnap. Let every colored man make up his mind on this, and live by it, and if needs be, die by it. This will put an end to the kidnapping and to slaveholding, too. … oh! That we had a little more of the manly indifference to death, which characterized the heroes of the American Revolution. (Douglass, "The True Remedy" 1).

Personal experiences of racialized violence thus shaped the positions of Douglass and Tubman. In his autobiography, *Narrative of the Life of Frederick Douglass, an American Slave* (1845), Douglass expands on this. He writes of his experience with Edward Covey, a slave-master, who held a reputation as a "nigger-breaker":

> he had used me like a brute for six months, and that I was determined to be used so no longer. With that, he strove to drag me to a stick that was lying just out of the stable door. He meant to knock me down. But just as he was leaning over to get the stick, I seized him with both hands by his collar, and brought him by a sudden snatch to the ground. By this time, Bill came. Covey called upon him for assistance. Bill wanted to know what he could do. Covey said, "Take hold of him, take hold of him!" Bill said his master hired him out to work, and not to help to whip me; so he left Covey and myself to fight our own battle out. We were at it for nearly two hours. Covey at length let me go, puffing and blowing at a great rate, saying that if I had not resisted, he would not have whipped me half so much. … The whole six months afterwards, that I spent with Mr. Covey, he never laid the weight of his finger upon me in anger. (Douglass, *Narrative* 61)

To Douglass, the encounter with Covey was "the turning-point" in his life because, as he observed later, "it rekindled the few expiring embers of freedom," and revived a sense of his "own manhood" (61). Similarly, for Tubman, it was a regained sense of one's humanity, self-defense, and a desire to affect change that influenced her perspective on violence and justice. In *Harriet Tubman: Myth, Memory, and History* (2007), Milton C. Sernett asserts that Tubman's frequent possession of a gun on her person reflects her "philosophy of righteous violence" (Sernett 72). This philosophy sought to avoid bloody horrors and insurgencies, but it was not opposed to resorting to violence, if needed, as a means of bringing about change or providing protection for one's self and community.

In the 1960s and 1970s, during the Civil Rights era, a similar philosophy of righteous violence resurfaced. As it is already well-documented, the prominent campaigns of the time, for example those organized by the National Association for the Advancement of Colored People (NAACP) and the Southern Christian Leadership Conference (SCLC), promoted nonviolence. Dr. Martin Luther King, Jr., a Christian minister and leader of SCLC, maintained that "constructive ends can never give absolute moral justification to destructive means, because in the final analysis the end is preexistent in the means" (King Jr. and West 41), and NAACP insisted that it "cannot support any sentiment calling for the use of violence to correct injustice" (Ivy 327). However, not everyone within these organizations shared this view. Robert F. Williams, President of the NAACP chapter of Monroe, North Carolina, encouraged Black people to arm themselves as protection from white terrorism. He believed that non-violent strategies combined with armed-defense in his county confirmed that Black people had "the willingness and readiness to fight and defend" themselves because they "didn't appear on the streets of Monroe as beggars depending upon the charity and generosity of white supremacists. We appeared as people with strength" (Williams 31).

Defenders of the right to bear arms in civil rights activism, like Williams, inspired the Black Power movement. Proponents were also influenced by the scholarly work of Afro-diasporic activists and intellectuals, including Marcus Garvey, Claude McKay, and Frantz Fanon. Fanon, a French-Martiniquais psychiatrist, emerged as a particularly important figure in the movement because of the uniqueness of his scholarship, namely his combination of medical science and political theory. Fanon's work with colonized subjects in Algeria led him to the conclusion in his book, *The Wretched of the Earth* (1961), that violence was necessary for the achievement of decolonization mainly because colonization is maintained through violence and thus violence, in the hands of the oppressed, allows them to speak the language of the oppressor. Fanon's work did not address the Black American struggle; it was specific to the political situations in the Antilles and Algeria, places where he had worked and lived. Furthermore, in *Black Skin, White Masks* (1952), he maintains that his work is born out of observations "concerning the black man at *home*" and not the Negro elsewhere (Fanon, *Black Skin* 14). Nonetheless, irrespective of Fanon's specificity and the fact that English translations of his work, initially *Wretched*, were not published in the United States until 1965, supporters of Black Power adapted Fanon's theory. They especially gravitated towards his theorization of violence in "Concerning Violence," the first section of *Wretched.* The essay articulated the benefits of armed resistance in the struggle for decolonization. In the hands of Black Power activists, the theory gave contexts for understanding inequalities and discriminations suffered by Black Americans. Fanon's insight as a psychiatrist explained the psychological impact of racism; his focus on colonialism also provided a theoretical paradigm to understand the political situation in the United States, namely, the U.S. as a repressive colonial system and Black Americans as colonized subjects.

The influence of Fanon in the Black Power movement is apparent in the writings of a number of influential activists. In *Revolutionary Suicide* (1973), Huey P. Newton, for example, credits Fanon for his understanding of revolutionary violence; he lauds Fanon for the realization that "Black people had been stripped of their birthright and their dignity, not by philosophy or mere words, but at gunpoint" (Newton, *Revolutionary Suicide* 111); similarly, in *Black Power: The Politics of Liberation in America*

(1967), Charles Hamilton and Kwame Turé cite *Wretched* as an inspiration. They adapt Fanonian theory to understand that "Black people are legal citizens of the United States .... Yet, they stand as colonial subjects in relation to the white society" (Hamilton and Turé 5). Likewise, Eldridge Cleaver's focus on the psychology of the Black subject under racial duress in *Soul on Ice* (1965) reflects his familiarity with Fanon's work. Maxwell Geismar notes this in his introduction to Cleaver's book by stating that "in a curious way, Cleaver's book has definite parallels with Fanon's *Black Skin, White Masks*" because both addressed the problem of the "black soul which has been 'colonized' – more subtly perhaps in the United States for three hundred years" (Geismar 16).

Fanon was not the only scholar from the African diaspora to have influenced the development of the Black Power movement in the United States. The movement itself was initiated by the actions of Kwame Turé (then Stokely Carmichael), a student from Trinidad and Tobago. In 1966, James Meredith, a student activist from the Mississippi Delta, was ambushed, shot, and hospitalized during a demonstration. Civil Rights advocates from across the country gathered around his hospital bed, among them Martin Luther King, Jr. and Turé. In defiance, they vowed to continue Meredith's march. King's person and iconography provided the necessary gravitas and publicity but it was Carmichael and his group, the Student Non-Violent Coordinating Committee (SNCC), who took action. Although protests in the South were often met with violence and terror, both King and Turé stressed nonviolence. On the day of the march, however, Turé signaled a change in direction when he took to the podium and told the crowd: "... this is the twenty-seventh time I've been arrested. I ain't going to jail no more. The only way we gonna stop white men from whuppin' us is to take over. What we gonna start saying now is 'Black Power!'" (Joseph 2). Turé's words reflected his experience as a Black international student in America during the 1960s and 1970s. Thus, as he chanted "Black Power" alongside the crowd, it was inevitable that the movement he was calling for would be global in its nature.[2]

The change Turé called for implicated deviation from traditional civil rights methodologies. King's insistence on nonviolence, love, and the redemption of white racists reflected his Christian beliefs. However, for Turé and his colleagues, continual racial injuries against Black people were evidence that King's strategies were no longer tenable. The quest for Black Power, therefore, was centered on the need "to radically redefine the relationship between blacks and American society" and to usher in "a militant new race consciousness that placed Black identity as the soul of a new radicalism" (Joseph 3). Redefinitions of Blackness was at the heart of the Black Power movement because it was thought necessary for the Black community "to reclaim their history, their culture; to assert their own sense of community and togetherness" before

2 The foundation of the Black Panther Party, for which Turé temporarily served as "Honorary Prime Minister," reflected this: the Party had visible presence in many countries in Asia, Africa, Europe, and the Middle East. Its international office, or its "Embassy," was established in 1970 in Algeria and under the leadership of Eldridge Cleaver.

they could have a "positive image of itself that *it* created" (Hamilton and Turé 37; my emphasis) [sic]. In essence, the movement sought to eradicate the problem of double consciousness that W.E.B. Du Bois had described as a "peculiar sensation" suffered by Black people when they look at themselves "through the eyes of others, of measuring one's soul by the tape of a world that looks on in amused contempt and pity" (Du Bois 2). Black Power encouraged Black people to own their political destinies without the intervention of white America.

This idea was antithetical to mainstream civil rights organizations, namely King's Southern Christian Leadership Conference (SCLC) and the National Association for the Advancement of Colored People (NAACP). To the NAACP in particular, Black Power represented violent, angry, and racist ideologies – perceptions that they drew on in their critique of the movement. For example, the November 1967 edition of *The Crisis*, the organization's official magazine, included an editorial, entitled "A Measure of Justice in Mississippi." The piece interpreted ideologies of Black Power as a "wailing of defeat" coming from "misguided black advocates of apartheid who have been convinced of their inability to compete in open market with other Americans and, … [are] seeking refuge in racialism" (*The Crisis* 439). To the NAACP, Black Power's refusal to collaborate with white liberals in the fight for civil rights equated the racial discrimination experienced by Blacks in the South and the rest of the country. As such, they asserted:

> We in the NAACP, as well as others, fought segregation because we had faith in our ability, given equal opportunity and fair ground rules, to compete with and achieve, on a man-to-man basis, with any other American of whatever origin. … But we have never fostered xenophobia … to be proud of one's self, or one's race, does not require, or justify hatred of other peoples. It is among defeated people that the merger of racial pride and racial hatred is commonly found. (*The Crisis* 440)

The NAACP's position reflected their politics and organizational history. Namely, it was interracial from the outset (its founders included white civil rights activists, such as Mary White Ovington and Henry Moskowitz) and its members prized formal education. Unlike Black Power, therefore, the image of NAACP was built on Black respectability. The prominence of Du Bois in the organization particularly cemented this. As the first African American to earn a doctorate from Harvard University, Du Bois encouraged intellectual, as a well as political, engagement with civil rights issues. He used his various publications, including his editorship of *The Crisis*, to analyze conditions of Black American life. He proposed solutions, such as emphasis on the 'Talented Tenth,' a distinguished class of exceptional men in the Black community who could be pillars and leaders of the Black community. The leadership of Martin Luther King Jr. and his iconography a generation later exemplified this. However, to Black Power activists, this idea was exclusive and elitist mainly because it encouraged white paternalism. Therefore, they encouraged inclusion by emphasizing community efforts and forming alliances with anticolonial movements in Africa, Asia, and Latin America.

2.

Africa served as an inspiration to Black Power advocates because of the historical and cultural connections between Black America and the African continent. Revolutionary leaders and politicians, whose ideas and movements had achieved tangible changes lived and worked in Africa. This included Kwame Nkrumah's successful leadership in the independence of Ghana from British rule in 1957. Nkrumah's ideas attracted Black Power advocates because he considered the concerns of the African diaspora. Particularly, Nkrumah extended invitation to all civil rights activists in the diaspora to come to the continent to learn about the strategies that had worked there. Leaders of Black Power, including Turé, accepted the invitation. Visiting Africa allowed Turé and other proponents of Black Power to better understand the project and aims of the Black Power movement. In his essay, "From Black Power to Pan-Africanism," Turé writes that he realized what the shared common roots between Black Power and Pan Africanism included because both movements "saw and felt the oppression of their people and pledged their lives to end that suffering ("From Black Power to Pan-Africanism" 224). Consequently, he concluded: "Black Power really means African Power" and therefore, the work of the movement could not be confined to the United States alone (224).

Experiencing African decolonization firsthand also emboldened Black Power advocates and affirmed revolutionary tactics proposed by Fanon. They saw how Fanon's radical tactics had given African leaders confidence to know that they can "fight their own battles and show that after all, the black man is capable of managing his own affairs" (Nkrumah 302). In his book, *American Africans in Ghana: Black Expatriates and the Civil Rights Era* (2012), Kevin Gaines argues that Africa provided Black American activists refuge from racial constraints of American culture (179). This was particularly true for trailblazers of the Black Power movement, such as Malcolm X.

Malcolm X died in 1965 and thus in many ways, his work cannot be easily situated within the classical period of the Black Power movement that lasted roughly from 1966 to 1975. However, his ideas closely reflected Black Power sentiments and were fundamental to the movement and its aims. This was particularly true for his thoughts on revolutionary violence. Like Fanon, Malcolm X believed violence could not be ruled out of the fight for Black freedom, which had to be achieved by "any means necessary," a phrase he often used and which became a Black Power mantra. He expressed this idea powerfully in "The Ballot or the Bullet," a speech delivered in 1964 at Cory Methodist Church in Cleveland, Ohio: "If they draft you, they send you to Korea and make you face 800 million Chinese. If you can be brave over there, you can be brave right here. And if you fight here, you will at least know what you're fighting for. … Well, I am one who doesn't believe in deluding myself" (X 117). Black Americans, he argued, were already speaking the language of violence, but not to advocate for their right and instead, to advance the interests of the oppressor. Thus, in his speech, Malcolm X warned: "If you don't take this kind of stand, your little children will grow up and look at you and think 'shame'" (123). Like Fanon, the violence Malcolm X encouraged was not senseless or without aim: it was self-defense. As such, Malcolm concluded: "I'm nonviolent with those who are nonviolent with me. But when you drop that violence on me, then you've made me go insane, and I'm not responsible for what I do. And that's the way every Negro should get" (123).

Malcolm X does not name Fanon as an inspiration in "The Ballot or the Bullet" nor does he cite him explicitly anywhere in his work. However, as the historian Peter Louis Goldman asserts, he was "a Fanoniste without having read Fanon because he lived in spirit if not in literal fact of the native quarters and understood its vocation for destruction" (Goldman 185). This unique perspective may have begun early in Malcolm X's life because his family experienced extreme racial violence and because he had been exposed to Black Radicalism in the figure of Marcus Garvey, through his parents. Malcolm X's mother, Louise Little, a Grenadian immigrant, alongside his father, Earl Little, supported Garvey's Back to Africa movement. In his autobiography, Malcolm X recalls that his father, a Baptist minister, was an organizer for Garvey's Universal Negro Improvement Association (UNIA). Earl Little dedicated his life to advance the philosophy that "freedom, independence, and self-respect could not be achieved by the Negro in America and therefore the Negro should leave America to the white man and return to his African land of his origin" (Haley and X 2).

Thus, whilst Malcolm X may not have had direct contact with Fanon or his work, their ideas converged due to the similarities of their experiences living under oppressive and violent conditions and, perhaps, Malcolm X's exposure to Black radical politics through his parents at an early age. Nonetheless, it is clear that even in their different societies, injustice and oppression had the same operative powers, for example the misuse of religion to keep the oppressed subservient. With reference to colonial Algeria in *The Wretched of the Earth*, Fanon, like Marx, believes religion to be the "opium of the people" because it weakens the agency of the colonized, thus influencing them to think that only God can fashion their future (Marx 244). In his autobiography, Malcolm X makes a similar point but with a specific reference to Christian religion: The political docility of Black Americans, he contends, is "the greatest miracle Christianity has achieved in America" (Haley and X 247). Christianity's emphasis on forgiveness and rewards in the afterlife, Malcolm X believed, encouraged Black people to remain peaceful "while catching centuries of hell … in the white man's heaven" (Haley and X 247). According to Fanon, this happens because the primary characteristic of the oppressed is their hyper-spirituality, customs, and traditions that "are the very sign of that poverty of spirit and of their constitutional depravity" (Fanon, "Concerning Violence" 6). Malcolm X thus proposes a solution that reflects his estrangement from the Nation of Islam in 1964, namely demarcating religion to the private sphere, and politics to the public sphere:

> My religion is still Islam. That's my personal belief. Just as Adam Clayton Powell is a Christian minister who heads the Abyssinian Baptist Church in New York, but at the same time takes part in the political struggles to try and bring about rights to the black people in this country … we don't mix our religion with our politics and our economics and our social and civil activities – not any more. We keep our religion in our mosque.

> After our religious services are over, then as Muslims we become involved in political action, economic action, and social and civic action. (X 115)

This statement critiques King's civil rights campaign and warns Blacks in the South, majority Christians, to not exchange their religious faith for their freedom. This is because, he believed, when religion is mixed with politics, it has the potential to discourage progress by pitching individuals and groups against each other, causing them to forget that Black people will "catch hell whether you're a Baptist, or a Methodist, or a Muslim, or a nationalist. Whether you're educated or illiterate, whether you live on the boulevard or in the alley" (X 116). Malcolm X's complicated history with the Nation of Islam led him to this conclusion. The Nation, under the leadership of Elijah Muhammed, appeared imbalanced in its dealings with politics and religion. According to Louis A. DeCaro, the organization was less concerned with Black nationalism than it was with creating a rebellion against Christianity. As a result, it was "aggressively and openly anti-Christian" (DeCaro 3). This turned the focus of the organization to religion and not on civil rights. Therefore, when he departed from the Nation, Malcolm X concluded that religion, when practiced privately, allowed individuals to concentrate on social justice, as it concerns *all* Blacks and minorities. Knowing that this separation between religion and politics would be problematic for some people, Malcolm X suggested a compromise which he called the "gospel of Black nationalism" (X 128). This had the potential to be inclusive: "Billy Graham comes in preaching … he evangelizes the gospel, he stirs everybody up, but he never tries to start a church … and in this way the church cooperates with him" (X 128).

Fanon too was intolerant of such middle grounds: his goal was for the oppressed to recognize that Christian religion controls them by forcing them to turn the "other cheek" and to forgive trespasses and insults "without shrinking" (Fanon, "Concerning Violence" 66). Only when the oppressed has come to this realization that he can be armed to fight back. Malcolm X concurs, but mindful of mistrust of the Black Power movement among Black Christians in the South, he reinforced the idea that the Black Power movement is not oppositional to King's campaign and his Christian message of love and peace. On the contrary, readiness to use armed resistance does not advocate violence for violence's sake, it entails the belief that Black freedom cannot be compromised.

However, irrespective of noble intentions, violence in the political philosophy of Black Power is, to some people, the primary factor for the demise of the movement. Curtis J. Austin in *Up against the Wall: Violence in the Making and Unmaking of the Black Panther Party* (2006) asserts that an "exaggerated paramilitary image … portrayed the group's members as gun-toting thugs out to kill white people" (Austin 89). The media seized on this and perpetuated this image, using it "to strike fear in both the white and black public, and to help justify the police repression" (89). This was the case in 1967, when the Black Panther Party invaded the California Capitol to protest racist legislations. The media's focus was not on the grievances of the Party, but on the iconic image of armed men and women in military formation, dressed in Black leather and beret. In that moment, those who watched them from the steps of the Capitol learned little about the Party's dedication to feeding the poor, providing healthcare and education on civil rights in marginalized communities. Yet, these were fundamental parts of their existence. The Party's Ten Point Program, which included campaigning for economic and employment opportunities, decent housing and education, and adequate healthcare for Black people, sought to address what King identified as the three evils of American society – racism, poverty, and war (King Jr.). These, however, were lost in the discourse as the media and the public focused on the image and rhetoric of violence. For Austin, even though the language of violence was grounded in hyperbole and sought to bring attention to the movement and its causes, authorities took them seriously and devised ways to disband the Black Panther Party specifically and the Black Power movement generally (94).

Certainly, the movement's emphasis on violence may have contributed to its demise. In the 1960s and 1970s, violence was a reality for many Black Americans, especially those living in the South. For such people, the ultimate goal of any civil rights campaign was to stop violence, improve the Black community's relations with the U.S. government, and strengthen Black American citizenship. For such people, violence in the rhetoric and actions of some groups, for example the "Kill the Pigs" campaign by the Black Panther Party, may have alienated them from the movement.[3] However, it is important to remember the movement was heterogeneous in its reception and its work. Therefore, it also attracted many people. Particularly for youths frustrated by lack of change or legislations that had no real power, Black Power provided opportunities for young people to affect real change. It was also a lifeline in Black communities: the outreach programs, for example, attended to the material needs of people in marginalized conditions and the ideologies gave voice to thoughts and feelings of oppressed and marginalized people. For many, these factors, and not necessarily the advocation of violence, made the movement revolutionary.

Works cited

Austin, Curtis J. *Up Against the Wall: Violence in the Making and Unmaking of the Black Panther Party*. U of Arkansas P, 2008. Print.

Brown, H. Rap. *Concise Oxford Dictionary of Quotations*. Oxford UP, 2006. 44. Print.

Carmichael, Stokely. "From Black Power to Pan-Africanism." *Stokely Speaks: From Black Power to Pan-Africanism*. Chicago: Chicago Review Press, Incorporated, 1970. 221–255. Print.

3 "Kill the Pigs" was a campaign by the Black Panther Party against police brutality. It was widespread in *The Black Panther*, the Party's newspaper. In articles and pictorials, police were caricatured as pigs and activists were encouraged to violently retaliate against any form of harassment from them.

Commonwealth of Massachusetts. "Legal History." Massachusetts Declaration of Rights – Article 17. 13 Jan. 2020. Print.

The Crisis. Editorial. "A Measure of Justice in Mississippi." *The Crisis* (November 1967): 438–441. Print.

Davis, Angela. *The Black Power Mixtape 1967–1975*. (2011) Bo Holmström. 1972. Documentary.

DeCaro, Louis A. *Malcolm and the Cross: The Nation of Islam, Malcolm X, and Christianity*. New York: NYU Press, 2000. Print.

Douglass, Frederick. *Narrative of the Life of Frederick Douglass, an American Slave*. New York: Blackberry Publishing, 2019. Print.

———. "The True Remedy for the Fugitive Slave Act." *The Frederick Douglass Paper* (9 Jun. 1854): 1. Print.

Du Bois, W.E.B. *The Souls of Black Folk*. New York: Dover Publications, 2012. Print.

Fanon, Frantz. *Black Skin, White Masks*. New York: Grove Weidenfeld, 1967. Print.

———, ed. "Concerning Violence." *The Wretched of the Earth*. New York: Grove Weidenfield, 1961. 34–106. Print.

Gaines, Kevin. *American Africans in Ghana: Black Expatriates and the Civil Rights Era*. U of North Carolina P, 2012. Print.

Geismar, Maxwell. "Introduction." Eldridge Cleaver. *Soul on Ice*. New York: Delta, 1991. 16–17. Print.

Goldman, Peter Louis. *The Death and Life of Malcolm X*. Chicago: U of Illinois P, 1979. Print.

Haley, Alex, and Malcolm X. *The Autobiography of Malcolm X*. New York: Ballantine Books, 1981. Print.

Hamilton, Charles V., and Kwame T. Turé. *Black Power: Politics of Liberation in America*. New York: Vintage Books, 2011. Print.

Ivy, James W. "The Robert Williams Case." *The Crisis* (Jun.–Jul. 1959): 325–330. Print.

Joseph, Peniel E. *The Black Power Movement: Rethinking the Civil Rights-Black Power Era*. New York: Routledge, 2006. Print.

King Jr., Martin Luther, and Cornell West. *The Radical King*. Boston: Beacon Press, 2016. Print.

King Jr., Martin Luther. "Martin Luther King Jr. Saw Three Evils in the World." April 2018. *The Atlantic* (13 Feb. 2020): n. pag.

Marx, Karl. "A Contribution to the Critique of Hegel's Philosophy of Right (1843)." *Karl Marx: Early Writings*. Ed. Karl Marx. London: Penguin, 1992. 243–258. Print.

Newton, Huey P. "Firing Line: How Does it Go with the Black Movement?" Huey P. Newton; William F. Buckley. 23 Jan.1971. TV Interview.

———. *Revolutionary Suicide*. New York: Penguin, 1973. Print.

Nkrumah, Kwame. "Independence Speech." *The Ghana Reader: History, Culture, Politics*. Ed. Kwasi Konadu and Clifford C. Campbell. Durham, NC: Duke UP, 2016. 301–302. Print.

Northup, Solomon. *Twelve Years a Slave*. New York: Atria Books, 2013. Print.

Sernett, Milton. *C. Harriet Tubman. Myth, Memory, and History*. Durham: Duke UP, 2007. Print.

United States Constitution. "United States of America 1789 (rev. 1992)." Constitute Project. 14 Jan. 2020. Print.

Williams, Robert Franklin. *Negroes with Guns*. Detroit: Wayne State UP, 1998. Print.

X, Malcolm. "The Ballot or the Bullet." *Great Speeches by African Americans: Frederick Douglass, Sojourner Truth, Dr. Martin Luther King, Jr., Barack Obama, and Others*. Ed. James Daley. New York: Dover Publications, 2012. 115–131. Print.

Revolutionary Alliances: Black Power, Brown Power, and Radical Ethnic Nationalism (1966–1973)

JEFFREY O.G. OGBAR

On February 17, 1969, in the freezing temps typical of Chicago's winter, young grassroots activists hosted a two-day meeting at the Olivet Presbyterian Church to discuss the pressing issues of poverty, racism, police brutality, and other exigences faced by the community. Although firmly grounded in the basic ideological thrust of the historic moment and the Black Power movement, it was focused on issues broader than the Black community in Chicago. The gathering's name, the Third World Unity Conference, was much more capacious than the community in which the meeting was held. It was a bold, audacious, and important nod to a struggle that aligned itself with people across national boundaries and races. Implicit with the term "Third World" was an anti-imperialist politics that was inherently anti-racist and, often anti-capitalist. The conference was co-sponsored by Black, Active, and Determined, a majority-Black organization, and the Young Lords, a largely Puerto Rican group. Formerly a street gang, the Young Lords had recently become politicized during the Black Power era and the general political activism of the late 1960s. These organizers understood that their circumstances in the mobilization for justice was stronger for alliances. No advocate of revolutionary solidarity was as prominent as the featured speaker, Fred Hampton. The 21-year-old charismatic Chairman of the Illinois Chapter of the Black Panther Party, Chairman Fred, as he was known, insisted that strategic and genuine alliances across racial and ethnic lines were critical to any revolutionary movement. "We say All Power to the People – Black power to Black people, and Brown power to Brown people, Red power to Red people and Yellow power to Yellow people. We say White power to White people" (Hampton 72). The sentiment of revolutionary nationalism struck a chord beyond the Black Panthers. Within days, the Young Lords adopted the Ten-Point Program of the BPP. By the end of the month, Hampton celebrated the formation of a "Rainbow Coalition" of groups all centered on organizing their communities on revolutionary principles of class-based, anti-racist, and anti-imperialist struggle. In addition to the Young Lords, two white groups, the Young Patriots and Rising Up Angry joined the coalition (Fernandez 41–42; Ogbar, "Puerto Rico" 155–157).

While this formation of the Rainbow Coalition was a powerful and bold step in radical struggle during the era, it was not the first formation of alliances and efforts at solidarity across racial and ethnic lines during the Black Power movement. Black communities were being ideologically transformed across the country, and other marginalized and racially oppressed peoples were acting upon shared commonalities with them. As evinced in the story of the Panthers in Chicago, the Black Power movement had a profound impact on the formation of the symbolism, rhetoric, and tactics of radical activism outside of the African American community during the Long Sixties.

Scholars have long credited the Civil Rights movement for fomenting the emerging movements of women, gays, and others in the late 1960s and early 1970s. While the Black struggle for civil rights undoubtedly affected the growing efforts of other marginalized and oppressed groups in the United States, it was the Black Power movement that had some of the most visible influences on the radical activist struggles of Latinos, Asians, and Native Americans, giving rise to a visible movement of radical ethnic nationalism. By 1968, young activists from outside the Black community had been impressed and inspired by the militancy, political analysis, organization as well as symbolism of Black nationalists and Black Power advocates. No organization influenced these burgeoning militants more than the Black Panther Party (BPP).

The Nation of Islam, the chief benefactor of the Black Power movement and largest Black nationalist organization in the country, long embraced all people of color as members of the family of Black humanity. Still, the language, symbolism, and general cosmology of the Nation was particularly geared toward African Americans. There were, however, Latinos, Asians, and other non-African Americans who joined the Nation. But for non-African Americans, the Black Power movement demonstrated that ethnic nationalism had incredible potential for political mobilization and resistance to the oppression and marginalization that they experienced. For many, the BPP, in particular, embodied and represented the model for revolutionary struggle, resistance, and radical chic.[1]

The Black Panther Party experienced precipitous growth in 1968 with over thirty chapters emerging across the country. While thousands of African American militants were willing to embrace the BPP as a vanguard organization to lead the national struggle against oppression, non-African Americans took notice. Conditions that gave rise to the radicalism that characterized Black Power similarly catapulted other minorities and even poor whites into militant activism in the late 1960s. Along with Black people, other people of color languished under the domination of white supremacy in the United States for over one hundred years. It was the militant call for Black Power that reverberated in the barrios and ghettoes throughout the country, which engendered such organizations as the Brown Berets, Young Lords, Red Guard, American Indian Movement, and other organizations that joined the chorus for liberation and radical political activism.[2] By 1967, the L.A.-based Brown Berets had become the first major organization to model itself after the BPP, emerging as the self-described "shock troops" for a burgeoning Chicano civil rights movement.

---

1 For more information on the degree to which some people read the Black Panther Party as the epitome of cool, cf. Tom Wolf's critical book, *Radical Chic and Mau-Mauing the Flak Catchers*.

2 The literature on what I call radical ethnic nationalism has grown over recent years. Cf. Ogbar, *Black Power*; Pulido; Fujino; Castro; Fernandez.

Several factors fed into Chicano nationalism and the Chicano Power movement, including an impassioned identification with *Aztlan*, the mythic homeland of ancient Aztecs. It was this land in the southwest of the United States that provided livelihood for the ancestors of Chicanos, long before there was a United States. As many Chicanos stated: "We did not cross the border. The border crossed us" (*La Causa* 1). By the late 1960s, East Los Angeles emerged as home to one of the largest Spanish-speaking communities in the world and a center of increasing political activism. Chicanos in the city suffered from police brutality and widespread discrimination in housing, education, and employment, as was the case for Chicanos throughout the Southwest. Although Chicanos were the second largest ethnic group in the state of California, they had only one state assemblyman and no state senators. In L.A., there were no Chicano city councilmen or representatives on the L.A. county board of directors. By 1970, a full eighty percent of Chicanos were high school dropouts, a rate higher than any ethnic group in the city.[3]

In 1967, an exceptional high school student, David Sanchez, organized the Young Citizens for Community Action in East L.A. (YCCA). Attempting to meet the needs of the surrounding community, YCCA surveyed the dilemmas of education in E.L.A. and sought Chicano representation on the LA Board of Education, campaigning for Julian Nava. Initially a liberal, youth-oriented reformist organization, the YCCA quickly became affected by the wave of radicalism that swept the country. With the help of Father John Luce, YCCA opened a coffee shop, La Piranya, in September 1967, which provided a meeting place for Chicano youth and others who read poetry, held meetings and informal political discussion groups (Ogbar, *Black Power* 161). There, young Chicanos would discuss the tumultuous political and social climate that had given rise to Black Power, student radicalism and a generally militant mood among many young people. Police brutality, poverty, and pervasive discrimination against Chicanos were issues of frequent debate.

On November 24, 1967, police officers were called to a civil disturbance in East L.A. Upon arrival, police beat one man, who was Chicano, unconscious. According to eyewitnesses, his wife and daughter were also beaten, pulled by the hair to a squad car where they were arrested and taken to jail. Similar stories of police brutality had been long known in Black and Chicano communities in LA. It was the new militant climate, however, that moved Sanchez and other members of YCCA to seek redress by placing police brutality central to the agenda of Chicano activism (Marin 123–124).

On December 3, David Sanchez formed the first unit of the Brown Berets, which demonstrated in front of the East Los Angeles Sheriff Station and the Hollenbeck Division of the Los Angeles Police Department. In addition to creating a formal organization to protest police brutality and the general oppression of Chicanos, Sanchez developed a uniform for its membership. He purchased twelve brown berets, which each member wore as his new uniform, demonstrating to spectators that the group was uni-

3 "Border Crossings" (22); "The Los Angeles Chicano Area-Cultural Enclave" (12).

fied and militant (Marin 124–125). Many observers also knew that the beret had been derived from the uniform of the Black Panther Party for Self-Defense.

The Black Panther Party adopted the Black beret as part of its uniform in 1966, along with the Black leather jacket, Black slacks, and power blue shirt and Black shoes (Seale 115). While Black militants before the Party wore sunglasses and leather jackets, the beret was unique to the party formed by Seale and Newton. Soon, the hat became an icon of militancy and radicalism throughout the country. For Sanchez, the beret symbolized "the dignity and pride in the color of my skin and my race" (Ogbar, *Black Power* 161). Also, it represented a dual identification with the program of the Panthers, replacing the Black beret of the Panthers with the brown color of Chicano people. Although the Brown Berets may not have been as ideologically revolutionary as the Panthers, the similarities with the Panther Party were not by chance or solely superficial (Pulido 7).

The Brown Berets, like other organizations and Latino leaders of its era, were affected by the rhetoric of cultural nationalism as well as revolutionary discourse in Black circles. La Piranya served as a meeting place for many of the leaders of the Black Power Movement, including H. Rap Brown, Stokely Carmichael from the Student Nonviolent Coordinating Committee (who also served as honorary officials of the BPP), and Maulana Karenga, from the U.S. organization. Books and tapes by and about Malcolm X were exchanged and, like Black people, many Mexican Americans moved toward a salient racial and cultural affirmation that did not pedestalize white people (Ogbar, *Black Power* 161).

This Mexican American brand of cultural nationalism was led by Denver-based Rodolfo "Corky" Gonzales who helped popularize the term Chicano, supplanting Mexican American. While there are different explanations of the origin of the word,[4] according to Gonzales, Chicano was a name with deep historical meaning, rooted in a rich and proud tradition. Like the Nation-inspired rejection of the term Negro, Mexican American, to Gonzalez and others, reflected a confused, culturally ignorant assimilationism, wedded to the system of oppression and exploitation that trampled upon the rights of the brown masses. These "Anglo-prones" eagerly defended white supremacy, even to the extent that they accepted their own inferiority. The acceptance of their inferiority was indicative in their eagerness to jettison any cultural trappings of their Mexican heritage and their willingness to idealize whiteness. Speaking Spanish was

4 Some have argued that the word Chicano evolved from sixteenth-century Castilian pronunciation of Mexico, where the "x" had a "sh" sound: Meh-shee-ko. For the people: Meh-shee-kanos, from which "Chicanos" emerged among isolated rural peasants whose pronunciation was unmodified into the nineteenth century. Conservative and moderate Mexican Americans, hostile to the new word for identity, however, insisted that the word is a Castilian word, meaning "one who practices fraud." Still, others said that it was a blend of two words, reflecting the demographic make up of the new militants: Mexicano and Chico, literally meaning "Young Mexican." Yet, others argued that it had historically been a pejorative term for poor Mexicans. Cf. Castro (131); "The Los Angeles Chicano Area – Cultural Enclave" (12); Acuña (338).

discouraged, as were holidays, rituals, and other examples of culture from Mexico. For Gonzalez and others, Chicano was a proud example of self-determination (Carranza 4–5; Castro 13).

Like the newly popularized word Black, Chicano came from the people, not their oppressors. It was a word that the people chose to use for definition and identity. It also spoke to the myths that characterized cultural nationalist traditions, an essential part of nationality formation, as explained by political scientist Karl Deutch (Schafer 41–47). And like Black nationalism, Chicano nationalism celebrated a past that produced an almost Edenic pre-European contact world that provided a source of pride, historical connection, and affirmation that fundamentally undermined the history lessons taught in schools. In these lessons, non-Europeans were perennially marginalized, relegated to secondary roles and as backdrops to the stage of European history and civilization.

People of Mexican descent in the United States, had, like other people of color, sought to approximate the cultural standards of white Americans, despite the overt hostility they received from whites. From the European standard of beauty to the pride that people took in exclaiming European ancestry (or denial of Indian/African ancestry), Mexican people experienced the psychological effects of racism, as had Black people. In a culture where Spanish ancestry and white skin had benefits, Chicano cultural nationalists insisted that they were a "bronze" people, whose native ancestors built great monuments and civilizations, such as Aztlan. The Aztecs were revered for their cultural and material achievements. Some nationalists even dropped their Spanish names, considered symbols of European imperialism and conquest of the Aztec empire. But like the Black nationalist adoration of ancient Egypt, the Swahili, or West African empires, Chicano nationalists conveniently overlooked the imperialistic nature of their ancestors who built massive empires on the backs of subjugated, hyper-exploited, and oppressed victims. But in a political climate that saw Black nationalists bicker over the role of cultural and revolutionary nationalism, many Chicano nationalists easily merged the two types of nationalisms. The Brown Berets, for example, simultaneously acknowledged the history of Aztlan, and the need to destroy imperialism. Despite their tolerance for cultural nationalism, they were largely ideologically aligned with the Black Panther Party.

The Berets created titles for their leadership that mirrored the Black Panther Party: Minister of Information, Minister of Defense, Minister of Education, and Prime Minister, among other titles. They also adopted eight points of attention, which listed the Party's eight points verbatim:

(1) Speak politely to the people
(2) Pay family for what you buy from the people
(3) Return everything you borrow
(4) Pay for anything you damage
(5) Do not hit or swear at the people
(6) Do not damage property or possessions of the people

(7) Do not take liberties with women
(8) When working for the people do not get loaded. (Marin 128)

The Brown Berets, who adopted a "13 Point Program," modeled after the Panthers' Ten-Point Platform and Program, demanded eight of the ten demands of the Party, including "an end to the robbery of our community by the capitalist businessmen," exemption for all Chicanos from military service, the release of all Chicanos from jails, and the immediate end to police brutality (*La Causa* March 1969).

Despite arrests of their leadership, the bombing of their headquarters, and factionalism, the Brown Berets continued for two more years until they disbanded in the fall of 1972. At a press conference in October that year, David Sanchez announced that the organization of ninety chapters and 5,000 members would dissolve so as to avoid further disruption of the Chicano Power movement by police infiltrators. Subsequent U.S. Congressional hearings on the FBI and COINTELPRO confirmed that the Brown Berets were targeted for neutralization. As the hearings revealed, neutralization included, at times, extra-legal activities such as break-ins, false correspondence, wiretaps, beatings, and even murder.[5]

The Chicano Power movement was diverse and adopted its own symbols and ideals that embodied the ethos of self-determination and radicalism. Aztlan, as homeland of Chicanos, both affirmed their right to the land where they lived, superceding and rejecting the white nativist exhort to "go back to where you came from," and also dismissing any notion that America was a white man's country. Some activists held placards that read "Aztlan: Love it or Leave it" (Acuña 348). Chicano cultural nationalism simultaneously undermined the traditional Mexican racial and social hierarchy that made Spanish ancestry a source of pride and privilege. White skin had long symbolized prestige in Mexico, as it had in the United States. Chicano nationalists, however, departed from this paradigm and conspicuously celebrated a "bronze" nation that derided Europeans as foreigners. This put white Americans into the position of explaining their right to the land in North America.

Of all of the radical organizations that emerged in the late 1960s, none had as intimate ties with the BPP or the Black Power Movement as the largely Puerto Rican Young Lords Organization. By the 1940s, large communities of Puerto Ricans were established in New York and a few other cities, attracted by the prospect of jobs. While New York had been a point of entry for many European newcomers, most Puerto Ricans experienced the limitations of not only being an immigrant group, but of not being white. White supremacy allowed economic mobility, social intercourse, and political opportunities for Jews, Irish, Italians, and other whites that Puerto Ricans could not easily access. A mixture of African, Spanish, and native Taino peoples, Puerto Ricans found discrimination pervasive. Like other economically marginalized groups, poor Puerto Ricans soon experienced the pathologies that typically develop in circum-

5 "Police Spying on LA Activist Groups," *Los Angeles Times* 19 July 1978. There is a growing body of literature on the illegal activities of the FBI and its program, COITELPRO. Cf. Churchill and Vander Wall; Glick.

stances of concentrated urban poverty, material deprivation, and oppression. High school dropout rates were higher than any other ethnic group in NYC, while unemployment and underemployment, police brutality, and gangs provided a backdrop to Spanish Harlem by 1968, the year that students established the Puerto Rican Student Association at City College as a Puerto Rican independence organization. That same year, Eduardo "Pancho" Cruz founded the Puerto Rican Student Union, which helped lead the City College Campus Strike in 1969. The strike was almost identical to the Third World Liberation Front of the Bay Area. Like the one in California, it began with activities initiated by Black students for a Black studies department, more Black faculty and Black students. Inspired by the rhetoric of Black Power, Puerto Rican students formed the PRSU and contributed to the efforts of the student strike, which eventually made broader demands to include a general ethnic studies department.[6]

A different type of politicization was developing among Puerto Ricans in the Windy City. Chicago, like New York and other major U.S. cities, suffered from a pervasive and destructive gang problem. While gangs were generally composed along racial and ethnic lines, they were most likely to engage in criminal behavior against people of the same ethnicity, although gang rivalry also transcended ethnic lines (cf. Short and Strodtbeck; Downes; Vigil). The politically charged climate of the late 1960s, the ubiquitous influence of the Black Power movement, and the nature of urban rebellions forced many Black gang members to reconsider their activities. Many abandoned gang life and joined the Nation of Islam. Others were attracted to the Panther Party or any of the scores of largely local nationalists and Black Power organizations in cities across the country. For Puerto Ricans, the process of politicization was similar. But unlike any major Black Power organization in the country, the leading Puerto Rican radical organization would have its roots in gang culture.

In 1959, seven Chicago Puerto Rican youths formed the Young Lords to defend themselves against attacks from surrounding white gangs. Largely engaged in battles with Italians, "Billigans" (Appalachian whites) and other Latinos, the Lords continued to grow in the early 1960s when "Cha" Jimenez was elected chairman of the organization. After a brawl at a YMCA in 1964, the new chairman was sent to prison for a year. Other Lords were subsequently sent to prison for various crimes and the gang dwindled in number. By 1967, the members opened a cafe, Uptight #2, where they talked about the general political and cultural upheaval in the country, as well as more mundane topics (Ogbar, "Puerto Rico"). In 1968, Cha returned to Chicago with renewed vigor and increased political consciousness. Affected by the Civil Rights movement and the new rhetoric of Black Power, Jimenez brought new members into the organization and began developing community programs such as a community summer picnic, a drug education program, and a Christmas giveaway of food and toys for impoverished people in the Puerto Rican community. The Lords even began a dialogue with the largest street gang in the country, the notorious Black Stone Rangers

6 Flyer, Nov. 1971, UCBSPC, Box 18, folder 33, Young Lord Organization.

and co-sponsored a "Month of Soul Dances" with them.[7] While these efforts impressed many liberals, Illinois deputy chairman Fred Hampton and the local Panthers hoped to make the Lords into revolutionaries.

In accordance with the Party's theories of class, the Panthers viewed the politicization of the Young Lords as an essential step in the political transformation of the country's internal colonies. The urban rebellions that often included the poorest and most maligned elements in the community were the precursor to revolution, argued the Party. The lumpen had guns and were not afraid to use them. Unfortunately, the Panthers explained, they were not yet politically sophisticated enough to aim in the direction of the "pig power structure" more frequently. These rebellions, insisted Huey Newton, were "sporadic, short-lived, and costly in violence against the people" (Newton 11). The task of the Panthers was clear: "The Vanguard Party must provide leadership for the people. It must teach correct strategic methods of prolonged resistance through literature and activities. If the activities of the Party are respected by the people, the people will follow the example" (11). The efforts of the Lords and the Rangers had been, to the Panthers, indicative of the political transformation that would make inadvertent agents of oppression into agents of liberation. The Lords, Rangers, and other street gangs could be made into harbingers of freedom, justice, and power for the people.

As Hampton began dialogue with Jeff Fort, the leader of the Black Stone Rangers, he also met with Jimenez, who was warmer to the idea of revolution than had been Fort. Impressed with the bold and brash militancy that characterized the Panthers, Jimenez envisioned a Puerto Rican revolutionary organization that could realize liberation for Puerto Ricans both on the island and in the mainland. Lords began to realize that they had been acting more like social workers by only addressing the symptoms and not the cause of social illness. By spring 1969, therefore, the Lords had officially joined a pact with the Panthers, and the Young Patriots, a gang of white Appalachian youths from the city's Uptown section on the North Side.[8]

In this new "Rainbow Coalition," the Lords and Patriots dutifully modeled themselves after the Panther Party, which they believed was the vanguard. In their respective communities, the Lords and Patriots held political education classes, organized free breakfast programs for poor children, and monitored police activities, in an attempt to curb police brutality. They created an organizational structure that reflected Panther influence, which included Ministers of Information, Defense, Education, and a Central Committee with field marshals. The Patriots developed an 11-Point Program and Platform that borrowed heavily from the Panthers, as did the Lords' 13-Point Program and Platform.[9] All three organizations sponsored events together, providing joint speakers and joint security. It seemed odd for some Black nationalists to see Fred

7 Flyer, n.d., UCBSPC, Box 18, folder 33, Young Lord Organization.

8 Flyer, n.d., UCBSPC, Box 18, folder 33, Young Lord Organization; cf. Hilliard and Cole (229).

9 Flyer, n.d., UCBSPC, Box 18, folder 33, Young Lord Organization.

Hampton give a typically awe-inspiring speech on revolutionary struggle, while white men wearing berets, sunglasses, and Confederate rebel flags sewn into their jackets helped to provide security for him.

By 1969, the Young Patriots and Young Lords were nationally known through their Rainbow Coalition, which was featured in articles in the *Black Panther* and other alternative newspapers. Also, that year, the Coalition sent representatives to the annual convention of the SDS, where Joe Martinez, an SDS member from Florida, met with Young Lords founders and was granted permission to start a branch in New York.

In New York, Puerto Rican nationalism was still on the rise. In the context of the militant student protests, some students at City College formed the Sociedad de Albizu Campos (SAC) that hoped to bring together the militancy of college radicals with that of the ghetto in early 1969. In a struggle to bridge the chasm between unorganized street militancy and that of the college campus, community-based activists Pablo "Yoruba" Guzman and David Perez joined SAC and became the links to the ghetto that the organization desired. Yoruba, with an Afro and dark skin, had a strong cultural nationalist affinity to both Africa and Puerto Rico. Perez, who was born in Puerto Rico and raised in Chicago, had involved himself in radical politics before moving to New York. Simultaneously, SAC members were reading the *Black Panther* newspaper regularly and learned of the Rainbow Coalition established by Fred Hampton. After merging with other local Puerto Rican activist organizations, SAC met with Martinez and on July 26, 1969, a coalition was formed in New York that became the New York State Chapter of the Young Lords Organization (Ogbar, *Black Power* 180). In addition to these efforts, Carlos Russell, as discussed by Matti Steinitz in this volume, emerged as a transnational ambassador of Black Power in New York. As an Afro-Panamanian activist, Russell was able to bridge African American, Afro-Latino and Afro-Caribbean experiences and served as a mentor to the founders of the NYC chapter of the Young Lords at Brooklyn College.[10]

The Young Lords from New York spread to several cities along the east coast, including Philadelphia, Newark, and Bridgeport, Connecticut. Within weeks, the Lords captured the headlines. In agreement with the Panther dictum to serve the people by meeting the people's basic needs, Lords asked local residents what they wanted. People informed the Lords that they wanted cleaner streets. The Lords swept streets in Spanish Harlem and put trash piles in the middle of the street, demanding that the city pay more attention to the barrio. The images of radicals working for the people impressed many who eagerly joined the fledgling organization.[11] Young Lords' activities extended into the Lincoln Hospital where a group of 100 men and women took it over on July 17, 1970, to protest inadequate health care for the poor and ongoing neglect

---

10 For more information on the rise of the Young Lords, cf. Miguel "Mickey" Melendez, a former member; Ogbar ("Puerto Rico"); Wanzer-Serrano (who also published *The Young Lords: A Reader* under the surname Enck-Wanzer.) Cf. Morales; Fernandez (41–42).

11 Felipe Luciano, speech, St. Lawrence University, April 1997.

from the city government. Though they were eventually expelled by the police, the act brought attention to insufficient medical care in poor communities. In response, the mayor of New York, John Lindsay, promised community activists that the city would build a new hospital on East 149th street to replace the dilapidated Lincoln. The new hospital opened in 1976 (Ogbar, *Black Power* 180).

As adherents of Puerto Rican independence, the Lords denounced the cardinal "three evils" of revolutionary nationalists: capitalism, racism, and imperialism. They sponsored free breakfast, drug detoxification, and garbage clean-up programs in chapters in several states. The activities of the Young Lords were particularly numerous along the East Coast in every major Puerto Rican community. They brought attention to police brutality, worked closely with students on college and high school campuses, and even found success organizing in prisons. During the Attica Prison uprising in September 1971, insurgents issued a list of over twenty demands to prison officials that included a request for the presence of the Young Lords and the BPP to serve as observers and advisors. In many cities, Lords worked in alliances with Black Power advocates and helped realize more community control of police, political reform, and political mobilization for poor and working-class people. And like the Brown Berets, the Young Lords were able to work with organizations openly hostile to the Black Panthers, despite their official pact with the Party. In the early 1970s, the Young Lords in Newark, New Jersey established an alliance with the Committee for a Unified Newark, led by Amiri Baraka, a leading cultural nationalist (Woodard 138–140).

For the Young Lords and other revolutionary nationalist organizations, various communities of color in the U.S. provided cheap labor and resources for the capitalists. Influenced by a theoretical rubric of racism, the capitalists found cheap, expendable labor that provided for increased quality of life for whites by expanding the white middle class considerably. Increased numbers of people of color in urban areas allowed working class whites to assume higher social-economic status. But since racism was very real, working-class whites, often beholden to white supremacy, out of ignorance and cultural tradition, were intolerant of considering the affinities that they shared with working class people of color. The Young Patriots hoped to demonstrate, however, that working class and poor whites could be mobilized and, indeed, follow a revolutionary program led by a Black organization. But while the Patriots, Rising Up Angry, White Panthers of Michigan modeled themselves after the BPP, the Party and Black Power had a special resonance for radicals of color.

Class exploitation was a major concern for leftists; however, the highly racialized climate of the U.S. made interracial political organization difficult, particularly with working-class whites, considered by many people of color to be a more overt and crude group of racists than the capitalist class. Moreover, the U.S. tradition of class exploitation was significantly bolstered by white supremacy, which had profound psychological and cultural ramifications (cf. Roediger). People of color who were involved in leftist liberation movements of the era were committed to liberate themselves along class and cultural lines simultaneously.

As they rejected terms such as Negro, Oriental, and Spanish, Blacks, Asians, and Chicanos conspicuously celebrated their ethnicity in ways they never had. Part of the drive to adopt new terms for identification grew out of the common call for self-determination. The Nation of Islam had long derided Black people for allowing whites to define them as Negroes. Black was the term chosen by the people, not outsiders. Moreover, it was an inherently defiant term that rejected the negative associations with Blackness that were pervasive in American culture. For Chicanos and Asians, the effort for self-identification was two-fold. It also marked a departure from the old manner in which people viewed these groups.

Black nationalism in general embodies a salient rejection of whiteness and the authority and power that it assumes. Part of this authority of whiteness is the assumption that white power is natural or that white is inherently superior. Many Black nationalists were careful to denigrate whiteness while also celebrating Blackness. Blackness had been lifted from the murky world of shame, blight, and despair, while whites were openly called racial epithets and ridiculed. Clearly, the language, symbols, and tactics of the Black Power movement significantly shaped the scope of the era's radicalism. And while Black Power had a special connection to other people of color, it also formed white radical activities.

The Chicano Power movement and Puerto Rican nationalism were not solely dependent on Black Power for symbolism, political direction, or motivation. In fact, the movements necessarily influenced each other in alliances, networks, conferences, and general dialogue. Furthermore, the international dynamics that influenced Black Power similarly formed Latino and Asian struggle in the U.S. Mao Zedong was an inspiration to Panthers as well as the Red Guard. Brown Berets and Young Lords had a particular affinity with Che Guevara who was also an adored icon for the Panthers. The symbiotic relations were dynamic and fundamentally invigorated all the involved movements. Still, the Black Power movement helped form a period of social and cultural transformation that would have substantive effects on the cultural and political landscape of the country.[12]

Black nationalists and Black Power advocates, by example, demonstrated the humanity of white people in ways that Martin L. King, Jr. and non-violent integrationists did not. Integrationists on a very basic and fundamental level acquiesced to white supremacy by allowing whites to maintain an aura of power, prestige, and social position of desirability. Despite the overt challenges to the authority of racist laws, there was a pervasive assumption that moderate and liberal whites in the North could be persuaded to assist the Southern-based freedom movement. Civil rights leaders constantly made appeals to white lawmakers, capitalist power brokers, and general white liberals for moral and material support.

The NAACP argued that it was psychologically damaging to a Black child to be segregated in public school. No mention was ever made of how psychologically dam-

12 Cf. Fernandez; Ogbar (*Black Power*, especially 159–189); Pulido.

aging racial segregation was for white children. The implicit belief was that a white presence made things better. As Richard Newman, a professor at Boston University in the late 1960s pointed out, "when civil rights leaders called for integration of higher education, they were not hoping to send more whites to Howard University. They wanted more Blacks at ['white' colleges]" (Newman, interview with author). Integration was a one-way street that assumed that the white mainstream was normative and desired.

Black power rejected the idea that white people's acceptance was desirable. Other people of color and even some poor whites, informed and significantly affected by Black Power also formed ethnic nationalist paradigms of resistance. Moreover, with their Black counterparts, these ethnic nationalists together organized in their communities across the country, changing the social, political, and cultural landscape. Furthermore, most of these ethnic nationalists copiously developed a theoretical construct of radical self-determination that was not dependent on xenophobia. The radical ethnic nationalism of the Panthers, Lords, or Berets reflected a conscious effort to culturally affirm people who languished under a dehumanizing system of racial oppression, while it also refused to pander to the convenient race-only discourse that attracted many. These proponents of radical ethnic nationalism glorified their ethnicity while they eagerly embraced a polysemic nationalist framework that pulled from Fanon, Marx, Lenin, and Mao. Also, they were significantly influenced by the political analysis of the BPP and its thesis of revolutionary struggle. But as seen above, Black Power's influence on non-African Americans altered the popular discourse and public discussion of identity and equality in the U.S. in interesting ways. Outside and inside of the radical leftist ethnic nationalist communities were militants who rebuked whiteness and the implications of whiteness such as attaining status based on the subjugation of non-whites. In this contextual framework, many militants sought to "humanize" whites by stripping them of any trappings of cultural prestige or supremacy. The cornerstone to this was a rejection of integration.

Radical ethnic nationalism attempted to overturn the white supremacy that had historically denigrated people of color in every arena of American life. To that end, whites were criticized in ways that they had never been. They were ridiculed for their smell, lack of rhythm, lack of hygiene, lack of morality, lack of beauty and, ultimately, lack of humanity. While this may appear anathema to the ideals of Panther transracialism, the ridicule of whites by some ethnic nationalists was an attempt to reconcile the new self-love in the midst of generations of self-hate. Whites were virtually pushed off their pedestal of whiteness and all the implied honor, prestige, and respect that skin-privilege conveyed. Black power and radical ethnic nationalism revealed the vulnerability of whiteness. Whiteness was not sacrosanct or without flaw. It was corrupt and inextricably bound to the frailties of humanity. Beyond the cultural and psychological effects that radical ethnic nationalism introduced to the new left of the late 1960s and early 1970s, the movement was a truly unique phenomenon. There are no major examples of other ethnic nationalist struggles that have established alliances as had young radicals of the Black Power era. African American, white, Puerto Rican,

Chicano, Asian, and Native American radicals merged ethnic nationalist rhetoric with a struggle that emphasized class conflict and interracial coalitions. When the Panther Party coined the slogan "all power to the people," it was attempting to broaden the call for Black Power by transcending race. According to Party chairman Bobby Seale, interracial coalitions are powerful examples of the people gaining strength in numbers in their efforts against the "power structure's oppression" (Seale 210–211). Unique among political movements anywhere, this was an example of a radicalism that adapted to the highly racialized climate of the United States, while adhering to the fundamental principles of leftist theories that generally criticized nationalism as bourgeois efforts to subvert true radicalism. At the center of this movement was the Black Power movement that provided the earliest examples of cultural nationalism and political organization around ethnic nationalist causes. More specifically, the Black Panther Party served as a paradigm of radical ethnic nationalism and a vanguard party for the revolutionary nationalist movement. The Panthers provided an appeal that was unprecedented in the annals of radical struggle.

Though considered a Black hate group by some whites, an irresponsible, careless, and disorganized band of immature radicals by some leftists, or too conciliatory to white radicals by some Black nationalists, the Panthers' impact was indelible. A group that reached a peak membership of five thousand members, the Party not only influenced radicals from every ethnic community in the United States, it also inspired marginalized and oppressed people worldwide who created Black Panther Parties. Australian Aborigines, Sephardic Jews in Israel, Blacks in Britain, Polynesians, and the Dalit in India all formed organizations that carried the name of the BPP, evoking the radical ethnic discourse of the organization. The legacies of the Black Panthers in particularly, and the Black Power movement in general, are considerable. These legacies reach across borders in the Americas as well. From Bermuda, through Cuba, Puerto Rico, and Panama, the associated language, aesthetics, music, and politics found their way via organizations like the Young Lords and other radical U.S.-based groups.

Works cited

Acuña, Rodolfo F. *Occupied America: A History of Chicanos*. Boston: Addison-Wesley Educational Publishers, Incorporated, 1997. Print.

"Border Crossings." *L.A. Weekly* (Jun 24–30, 1988): 22. Print.

Carranza, Elio. *Pensamientos on Los Chicanos: A Cultural Revolution.* Berkeley: California Book Company, 1969. Print.

Castro, Tony. *Chicano Power: The Emergence of Mexican America*. Bloomington: iUniverse, 2013. Print.

Churchill, Ward, and Jim Vander Wall. *Agents of Repression: The FBI's Secret Wars against the Black Panther Party and the American Indian Movement.* Boston: South End Press, 1988. Print.

Downes, David M. *The Delinquent Solution: A Study in Subcultural Theory.* New York: Free Press, 1966. Print.

Fernandez, Johanna. *The Young Lords: A Radical History.* Chapel Hill: U of North Carolina P, 2020. Print.

Fujino, Diane C. *Samurai among Panthers: Richard Aoki on Race, Resistance, and a Paradoxical Life.* Minneapolis: U of Minnesota P, 2012. Print.

Glick, Brian. *War at Home: Covert Action against U.S. Activists and What We Can Do About It.* Boston: South End Press, 1989. Print.

Hampton, Fred. "You Can Murder a Liberator, but You Can't Murder Liberation." *The Black Panthers Speak.* Ed. Phillip Foner. Boston: De Capo Press, 1995. Print.

Hilliard, David, and Lewis Cole. *This Side of Glory: The Autobiography of David Hilliard and the Story of the Black Panther Party.* Boston: Little, Brown and Company, 1993. Print.

La Causa 1.1 (23 May 1969): 1. Los Angeles, California. Print.

La Causa 1.9 (Mar. 1970): 10. Los Angeles, California. Print.

"The Los Angeles Chicano Area – Cultural Enclave." *San Francisco Chronicle* (10 Oct. 1970): 12. Print.

Luciano, Felipe. Speech, St. Lawrence University, April 1997.

Marin, Marguerite Viramontes. *Protest in an Urban Barrio: A Study of the Chicano Movement.* Ph.D. Dissertation. University of California, Santa Barbara, 1980. Print.

Melendez, Miguel. *We Took to the Streets: Fighting for Latino Rights with the Young Lords.* New Brunswick: Rutgers UP, 2005. Print.

Morales, Iris. *Through the Eyes of Rebel Women: The Young Lords 1969-1976.* New York: Red Sugarcane Press, 2016. Print.

Newman, Richard. Interview with Author. Cambridge, MA, 4 Aug. 1999.

Newton, Huey P. *Essays From the Minister of Defense.* Pamphlet, 1967. Print.

Ogbar, Jeffrey O.G. "Puerto Rico en mi Corazón: The Young Lords, Black Power, and Puerto Rican Nationalism in the U.S., 1966–1972." *CENTRO: Journal of the Center for Puerto Rican Studies* 18.1 (2006): 148–169. Print.

———. *Black Power: Radical Politics and African American Identity.* Baltimore: Johns Hopkins UP, 2019 [2004]. Print.

Pulido, Laura. *Black, Brown, Yellow, and Left: Radical Activism in Los Angeles.* Berkeley: U of California P, 2006. Print.

Roediger, David R. *Wages of Whiteness: Race and the Making of the American Working Class.* New York: Verso, 1991. Print.

Seale, Bobby. *Seize the Time: The Story of the Black Panther Party and Huey P. Newton.* Baltimore: Black Classics Press, 1991. Print.

Shafer, Boyd C. *Nationalism and Internationalism: Belonging in Human Experience.* Malabar, FL: Krieger Pub. Co, 1982. Print.

Short, James F., and Fred L. Strodtbeck. *Group Process and Gang Delinquency.* Chicago: U of Chicago P, 1974. Print.

Vigil, James Diego. *Barrio Gangs: Street Life and Identity in Southern California.* Austin: U of Texas P, 1988. Print.

Wanzer-Serrano, Daniel, ed. *The New York Young Lords and the Struggle for Liberation*. Philadelphia: Temple UP, 2015. Print.

Wolf, Tom. *Radical Chic and Mau-Mauing the Flak Catchers*. New York: Picador, 2009. Print.

Woodard, Komozi. *A Nation Within a Nation: Amiri Baraka (LeRoi Jones) and Black Power Politics*. Chapel Hill: U of North Carolina P, 1999. Print.

The United States, American Black Radicalism, and the Anti-Imperialist Struggle in Latin America: A Study of Stokely Carmichael's 1967 Visit to Cuba

VALERIA L. CARBONE

When Stokely Carmichael was invited to visit Cuba to attend a conference of the Organization of Latin American Solidarity (OLAS) in July 1967, he had already gained himself an international reputation – not only as the young leader of SNCC who had popularized the slogan "Black Power" a year earlier but also as an advocate of the radical view that black communities constituted "internal colonies" which were part of a worldwide revolution against a "system of international white supremacy coupled with international capitalism" (*Digital SNNC Gateway*). In many ways the evolution of Stokely Carmichael from community organizer in the Deep South to one of Black America's most visible representatives on the world stage mirrored the shift from the U.S.-centered agenda of the Civil Rights Movement to the global outlook that defined the Black Power movement.

By the mid-1960s, the Civil Rights Movement seemed to have reached the height of success that followed decades of black activism. The struggle to end racial segregation and acquire civic and political rights had intensified in a context of racial violence and opposition to the white establishment that decisively challenged the racial status quo in every corner of the country. This movement achieved an ever-increasing support in the media and in public opinion which forced action in the U.S. Congress. Responding to this effervescent situation, a series of Civil Rights Acts were passed in 1957, 1960, and 1964, the first ones since Reconstruction (1863–1877). Even though they were presented as major legal promises regarding the integration of African Americans in education and public spaces, they ended up being mostly ignored or poorly implemented. An exclusive product of black activism and a more explicit and definite legislation related to the political rights of the black community, the Voting Rights Act of 1965 was passed by the Congress to make up for what the previous acts failed to accomplish.

Perhaps because of these legal achievements of a non-violent mass movement, the years between 1954 and 1965 are generally considered the "heroic phase" of the Civil Rights Movement (Rustin). However, as Peniel E. Joseph has emphasized, such characterization removes important political organizations and figures that went beyond the call for upholding African Americans' civil rights to advocate radical and systemic social, political (and economic) change from the spotlight. Joseph states that "rather than being viewed as an alternative to the ineffectiveness of civil rights demands in critical areas of American life" (Joseph 3), Black Power has been blamed, rather conveniently, for the failures of the Civil Rights Movement and nonviolence to achieve more substantive change.

In the following pages, I attempt to explore one case that prominently shows the transnational influence of Black Power and the impact of the African American struggle in the liberation movements of Latin America. I further highlight the influence of the Cuban revolution on the Black struggle for freedom and equality in the United States and worldwide. The analysis focuses on Stokely Carmichael's trip to Cuba in 1967, in the larger context of the "Third World" national liberation movements across Latin America, Africa, and Asia. This approach illustrates the transnational aspect of the African American freedom struggle and its complex ties with various anti-colonialist and anti-imperialist movements abroad.

Stokely Carmichael and the rise of Black Power

While Stokely Carmichael was not the sole facilitator behind the transformations within the black movement, nor can he be credited as the founder of the Black Power movement, he indeed served "as the charismatic catalyst to commence the Black Power phase of the evolution of the movement" (Stewart 436).

Carmichael began his activism as a high school student, where he led picket-lines, sit-ins, and rallies. Later, he joined in freedom rides, organized registration campaigns, and in 1960 became an active member of the Congress of Racial Equality (CORE). He contributed to the consolidation of the first black political party of Mississippi (the Lowndes County Freedom Organization), and, by 1967, he was one of the most celebrated leaders of the Student Non-Violent Coordinating Committee (SNCC), along Ella Baker. After more than a decade of non-violent struggle, it was evident to Carmichael that racial integration could only materialize for a few middle-class blacks who had the socio-economic means to integrate into the system. For the poor blacks of the rural south and the urban ghettos, integration was not just insufficient but unfeasible.

With the release of *Black Power: The Politics of Liberation* (1967), Carmichael and political scientist Charles Hamilton became the key thinkers behind a revised concept of modern black nationalism, of which Marcus Garvey is considered the founder.[1] They pointed out that Black Power meant much more than "self-defense" and "armed resistance." They believed that Black Power was about the capacity of the black com-

1 In the 1920s, Marcus Garvey (1887–1940) initiated the first significant Black mass movement, subsequent to which the Universal Negro Improvement Association (UNIA) became one of the most important diasporic organizations in the United States and Latin America. Carmichael considered Garvey a pivotal influence in his vision of Black Power. In Carmichael's words, Garvey had "built the largest mass black nationalist organization in U.S. history – Afro-Americans, West Indians, and Afro-Latinos – in the early twentieth century" (Carmichael and Thelwell 789).

munity as a collective to "take matters into their own hands" (Carmichael and Hamilton vii). This meant that it should struggle for full political and economic autonomy *of* and *for* black people, to take charge of their communities, organizations, and institutions and to strengthen their base of political, economic, and social power. It didn't mean "merely putting black faces into office. Black visibility is not Black Power .... The power must be that of a community, and emanate from there" (44–46). In other words, Black Power meant black self-determination and needed to result into "full participation in the decision-making processes affecting the lives of black people, and recognition of the virtues in themselves as black people" (47) or it was not Black Power at all.

Whereas Black Power challenged the ideal of "integration" as understood in the sixties (cooptation and assimilation), it could not be reduced in any way to the ideology of "separatism." Instead, it implied giving rise to a sense of pride, self-esteem, and identity among black Americans to allow them to accept their blackness as a tool to fight for political, economic, and social power. According to Carmichael and Hamilton, black Americans were subject to internal colonialism, the highest expression of institutional racism that historically and systematically relegated Blacks to a place of subordination (5–6; 23). The authors held that Black Power was, at its heart, a liberation movement similar to those pursued by what they considered to be "Third World" nations in the fight against imperialism and colonialism. Hence, it was necessary to set up relationships, ties, and alliances with them (xi).

Towards 1967, and as a result of growing dissatisfaction with organizations and leaders who preached moderation, gradualism, and caution against the demands of the black movement, Black Power ideals became very popular among African Americans. Black radicals as Carmichael showed dissatisfaction with non-violence and civil disobedience strategies, which had led to few concrete changes after a decade of mass mobilization. From the moment the movement was born it was attacked and distorted. Both from inside and outside the movement, Black Power was denounced as being synonymous with "violence," "anti-whiteness," "anti-systemic struggle," separatism, black racism, and "black supremacy" (Hamilton 22). The fear of Black Power as a threat to national security increased even further when Carmichael traveled to Cuba which he considered the cradle of the coming revolution.

Washington – Havana relations after the Cuban Revolution

In 1959, the revolution led by Fidel Castro toppled dictator Fulgencio Batista. At first, Washington was deeply concerned about the developments in Cuba as a country of great importance to the United States due to its geostrategic condition and economic significance. The concern did not have only to do with the fact that the United States had a military base in Guantánamo since 1903. Rather, it was because, at the time of the revolution, the value of American investments in Cuba (in sugar plantations, mines, public utility companies, finance and manufacturing facilities) exceeded those in other Latin American countries. The United States received around two-thirds of Cuban sugar exports and provided three-quarters of their imports (Domínguez 184). By 1958, the total amount of American investment in the country was U.S.$ 1,001 million, an amount only surpassed in all Latin America by Brazil (1,411 million) and Venezuela (1,308 million) (Moreno 481–482). This meant that the U.S. controlled over 42% of the sugar production, 47.2% of the land allocated to that crop, 90% of the electricity and telephone services, 50% of the railway system, and 23% of the non-sugar industries in Cuba. This was compounded by the dependency on, and high concentration, of foreign trade dominated by the United States of America: 72% of exports and 71% of imports (482).

Four years later, Cuba had become a socialist country mirroring the Soviet model, and had become a diplomatic, strategic, commercial, economic, and military ally of the Union of Soviet Socialist Republics (U.S.S.R.). That led to the definite rupture in U.S.-Cuba relations that had already started when Castro took office in 1959 (Carbone 285). Back then, the U.S. government had already begun to apply tactics of political and economic pressure: they prohibited foreign trade with Cuba, declared a commercial and financial embargo, fostered the emigration of Cubans, and, in 1961, ended diplomatic relations with Havana. After that, the U.S. government began plans for covert assistance (recruitment, financing, training, logistics, and armed support) to anti-Castro migrants that led to the Bay of Pigs Invasion (1961). Conflict escalated in the Cuban missile crisis (1962), while Cuba put in motion its "export the revolution" policy, and the United States – following the guidelines of the policy of containment – implemented its double policy of "no to a Second Cuba" and the Alliance for Progress (Carbone 289–292).

Lyndon Johnson's administration (1963–1967) adopted more aggressive policies that led to the implementation of hemispheric and global actions against Cuba. This included the strengthening of the embargo that added to Cuba's political isolation, undercover operations to topple Castro from abroad (Dumbrell 141), and the reinforcement of political and diplomatic ties with regional allies through the Organization of American States (OAS).

In this context, the Cuban government organized the first Conference of the Organization of Latin American Solidarity (OLAS), which was held between July 31st and August 8th, 1967. OLAS welcomed representatives of revolutionary, nationalist, and anti-imperialist movements in Latin America and other parts of the world (such as African countries and Vietnam) that shared, to a greater or lesser extent, the strategic goals of the Cuban Revolution.

OLAS identified U.S. imperialism and "its servants, the governments settled in each country to repress the peoples, serve imperialism and stand for the criminal interests of national oligarchies" as the enemy to combat (OLAS 13). It also endorsed "the peoples' right to oppose the violence of imperialism and reaction with revolutionary violence" (*Granma* 5). In the course of the conference, approximately 700 delegates from 85 organizations debated issues such as the status of the revolutionary struggle in

Latin America, the policies and actions of the United States in the region, the role of local oligarchies allied to the White House, the role of armed struggle and other forms of revolutionary struggle, and, above all, the importance of reaching regional and international "anti-imperialist solidarity" (5).

On their first statement, the OLAS evaluated the strategies applied so far and decided on armed struggle and guerrilla warfare as fundamental methods to expand the revolution. Another aspect emphasized was the policy of "Latin American solidarity" and of the "Third World" in the fight against imperialism and colonialism, and the need to lend a "brotherly hand to the people of the United States," urging them to fight against the "repressive politics of imperialist monopolies." Most importantly, they agreed to strengthen bonds with black America, "which in turn, suffers class exploitation, deprivation, unemployment, racial discrimination, and denial of the most basic human rights, and make up an important force to be considered within the context of the revolutionary struggle"[2] (OLAS 1). With these in mind, Carmichael was invited on behalf of an African American community that waged its own struggle in the heart of the United States of America.

Carmichael's message from Havana

Since 1964, the United States had witnessed multiple waves of unrest and uprisings staged mainly by black youth, among which the Watts riots of 1965 and the Detroit riots of 1967 were probably the best known. They all had deep and persistent structural causes: abuse of power on the part of the white community, the rampant powerlessness of the black community, police repression, poverty, unemployment, racial discrimination and racial profiling, political exclusion, and the constant and systematic inequality with regard to living conditions, housing, health, and education in the poorest neighborhoods inhabited by Blacks and Latinos (Kerner Commission 1–5).

The Cuban revolution was central to the black struggle and had already made Cuba a repository of support during the age of civil rights. As a result, in April 1960, many intellectuals – including prominent African Americans – funded the Fair Play for Cuba Committee (FPCC) to denounce the U.S. government's actions towards Cuba and the possibility of military intervention.

The FPCC is relevant both in the history of the transnational dimension of the black movement and in the analysis of the connections and mutual influences between the African American struggle and (Afro-)Caribbean movements. Based on the premise that many Americans saw the Cuban revolution as "a symbol and the hope for their own liberation from political, economic and racial oppression" (*The New York Times*, "Policy on Cuba" 2), the organization established several chapters in the United States and Canada. Among its approximately 7000 members were notable figures such as

2 In its draft agenda, the OLAS proclaimed its "support of the Negro people of the United States in their struggle against racial discrimination and in defense of their civil rights and liberty" (*Granma*, "The Duty of" 5).

William Appleman Williams, C. Wright Mills, Norman Mailer, Truman Capote, Jean-Paul Sartre, Allen Ginsberg, Simone de Beauvoir, Waldo Frank, Alan Sagner, Carleton Beals; and African-American intellectuals and activists such as writers James Baldwin, Leroi Jones (Amiri Baraka), John Oliver Killens, journalist William Worthy, the president of the Monroe chapter of the National Association for the Advancement of Color People (NAACP) Robert F. Williams, journalist Richard Gibson, historian John Henrik Clarke, and actor-director Julian Mayfield.

In October 1960, FPCC sponsored a group of black writers and activists to travel to the island. Among them were Harold Cruse, Julian Mayfield, Tom Feelings, Robert F. Williams, LeRoi Jones, and John Henrik Clarke. This trip was organized "in view of Cuban Premier Fidel Castro's desire to show appreciation for Harlem hospitality" (*The New York Times*, "Negroes Offered Tour" 33), in reference to Castro's famous stay at the Theresa Hotel in Harlem in September 1960, when he participated in the General Assembly of the United Nations. During his stay in Harlem, "thousands of black and Latino harlemites surrounded the hotel, cheering and carrying pro-Cuban signs" (Marable 12). This incident earned him countless compliments and visits from figures like Malcolm X, Joseph and John X (Nation of Islam), Langston Hughes, Leroi Jones, Joseph Overton (president of the New York chapter of the NAACP), and Jackie Robinson. Juan Almeida Bosque, the commander of the Afro-Cuban army, became quite a celebrity himself, with crowds of people cheering him in the streets (Cohen). Years later, Cuba would become a safe haven to black politicians and activists like Robert F. Williams (who edited *The Crusader* newspaper and hosted radio shows at Radio Free Dixie from Cuba), members of the Black Panther Party such as Eldridge Cleaver and former member of the militant Black Liberation Army Assata Shakur, who found exile in Cuba after successfully escaping from a New Jersey prison in 1979.

As stated above, Carmichael was not the first African American to travel to post-revolutionary Cuba. Others had broken ground for his visit, albeit not on purpose. In this scenario, Carmichael – portrayed by the Cuban newspaper *Granma* as "the best of the Negro people's struggle in the United States" (Meluzo 2) and introduced to 400,000 people by Castro as "one of the most distinguished pro-civil rights leaders," – arrived in Havana as an "honorary delegate" (Tom Reston n. pag.). As he had stepped down from his position as chair of SNCC a couple of months earlier, he was not representing any particular organization, but still was given the status of "honorary delegate" when he traveled with SNCC's Elizabeth Sutherland Martínez, Julius Lester, and George Ware. Carmichael was warmly welcomed and participated in all kind of activities including a three-day tour of the island with Castro himself – an experience he later described as "the most educational, most interesting and best apprenticeship of my public life" (UPI, "Carmichael Learns" 15).

Once in Cuba, Carmichael's rhetoric in Havana seemed to be more directed to black Americans in the United States and the U.S. establishment than to establishing solidarity and mutual support with representatives of other movements present at the Conference. The leader spoke about the importance of black Americans' union to

Third World liberation movements in their fight against a common enemy: capitalism and American imperialism (*The New York Times*, "Negroes Ready" 19). He also referred to the African American struggle as a two-front struggle: "... the fight against racism and the fight against capitalism: [because] racism is a result of capitalism" (Goshko 1). He added that if African Americans pretended to internationalize their struggle and turn Che Guevara's words to create "one, two, many Vietnams" (Guevara n. pag.) into a reality, first they had to acknowledge that "Detroit and New York are also Vietnam" (*The New York Times*, "Carmichael Urges" 10).[3] That was why black people were refusing to take up arms against the Vietnamese, who were also fighting against the ones that exploited and oppressed them both (Meluzo 2).

When Carmichael was asked about a possible (and effective) coordination of the black struggle in the United States with that of "Third World" countries, he replied: "our very presence here [in Cuba] indicates that ... the joint struggle of the people against the United States will destroy the monster" (Meluzo 2). But his presence in Havana meant more than that. Carmichael not only claimed that black America saw the Cuban revolution as a source of inspiration and its leaders as role models[4]; more importantly, he admitted that he was on the island to "learn."

Carmichael repeatedly stressed that the black community needed to adopt the tactics of the Cuban revolution, including armed struggle and urban guerrilla warfare (*Los Angeles Times*, "Carmichael Message" 10). He further pointed out that the liberation revolution was already underway in the United States and that it had to happen "by any means necessary" (Menéndez 25). As he put it, "in Newark we applied war tactics of the guerrillas. We are preparing groups of urban guerrillas for our defense in the cities. The price of these rebellions is a high price that one must pay. This fight is not going to be a simple street meeting. It's going to be a fight to the death" (*The New York Times*, "Carmichael Is Quoted" 22)[5].

In his last speech in Havana, Carmichael stressed once again the notion of a common enemy (U.S. capitalism and imperialism), the concept of a hemispheric struggle, and that black Americans were part of the "Third World"'s international resistance movement. They were to mobilize to control their communities "as you are moving to wrest control of your countries – of the entire Latin continent – from the hands of foreign imperialist powers" (Carmichael 2–4). He emphasized that Cuba was "a shining

3 The 1967 Detroit (Michigan) riots were among the most violent and destructive since the summer's riots began in 1964. By the time the bloodshed, burning, and looting ended, 43 people were dead, 342 injured, nearly 1,400 buildings burned, and 7,000 National Guard and U.S. Army troops had been called into service.

4 "[Carmichael] said that the guerrilla leader (Ernesto Che Guevara) was an inspiration to American negroes. ... In a salute to the Solidarity organization, Mister Carmichael said that 'Negroes in the United States feel that your victory is a victory for us because your unlimited courage inspires us'" (*The New York Times*, "Carmichael Is Quoted" 22).

5 The Newark (New Jersey) riots took place in July 1967 in one of the city's largest ghettos. Over the four days of rioting, looting, and property destruction, 26 people died and 1,500 were injured.

example of hope" in the hemisphere and that black Americans looked forward to the day "when a true United States of America will extend from Tierra del Fuego to Alaska, when those formerly oppressed will stand together, a liberated people" (2–4). Carmichael's anti-imperialist, anti-colonialist, and mainly, anti-capitalist speech, voiced the struggle of the oppressed. He preached international and anti-imperialist solidarity and presented the Cuban Revolution as a model to be followed by liberation movements throughout the hemisphere.

The American press

While in Cuba Carmichael was praised and celebrated (*La Vanguardia,* "Castro elogia" 19), the American press did not pay as much attention to the OLAS as to Carmichael's role in it. One of the most popular and well-known African American leaders of the time, Carmichael was discredited by some journalists who sought to minimize his relevance in the black community. *The New York Times*, for example, disqualified him, claiming that the black leader did nothing but "preach a gospel of hatred and violence" (*The New York Times*, "Soviet is Assailed" 6).

James Reston, whose reports from Havana were replicated by countless U.S. newspapers, claimed that Carmichael was misleading Castro and the other revolutionary communists about the condition and power of black people in the United States. He claimed that neither Black Power politics nor Carmichael had popular support among black Americans and that – while in Havana – he was operating "not only outside the legal framework of the United States government but outside the structure of the Negro protest movement" (James Reston, "Havana: Stokely" 36). Similarly, other newspapers characterized him as an "extremist leader" (Goodsell 1) and a militant Black Power advocate "who has done more, perhaps, than any other man to disrupt the harmony between the races" (*Gadsden Times*, "Carmichael's Cuba" 3). This highly contrasted with the portrayal of African American newspapers that did not hesitate to acknowledge and highlight Carmichael's leadership role in the black community (*St. Petersburg Times* 9).

James Reston and many other journalists' main concern was the possibility that Carmichael could forge an alliance with the radical revolutionary communists in Latin America (J. Reston, "Havana: Stokely" 36). Reston stated, for example, that Castro viewed the racial riots in the United States as one front in a worldwide struggle for the liberation of oppressed people, and concluded that even though,

> [Castro] did not say or implied that Negro revolution in America was led or even influenced by Communists, he linked the fight in Detroit, the war in Vietnam and the guerrilla uprisings in Bolivia, Venezuela, Peru, Colombia and Guatemala as different battles in a common struggle against the United States government. (James Reston, "Havana: The American Negro" 23)

Later on, *The New York Times* seemed to consider the urban riots – which had been defined a few days before as being orchestrated by Castro "in revolutionary terms" –

as a "coincidence that has played into Premier Castro's hands" (*The New York Times*, "Havana's Other Vietnams" 10). *The New York Times* certainly was not the only media outlet to focus on the tie between Carmichael and Castro, between the black movement and the Cuban revolution, and between the urban riots and communism. Even though Castro himself said that any suggestion linking him with the racial unrest in the United States was ridiculous (UPI, "Fidel Gives Blessing" 14), many newspapers devoted pages to just that.

The Washington Post, for one, dedicated an article to prove the "long-lasting alliance" between SNCC and Castro. According to Rowland Evans and Robert Novak, the link between both sides dated back to at least 1964. In their view, the link was a direct consequence of the "deep disillusionment over Vietnam and civil rights" that had been brought forth by "radical intellectuals" associated with the island and the organization (Evans and Novak 17).[6] Although Rowland and Novak admitted that they had no documentary evidence to support their claims, they speculated where the organization's funds came from: "SNCC's treasury – empty since the disaffection of White liberal contributors – suddenly began to fill again. It is believed by many close to SNCC that the new money came from Cuba" (Evans and Novak 17). In their view, this was enough proof that Carmichael and SNCC were Castro's arm in the United States.

Moreover, *Los Angeles Times* published an article in which Drew Pearson emphasized that race riots in the United States were the preface to a revolution and that, as a possible revolutionary focus, the Cuban leader was requesting as much support as possible (*Los Angeles Times*, "Castro sees Revolution" 23). In this sense, Pearson repeatedly claimed that Carmichael had been working as an undercover agent for the revolution (Pearson 5). Overall, the unfounded notion that communism was behind urban riots and that the rioters were encouraged, sponsored, and led by Carmichael and other Black Power activists who were "subsidized by some communist country" (*La Vanguardia*, "Washington" 21) was accepted and promoted by American media and the international press ("Parece confirmarse" 11).

Paul Rogers, the Republican representative of Texas, got behind the idea that Carmichael was an instrument of Castroism. He proclaimed that not taking punitive measures against Carmichael meant giving Cuban subversion in the United States a free pass (*The Baltimore Afro-American* 1). Following Rogers's claims, the U.S. press proceeded to press for sanctions, the seizure of Carmichael's passport, and his arrest on charges of treason and sedition.[7] Furthermore, Joe Pool, a Democratic representative, introduced a constitutional amendment to Congress to enable stripping Carmichael of his citizenship (*The New York Times*, "Congress Gets Bill" 21). And finally,

6 "By the time of the Mississippi Summer Project in 1964, SNCC's admiration for castroism was apparent. SNCC workers were distributing propaganda and material printed in Cuba by exile (Robert) Williams advocating guerrilla warfare by American Negroes and describing how Molotov cocktails could be used in American cities" (Evans and Novak 17).

7 Carmichael was also charged with "seditious conspiracy, for making threats against the President, for rebellion or insurrection and for advocating the overthrown of the government" (Warde 10).

in August of 1967, the Senator from Alabama, Leland Childs, presented a resolution to forbid his return to the United States (*Associated Press*, "Don't Let Carmichael" 3).

Connections and implications

In 1967, Willard Edwards, a reporter for the *Chicago Tribune*'s Washington bureau, stated that Carmichael's actions were proof of the danger that Cuba represented as a bastion of communist aggression that supported the internationalization of guerrilla warfare throughout the Western Hemisphere. Carmichael himself, Edwards wrote, "clarified the purpose of the so-called Latin American solidarity meeting he is attending – to organize, under communist guidance, revolution in both Americas" (Edwards 4).

Edwards's words mirrored the views of numerous politicians who stressed the idea that Carmichael's trip was proof of the influence of communism on the riots and urban uprisings that had taken place in the United States since 1964. In view of the "evidence regarding the possibility that American nationals, who are Castro-trained guerrillas, have been and are even now operating to foment and exploit riot situations in cities in the United States," Armistead Selden, Democratic representative from Alabama and president of the House Subcommittee on Inter-American Affairs, demanded an investigation into Carmichael's relations with revolutionary Cuba (*Gadsden Times*, "Carmichael's Cuba" n. pag.). To Selden, Carmichael's statements and actions in Cuba posed serious questions on the scope of Castro's aid to the urban rebellions in the United States. But to many others, Carmichael's trip symbolized the integration of the United States, through black activism and Black Power, to the struggle of Third World countries (Ryan, "Stokely" 16).

Carmichael's presence in Havana was the cause of controversy even one year later. On the one hand, a month after the assassination of Martin Luther King, Jr. (April 4th, 1968) and of the violent riots that followed, the media commonly blamed Cuba for the uprisings caused by the sheer anxiety and disbelief over the assassination of one of the century's most important African American leaders. Nevertheless, and as some finally concluded, the urban riots were not caused by foreign interference from Cuba, Moscow, or Beijing. They were nothing but the expression of ongoing socio-economic crises, the structural racism ingrained in American society, and the lack of suitable response from the Johnson administration (Trohan 4).

On the other hand, Carmichael's trip coincided with a new era of Black activism and organization in the Anglophone Caribbean, where the political, social, and economic oppression of the populations in many cases did not come to an end with the shift from British colonial rule to "black governments." Mostly, these governments were led by Afro-descendant parties or leaderships which had assumed power between the late 1960s and early 1970s but still responded and protected the interests of the "white" political establishment and the foreign capital. As it was maintained in a 1972 CIA memorandum, "for the most part, Caribbean Black Power movements are home-grown, deriving primarily inspiration from U.S. Black Power leaders and the revolutionary rhetoric of Fidel Castro." It also referred to some evidence that foreign Black Power groups were providing a certain degree of logistical and financial support to Black Power organizations in the Caribbean (Central Intelligence Agency 14).

In the short term, the parallel influences of Black Power and the Cuban Revolution propelled the emergence of anti-racist and anti-establishment movements in the British Caribbean. This included, among others, the Afro-Caribbean liberation movement in Antigua, the Black Beret Group in the Bermudas (led by one of the most active afro-Caribbean leaders of the time, Roosevelt Brown), the National Joint Action Committee in Trinidad and Tobago, the People's Progressive Movement in Barbados, the African National Union in Jamaica (led by Marcus Harvey, Jr.), the Antillean Black Power Organization in Curacao, the Black Socialist Party in Dominica, the African Society for Cultural Relations with Independent Africa in Guyana, the Forum in St. Lucia, the Black Power Party in Montserrat, the Black Power Group in St. Kitts and Maurice Bishop's New Jewel Movement's in Grenada. Most of these movements distinguished "between the black power they advocate[d] and the black power advocated by the black Establishment" (Johnson 1). At the same time, however, they established solidarity ties among themselves and with various black organizations in the United States, such as the Black Panther Party and the Republic of New Africa.

Final considerations

The visit of one of the leading Black Power advocates to Cuba in mid-1967 had a range of expected and unexpected repercussions at different levels. In a scenario dominated by Cold War policies and the total disruption of foreign relations between the United States and Cuba, Carmichael's figure was instrumental in creating a peculiar space for meetings and discussions between Black Power figures and revolutionaries in other nations. By studying his legacy, we can better appreciate the full complexity of the 1960s and '70s that provided the African American struggle with a platform that contextualized it and connected it with the global struggle against U.S.-led imperialism and colonialism.

On the one hand, Carmichael's visit to Cuba was an attempt to set up links between the Black movement in the United States and other anti-imperialist, nationalist, and anti-capitalist movements across the Americas and beyond. The time he spent in Cuba underscored potential sympathies and ideological synergies between an increasingly radicalized bBlack movement in the United States and the revolutionary Cuba that served as its political model. But it also revealed the Cuban support and endorsement of the African American community in its struggle. At least, at a symbolic and rhetorical level, it implied the first step toward rapprochement between liberation movements in Latin America and the black movement in the United States. To Castro, this "revolutionary rapprochement" was natural and spontaneous, since – as he claimed on his OLAS closing speech – it would be "from this black community, being the most exploited and repressed, the most brutally mistreated sector in the United

States, [from where] the revolutionary movement in that country will arise" (Castro 4). In Castro's view, it was the "vanguard of a fight called upon liberating, one day, the whole North American society" (4).

On the other hand, Carmichael's trip fueled the worst fears of conservative groups in the United States. According to many mainstream U.S. news outlets, the trip revealed connections and mutual admiration between Carmichael and Castro. The U.S. media strived to sketch it as the most blatant evidence of the ties between the Black Power movement and the Cuban revolution, of the influence of Castroism on the urban riots in the United States, and the infiltration of communist agents into North American soil. With Castro's public statements in which he labelled Carmichael's visit an act of "revolutionary internationalism" and highlighted the ties between the struggles in the United States and the "Third World" he further fueled these fears.[8] He also reinforced the views upheld by leaders like H. Rap Brown (president of SNCC and member of the Black Panther Party) who emphasized the influence of the Cuban Revolution and the anti-imperialist fight in the black movement.

All this led to a hardening of diplomacy between the parties and the disclosure of political and ideological divergences. The OLAS concluded with irreconcilable disagreements regarding the strategies that liberation movements should adopt. There was an explicit condemnation of the U.S.S.R.'s "peaceful coexistence" policy and their attempts to establish political, diplomatic, commercial relations and agreements with Latin American governments that opposed the Cuban regime (*The New York Times*, "Fireworks in Havana" 36). Likewise, the "moderate" sectors that were inclined towards alternative forms of struggle to armed revolution were expressly condemned (*The Tuscaloosa News* 15).

Eventually, the OLAS began to crumble from within: the communist parties from Colombia and Venezuela demanded a new Conference to debate the strategies proposed by Cuba (Ryan, "Negro Rioting" 11), while Cuba and twenty-seven other countries presented a motion to condemn Colombia and Venezuela for "treason" (UPI, "Conference" 12). When the OLAS finally fell apart, Carmichael went on his way. He traveled to Moscow and China (Carmichael and Thelwell 594), North Vietnam, Algeria, Guinea and Tanzania (596–638). But none of these places nor any of the statements he made while on this tour (not even the speeches he delivered in Vietnam, where the United States had waged a decade-long war) were as impactful as the ones he had made in Cuba.

---

8 As Castro observed, "We [Cubans] believe that the attitude of this revolutionary North American leader [Carmichael] is a great lesson, a great example of militant internationalism, something inherent to revolutionaries. And there is no doubt that we agree much more with this kind of revolutionary than with super theorizers, who are revolutionary by word and bourgeois by deed. Such level of internationalism is not proclaimed, it is practised! And black people in the United States are resisting to that matter. … We believe that, if there is a country where the struggle is tough, the fight is difficult, that is the United States. And it is there where we have North American revolutionaries providing us with examples and lessons" (4).

When Carmichael finally returned to the United States, he had to face the consequences. Upon landing on American soil, he was stripped of his passport, the State Department demanded Congress to impose sanctions on Carmichael, and two members of Congress asked for his arrest (*The Spokesman-Review* 1). Even the executive board of SNCC passed a condemnatory resolution for the words and actions of his former president abroad (*Gadsden Times*, "Stokely Carmichael Faces" 57).

Nonetheless, Carmichael's trip had a powerful impact domestically. Not only did it promote discussions on U.S. American citizens' rights to travel to countries with which the government had no diplomatic relations; it further turned the (possible) influence of communism on the socio-political movements of the time into a much-debated topic. The perceived threat led to a massive increase in government surveillance and state repression aimed at "exorcising" the communist seed in the black movement. Since the late 1950s, the FBI Counterintelligence Program (COINTELPRO) had been involved in surveillance, infiltration, discrediting, and elimination of individuals and groups associated with the anti-war or counterculture movement, unions, or New Left organizations, that were deemed "radical," "subversive," or a threat to the status quo. In the 1960s and early 1970s, COINTELPRO's main goal was the disruption of organizations that identified, first with the civil rights movement and, later, with Black Nationalism, Black Power, and the Black Panther Party and the elimination of its members.

Many years later, in his autobiography *Ready for Revolution*, Carmichael recalled his trip to Cuba as "an incredible moment, more than just exciting. It was," he continued, "eye-opening, inspiring, and mind-blowing" (Carmichael and Thelwell 583). It was the moment the international struggle became tangible to him, "no longer an abstraction" (584). He would also reflect on what he still considered the "obvious similarities" (588) between the experiences and situations of Latin Americans and African Americans, both oppressed by the similar forces – capitalism and American imperialism – and thus party to the same struggle. For this reason, Carmichael still called for "unity of the oppressed and the victory of the world revolution. And, of course," he further observed, "I expressed my respect, solidarity, and undying support for the courageous Cuban people and their revolution. True then, true now" (588).

Works cited

Associated Press. "Don't Let Carmichael Back in, Senate says." *Associated Press* (24 Aug. 1967): 3. Print.

The Baltimore Afro-American. "Many on Warpath for Stokely's Scalp." *The Baltimore Afro-American* (26 Jul. 1967): 1. Print.

Carbone, Valeria L. "Cuando la guerra fría llegó a América Latina." *Invasiones Bárbaras en la Historia Contemporánea de los Estados Unidos*. Ed. Fabio Nigra and Pablo Pozzi. Buenos Aires: Maipue, 2009. 275–296. Print.

Carmichael, Stokely. "Black Power and the Third World." 1967. *Freedom Archives*. Ed. Third World Information Service. 2–4. Web. https://www.freedomarchives.org/Documents/Finder/Black%20Liberation%20Disk/Black%20Power!/SugahData/Books/Carmichael.S.pdf.

Carmichael, Stokely, and Charles V. Hamilton. *Black Power: The Politics of Liberation in America*. New York: Vintage Books, 1967. Print.

Carmichael, Stokely, and Ekwueme Michael Thelwell. *Ready for Revolution: The Life and Struggles of Stokely Carmichael (Kwame Turé)*. New York: Scribner, 2003. Print.

Castro, Fidel. "Discurso pronunciado en la Clausura de la Primera Conferencia de la OLAS." *Punto Final* 35 (1967): 2–12. Print.

Central Intelligence Agency. *Interrelationship of Black Power Organizations in the Western Hemisphere*. United States. 1972. Web. https://link.gale.com/apps/doc/CK2349563258/USDD?u=roosesc&sid=USDD&xid=ec48a24f.

Cohen, Steven. "When Castro Came to Harlem." *The New Republic* 21 (Mar. 2016): n. pag. Web. https://newrepublic.com/article/131793/castro-came-harlem.

Digital SNCC Gateway. "Stokely Carmichael goes to Cuba." N.d. Web. https://snccdigital.org/events/stokely-carmichael-goes-cuba/.

Domínguez, Jorge. "Cuba. 1959–1990." *Historia de América Latina. México y el Caribe desde 1930*. Ed. Leslie Bethell. Barcelona: Crítica, 1988. 183–227. Print.

Dumbrell, John. *President Lyndon Johnson and Soviet Communism*. Manchester: Manchester UP, 2004. Print.

Edwards, Willard. "Carmichael Spotlights Red Cuba." *The Spokesman-Review* (2 Aug. 1967): n. pag. Print.

Evans, Rowland, and Robert Novak. "Inside Report: SNCC in Havana." *The Washington Post* (3 Aug. 1967): 17. Print.

Gadsden Times. "Carmichael's Cuba Trip Spells Trouble." *Gadsden Times* (3 Aug. 1967): 3. Print.

———. "Stokely Carmichael Faces SNCC Reprimed." *Gadsden Times* (16 Aug. 1967): 57. Print.

Goodsell, James Nelson. "Castro and Viet Cong: Cuban Celebrations Link Anti-U.S. Sentiment in Vietnam, Black Power and Revolution." *The Christian Science Monitor* (28 Jul. 1967): 1. Print.

Goshko, John M. "Carmichael Lauds Cuban Communism: Carmichael Praises Castro's." *The Washington Post* (2 Aug. 1967): 1. Print.

Granma. "The Duty of Every Revolutionary is to Make Revolution." *Granma* (26 Feb. 1967): 5. Print.

Guevara, Ernesto. "Mensaje a los pueblos el mundo a través de la Tricontinental." *Marxist Internet Archives*. 16 Apr. 1967. Web. https://www.marxists.org/espanol/guevara/04_67.htm.

Guridy, Juliet, and Frank Hooker. "Corrientes de pensamiento político afrolatinoamericano." *Estudios afrolatinoamericanos: una introducción*. Ed. Alejandro de la Fuente and George Reid Andrews. Ciudad Autónoma de Buenos Aires: CLACSO, 2018. 219–267. Print.

Hamilton, Charles. "An Advocate of Black Power Defines It." *The New York Times* (14 Apr. 1968): 22. Print.

Johnson, Thomas A. "Black Power Flourishing in Caribbean." *The New York Times* (24 Apr. 1970): 1. Print.

Joseph, Peniel E. *The Black Power Movement: Rethinking the Civil Rights-Black Power Era.* New York / London: Routledge, 2006. Print.

Kerner Commission. *Report of the National Advisory Commission On Civil Disorders*. U.S. G.P.O.: Washington: United States, 1968. Print.

La Vanguardia. "Castro elogia a Carmichael y rinde homenaje a los negros norteamericanos." *La Vanguardia* (28 Jul. 1967): 19. Print.

———. "Parece confirmarse que la racha de violencias raciales no surgió espontáneamente." *La Vanguardia* (4 Aug. 1967): 11. Print.

———. "Washington: Stokely Carmichael se dispone a continuar sus campañas anti-norteamericanas en el extranjero." *La Vanguardia* (12 Oct. 1967): 21. Print.

Los Angeles Times. "Carmichael Message Asks Negro Revolt." *Los Angeles Times* (18 Aug. 1967): 10. Print.

———. "Castro Sees Revolution in U.S. on Racial Issue." *Los Angeles Times* (11 Aug. 1967): 23. Print.

Marable, Manning. "Race and Revolution in Cuba." *Souls* 1.2 (1999): 6–17. Print.

Meluzo, Pedro. "When the United States Has 50 Vietnams Inside and 50 Outside, This Will Mean the Death of Imperialism." *Granma* (13 Aug. 1967): 2. Print.

Menéndez, Mario. *Entrevista a Stokely Carmichael, en La Habana (Cuba). Ninety-First Congress, Senate, Committee on the Judiciary: Testimony of Stokely Carmichael.* United States Senate. Washington D.C.: Government Printing Office, 1970. 21–29. Print.

Moreno, George Carriazo. "Las relaciones económicas Cuba-Estados Unidos: una mirada al futuro." *Estudios Internacionales* 26.103 (1993): 480–499. Web. http://www.revistaei.uchile.cl/index.php/REI/article/download/15387/28493.

The New York Times. "Carmichael Is Quoted as Saying Negroes Form Guerrilla Bands." *The New York Times* (26 Jul. 1967): 22. Print.

———. "Carmichael Urges a 'Vietnam' in U.S." *The New York Times* (28 Jul. 1967): 10. Print.

———. "Fireworks in Havana." *The New York Times* (10 Aug. 1967): 36. Print.

———. "Havana's Other Vietnams." *The New York Times* (2 Aug. 1967): 10. Print.

———. "Negroes Offered Tour of Cuba." *The New York Times* (11 Oct. 1960): 33. Print.

———. "Negroes Ready for War in U.S., Carmichael Says." *The New York Times* (3 Aug. 1967): 19. Print.

———. "Policy on Cuba Scored." *The New York Times* (6 Apr. 1961): 2. Print.

———. "Soviet is Assailed at Parley in Cuba." *The New York Times* (4 Aug. 1967): 6. Print.

———. "Congress Gets Bill to Strip Carmichael of Citizenship." *The New York Times* (16 Aug. 1967): 21. Print.

OLAS. "Discurso pronunciado por el Presidente de la República y miembro del Buró político del partido comunista de Cuba, Dr. Osvaldo Dorticos Torradoolas." *Actas Primera Conferencia de la Organización Latinoamericana de Solidaridad.* Organización Latinoamericana de Solidaridad: Havana, 1967. 13–20. Print.

Pearson, Drew. "Stokely Eyed for Treason." *The Tuscaloosa News* (9 Aug. 1967): 5. Print.

Reston, James. "Havana: Stokely Carmichael's Game." *The New York Times* (2 Aug. 1967): 36. Print.

———. "Havana: The American Negro and Communist Strategy." *The New York Times* (28 Jul. 1967): 23. Print.

Reston, Tom. "Habana 1967: The OLAS Conference Defines Revolution." *The Harvard Crimson* (17 Nov. 1967): n. pag. Web. http://www.thecrimson.com/article/1967/11/17/habana-1967-pway-at-the-top/?page=single.

Rustin, Bayard. "From Protest to Politics: The Future of the Civil Rights Movement." *Commentary* 39.2 (Feb. 1965): 25–31. Print. http://www.commentarymagazine.com/article/from-protest-to-politics-the-future-of-the-civil-rights-movement/.

Ryan, William L. "Negro Rioting a Windfall for Castro, Meeting to Open." *Sarasota Herald-Tribune* (29 Jul. 1967): 11. Print.

———. "Stokely Planning to Return Home." *The Spokesman-Review* (2 Dec. 1967): 16. Print.

Stewart, Charles J. "The Evolution of a Revolution: Stokely Carmichael and the Rhetoric of Black Power." *Quarterly Journal of Speech* 83.4 (1997): 436. Print.

St. Petersburg Times. "Castro Laud Carmichael." *St. Petersburg Times* (27 Jul. 1967): 9. Print.

The Spokesman-Review. "U.S. Passport Seized as Stokely Returns." *Associated Press* (12 Dec. 1967): 1. Print.

The Tuscaloosa News. "Latin Reds Talk Over Differences." *Associated Press* (3 Aug. 1967): 15. Print.

Trohan, Walter. "Report From Washington: Kerner Holding Out for Honest Report on Riots." *The Chicago Tribune* (7 Feb. 1968): 4. Print.

UPI. "Carmichael Learns More From Castro." *Washington Afro-American* (8 Aug. 1967): 15. Print.

———. "Conference in Cuba Draws to a Close." *Sarasota Herald-Tribune* (11 Aug. 1967): 12. Print.

———. "Fidel Gives Blessing to Negro Rioting." *The Bryan Times* (27 Jul. 1967): 14. Print.

Warde, Philip. "Congressmen Seek Trial for Carmichael." *The Chicago Tribune* (13 Aug. 1967): 10. Print.

Black Movements in Latin America, 1970–2000

GEORGE REID ANDREWS

An observer looking at any Latin American country in 1970 would have had little reason to foresee the imminent appearance of Black political and cultural movements later in the decade. Most Latin American societies thought of themselves at that time as "racial democracies" based on histories of *mestizaje* [race mixture] that had supposedly obliterated identifiable racial groups and had achieved high levels of inter-racial *convivencia* [people of different races living together with relative equality and harmony] (Alberto and Hoffnung-Garskof). According to both Marxist and liberal modernization theory, the two approaches that dominated social-science thinking in the region, the structuring categories of Latin American life were not racial but rather class-based. Individuals found their places in society not on the basis of racial identities but rather on the basis of class, as workers, peasants, white-collar professionals, etc.

The same was true of politics, where the great debates of the post-war period centered on class issues: how much relative weight should workers, peasants, members of the middle class, national elites, and foreign investors have in national politics, and how should the benefits of economic development be distributed? Populist political movements – Peronism in Argentina, *trabalhismo* in Brazil, the Partido Revolucionario Institucional in Mexico, and Cuba's newly installed socialist government – all claimed to represent the interests of workers, peasants, and the poor, and to varying degrees actually sought to do so. Fearing that populist movements might open the way for Cuban-style socialism, in the 1960s and 1970s authoritarian regimes seized power in Argentina, Brazil, Chile, Uruguay, and other countries, repressing popular movements and imposing military discipline on their societies.

For these reasons, the 1970s would seem to have offered an unlikely setting for the rise of racially defined Black (or indigenous) political movements. Yet, with the benefit of a half-century of hindsight, we now know that the 1970s marked the starting point of an extended trajectory of mobilization by those racial groups that had previously been excluded from national life. By the early 2000s, that mobilization had produced some major policy initiatives aimed at achieving racial democracy and equality, resulting in profound shifts in regional thinking about race (Hernández; Paschel, "Rethinking").

As the essays in this volume make clear, the U.S.-based Black Power movement played a significant role in the rise of Black movements in Latin America. Activists often cited the importance for them of writings by Eldridge Cleaver and Malcolm X. For Carlos Alberto Medeiros (see his essay in this volume), "you take a kid like I was at that time, coming into contact with that work, with that Malcolm X thing …. This has a very strong impact, because it really hits you inside and makes you raise your head" (Contins 133). Twenty-five years after his 1969 visit to the headquarters of the Black Panther Party in Oakland, Afro-Brazilian leader Abdias do Nascimento recalled its effects on him: "Very impressive, for me, that visit to Black Power, because I saw how well they were doing, [and how] militarily prepared [they were]. When I arrived, I saw that everyone was armed and ready to receive me. On guard, with everyone armed. For somebody from Brazil, this was impressive" (Contins 29; cf. *Afro-Latino-América* 68–69).

Yet, Black Power, important as it was, was not the only force behind the rise of Black movements in the region. Recent scholarly research and *testimonios* and analyses written by participants in those movements provide a broad and expansive picture of how and why Black movements appeared in Latin America at that time. Who took part in those movements, and for what reasons? Centrally important, for the purposes of this volume, is the question of Afro-Latin American movements' connections with larger diasporic waves of mobilization at that time. To what degree were Afro-Latin American movements influenced and inspired by similar mobilizations in the United States and Africa, and to what degree were they products of local experiences of organization and struggle?

The answer, inevitably, is that both dimensions – the local/national, and the transnational – were necessary conditions for the rise of Afro-Latin American political mobilization in the 1970s and 1980s (Paschel, *Becoming*). Also inevitably, but perhaps not as obviously, the cross-national roots of Afro-Latin American movements reached well beyond their connections to movements in other countries to include a broad spectrum of transnational actors: the Catholic church and other religious organizations; private and public foundations; multilateral development agencies; not to mention cross-border collaborations among Black movements within Latin America itself. This essay seeks to survey some of the principal forces driving the creation and diffusion of Black movements in the region, and some of the most consequential interactions between local/national and transnational spheres of action.

Local conditions

A history of movements

Perhaps the most important finding of recent research on Black social and political mobilization is how "thick" the historical record of that mobilization is, and how far back that record extends. Under slavery, hundreds of thousands of enslaved Africans and Afro-Latin Americans fled to join the networks of runaway communities – *quilombos* and *mocambos* in Brazil, *palenques* and *cumbes* in Spanish America – that embraced most of Latin America. Though never knit together in any formal associational structure, each such community represented a node of resistance to enslavement. And while most of those communities were eventually suppressed, enough of them survived to form a continued presence into the twentieth and twenty-first centuries, and indeed managed to make racism a central political issue around which present-day Black movements have mobilized (Helg 43–63; Offen).

Within the boundaries of slavery, Africans and their descendants found potent organizational vehicles in Catholic religious brotherhoods and colonial militias. Both forms of mobilization provided state-authorized venues within which free and enslaved people could gather to discuss their individual and collective needs and to carry out projects of collective advancement. Black militiamen in Mexico, for example, succeeded in winning tax exemptions not just for themselves and their families but for the entire free Black population (Vinson 132–172). Black militias also proved to be of crucial importance during the Spanish American independence wars, again winning major advances for the enslaved and free Black populations: the end of the slave trade, the gradual abolition of slavery, and the striking down of colonial racial laws (Andrews, *Afro-Latin America* 53–84; Helg 197–219).

The striking down of those laws opened the way for Black enfranchisement and participation in nineteenth- and twentieth-century electoral politics. Confronting continuing racial prejudice and discrimination, Afro-Latin Americans also organized and joined an extensive network of social clubs and civic organizations, reported on by the Black newspapers that flourished in Argentina, Brazil, Cuba, Panama, and Uruguay.[1] Newspapers published in predominantly Black regions of Colombia did not adopt an explicitly racial identity but expressed a rhetoric of citizenship and civic equality that clearly reflected the interests of those regions' Black working and middle classes (Crawford; Flórez-Bolívar).

In Brazil, Cuba, and Uruguay, Afrodescendant activists formed political parties – the *Frente Negra Brasileira*, the *Partido Independiente de Color*, and the *Partido Autóctono Negro* – that sought to more fully integrate people of color into national political and economic life. Though none of those parties achieved electoral success, their programs were at least partially adopted by the populist parties and movements that came to power in the region during the 1930s and 1940s. Appealing directly to the racially mixed *pueblo*, populist governments invoked the idea of racial equality (first enunciated as a national value during the independence struggles of the 1800s) while simultaneously undertaking programs of state-led industrial development and social provision that had powerful effects in the region.

Access to education

As a result of those programs, between 1945 and 1980 Latin American societies experienced what economists Luis Bértola and José Antonio Ocampo describe as a "golden age" of economic growth and development (Bértola and Ocampo 175). Latin American economies achieved some of the highest growth rates in their history, in many cas-

1 Cf. Geler; Alberto (*Terms of Inclusion*); Pappademos; Andrews ("Afro-World"); Alberto, Andrews, and Hoffnung-Garskof.

es equaling rates in Europe and the United States at the same time. In most countries, programs of state-led economic development also included provisions for expanded social spending on public goods such as housing, transportation, health, and education (191–197).

Afro-Latin Americans benefited directly from post-war efforts to expand access to education, entering secondary and university education in historically unprecedented numbers (Andrews, *Afro-Latin America* 162–163). Their experiences in those schools were deeply contradictory. On the one hand, the educations they received greatly increased their human and cultural capital, empowering them to compete for better jobs and to analyze and make sense of the world surrounding them. But many Afro-Latin Americans also recall their school years as the setting in which they first became conscious of racial difference and racial prejudice. For Afro-Brazilian activist Nilma Bentes, "school is the place where you first learn that discrimination exists, that the issue of blackness exists" (Alberti and Pereira 40). "During the brief time that I went to school I suffered a great deal," recalled Afro-Uruguayan dancer and writer Rosa Luna. "Racism attacks you from when you're little, and I can tell you this because I suffered it in the flesh, beginning in school, like many, many others" (Andrews, *Blackness* 91).

At the university level, future activists found themselves in programs in which they were one of only a handful of Black students. "For black people who are studying, most of the time they find themselves to be the only black person in their classrooms, and … they are looked at constantly as the Other," recalled Brazilian public-health official Maria Inês Barbosa. "Because of that scrutiny, we ha[d] no choice but to be above average because if not, it will not be enough, race and racism will not allow you to progress, despite your diplomas." In order to escape that isolation, in the mid-1970s, Barbosa joined the *Centro de Cultura e Arte Negra* in São Paulo, where the members "were all university students, male and female, and that became very important to me," and then, in 1978, the newly formed *Movimento Negro Unificado* (MNU).[2]

In São Paulo, poet Luis Silva (Cuti) explains, "the Black movement was made basically by university students who were confronting the problem of the university and who were reading[;] they were people who read and who made contact" (Alberti and Pereira 77). In Colombia, one of the seminal Black Consciousness organizations was the *Centro de Estudios Soweto*, founded in 1976 by undergraduates studying at the Technological University of Pereira (Agudelo 173–174; Paschel, *Becoming* 66; Perea's essay in this volume). Members of that early organization went on to found *Cimarrón* in 1982. Similarly, the *Proceso de Comunidades Negras* (PCN), today the most important Black organization in Colombia, was created in the early 1990s by university students and recent graduates in the port city of Buenaventura (Agudelo 182). "During the 1980s the Afro-Ecuadorian movement built its organizations on the basis of student groups in Quito and Guayaquil" (Antón Sánchez 116). Similar groups

2 Rahier ("Interview" 217–218); on the MNU, cf. Pereira (247–287); Alberti and Pereira (148–163).

formed in the 1970s among university students and intellectuals in Costa Rica, Cuba, and other countries.

Political openings

Further promoting the formation of new Black movements were the political transitions occurring in many Latin American countries. Those transitions opened new windows of opportunity for civil-society movements to take part in national debates and to connect to both political parties and state institutions.

One of the most dramatic such openings occurred in Panama, where during the 1970s the military-populist regime of Omar Torrijos sought to mobilize support for a national campaign to renegotiate the Panama Canal treaties and take control of the canal. Torrijos's active pursuit of political partners in the Afro-Antillean and Afro-Panamanian populations led to the formation of a number of new organizations: the *Unión Nacional del Negro Panameño* (UNEP), *Acción Reivindicadora del Negro Panameño* (ARENEP), the *Asociación de Profesionales, Obreros, y Dirigentes de Ascendencia Negra* (APODAN), the *Congreso del Negro Panameño*, and others. Mobilizing supporters both in Panama and in the Afro-Panamanian diaspora in the United States, these organizations played a significant role in getting the 1977 Panama Canal treaties approved in both nations, while simultaneously seizing "the opportunity to place high on the political agenda discussions of national, ethnic and racial identity" (Priestley 61; cf. Steinitz in this volume).

In Ecuador, the initial political opening was the land reform of 1964, which opened the door for indigenous and Black peasant associations to press the national state for the redistribution of hacienda lands. That process of peasant mobilization, and the return to civilian rule in 1979, led to the formation in 1986 of the *Confederación de Nacionalidades Indígenas del Ecuador* (CONAIE), followed by a series of CONAIE-led "popular uprisings" in the 1990s and early 2000s. Those uprisings removed two presidents from power and produced new constitutions (1998, 2008) that declared Ecuador to be a plural, multicultural state (cf. Becker; Rahier, "Afro-Ecuadorian").

That process of indigenous mobilization had major consequences for the country's Black movement. First, and most obviously, the constitutional recognition of Ecuador as a multicultural state and society meant recognition not just of indigenous rights but of Black rights as well, eventually codified in the 2006 *Ley de Derechos Colectivos del Pueblo Afroecuatoriano*. As a result of those constitutional provisions, scholar and activist Jhon Antón Sánchez suggests, Ecuador is now "in the vanguard" of defining and protecting Afrodescendant rights in Latin America, enabling Afro-Ecuadorians to "successfully demand policies for their socioeconomic, political and cultural inclusion."[3]

3 Antón Sánchez (237); De La Torre and Antón Sánchez (179); for a less optimistic reading of the Ecuadorian experience, cf. Walsh ("Afro In/Exclusion"; "Affirmative Action(ing)s").

Second, the achievements of indigenous movements provided further impetus to Black peasant associations in Esmeraldas and the Chota Valley. While urban-based Black organizations in Ecuador found it very challenging to recruit members among poor Black urbanites, Afro-Ecuadorian subsistence farmers were much more likely to recognize the potential benefits of collective action. "Talking with these people," reports Antón Sánchez, "they express forcefully that organizing is perhaps the best way" to achieve their goals (Antón Sánchez 253).

In Colombia, the political opening was created by the Constitutional Assembly of 1991 and, as in Ecuador, the writing of a new constitution. Also, as in Ecuador, indigenous movements took the lead in demanding multicultural legal status and constitutional protection of their collective land rights. Allying closely with the indigenous movement, the Black peasant associations of the Pacific coast successfully sought similar protections, which were then further guaranteed in Law 70 of 1993. By 2014, almost all of the majority-Black counties along the Pacific coast had received official title to their lands. That has not prevented, however, massive incursions into the region by drug traffickers and right-wing paramilitary groups; and as Paschel cogently notes, the focus on Black land rights has led to "a limited and geographically specific notion of blacks as rural and as from the Pacific coast that persists within state institutions today" (Paschel, *Becoming* 112), limiting the potential impact of urban-based Black organizations.

Brazil and Uruguay offered yet another form of political opening, namely, the transition from military dictatorship to civilian democracy. In both countries, that transition generated a process of civil-society mobilization in which Black organizations actively participated. This process was more pronounced in Brazil, where the transition began in the late 1970s and extended until 1985. When the dictatorship lifted restrictions on political parties in 1979 and allowed them to mobilize and campaign relatively freely, most of those parties actively sought support from Black organizations and activists. That process of recruitment did not translate into electoral success for Afro-Brazilian candidates; but it did contribute to a historic moment in which Brazilian media, academia, and political parties proved much more receptive than in the past to Black movements' analyses and denunciations of racial inequality, discrimination, and prejudice. Some state and municipal governments created new agencies specifically charged with attention to Afro-Brazilian issues and demands; two such institutions at the national level, the *Fundação Cultural Palmares* (created in 1988) and the *Grupo de Trabalho Interministerial* (1995) kept issues of race on the public agenda, eventually producing the federal government's first formal commitment (in 1996) to affirmative action and other racially compensatory policies.[4]

The importance for Black mobilization of these moments of political transition becomes even clearer when we consider the counter-case of Cuba. As in other Latin American countries, the rapid expansion of the educational system after 1959 created a

4 Alberti and Pereira; Paschel (*Becoming*); on comparable developments in Uruguay, cf. Andrews (*Blackness* 144–155).

new generation of Afro-Cuban high-school and university students, some of whom went on to create the same sorts of study groups and cultural institutions found in Brazil and Colombia. During the 1970s, members of the *Grupo de Estudios Afro-Cubano* read Fanon and Malcolm X, listened to African American soul music, and debated the position of Black people in Cuban society and culture; during that same decade, Afro-Cuban artists formed the *Grupo Antillano* to explore Black themes in their own work and to connect to artistic currents in the Caribbean and the African diaspora more generally. In the face of a fully consolidated authoritarian government, however, those organizations were either actively repressed or quietly marginalized and silenced (Sawyer 67–68; De La Fuente; cf. essay by Alberto Abreu in this volume). Not until the Special Period of the 1990s did political space open for the rise of new Afro-Cuban cultural and political movements (Fernandes; Saunders; Perry, *Negro*).

Transnational conditions: *Black Pau*[5] [Black Power] and African liberation

Local conditions – longstanding histories of Black mobilization, the expansion of high-school and university education among young Afro-Latin Americans, and national processes of political opening and transition – provided starting points for a new wave of Black mobilization in the 1970s, 1980s, and 1990s. That wave was then made even more intense by international conditions that fostered the rise and spread of Black movements.

As they gathered to read, study, and discuss the situation of Black people in their respective societies, Afro-Latin American students and intellectuals were profoundly influenced by the works of canonical diasporic writers from across the Atlantic world: Frantz Fanon, Malcolm X, Eldridge Cleaver, Angela Davis, Aimé Cesaire, Léopold Sédar Senghor, and others. Equally important, if not more so, were the visible political achievements of Black movements in the United States and Africa. Afro-Latin American writers and intellectuals had been paying close attention to racial conditions and Black movements in the United States since the early 1900s. Indeed, the very concept of racial democracy, jointly constructed by elite white intellectuals and marginalized Black intellectuals, had been built in large part on the sharp contrasts between U.S. racial segregation and more fluid models of racial co-existence in Latin America (Seigel 179–205; Alberto and Hoffnung-Garskof). When, therefore, the U.S. civil rights movement began to win major political victories in the 1950s and 1960s, starting to dismantle the legal structures of segregation, politically active Afro-Latin Americans drew direct inspiration from those events (Pereira 168–216).

Especially for young Afro-Latin Americans, and as abundantly evidenced by the essays in this volume, U.S. Black Power and Black nationalist movements were in some ways even more appealing and influential than the civil rights movement. Equally inspiring were cultural expressions of North American Blackness. Carlos Alberto Medeiros recalls buying *Ebony* magazine at a newsstand in Rio de Janeiro and mar-

5 Cf. McCann.

veling at the ideas and images presented in its pages. Seeing Afro hairstyles, he recalls, was "love at first sight" (Alberti and Pereira 70; cf. essay by Medeiros in this volume). Young Afro-Brazilians flocked to Black Rio, Black São Paulo, and Black Bahia dances to hear African American soul and funk music and to watch films like *Shaft* and *Wattstax* (McCann; Alberto, "When Rio"). Bahian activist and cultural entrepreneur Antonio Carlos "Vovô" dos Santos was powerfully affected by the music of James Brown and its message of Black pride. When dos Santos and his friends decided in 1974 to create an all-Black Carnival *bloco*, they initially planned to name the group *Poder Negro* [Black Power]. Informed by the Federal Police that this would not be viewed kindly by the authorities, they opted instead for the Yoruba name under which the *bloco* is now internationally famous, Ilê Aiyê (Alberti and Pereira 144).

The choice between *Poder Negro* and Ilê Aiyê reflects the impact on Afro-Latin American activists of national liberation and anti-apartheid struggles in Africa. In Colombia, students at the Technological University of Pereira formed the Centro de Estudios Soweto, recalls Juan de Dios Mosquera, because "the struggle in South Africa influenced us a lot, the debates they had within the movement in South Africa and the Negritude movement also influenced, Amilcar Cabral, Aimé Césaire, also Frantz Fanon. The process of decolonization in Africa influenced us a lot" (Paschel, *Becoming* 77). The same was true in Brazil, where activists in Rio de Janeiro founded the Sociedade de Intercâmbio Brasil-Africa in 1977.[6] In Uruguay, the local Black press followed events in Africa closely and celebrated the historic day in 1990 when Nelson Mandela was released from prison (Andrews, "Afro-World" 102–103).

The Catholic Church

Speaking in the early 1990s, Afro-Brazilian activist Amauri Mendes recalled how difficult it had been, in the 1970s, to create the first Black organizations:

> It is one thing to take part in conventional politics, through parties or the more established labor unions, which already exist. It's another thing to be an activist in a movement like ours, the Black Movement, or the community movement (*movimento comunitário*). There are no resources, no institutional credibility, like there are in the labor movement or in the parties …. Really, as an old friend of mine used to say, we have to kill a lion every day [in order to survive and function]. (Contins 46)

In the initial absence of that organizational structure, the Liberation-Theology wing of the Catholic church played an essential role in helping Black organizations establish themselves. One of the core elements of Liberation Theology was the idea that, in order to realize their full individual and collective promise, poor people needed to create organizations through which they could demand social and economic justice. Priests and nuns committed to that project devoted themselves to fostering social mobilization in poor communities. While much of that mobilization was initially conceived in class

6 Alberto (*Terms* 260–269); cf. *Afro-Latino-América* (82–83; 93–98; 101–102).

terms, focusing on the rural and urban poor, it gradually evolved to include organizing along racial lines as well.[7] Beginning in the 1970s, national churches created Black Pastoral organizations aimed at guiding local groups in their efforts to address issues of racial inequality and discrimination. The Church convened international meetings of those national organizations in 1980 (in Colombia), 1983 (in Ecuador), and 1986 (in Brazil), further promoting cross-national sharing of local experiences, tactics, and strategies (Antón Sánchez 103).

In Colombia during the 1970s, Catholic priests and missionaries worked with subsistence farmers and forest dwellers in the Pacific coastal regions to form peasant associations aimed at defending their lands from encroachment by lumbering and mining companies. Those associations were initially focused on questions of land rights and economic development, but by the 1980s and 1990s they were thinking of themselves increasingly in racial and cultural terms, as Black communities facing existential threats. "Nearly every activist" that Tianna Paschel interviewed for her research on those organizations "began his or her political trajectory in the Church" (Paschel, *Becoming* 70; cf. Agudelo 176–178).

Catholic missionaries and clerics were similarly crucial in the formation of peasant associations in Ecuador. Priests of the Comboni missionary order also created a series of Afro-related organizations, including the *Pastoral Afroecuatoriana* (1978), the *Movimiento Afroecuatoriano Consciencia* (1981), and the *Centro Cultural Afroecuatoriano* (1984). As in Colombia, these entities initiated a generation of Afro-Ecuadorian activists that included Jaime Hurtado (assassinated in 1999 during his campaign for the presidency), future cabinet secretary Alexandra Ocles, and others (Johnson; Antón Sánchez 103–105).

In Uruguay, Franciscan missionaries provided financial and logistical support for the Afro-Uruguayan organization *Asociación Cultural y Social Uruguay* (ACSU), seeing in it a potential vehicle for organizing in the center-city neighborhoods of Montevideo. When ACSU failed to play that role, the friars shifted their support to a group of younger members of ACSU, who split off in 1988 to form Organizaciones Mundo Afro. The Franciscans were instrumental in connecting the new organization to potential sources of funding, including foreign foundations and the United Nations Development Program (Andrews, *Blackness* 145–147). Like the Church, those international funders proved crucial in sustaining Black organizations.

International funders

While Church institutions did provide significant levels of material and advisory assistance to nascent Black movements, their resources were limited. Consequently, from the very beginning, Black activists reached out to other possible sources of support. Afro-Brazilian activists in Rio de Janeiro and Salvador recall the warm reception they

7 For a thoughtful portrayal of that evolution, focusing on Afro-Brazilian priest and activist Frei Davi Raimundo dos Santos, cf. Kramer.

received at the *Instituto Cultural Brasil-Alemanha* (ICBA) in those cities. ICBA staff encouraged them to use the institutes' libraries and provided a welcoming venue for their meetings. The German libraries were particularly rich in materials on Africa, the activists recall; and it was through meetings at the Rio ICBA that the *Sociedade de Intercâmbio Brasil-Africa* (SINBA) was first established (Contins 129; Alberti and Pereira 76–77).

Participants in SINBA went on to create one of the most important of the Afro-Brazilian organizations, the *Instituto de Pesquisa das Culturas Negras* (IPCN). The U.S.-based InterAmerican Foundation provided funds for IPCN to buy a building to house its headquarters, as well as grants to several Carnival groups and a Candomblé congregation in Salvador. Largely in response to those grants, in 1977 the military government suspended the foundation's operations in Brazil, forcing it to leave the country for several years (Pereira 201–206). During the 1980s, the Ford Foundation, which had a longstanding interest in the promotion of racial equality in the United States, began to take a more active role in the financing of scholarship and activism on racial inequality in Brazil. Ford was in turn followed by European foundations and, in the 1990s and early 2000s, by the Inter-American Development Bank, the World Bank, and the United Nations Development Program, all of which provided grants, loans, and contracts in support of Black and indigenous organizations (cf. Davis, Paschel, and Morrison).

Activists and scholars continue to debate the impacts of that transnational financial support. Clearly, it was instrumental in helping specific Black organizations survive and, after 1990, become more "professionalized." Many activists suggest, however, that that very process of professionalization (or, as some called it, NGO-ization) worked to widen the gap between organizations receiving international funding and the predominantly poor populations that they sought to represent. Many Afro-Latin Americans came to see the Black organizations as "closed clubs" more dedicated to the financial support of their staffs than to the improvement of their communities (Antón Sánchez 257; Andrews, *Blackness* 153). It also led, some observers suggest, to bitter rivalries among the organizations as they competed against each other for political influence and financial survival.

Cross-national contacts and conferences

If activist judgments on the effects of international funding are mixed, their judgments on a final area of cross-national contact and influences are entirely positive. These are the international meetings among Afro-Latin American organizations and activists that began in Cali, Colombia, in 1977 and that continue to the present. Working in conjunction with local Black organizations, Afro-Colombian author and activist Manuel Zapata Olivella gathered some 150 delegates from Latin America, the Caribbean, Africa, and the United States for the first *Congreso de la Cultura Negra de las Américas* (Correa Ochoa; Valero). Subsequent conferences were held in Panama City in 1980 (organized by Panamanian sociologist Gerardo Maloney), São Paulo in 1982 (organized by Abdias do Nascimento), and Montevideo in 1994 (organized by Romero Rodríguez, head of *Organizaciones Mundo Afro*). Each of these meetings generated enormous ferment and excitement among the participants, providing opportunities to share tactics and strategies and to discuss the challenges facing Black populations in different national contexts (Davis, Paschel, and Morrison; Nascimento).

Probably the most consequential of those international meetings was the *Conferencia Regional de las Américas*, held in Santiago, Chile, in 2000 in preparation for the UN World Conference on Racism held in South Africa the following year. At the Santiago meeting, Black organizations from around the hemisphere pressured their national governments to make serious commitments to combat racism and inequality. Confronting not only their own Black movements but a broad transnational front of Black activism from the region as a whole, a number of governments did in fact make such commitments, which in turn paved the way for affirmative action and other policies adopted in Brazil, Uruguay, Colombia, and other countries in the first two decades of the 2000s (Alberti and Pereira 358–391; Paschel, *Becoming* 122–132).

The local and the transnational: Black feminism

As we have seen, local and transnational conditions interacted in crosscutting ways to produce the Black movements of the late 1900s. Nowhere is this clearer than in the rise of Black women's organizations in the region.

Women had participated in Afro-Latin American civil and social organizations since their beginnings in the Catholic lay brotherhoods of the late colonial period. While white brotherhoods admitted women as non-voting dependents of male members, Black brotherhoods accorded women equal status as voting, dues-paying members. And "while supposedly occupying a secondary, auxiliary role in the Black social clubs and civic organizations" of the late 1800s, "women were in fact largely responsible for the maintenance of those organizations" (Andrews, *Blackness* 47; cf. Alberto, *Terms* 135).

This early pattern continued into the late 1900s. Discussing Black organizations in Ecuador, Antón Sánchez identified the "organizational capacity of Afro-Ecuadorian women" as one of the movement's "greatest strengths .... The political role [*protagonismo*] of Afro-Ecuadorian women has eclipsed that of the men" (Antón Sánchez 119–120). Escobar similarly comments on "the unusually high profile of women in some sectors of the black movements .... This is particularly the case with PCN [Proceso de Comunidades Negras, the country's principal Black organization], where women are among the most prominent, articulate, and well-regarded leaders" (Escobar 237).

That leadership role derived in part from a greater willingness to take on the day-to-day work involved in running any kind of organization. Anthropologist Kiran Asher found that

> it was mostly women who answered telephones, managed the books, and took care of running the offices at the PCN, Cococauca, and OBAPO [Organización de Barrios

> Populares del Chocó]. Many women in the PCN told me that it was mostly women who organized workshops, meetings, and mobilizations, often on shoestring budgets. They bought supplies, cooked and served food, and cleaned up after gatherings. When there was no running water at the Buenos Aires Palenque, it was the women who figured out how to address the problem. (Asher 137)[8]

As they carried out that work, however, many women felt that the organizations they were supporting were not paying sufficient attention to questions of gender or to such "women's" issues as domestic violence or reproductive health. At the same time, feminist movements and organizations run by middle- and upper-class white women were far more receptive to those issues but then tended to default on questions of race, declining to take up the class- and race-based challenges faced by poor Black women (Caldwell; Roland).

Developing the idea of "triple discrimination" (discrimination based on class, on race, and on gender), Afro-Brazilian theorists like Beatriz Nascimento, Lélia Gonzalez, Sueli Carneiro, and Edna Roland were anticipating the concept of intersectionality even before that concept had been formally articulated (by legal scholar Kimberlé Crenshaw, in 1989) (Paschel, "Rethinking" 212–214). Partly in response to that theorizing, but mainly in response to the everyday challenges of their lives, during the 1980s and 1990s Black women began to form their own organizations: *Geledés*, *Casa Dandara*, *Criola*, *Nzinga*, and *Fala Preta* in Brazil; the *Red de Mujeres Negras* in Colombia; the *Grupo de Apoyo a la Mujer Afrouruguaya* (GAMA) in Uruguay; the *Unión de Mujeres Negras de Venezuela*; the *Movimiento de Mujeres Negras de Esmeraldas* in Ecuador; and others. In 1988, Afro-Brazilian activists held the first *Encontro Nacional da Mulher Negra.* Four years later, in 1992, Black women's organizations from around the region met in the Dominican Republic for the first *Encuentro de la Mujer Negra.* At that meeting, activists created the transnational *Red de Mujeres Afrolatinoamericana, Afrocaribeña y de la Diáspora* (RMAAD), which continues to the present. Several members of RMAAD and other Afro-Latin American women's organizations attended the UN Conference on Women, held in 1995 in Beijing, which lent further impetus to Black feminist mobilization in the region (González Zambrano).

In these Black feminist organizations, we can see all the elements that went into the making of Afro-Latin American movements more broadly: the building on the historical foundation of previous mobilizations; the rise of a new generation of Afrodescendant intellectuals and professionals; the importance of national-level political openings; the influence of diasporic thinkers and events, including those associated with Black Power; support from international funders; and the role of cross-border contacts and collaborations within the region itself. Between 1970 and 2000, all of these elements came together to produce a wave of Black mobilization that, by the early 2000s, had definitively changed the political landscape of the region.

---

8 Cf. Keisha-Khan Perry's portrayal of women as "the black movement's foot soldiers" (*Black Women* 55–86).

Works cited

Afro-Latino-América. São Paulo: Fundação Perseu Abramo, 2014. Print.

Agudelo, Carlos. *Retos del multiculturalismo en Colombia: Política y poblaciones negras*. Medellín: La Carreta, 2005. Print.

Alberti, Verena, and Amilcar Araujo Pereira, eds. *Histórias do movimento negro no Brasil: Depoimentos ao CPDOC*. Rio de Janeiro: Pallas, 2007. Print.

Alberto, Paulina L. *Terms of Inclusion: Black Intellectuals in Twentieth-Century Brazil*. Chapel Hill: U of North Carolina P, 2011. Print.

———. "When Rio Was Black: Soul Music, National Culture, and the Politics of Racial Comparison in 1970s Brazil." *Hispanic American Historical Review* 89.1 (2009): 3–39. Print.

Alberto, Paulina L., George Reid Andrews, and Jesse Hoffnung-Garskof, eds. *Voices of the Race: Black Newspapers in Latin America, 1870–1960*. New York: Cambridge UP, 2022. Print.

Alberto, Paulina L., and Jesse Hoffnung-Garskof. "'Racial Democracy' and Racial Inclusion: Hemispheric Histories." *Afro-Latin American Studies: An Introduction*. Ed. Alejandro de la Fuente and George Reid Andrews. New York: Cambridge UP, 2018. 264–316. Print.

Andrews, George Reid. *Afro-Latin America, 1800–2000*. New York: Oxford UP, 2004. Print.

———. "Afro-World: African-Diaspora Thought and Practice in Montevideo, Uruguay, 1830–2000." *The Americas* 67.1 (Jul. 2010): 83–107. Print.

———. *Blackness in the White Nation: A History of Afro-Uruguay*. Chapel Hill: U of North Carolina P., 2010. Print.

Antón Sánchez, Jhon. *El proceso organizativo afroecuatoriano: 1979–2009*. Quito: FLACSO. Print.

Asher, Kiran. *Black and Green: Afro-Colombians, Development, and Nature in the Pacific Lowlands*. Durham: Duke UP, 2009. Print.

Becker, Marc. *Pachakutik: Indigenous Movements and Electoral Politics in Ecuador*. Lanham: Rowman & Littlefield, 2011. Print.

Bértola, Luis, and José Antonio Ocampo. *The Economic Development of Latin America since Independence*. New York: Oxford UP, 2012. Print.

Caldwell, Kia Lilly. *Negras in Brazil: Re-Envisioning Black Women, Citizenship, and the Politics of Identity*. New Brunswick: Rutgers UP, 2007. Print.

Contins, Márcia. *Lideranças negras*. Rio de Janeiro: Aeroplano, 2005. Print.

Correa Ochoa, Laura. "Manuel Zapata Olivella and the First Congress of Black Culture of the Americas." Cali, Colombia, 1977. Unpublished, 2019.

Crawford, Sharika. "'Under the Colombian Flag': Nation-Building on San Andrés and Providencia Islands, 1886–1930." PhD dissertation. University of Pittsburgh, 2009. Print.

Davis, Darién, Tianna Paschel, and Judith Morrison. "Pan-Afro-Latin African Americanism Revisited: Legacies and Lessons for Transnational Alliances in the New Millennium." *Afro-Descendants, Identity, and the Struggle for Development in the Americas*. Ed. Bernd Reiter and Kimberly Eison Simmons. East Lansing: Michigan State UP., 2012. 19–48. Print.

De la Fuente, Alejandro, ed. *Grupo Antillano: The Art of Afro-Cuba*. Pittsburgh: Caguayo, 2013. Print.

De la Torre, Carlos, and Jhon Antón Sánchez. "Afro-Ecuadorian Politics." *Comparative Racial Politics in Latin America*. Ed. Kwame Dixon and Ollie A. Johnson III. New York: Routledge, 2019. 163–182. Print.

Escobar, Arturo. *Territories of Difference: Place, Movements, Life, Redes*. Durham: Duke UP, 2008. Print.

Fernandes, Sujatha. *Cuba Represent! Cuban Arts, State Power, and the Making of New Revolutionary Cultures*. Durham: Duke UP, 2006. Print.

Flórez-Bolívar, Francisco. "En sus propios términos: Negros y mulatos y sus luchas por la igualdad en Colombia, 1885–1947." PhD dissertation. University of Pittsburgh, 2017. Print.

Geler, Lea. *Andares negros, caminos blancos: Afroporteños, Estado y Nación. Argentina a fines del siglo XIX*. Rosario: Prohistoria, 2010. Print.

González Zambrano, Catalina. "Mulheres negras em movimento: Ativismo transnacional na América Latina (1980–1995)." PhD dissertation. Universidade de São Paulo, 2017. Print.

Helg, Aline. *Slave No More: Slave Liberation before Abolitionism in the Americas*. Trans. Lara Vergnaud. Chapel Hill: U of North Carolina P, 2019. Print.

Hernández, Tanya Katarí. *Racial Subordination in Latin America: The Role of the State, Customary Law, and the New Civil Rights Response*. New York: Cambridge UP, 2013. Print.

Johnson, Ollie A. "Black Activism in Ecuador, 1979–2009." *Comparative Perspectives on Afro-Latin America*. Ed. Kwame Dixon and John Burdick. Gainesville: U of Florida P, 2012. 176–197. Print.

Kramer, Jane. "Letter from the Elysian Fields." *New Yorker* (2 Mar. 1987): 40–75. Print.

McCann, Bryan. "Black Pau: Uncovering the History of Brazilian Soul." *Journal of Popular Music Studies* 14 (2002): 33–62. Print.

Nascimento, Elisa Larkin. "Pan-Africanism and Latin America." *Comparative Racial Politics in Latin America*. Ed. Kwame Dixon and Ollie A. Johnson III. New York: Routledge, 2019. 64–85. Print.

Offen, Karl. "Environment, Space, and Place: Cultural Geographies of Colonial Afro-Latin America." *Afro-Latin American Studies: An Introduction*. Ed. Alejandro de la Fuente and George Reid Andrews. New York: Cambridge UP, 2018. 486–533. Print.

Pappademos, Melina. *Black Political Activism and the Cuban Republic*. Chapel Hill: U of North Carolina P, 2011. Print.

Paschel, Tianna S. *Becoming Black Political Subjects: Movements and Ethno-Racial Rights in Colombia and Brazil*. Princeton: Princeton UP, 2016. Print.

———. "Rethinking Black Political Mobilization in Latin America." *Afro-Latin American Studies: An Introduction*. Ed. Alejandro de la Fuente and George Reid Andrews. New York: Cambridge UP, 2018. 222–263. Print.

Pereira, Amilcar Araujo. *O mundo negro: Relações raciais e a constituição do movimento negro contemporâneo no Brasil*. Rio de Janeiro: Pallas, 2013. Print.

Perry, Keisha-Khan. *Black Women against the Land Grab: The Fight for Racial Justice in Brazil*. Minneapolis: U of Minnesota P, 2013. Print.

Perry, Marc D. *Negro Soy Yo: Hip Hop and Raced Citizenship in Cuba*. Durham: Duke UP, 2015. Print.

Priestley, George. "Antillean-Panamanians or Afro-Panamanians? Political Participation and the Politics of Identity during the Carter-Torrijos Treaty Negotiations." *Transforming Anthropology* 12.1–2 (2004): 50–67. Print.

Rahier, Jean Muteba. "Afro-Ecuadorian Community Organizing and Political Struggle: Influences on and Participation in Constitutional Processes." *Comparative Perspectives on Afro-Latin America*. Ed. Kwame Dixon and John Burdick. Gainesville: U of Florida P, 2012a. 198–218. Print.

———. "Interview with Maria Inês Barbosa, Former Vice-Minister, Secretaria Especial de Políticas de Promoção da Igualdade Racial (SEPPIR), Brazil." *Black Social Movements in Latin America: From Monocultural Mestizaje to Multiculturalism*. Ed. Jean Muteba Rahier. New York: Palgrave Macmillan, 2012b. 213–224. Print.

Roland, Edna. "O movimento de mulheres negras brasileiras: Desafios e perspectivas." *Tirando a máscara: Ensaios sobre o racismo no Brasil*. Ed. Antonio Sérgio Alfredo Guimarães and Lynn Huntley. São Paulo: Paz e Terra, 2000. Print.

Saunders, Tanya L. *Cuban Underground Hip Hop: Black Thoughts, Black Revolution, Black Modernity*. Austin: U of Texas P, 2015. Print.

Sawyer, Mark. *Racial Politics in Post-Revolutionary Cuba*. New York: Cambridge UP, 2006. Print.

Seigel, Micol. *Uneven Encounters: Making Race and Nation in Brazil and the United States*. Durham: Duke UP, 2009. Print.

Valero, Silvia. *"Los negros se toman la palabra": Primer Congreso de la Cultura Negra de las Américas*. Bogotá: Editorial Pontificia Universidad Javeriana, 2020. Print.

Vinson, Ben. *Bearing Arms for His Majesty: The Free-Colored Militia in Colonial Mexico*. Stanford: Stanford UP, 2001. Print.

Walsh, Catherine. "Affirmative Action(ing)s and Postneoliberal Movement in South America and Ecuador." *Cultural Dynamics* (2014): 1–23. Print.

———. "Afro In/Exclusion, Resistance, and the 'Progressive State: (De)Colonial Struggles, Questions, and Reflections." *Black Social Movements in Latin America: From Monocultural Mestizaje to Multiculturalism*. Ed. Jean Muteba Rahier. New York: Palgrave Macmillan, 2012. 15–34. Print.

Black Power Cubano – African American and Afro-Cuban Movements between Solidarity, Repression, and Contradictions[1]

ALBERTO ABREU ARCIA

Very little research has been done on the movement known as *Black Power Cubano.* This group was made up of young Afro-Cuban men and women from the intellectual field and other circuits close to the political and diplomatic structures of revolutionary Cuba. They fell out of favor with the regime when, inspired by the black movement of the 1960s in the United States, they began to address the taboo subject of racism in a socialist state. There is only scarce research on the impact that their encounters with radical Black Power and Black Panther leaders and activists who visited or escaped to Cuba had on their awareness of racial identity. Obviously, the history of relations between black movements in Cuba and the United States is inseparable from the extremely strained relations between both states after the Revolution of 1959 and the failed U.S. invasion at the Bay of Pigs of 1961. It is also intrinsically linked to the political pacts and alliances forged in the 1960s between a very influential part of the African American movement and the Cuban government which continue to this day.

While aspects of this transnational alliance have been analyzed by Ruth Reitan (1999) and others, little is known about the practices of political and ideological intimidation that suppressed the small burgeoning Afro-Cuban movement. These intimidation tactics culminated in the nefarious provisions on cultural policy emanating from the *Primer Congreso de Educación y Cultura* [First Congress of Education and Culture] (1970) that institutionalized a series of repressive regulations and symbolic violence, which led to the devaluation of many artistic expressions and religious practices that bore the imprint of Cuban *black popular culture.* In what follows, I will attempt to explore some gestures that highlight the influence of the U.S. Black Power movement and organizations such as the Black Panthers on the will of Afro-Cuban intellectuals of those years to articulate an autonomous racial discourse.

Between 1959 and 1961, the heated debates on racial non-discrimination, racism, and the place of blacks and *mulatos* in the nascent revolutionary society dominated a good part of the speeches of Fidel Castro and other political leaders such as Ernesto Che Guevara, Carlos Rafael Rodriguez, and others who hinted at how blacks and *mulatos* had benefitted from the new laws dictated by the Revolution that sought equity and social justice. It was a discussion that reached magazines, newspapers, and other mass media and in which Afro-Cuban intellectuals such as Juan René Betancourt,

1 Translation by Ann-Kathrin Lauer and Matti Steinitz.

Salvador Gastón Agüero, Nicolás Guillén, Elias Entralgo, among others, participated. In 1961, Afro-Cuban communist Walterio Carbonell, a friend and admirer of Fidel Castro, published his influential essay *Cómo surgió la cultura nacional* [How the national culture emerged] (1961), in which he traced African contributions to Cuban national culture and analyzed power relations in nineteenth-century Cuba from a Marxist perspective, arguing that the fundamental contradiction of Cuban society at the time was the relationship between slaveholders and the enslaved, rather than that between the metropolis and the colony. In the 1960s, his considerations on the birth of Cuban nationality aroused controversy among Cuban intellectuals, constituting one of the reasons for his exclusion from these circles later in the decade. Starting with the process of Sovietization of Cuban culture, the simple and politically comfortable perception inherited from Marxism that racism was solely a product of capitalism became generalized in both political and institutional academic discourse. If racism was the product of a society divided into classes, a phenomenon the country had left behind with the revolutionary triumph of January 1, 1959, then there was no reason for racism to exist.

In February 1962, Fidel Castro's government issued the *Second Declaration of Havana* affirming that the Revolution had eliminated in Cuba "discrimination based on race or sex." Overnight, without much effort, barely two years after coming to power, the nascent Revolution solves by decree the legacy of more than two centuries of slavery and colonial rule. Racism and racial discrimination in Cuba, a phenomenon strongly rooted in the popular imaginary, nationalist discourses, and the structures and models of thought of the Cuban nation, was declared overcome. This assertion was reproduced in political discourse, in official texts, in school teaching, and in all normative documents of the nascent Revolution. I agree with Alejandro de la Fuente when he observes that the "initial campaign against racism waned after 1962; there was a growing public silence around the issue except to highlight Cuba's success in this area" (356). What was the subject of a fruitful and stimulating debate in the early years of the Revolution became a taboo topic (356).

Historical alliances: Cuba and the African American freedom struggle

The image of Cuba as a country that had successfully overcome racism seduced many African American intellectuals and public figures who, between 1959 and 1961, visited the island at the invitation of the government as part of "Operation Truth" to learn about the achievements of the Revolution. As Cuban historian Alejandro de la Fuente points out, "Black journalists recognized the Revolution's efforts to eliminate racism and gave coverage to Fidel Castro's public statements against discrimination and racism" (380). The campaign was a success, especially in view of the comparisons between what the Cuban Revolution had achieved in its first two years of life, and the context of the struggle of African Americans in the United States. Of course, the climax of these attempts of the nascent Revolution to reach the sympathy of African American freedom fighters was reached in October 1960, when Fidel Castro at the head of the Cuban delegation to the United Nations decided to stay at the Theresa Hotel in Harlem where he also met Malcolm X. It was the beginning of a political pact between Cuba and U.S.-black radicals that extended into the twenty-first century.

In the 1960s, revolutionary Cuba became a source of inspiration and a safe haven for black radicals from the United States. The Cuban government was well aware that highlighting racial segregation in the United States and portraying itself as an uncompromising ally of the African American cause was of great use in the propagandistic confrontation between two models of society that characterized the Cold War. Tensions arose when these black expats from the United States started to criticize persistent patterns of racism in socialist Cuba. The first, and one of the most prominent African American refugees was Robert F. Williams, a NAACP organizer from Monroe, North Carolina, who had caused outrage within and outside the Civil Rights movement because of his advocacy for armed self-defense against the Ku Klux Klan and the racist local police force. Falsely accused of kidnapping, he arrived in Cuba in 1961 after spectacularly escaping from the security forces of the U.S. government. During his stay, the Cuban government granted him the facilities to host the Radio Free Dixie program, from which he broadcast is radical ideas to the south of the United States (Tyson). In 1965, Williams left Cuba after experiencing certain tensions with officials of the Ministry of the Interior. He continued his exile in China, from where he sent a letter to Fidel Castro in September 1966. María Isabel Alfonso has been able to trace these sources:

> In the missive, he refers to conflicts with Osmany Cienfuegos, Commander René Vallejo and Vice Minister of the Interior Manuel Piñeiro, who neglected and boycotted, according to Williams, his struggle for the Afro-American cause. He does not speak of racism in that letter, but I have found in the Robert Williams Papers archive other letters of his referring to the fact that he was discriminated against by Cuban authorities. (Alfonso 118)

The abrupt departure of Williams did not result in a rupture of the alliance between radical African American activists and the Cuban government. All to the contrary, in 1967, Black Power leader Stokely Carmichael was officially invited to attend the first OLAS [Latin American Organization of Solidarity] conference in Havana (cf. Carbone, "The United States"; and her essay in this volume). While praising the unity of anti-racist and anti-imperialist struggles in the United States and the Third World in his speech at OLAS, he was disappointed by the way in which the racial problem was treated in Cuba. For Carmichael, it was a mistake to think that the dissolution of social classes was the way to progressively eliminate racism. In 1968, the Cuban government enthusiastically invited the Black Panther Party's Minister of Information Eldridge Cleaver to Cuba when he had become a fugitive after an armed clash with Oakland police during which two police officers were wounded and the Party's youngest member Bobby Hutton was killed. Cleaver was welcomed as an exile and treated like a foreign dignitary until he decided to organize a Cuban chapter of the Black Panther Party, erroneously believing that Fidel Castro would support his idea of training African American revolutionaries for guerrilla warfare in the United States. Eventually, under pressure from the authorities, he had to leave the island and went to Algeria (Brent 174). While Carmichael and Cleaver openly criticized the persistence of racism under socialism, these tensions did not halt the influx of black fugitives from the United States. Still, there were significant differences in the way African American refugees were treated. In 1969, Black Panther William Lee Brent hijacked an airplane from Oakland to New York City and forced its landing in Cuba where he was not greeted with open arms but spent 22 months in an immigration jail. Although deeply critical of racial discrimination and the lack of freedom of speech in Cuba, he stayed as an exile until his death in 2006 (Brent). Today, the most prominent representative of the U.S. black radical exile community in Cuba is Assata Shakur, a former member of the Black Liberation Army (BLA), who was convicted for the murder of a New Jersey State Trooper in 1973 and managed to escape from prison in 1979, resurfacing in Cuba in 1984. In 2013, she was the first woman to be added to the FBI Most Wanted Terrorists list and there is a $2 million reward for her apprehension. Repeated demands for her extradition by U.S. authorities have been rejected by the Cuban government (Shakur).

Nationalism, *mestizaje*, and censorship in 1960s Cuba

The contradictions between the Cuban revolutionary government's external policy of embracing the African American freedom struggle in the United States and supporting anti-colonial movements in the Third World and its internal repression of critical black voices first came to display when the alternative publishing house *Ediciones El Puente* was disbanded in 1965. Founded in 1961, the self-financed publisher released the works of a group of young authors, mainly made up of women, gays, lesbians, and Afro-Cuban writers. This group included influential writers such as José Mario Rodríguez, Ana María Simo, Reinaldo García Ramos, Gerardo Fulleda, Eugenio Hernández, Rogelio Martínez Furé, Georgina Herrera, Belkis Cuza Malé, and Nancy Morejón. It was characterized by its inclusive aesthetics, the way it managed the inclusion of writing gestures and subjects that until then had been considered as subaltern by the codes of our literary canon (Abreu, *La cuentística*; Barquet).

It was the guardians of this canon who brought down this project on the basis of a series of false accusations still found in Cuban literary historiography. It is significant that one of the arguments used by literary critics in the 1970s and 1980s to justify the banishment of *Ediciones El Puente* from the nation's literary memory and dictionaries of Cuban literature aimed at mapping a genealogy of post-revolutionary literature was that this group of young writers wanted to foment a Black Power movement in Cuba. This accusation is only sustained by virtue of the prominent presence of black writers within that group, since at the time when Stokely Carmichael first issued his call for Black Power in 1966, official policy had already decreed the closure of *El Puente*. This argument, besides lacking the most elementary historical basis, illustrates the racist bases on which the post-revolutionary literary canon was built.

The desire to build a *different* nation and a new project of modernity based on ideas about nationalism, identity, and national culture which were summarized in the paradigm of a *mestizo* or *mulato* nation, subsumed all racial and cultural differences. As a consequence, the white Eurocentric cultural matrix continued to play its hegemonic and exclusionary role. This was achieved not only through a cultural policy that operated as a device of ideological integration, but also through a series of cultural aporias and blackmails that depicted manifestations of black popular culture as symptoms of cultural degradation. For example: while institutions such as *Departamento de Folklore del Teatro Nacional de Cuba*, *Instituto Nacional de Etnología y Folklore*, its magazine, *Etnología y Folklore* and the *Conjunto Folklórico Nacional* were created to rescue and preserve the African cultural heritage, they were also instrumental in reducing black popular culture to the condition of archive, folklore, patrimony – something archaic. This meant that the same movement which was committed to recognizing the contributions of the African component to the construction of the national identity implicitly carried a kidnapping of black Cuba's autonomy and cultural differences, of its secular gestures of counter-memory, interpellation, and resistance to the white hegemonic culture which had allowed it to survive for centuries.

The academic and institutional discourse – in complicity with the political field – constructed a series of metaphors-concepts of transculturation such as *color cubano*, *ajiaco*, *mulatez*, and *mestizaje* that responded to the political purpose of building a homogeneous national subject that allowed the nascent revolutionary state to reabsorb, from its center of power, the identity differences that were an obstacle to its unified exercise of power. Consequently, the discourses and practices related to the staging of blackness, be they religious or cultural, became incompatible with the paradigms of the new symbolic order coming from Marxist aesthetics and philosophy, and were stigmatized by the modernizing discourse of the Revolution under the argument that they were expressions of prejudice, ignorance, superstition, etc. So much so that it is possible, today, to read the concept of *black popular culture* as that *other* story suppressed by official history and post-revolutionary literate reasoning.

A burgeoning Afro-Cuban movement: the specter of *Black Power Cubano*

The contrast between Cuba's foreign policy, shaped by excellent relations and solidarity with leaders of the Black Power movement, the Black Panthers, and African nations on the one hand, and the tabooing of topics related to racism and blackness within the revolutionary society on the other, could not have been sharper. According to Clarisbel Gómez Vasallo, the attentive look of some Afro-Cuban intellectuals, academics, and artists to the struggle carried out by black men and women in the U.S. civil society allowed some of them to

> turn their eyes again to the interior of the Cuban society and to try to rescue the debate on the racial problem, but the efforts did not bear fruit. It was difficult that this could happen under the predominance of certain political and scientific criteria that denied the

> existence of tensions in the interracial relations of the country, with the canalization of these opinions in the Cuban popular ideology. (Gómez Vasallo 140)

In the midst of this scenario, the recently constituted *Instituto Cubano del Libro* published a group of texts including, in addition to African novelists, a compilation of essays by LeRoi Jones, James Baldwin, Stokely Carmichael, Martin Luther King, as well as the *Autobiography* of Malcolm X – books whose translation and dissemination fostered the process of racial consciousness among a group of young Afro-Cuban intellectuals of those years.

Displaying the contradictions between the militant anti-racism of the Black Power movement and the homogenizing nationalist impulse of the Cuban Communist Party, many of the African American leaders who were in Cuba expressed their criticism of the Cuban Revolution's treatment of racial issues. These were not well seen by the Cuban authorities. De la Fuente examines these tensions between the Cuban government and the leaders of the U.S. black movement in their transit through the island during these years: "In any case, the militants sent messages to ordinary Cubans that were not always convenient for the authorities: messages from fighters whose purposes, struggles and doctrines were defined in racial terms" (De la Fuente 287). This occurred in a politically complex scenario, just when "the Communist Party and the Cuban authorities were discouraging, if not repressing, Afro-Cuban cultural expressions such as their religiosity" (287). According to de la Fuente, the visit that Carmichael made to Cuba in 1967 had "a significant impact among Afro-Cubans, who 'apparently watched and listened to him with particular intensity.' Some adopted some of the external symbols of these militants – such as the Afro-style hair – and perhaps part of the essence of his preaching" (287).

Afro-Cuban intellectuals who lived through this period, such as Rogelio Martínez Furé, Nancy Morejón, Sara Gómez, and Gisela Arandia, confirmed to me in interviews and conversations that they started to wear an Afro in the 1960s. In Cuba, the Afro was referred to as the *espendrún*, a way of wearing the hair naturally that responded to the slogan "Black is Beautiful." It was popularized by numerous artists and African and African American political activists such as Miriam Makeba during the period she lived as an exile in the United States, Angela Davis, and musicians such as James Brown and The Jackson Five, as a way of vindicating black aesthetics against the dominant white beauty patterns. In the case of Cuba, Afro-feminist writer Inés María Martiatu tells us that Sara Gómez "was the first black woman in Cuba to wear her hair natural. She was congratulated by the then Afro-American student leader Stokely Carmichael as the first free head in Cuba" (Martiatu n. pag.). Poet Eloy Machado ("El Ambia") recalls his participation in a group of Afro-Cuban activists and thinkers who met to study and discuss texts "that dealt with black issues" (Howe, "La producción cultural" 88) by the likes of Malcolm X and Frantz Fanon. These gestures shed light on the ways the messages, texts, and conversations with the leaders of the Black Power movement had an impact on black Cubans in the 1960s.

As various accounts of the era suggest, some of these young Afro-Cuban intellectuals tried to elaborate a document on race and culture in Cuba to be discussed at the *Congreso Cultural* in Havana, 1968. De la Fuente notes that "unconfirmed reports assert that blacks tried to articulate, in various ways, some kind of autonomous discourse, but always met with official resistance" (387). In the following, I would like to investigate both the presumed existence of this "autonomous discourse" to which this quote alludes and the "official resistance" that suppressed the will of the Afro-Cuban intellectuals of the 1960s and 1970s to articulate an alternative to the official discourse on race.

Asked about the existence of a group referred to as *Black Power Cubano*, Cuban historian Juan F. Benemelis, who lives in exile, told me in an interview he gave me some years ago:

> There were two tendencies or aspects. One, let's call it cultural, whose actors came mainly from the field of ethnographic research and artistic and literary creation such as Sara Gómez, Tomas González, Pedro Pérez Sarduy (Abreu, "El Black Power" n. pag.).

According to Benemelis, members of the other, more politically oriented, side were much closer to the state structures in those first decades of the Revolution:

> In the case of ours, that is to say of this last group from which I come, we were political leaders and diplomats. We had a direct relationship with Africa and the Caribbean, with their leaders and thinkers. I, for example, worked at the MINREX [Foreign Ministry]. [Among the members of this line were] Manuel Casanova, Felino René Goyre, Iván Cesar Martínez, Juan Domenesch, who was the most fervent defender of *négritude* in the style of Cesaire and Senghor among us. There were also Ramiro de la Cuesta, Ernesto González, Walterio Carbonell, Santiago Boullón, Irmina Iglesias, Miguel Conill, Juan Bumell, Justo Fuente, Gerardo Cesar Proenza. Martha Jean Claude and René Depestre were very close to us. On the other hand, this group was joined by some plastic artists such as painter Juan Boza, and sculptors Kueneditt, Cobas, José Francisco Fowler, whose works dealt with themes related to the Afro-Cuban identity. We met at the house of a pianist, who was called Mario El Americano. Or at my house behind the *Arenal* movie theater. That was every Saturday night. (Abreu, "El Black Power" n. pag.)

Further on Benemelies clarifies:

> Another important fact was our personal relationship with Afro-American leaders from the United States who were in Cuba like Robert Williams, Brent of the *Black Panthers*. We met many of them. The discussions and personal conversations with other intellectuals and international black leaders were decisive. We were not in the mood for violent rebellion. The *Black Power* label was, on the one hand, a way of indicating a racial belonging, and on the other hand, it could be said that it was a symbolic way of calling attention to ourselves, making ourselves visible as a group. Which also shows you that we had reached a state of asphyxia in the search for a space to dialogue, to debate the issue. That moment was more neuralgic if we compare it with today. Regrettably, we did not achieve any space. (n. pag.)

Until today, Afro-Cuban intellectuals and artists who, during the second half of the 1960s and early 1970s, tried to build a racially differentiated place of enunciation within the intellectual field of the island refuse to write down their memories or speak publicly about those facts. For many, these are events whose evocation is traumatic. Afro-Cuban playwright Tomás González remembers:

> What was for me the possibility of living a happy and fulfilled life went to my head, like a kite of furious colors. [It all began when I presented] a paper written in two pages, in which I exposed my criteria on the problems for the development of national culture in our country. I said that blacks and whites were not in equal conditions for the integration of their cultural contributions. Racial discrimination cannot be erased with a decree. (González n. pag.)

In the referred document several examples were cited: "From the blonde doll in the arms of a black girl, how in a cast for a novel or for a classic the actors and actresses could not be black, the thousand ways of considering the black a savage and brute being that 'if he doesn't make it on the way in, he makes it on the way out.' The reaction against these arguments was extraordinary." He relates how:

> A majority of white Cubans were asking for me to be thrown to the lions of the Roman circus, with a thumbs down. Of course, this had serious consequences for me, I was left without employment and salary for some years, during the time that José Llanusa[2] was minister. For that speech I was considered as the leader of a *Poder Negro* [Black Power] movement in Cuba, in the style of [U.S.] Black Power and with ramifications in the 'negritude' of our friend Césaire, the great poet of Martinique. From that moment on, I was an outcast. In the midst of this dark time, one of my daughters died. Time went by and one day I was summoned to an ideological commission of the Party. … They would watch me for a long time. I worked for free at the theater and was not paid a salary. Not eight hours, but many more. … When they gave me a salary again, it was the minimum. All this happens until the arrival of Torquemada, who summons me to the Palacio del Segundo Cabo in Havana into a dark office, with a small lamp directed at my face. He told me that my Hamlet was *negrista* because the actors I had chosen were black. This time, I was transferred to keep me away from the theater. To go back singing in the Benny Moré band all over the country. (n. pag.)

It seems that Tomás González's account mixes two events: the 1968 *Congreso Cultural de La Habana* and the 1970 *Congreso Nacional de Educación y Cultura*. Inés María Martiatu, a personal friend of González and witness of those events, sheds light on those facts:

> At the preparatory seminar for the *Congreso Cultural de La Habana*, at the *Congreso Nacional de Educación y Cultura* and wherever he was heard, Tomás expressed his opinion about the way in which the contribution and presence of elements of the African Diaspora were relegated in the cultural field. He denounced the low percentage of blacks in the television image and in the National Ballet of Cuba or the uproar against works such as the brilliant *María Antonia* by Eugenio Hernández Espinosa. (Martiatu n. pag.)

González also lamented the existence of "only white and blond mannequins in the store windows and something he considered very serious, that no black dolls were manufactured in Cuba. Of course, the attacks were almost unanimous. Some people

2 Then Minister of Education and President of the Cultural Congress of Havana.

were against this views, and others simply did not want to get into trouble" (González n. pag.). Black artists and intellectuals, including Tomás González and Walterio Carbonell, had also debated in private and academic circles the presence and participation of Afro-Cuban intellectuals and the inclusion of African and black history in Cuba in the curricula of all levels of education. As a result of these demands, "they were repressed, they were accused of fomenting a 'Black Power' in Cuba," as Martiatu points out. She was told by Sara Gómez that

> Tomás González and ethnologist Alberto Pedro Díaz were summoned and warned by then Minister of Education José Llanusa for alleged activities diverging from the ideological line of the Revolution for having raised these and other demands. Party officials discussed these issues with Rogelio Martínez Furé, Tomás González and Alberto Pedro Díaz in individual interviews. Many more intellectuals and even black diplomats were involved in this process. Sara Gómez continued working at ICAIC [Instituto Cubano del Arte e Industria Cinematográficos] but her works were not exhibited. Alberto Pedro Díaz stayed at the *Academia de Ciencias* for many years. That experience is undoubtedly the reason why he did not want to publish any book and even left to his heirs the prohibition to do so after his death many years later. (Martiatu n. pag.)

On the other hand, Benemelis assured that other intellectuals such as Manolo Casanova, Santiago Boullon, Walterio Carbonell, and he himself also had papers prepared for the Congress. Regarding this, Inés Martiatu states: "I understand that Walterio suggested to Franqui the idea of taking this work commission to the congress, but Franqui was not the person to decide on this matter. He then presented it to Llanusa's people" (n. pag.).

The "Black Manifesto" and the silencing of Afro-Cuban voices at *Congreso Cultural de La Habana* (1968)

These accounts explain the paralysis, fear, and frustration that permeated the discussion of matters related to race in Cuba from the end of the 1960s until the first half of the 1980s. Until today, people assume a kind of myth or speculation around what Linda S. Howe and Carlos Moore have denominated the "Black Manifesto" (Howe, *Transgression*; Moore, *Castro*). Benemelis, for his part, assured me of the Manifesto's existence: "Yes, I remember that Manolito Casanova came to my house one afternoon carrying it. That was before the '68 congress. Walterio was very stimulated with this congress and with the idea of creating a commission to discuss the Cuban racial problem. The manifesto focused on issues related to the obstacles for *mulatos* and the quest for equality" (Abreu, "El Black Power" n. pag.). Consulted about the existence of this manifesto, Pedro Pérez Sarduy affirms that it is a paper of which he keeps a typed copy and where everyone "participated in the elaboration of ideas. Especially Sarita [Sara Gómez] who was very sharp. The so-called Black Manifesto was never such a thing .... It was a paper to the Congress" (Pérez).[3]

3 Consultation made via email on May 9, 2017.

The mentioned intellectuals envisioned the *Congreso Cultural de La Habana* held between January 5 and 12, 1968, to become a decisive platform for the staging of this autonomous discourse on blackness in Cuba. It is worth remembering that the convocation to this Congress was approved and signed by the militants, artists, and European intellectuals who attended the festivities of July 26 in Havana and the OLAS conference held between July 31 and August 10, 1967. The *Congreso Cultural* aimed to break the isolation of Cuban intellectuals by putting them in contact with the most radical currents of thought and the main avant-garde currents: "After the Tricontinental and OLAS, the *Congreso Cultural* marks the third stage of a long-term action to build a 'world front against imperialism'" (Gilman 118).

Carlos Moore, an exile and prominent critic of racism in Cuba,[4] holds that this group of young Afro-Cuban intellectuals and artists were excluded from the *Congreso Cultural* after the conference organizers became aware that they had been meeting to discuss the Cuban government's lack of action against racism, a problem the revolutionary leaders claimed to have solved with the abolition of racial segregation in the 1960s. In response to a rumor that these intellectuals had drafted a programmatic document on race and culture in Cuba for the Congress, Minister of Education José Llanusa called them to chapter in a private meeting a couple of days before the Congress began. After hearing their criticisms, Llanusa accused them of being "seditious" and told them that the "revolution" would not allow them to create a racial "gap" in the Cuban people. He explained that the very idea of their "black manifesto" was a provocation from which they would have to retract or face the consequences (Farber n. pag.).

The congress terminated the attempts of Afro-Cuban activists to put the issue of persistent anti-black racism on the agenda of Cuban government policy, and a long period followed in which the articulation of black perspectives retreated to the realm of culture. Between the 1970s and the first half of the 1980s, themes and issues related to Cuba's racial problems were addressed through the solitary work and gestures of resistance of black artists and intellectuals such as Sara Gómez and Nicolás Guillén Landrián in the cinema, the visual discourse of Manuel Mendive, the poems of Excilia Saldaña, Nancy Morejón, Pedro Pérez Sarduy, and Georgina Herrera, the narrative of Manolo Granados, the plays of Alberto Pedro, Gerardo Fulleda, Eugenio Hernández, Tomás González, and Alberto Pedro, and the research and teaching of Rogelio Martínez Furé. The approaches of these authors and artists to issues of black racial identity are not exempt from discursive veils, compromises, and negotiations with the hegemonic cultural canon. They also had to deal with the silence and indifference of critics

4 Carlos Moore, Afro-Cuban descendant of Jamaican migrants was living as a migrant in New York when the Cuban Revolution took place. As a staunch supporter, he returned to the island in 1961 and worked for the Cuban government as a translator for the ministries of Communications and External Affairs. When he started to criticize the persistence of racism under socialism, he was arrested and could only leave the island thanks to the intervention of Robert F. Williams on his behalf. As an exile in Paris, he got in touch with Malcolm X and other black radicals and made himself a name as an ardent critic of Cuban socialism from a Pan-African perspective (Moore, *Pichón*).

who refused to talk about them as Afro-Cuban authors. These creators, as a strategy, elaborated an ideo-aesthetic proposal that moved within the utopian and redemptive dimension of the post-revolutionary aesthetic discourse, while intersecting the political, the historical, and the conjunctural with the revaluation of the cultural and religious African heritage in Cuba. Their work remains a significant project insofar as it allowed the representation and consequent problematization of a group of themes and issues related to the survival of expressions of blackness.

Período especial and beyond: deepening inequalities and the re-emergence of an Afro-Cuban movement (1990s to the present)

Whereas the absence of discernible articulations of anti-racist critique in the 1970s and 1980s proved the effectiveness of the Cuban government's efforts to silence dissident voices from the black movement, the collapse of the Soviet Union heralded a new era in Cuban race relations. During the so-called *período especial* [special period], the economic situation deteriorated significantly, producing a profound crisis that disproportionately affected Afro-Cuban communities. Unequal access to remittances from abroad and opportunities in the rising tourism industry, the gentrification of mostly black neighborhoods in Havana, and other aspects contributed to the deepening of existing racial hierarchies and prejudices and a growing discontent among Afro-Cuban youth. It is in this context that several grassroots initiatives aimed at creating autonomous platforms of expression for Afro-Cuban dissident voices emerged, among them hip-hop bands, cultural groups, as well as anti-racist and Afro-feminist projects such as Sandra Abd'Allah Álvarez Ramírez' blog *Negra Cubana Tenía Que Ser* and the magazine *Afrocubanas* (Álvarez; Rubiera et al.).

Currently, what I call the Afro-Cuban movement is characterized by a deterritorialized geography. New groups such as *Alianza Afrocubana* are led by young people who bring their own visions and ways of conceiving not only their racial identity, but also the intersections between anti-racist struggle and sexual dissidence. The movement is not limited to the activism carried out from leftist positions, which, although recognizing the contributions of the Revolution in matters of racial equality, believe that these are not enough and maintain a critical stance in this regard. This movement also includes other groups of political dissidents such as *Comité Ciudadano por la Integración Racial* [Citizens' Committee for Racial Integration] and projects such as *Beyond Roots Cuba*, which is dedicated to promoting an aesthetic of the black body. It is not limited to the groups that operate on the island, but also encompasses actors and voices from the diaspora, from the public sphere of the blogosphere, and other social networks. It is typical of a post-national scenario and a region crossed by multiple intellectual and symbolic practices. As can be inferred, these subjects and social actors are not a uniform block, on the contrary: they make up a heterogeneous and complex map. They not only speak from different generational experiences, religious and political creeds, gender identities, and diverse enunciative media, but also come from the most dissimilar areas of society, culture, and knowledge. From this polyphony they articulate the story of their memories, as well as their questions, concerns, and proposals on the place and future of the racialized black body in the Cuban nation.

Breaking the taboo of talking about race in Cuba, these groups have addressed the manifold dimensions of persistent racism on the island. The innumerable investigations, academic theses, case studies, books, and articles that have appeared in the country since the 1990s devoted to the analysis of marginality, social exclusion, and the racial dimension in the processes of reproduction of poverty show alarming indicators for the black population. These phenomena have their origin in disarticulations and cumulative deficiencies – of all kinds – that feed back synchronically and diachronically.

Due to adverse socioeconomic and family conditions, all studies on social disadvantage and marginality show that blacks are overrepresented. The studies agree that the Afro-Cuban population is among the most vulnerable groups in the field of health, income, and housing conditions. In general, there is an above-average representation of black people in improvised housing and in shantytowns. Case studies of families living in poverty – among which the black and *mulato* population is in the majority – show the precariousness of their housing and the impairment of basic services to be an inherent characteristic of this condition. They are underrepresented in the completion of higher education and overrepresented in prisons. At the same time, they receive the least remittances from abroad. These indicators provide clear evidence of deep gaps in terms of equality. To these data we must add others such as the lack of material wealth, the overrepresentation of blacks in the poverty line, constituting a characteristic that affects black families throughout different generations because they are historically discriminated against and have the least resources. On the other hand, research carried out by the *Instituto de Antropología* found that blacks and *mulatos* are underrepresented in certain advantageous segments of the current Cuban labor structure, unlike whites who are not only more represented in the emerging sectors of the economy, but also have a majority presence as leaders, both in this sector and in the traditional – not revived – ones. Consequentially, the survival strategies of blacks depend more on personal effort and are carried out with scarce resources and without the support of remittances sent by relatives in exile. Against this backdrop it is no coincidence that black and *mulato* youth are among the most visible in the recent wave of protests (Albizu-Campos; Caño; Espina Prieto and Rodriguez Ruíz; Hernández)

Movimiento San Isidro and 11-J (2021): Afro-Cubans at the forefront and a silent global left

The current protests on the island were instigated by the human rights activism, performances of civil disobedience, and hunger strikes of Movimiento San Isidro (MSI). Founded in 2018 to protest Decree 349, a law issued by the current President Miguel Díaz-Canel that formalized censorship by restricting artistic freedom and expression,

MSI is a group of young activists, artists, and *raperos contestarios* [protest rappers] from the marginalized, majority-black San Isidro neighborhood of Havana. According to influential Afro-Cuban intellectual Roberto Zurbano, the MSI's universal demands for freedom were racialized by discriminatory denunciations in state-controlled media where they were portrayed as "marginal," "delinquents," "anti-Cubans," and "mercenaries of U.S. imperialism," leading the MSI to assume "a contestant anti-racism, perhaps the harshest and least addressed by the critical Cuban discourse of the 21st century" (Zurbano n. pag.). Luis Manuel Otero Alcántara and Maykel Osorbo, two of MSI's main protagonists, both black, are in prison since 2021 and are recognized as prisoners of conscience by Amnesty International, Human Rights Watch, and other human rights organizations. The struggle for their liberation has become one of the main demands of the recent protest wave, which reached its temporary peak in the events of July 11, 2021. During the popular revolt of July 11 (11-J), for the first time since the Revolution, thousands of Cubans took to the streets in different parts of the country protesting against the government of Díaz-Canel.

Considering the patterns of anti-black racism that can be discerned from the early years of post-revolutionary Cuba to the present, a question arises: what attitude have the different African American leaders, academics, activists, and left-wing movements assumed throughout these six decades in the face of the intransigent stance of the Cuban government? A government that refuses to recognize the existence of racism on the island, and whose practices are aimed at silencing the black voices that dare to denounce this problem and demand a public debate on this issue.

The rapprochement and political connections of the Cuban Revolution with the activists of the Civil Rights and Black Power movements in the 1960s laid the foundations for a kind of political pact or alliance that continues to this day. Activists, academics, and leaders of leftist African American social movements have acted as a key instrument for legitimizing the double discourse, contradictions, and paradoxes that characterize the Cuban government's position on racism and racial discrimination. If in terms of foreign policy Cuba has shown solidarity with liberation movements that fight against racism and racial discrimination worldwide – its explicit condemnation of South African apartheid, the massive military support to Angola and Ethiopia in the 1970s and 1980s – it has not done so at its domestic level. Cuba continues to ignore the issue of racial discrimination in the national agenda and does not engage in public debate about it. Throughout these last decades, I have heard intellectuals, artists, and independent black activists in Cuba complain about the little interest shown by their African American brothers and sisters in their official visits to the island, not only because they do not know them but also because there has been no will to establish a dialogue about the reality of black men and women in Cuba. Instead, African American visitors from the United States have shown more concern and complacency in meeting with official representatives of the country and in listening to versions of Cuba's race relations that they were offered by the state.

A palpable sign of this fact was in the reactions of disenchantment and discomfort generated within the different groups, projects, independent activists and intellectuals that make up the Cuban anti-racist movement by the silence of the leaders, activists, and social movements of the African American left in the face of the demonstrations that took place on July 11, 2021. These demonstrations were characterized by a strong black presence, highlighting the situation of poverty and marginalization in which the Afro-descendant population lives on the island – a problem to which we as Afro-Cuban activists, academics, and leaders have been calling attention for decades. Black Cubans also were highly affected by the fierce repression with which the state responded to these protests: young Afro-Cuban Diubis Laurencio died during the riots in La Güinera, one of the marginalized neighborhoods with a predominantly Afro-descendant population; a majority of those convicted to sentences of up to 30 years in prison for participating in the protests, among them several minors, are Afro-Cubans (Romero and Hall).

Considering the close ties between the Cuban government and the U.S. left, the popular uprisings of July 11 confronted activists in the United States with a series of political and ideological dilemmas. In a lucid article, James Buckwalter-Arias writes in the opening lines: "I am writing from the United States, where the left is going through a historic moment that should bring about understanding and solidarity among social movements on the island and in the mainland." He observes that if on the one hand "the U.S. left has the duty to show solidarity with Cubans who have taken to the streets to demand radical changes"; on the other hand it must recognize "that the interference of foreign powers, far from promoting the right of citizens to political self-determination, necessarily interferes with this right." The author hints at the left's single-minded focus on the "U.S. embargo's huge role in creating the economic desperation driving the protests without also wrestling with the complexity of the protest movement and the painful reality of the state repression that the protesters have faced" (Buckwalter-Arias n. pag.). His text, to some extent, attempts to dialogue with the op-ed by Afro-Cuban American scholar Odette Casamayor Cisnero in which she issued a call to the global left to reconsider their alignment with Cuban state repression and practice solidarity with the Cuban people:

> I can understand that, for the global left, if Cuba fails to cast the image of the socialist exception, where is then hope to be found? On what grounds to build utopia? The current situation in Cuba brings up uncomfortable emotions, steered by these questions. Thus, many on the Left are hesitant to listen to the claims of Cuban protesters over the state's official tale. … But I think the Cuban people deserve better. More solidarity, perhaps. … The lack of knowledge and disinformation are certainly some of the reasons precluding the global left from realizing that it is possible to choose humanitarian internationalism over a small-minded nationalism. State violence must be denounced everywhere, even in Cuba, the last rampart of leftist hopes. Acknowledging the mass nature of the protests in Cuba and explicitly condemning the state's repression of the protesters does not require lessening the vehemence of their calls for the U.S. to end the embargo, or muffling their adamant opposition to U.S. intervention in Cuban politics. But it does

> mean that more people within the global left must make a real effort to gain an understanding of the realities on the ground in Cuba. (Casamayor-Cisneros n. pag.)

Critical dialogues between Afro-Cuban dissidents and Black Lives Matter

Interestingly, there are significant similarities between Black Lives Matter (BLM) and *Movimiento San Isidro* in that both share the denunciation of racism in the centers of governmental power, as Buckwalter-Arias points out (n. pag.). He calls for a recognition of the fact "that on both sides some leaders incited more violence among civilians, justified police violence, and denigrated protesters," and emphasizes: "What is at stake in both countries is the survival of a political project in which many still believe and which others want to destroy" (n. pag.).

In response to the 11-J demonstrations in Cuba, Black Lives Matter issued a statement on July 15, 2021 in which they demanded from President Joe Biden to end the blockade but forgot to mention the historical and present violence suffered by black people on the island. The BLM statement provoked discomfort and great indignation across the heterogeneous Cuban opposition, especially in the critical left of the different Afro-Cuban groups that fight against racism and racial discrimination in Cuba (*Colectivo Cuba Liberación Negra*; Suárez). In an unpublished article entitled "BLM and some racial notes of July 11," young Afro-Cuban activist and sexual dissident Ulises Padrón Suárez gives voice to his astonishment when he was confronted with the position assumed by BLM in response to the popular demonstrations of 11-J: "Of all the statements from the left, or movements from this ideological orientation, the one I expected the most empathy with the cause of Afrodescendants, and Cubans in general, in the midst of the pandemic crisis and the protests of July 11, was precisely that of Black Lives Matter" (Padrón Suárez n. pag.). According to the author, Black Lives Matter "suffers from myopia in not denouncing the repression of the demonstrators that Sunday, in which a large number of people were black, from marginalized neighborhoods, who took to the streets to demand freedom, food and medicine" (n. pag.).

From his Twitter account, Raul Soublett Lopez, Afro-Cuban activist and coordinator of *Alianza Afrocubana*, questioned the statement of Black Lives Matter and accused it of being biased in favor of the government of the island and of not recognizing the fact that "many of those who took to the streets are black people who are tired of classist and racist policies, of the incapacity of the government" (Soublett López n. pag.). In the same vein, Hilda Landrove examines the different positions of the global left with respect to the popular demonstrations of 11-J in Cuba:

> Any critical perspective directed at a left muzzled by loyalty (affective or strategic) to the Cuban government, always navigates in turbulent waters. Faced with its incidence in the public debate, voices are raised accusing such perspective of being reactionary and disqualifying it for referring to something – authoritarianism, political repression, social exclusion – supposedly non-existent. (Landrove n. pag.)

Given the various criticisms of the first BLM statement, the organization issued a second document where, unlike the first one, it does take a stand in favor of the Afro-descendants repressed and detained during the demonstrations of 11-J:

> Black Lives Matter is committed to listening and uplifting the voices of our Afro-Cuban family as they call for change. And, we remain steadfast in our commitment to freedom for Black people everywhere – a liberation that can only be achieved when Black people around the world thrive, experience joy and are free from all forms of oppression and violence. (*Black Lives Matter*)

In this context, an online forum took place on July 26 (the historic national holiday of the Cuban Revolution) under the title "It's Time: The People, Cuba, and Radical Solidarity." Representing the Cuban side was the poet and essayist Nancy Morejón, who, since her participation in the efforts to include Afro-Cuban perspectives in the revolutionary agenda of the 1960s, has always refused any kind of militancy not only in the Cuban anti-racist movement, but also in Afro-feminism. Coincidentally, only a week earlier Morejón had published an article in *Granma*, the official organ of the Cuban Communist Party, denouncing the 11-J demonstrators as "malandrines" [crooks, miscreants] (Morejón n. pag.). The other guests were Liz Oliva Fernandez, host of the series "The War on Cuba" produced by staunch Cuban government supporters Oliver Stone and Danny Glover, and the intellectual and social activist Roberto Zurbano. BLM had been in charge of the selection and invitation of the panelists from Cuba. To a certain extent, this gives an idea of the points of view and perspectives from Cuba, that the sponsors of this meeting considered permissible or valid. Except for the intellectual Roberto Zurbano, known for his years of struggle and militancy within the Afro-Cuban movement, the other two people who participated in this online meeting had a view from outside the struggles, problems, and demands of the movement.

The meeting organized by BLM evidenced the complete ignorance of the African American left about the reality of blacks in Cuba, shedding a spotlight on the ruptures, disarticulations, and historical contradictions that have marked the relations between black radicals from the United States and non-officialist autonomous Afro-Cuban activism during the past six decades. In contrast to Zurbano's interventions where he reminded the other speakers of the uneasiness generated among many black Cuban leaders, intellectuals, and activists by the position assumed by the BLM in the face of the popular revolts of July 11, the interventions of Morejón and Oliva Fernández were cantinflesque and lacking in rigor. It was a debate marked by a position of arrogance and hegemony of the members of Black Lives Matter towards the points of view offered by the Cuban panelists. They reminded me of what Afro-Colombian activist Carlos Calderón Mosquera said to the African American delegation from the United States in one of the debates of the First Congress of Black Culture of the Americas held in Cali between August 24 and 27, 1977 and organized by Manuel Zapata Olivella: "You are not our masters," he warned them as he observed the air of superiority of the African American representatives in their interactions with the Latin American delegates (Valero 66).

Works cited

Abreu Arcia, Alberto. "El Black Power en la Cuba de los sesenta y setenta. Conversación con Juan Felipe Benemelis." *Afromodernidades.* 2012. Web. https://afromodernidades.wordpress.com/2012/09/19/afromodernidades/.

——. *La cuentistica de El Puente y los silencios del canon narrativo cubano.* Valencia: Aduana Vieja, 2014. Print.

Albizu-Campos Espiñeira, Juan Carlos. "Contrapunteo cubano de la muerte y el color." *Novedades en Población* 4.7 (2008). Print.

Alfonso, María Isabel. "Ediciones El Puente y las dinámicas raciales de los años 60: un capítulo olvidado de la historia literaria cubana." *Revista Temas* 70 (2012): 110–118. Print.

Álvarez Ramírez, Sandra Abd'Allah. *Negra Cubana Tenía Que Ser.* Barcelona: Wanafrica Ediciones, 2020. Print.

Barquet, Jesús, ed. *Ediciones El Puente en La Habana de los años 60. Critical Readings and Poetry Books.* Chihuahua: Ediciones del Azar A.C., 2011. Print.

Black Lives Matter @Blklivesmatter. "On Cuba: Our solidarity continues …" *Twitter.* 23 Jul. 2021. Web. https://twitter.com/Blklivesmatter/status/141 8642187802218496.

Brent, William Lee. *Long Time Gone: A Black Panther's True-Life Story of His Hijacking and Twenty-Five Years in Cuba.* New York: Time Books, 1996. Print.

Buckwalter-Arias, James. "La izquierda estadounidense ante los recientes sucesos en Cuba." *On Cuba.* 21 Jul. 2022. Web. https://oncubanews.com/cuba-ee-uu/la-izquierda-estadounidense-ante-los-recientes-sucesos-en-cuba/.

Caño, María del Carmen. "Relaciones raciales, proceso de ajuste y política social." *Revista Temas* 7 (1996) : 58–65. Print.

Carbone, Valeria L. "The United States, Black Power and the Third World: An Analysis of the Implications of Stokely Carmichael's Visit to Cuba in August 1967." *Revista Universidad de La Habana* 284 (2017): 51–67. Print.

Carbonell, Walterio. *Cómo surgió la cultura nacional.* Havana: Ediciones Yaka, 1961. Print.

Casamayor-Cisneros, Odette. "My Heart Aches for Cuba – and I Yearn for More Solidarity From the Global Left." *Truthout.* 18 Jul. 2021. Web. https://truthout.org/articules/my-heart-aches-for-cuba-and-i-yearn-for-more-solidarity-from-the-global-left/.

Colectivo Cuba Liberación Negra. "Declaración del Colectivo Cuba Liberación Negra." 31 Jul. 2021. Web. https://medium.com/@cuba.liberacion.negra/declaraci%C3%B3n-del-colectivo-cuba-liberaci%C3%B3n-negra-d33a545375a7.

De la Fuente, Alejandro. *Una nación para todos. Raza, desigualdad y política en Cuba 1900–2000.* Havana: Ediciones Imagen Contemporánea, 2014. Print.

Espina Prieto, Rodrigo and Pablo Rodriguez Ruíz. "Raza y desigualdad en la Cuba actual." *Temas* 45 (2006): 44-54. Print.

Farber, Samuel. "Cuba in 1968." 13 May 2018. Web. https://www.sinpermiso.info/textos/cuba-en-1968.

Gilman, Claudia. *Entre la pluma y el fusil. Debates y dilemas del escritor revolucionario en América Latina.* Buenos Aires: Siglo XXI Editores Argentina, 2003. Print.

Gómez Vasallo, Clarisbel. "Cuban Social Sciences in the Revolutionary Whirlwind. Relaciones interraciales y discurso científico-social." *Revista Universidad de La Habana* (Jan.–Jun. 2012): 139–140. Print.

González, Tomás. *Personal E-Mail*. 18 Jan. 2007.

Hernández, Rafael. "1912. Notas sobre raza y desigualdad." *Catauro. Revista Cubana de Antropología* 4.6 (2002). Print.

Howe, Linda S. "La producción cultural de artistas y escritores 'afrocubanos' en el período revolucionario." *Acta Literaria* 26 (2001): 77–88. Print.

——. *Transgression and Conformity. Cuban Writers and Artists after the Revolution*. Madison: U of Wisconsin P, 2004. Print.

Landrove, Hilda. "On Cuba: Caricatures of the Left and the Absent Cuban People." *NACLA*. 4 Oct. 2021. Web. https://nacla.org/cuba-caricatures-left-and-absent-cuban-people.

Martiatu, Inés María. "Tomás González, el autor como protagonista de su tiempo." Aug. 2008, unpublished.

Moore, Carlos. *Castro, the Blacks, and Africa*. Los Angeles: U of California P, 1989. Print.

——. *Pichón: Race and Revolution in Castro's Cuba*. Chicago: Chicago Review Press, 2008. Print.

Morejón, Nancy. "Malandrines." *Granma*. 19. Jul. 2021. Web. https://www.granma.cu/cuba/2021-07-19/malandrines-19-07-2021-17-07-28.

Padrón Suárez, Ulises. "BLM and some racial notes of July 11." Unpublished article.

Pérez Sarduy, Pedro. *Personal E-Mail*. 9 May, 2017.

Reitan, Ruth. *The Rise and Decline of an Alliance: Cuba and African-American Leaders in the 1960s*. East Lansing: Michigan State UP, 1999. Print.

Romero Negrín, Leonardo, and Alexander Hall Lujardo. "Dos jóvenes detenidos el 11-J replican a la revista 'Alma Mater.'" *Revista El Estornudo*. 8 Sep. 2021. Web. https://revistaelestornudo.com/dos-jovenes-detenidos-el-11-j-replican-a-la-revista-alma-mater/.

Rubiera Castillo, Daisy, Inés María Martiatu Terry, and Devyn Spence Benson. *Afrocubanas: History, Thought, and Cultural Practices (Creolizing the Canon)*. Washington: Rowman & Littlefield, 2020.

Shakur, Assata. *Assata: An Autobiography*. London: Zed Books, 2001. Print.

Soublett López, Raúl [@RaulSoublett]. "Según el gobierno en la protesta todos eran 'vándalos,' 'delincuentes,' 'marginados' ¿les suena el escenario? Muchas de los que salieron a las calles son personas negras que se cansaron de políticas clasistas y racistas, de la incapacidad gubernamental." *Twitter*. 16 Jul. 2021. Web. https://twitter.com/RaulSoublett/status/1416127935094923273.

Suárez, Yania. "Activistas antirracistas emplazan a Black Lives Matter desde Cuba." Diario de Cuba. 26 Jul. 2021. Web. https://diariodecuba.com/derechos-humanos/1627325554_32951.html.

Tyson, Timothy. *Radio Free Dixie: Robert F. Williams and the Roots of Black Power*. Chapel Hill: The U of North Carolina P, 2001. Print.

Valero, Silvia. *"Los negros se toman la palabra." Primer Congreso de Cultura Negra de las Américas: debates al interior de las comisiones y plenarias*. Bogotá, Cartagena: Universidad Javeriana, Universidad de Cartagena, CEA, 2020. Print.

Zabala Argüelles, María del Carmen. *Desigualdades por color de la piel e interseccionalidad: análisis del contexto cubano 2008-2018*. La Habana: FLACSO Cuba, Publicaciones

Acuario, 2020. Web. http://biblioteca.clacso.edu.ar/Cuba/flacso-cu/20201103111644/5-Desigualdades-color.pdf.

Zurbano, Roberto. "Contra la rabia política: una vacuna y una propuesta." *Afrocubanas*. 2021. Web. https://afrocubanas.com/2021/04/26/contra-la-rabia-politica-una-vacuna-y-una-propuesta/.

The Act and the Shadow: Social, Artistic, and Cultural Influences of the Black Power Era in Colombia

ÁNGEL PEREA ESCOBAR

"If I can move one grain of sand from one spot to another,
then the world will never be exactly the same."
Huey P. Newton (qtd. in Jeffries 120)

Identifying the traces of the Black Power movement's influence on Afro-Colombian individuals, communities, and movements in the broad context of the Civil Rights movement and its hemispheric popularization among the Afro communities of the Americas in the 1960s and 1970s is a difficult task. In regard to the Colombian cultural landscape, this task becomes even more difficult, given that these influences can be perceived in very different stages of the social and historical development of what we identify as Afro-Colombian socio-political and cultural movements. I will especially highlight this aspect due to its direct relation to a certain "Afro-American identity," a wide cultural field referring to the history of the African diaspora, with which the Colombian case shares an extensive field of modes and communication rituals to use James Baldwin's eloquent phrase.

Afro-Colombian social movements developed in the same historical period as the African American movements and, to a great extent and in a very evident way, have been encouraged and inspired by the latter, which implies the constant dialogue between African American, pan-African, and Afro-diasporic cultures. This dialogue, however, is not evident or patent in the sense that these mutual interactions have not been formally documented, despite the current trend among several local authors and researchers to document the history of socio-political and cultural Afro movements in Colombia. This gap accounts for the current need to establish a genealogy of the aforementioned influences, through a sort of 'observation archeology' as the method to gather pieces of scattered and fragmented information, and to attempt the study of non-specific and obscure historical documentation from different sources. The account of these influences is still expressed as a kind of oral history, which uses the testimonies that survive in the Colombian context. Thus, it is based on the experiences of those who acknowledge such influences as part of their personal history, even if these influences were not clearly expressed as a particular or concrete militancy in any social movement, back then or now.

Following the Panthers: a view from Black Bogotá

The approach of the present essay is certainly personal and hence subjective, since it arises from my own experience. I am able to acknowledge my own affiliation to what I have labelled "the African American school of thought," constituted by the political, social, and cultural events and scenarios that emerged during the 1960s and 1970s and that had a dramatic impact on the collective imagination of my generation's youth movements. A good deal of my own personal imaginary, my ideas of cultural formation regarding the African American substance, and my cultural heroes and heroines, come from this rich and complex universe, and it has been specifically expressed in the core of my professional activities as an artist, journalist, and cultural commentator.

I was just a kid when Bobby Seale and Huey P. Newton founded the Black Panther Party for Self-Defense in 1966. However, at home, my father was an activist for the Afro-Colombian cause, even though he, as a member of an ethnic minority under various forms of surveillance, was barred from broadly sharing his convictions, much less presenting his ideology in the public scene. From around 1968 onwards, I followed the latest feats of the Black Panthers as if they were a series of adventures published in weekly chapters in the local papers and told piecemeal on the radio news. In 1970, my father brought home a paper sheet, which he solemnly read in English and immediately translated to his two children in our living room; it was the Black Panther Party Ten-Point Program. I have never forgotten its point number one: "We Want Freedom. We Want Power to Determine the Destiny of Our Black Community. We believe that Black people will not be free until we are able to determine our destiny."[1]

The headlines of that period are a vivid reminder of critical events, such as the militant protest of the Black Panthers at the California state Capitol in 1967, armed and dressed in the outfits that would turn them into icons of a singular aesthetic that changed forever the image of young, urban, black men. Sensational news about the armed clashes in which leaders like Chairman Huey Newton and the Minister of Information Eldridge Cleaver engaged with the white police were widely broadcasted, followed by the development of the legal proceedings once the Black Panther Party was targeted as "the greatest threat to internal security of the country" by FBI director J. Edgar Hoover.[2] At home, conversations among adults about the ongoing "black revolution" were frequent. These talks sparked heated and passionate discussions. During memorable afternoons and evenings of polemic and contention, the form and substance of the events were endorsed or questioned by the participants, all of them members of the then small Afro community in Bogotá.

Obviously, these early influences were transmitted by my closest surroundings, which proves, for the purposes of the topic here, that the influence from both the spectacular emergence of an Afro-International movement during the second half of the

1 https://www.blackpast.org/african-american-history/primary-documents-african-american-history/black-panther-party-ten-point-program-1966/.

2 https://www.pbs.org/hueypnewton/people/people_hoover.html.

twentieth century and the emergence of the Black Panthers (as a singular expression of the former), among diverse individuals of the Afro-Colombian community was tangible, relevant, and encouraging. Very soon I would learn that everything that was discussed at home was just a reflection of a broader world movement, led by the African American youth, in an explosive and volatile manifestation of dissent, resistance, and revolutionary ambition. Thus, the sociocultural and political phenomenon represented by the Black Panthers became a rightful and common cultural heritage, resulting from the context in which my generation grew up. Many of my friends and acquaintances, including artists, thinkers, writers, social scientists, activists, and political leaders, either black, white, *mestizo* or any other color and from very different backgrounds, also acknowledge its ardent influence, even if many times this influence is manifested as a mere incidental reference in contemporary culture.

From the Harlem Renaissance to the Black Arts Movement

The present text explores how the influence of the Black Panthers – and in general the Black Power movement – has manifested itself in the Colombian environment as a key contributor to the emergence of an "attitude" that was both cultural and political. Of course, the conditions that marked the emergence of these movements in Colombia determined that the local Afro artistic and aesthetic expressions could never reach a level similar to the powerful African American demonstrations, linked to broad social movements or as an expression of them. This is partly due to the different social histories in the United States and in Colombia, but also because of the very different conditions of material development, artistic and creative production, unequal levels of access to an autonomous control of the means of production, and industrial development, among a myriad of other differences.

One of the most important features of the more radical and diverse Black Power movement of the 1960s and 1970s in the United States, which emerged from the Civil Rights movement and marked the beginning of a new era of Afro social movements, was that it encompassed all forces and spheres of society in black America. Artists and creators had a fundamental participation. The artists were activists on all fronts, whether they were adept at the integrationist ideas of the civil movement, the manifestations of cultural nationalism or the broader revolutionary ideas regarding the political connection with the proletarians and the "wretched of the earth" world-wide, as Frantz Fanon had it in his seminal book which inspired the Black Panthers and other black revolutionaries (see article by Owusu in this volume).

This activation did not come, however, from a cultural vacuum. Already in the early 1900s, between 1918 and 1937, the cultural movement better known as the Harlem Renaissance, gave an extraordinary boost to African American artistic, creative, and intellectual production. The creation of an independent publishing industry was decisive in the emergence of great figures who shook the American cultural scene. The Harlem Renaissance, as conceived by one of its luminaries, Alain Locke, provided

African Americans for the first time with the sense of "an expression of group and self-determination" (Locke 3) offered by cultural and artistic production.

The Harlem Renaissance laid the foundations for the 1960s during which a wave of black cultural nationalism found its expression in the emergence of the Black Arts Movement, a radical creative artistic collective founded by writers and intellectuals of the stature of LeRoi Jones, later better known as Amiri Baraka. The Black Arts Movement as one of the most important currents of the Black Power era was also crucial in establishing the academic programs of higher African American studies, then known as Black Studies. Of course, music, perhaps the most powerful expressive force in African American history, took its place in the battle, although the nature of its ambiguous relationship with the recording industry made it ride between two waters. The power of music was rightly reflected in its ability to give sound to the Black Arts Movement in an admirable way and with a performance that touched the highest creative peaks and accentuated the influence and leadership of African American artists in world music. Other artistic expressions, such as cinema, dance, theater, and dramaturgy, were also infused by the spirit of the Black Arts Movement. In the 1960s and 1970s, key decades in the internationalization of Black Power and the shaping of local Afro movements, the Black Arts Movement and its conceptualization of a "black aesthetic" spread globally and were incorporated to the arts and creative expressions in Africa and the diaspora, becoming a major and throbbing force to the underground movement, as well as the pop art culture worldwide.

New attitudes, old fears: Black Power as a threat to Colombian *mestizo* nationalism

In contrast to the U.S. context, where black culture and politics had gained national visibility between the 1920s and 1970s, in Colombia a dominant *mestizaje* discourse celebrated the indigenous and Hispanic roots of the nation while neglecting the very existence of a strong Afro-Colombian presence for most of the twentieth century. The disproportionate impact of social inequality on Afro-Colombians and the virulence of racist stereotypes in Colombian society were not addressed for a long time, not least due to the invisibilization of the black presence and the tabooing of *race* as a relevant social category. The consolidation of Colombian *mestizo* nationalism and the accompanying denial of the existence of Colombian racism have led to both a notorious neglect of the study of racial hierarchies and extremely difficult initial conditions for black anti-racist mobilization. Despite the fact that, based on its demography, Colombia is the second most important location for the African diaspora in Latin America after Brazil, and Afro-Colombians make up as much as 90 percent of the local population in some regions such as the Pacific Coast, blackness had no place in the construction of a cultural identity of the modern Colombian nation. Similar to other Afro-Latin American contexts, critical discourses on race associated with the United States were denounced as "foreign" ideologies without any connection to Colombian reality (Mosquera Rosero-Labbé, Laó-Montes, and Garavito). While the adaptation of Afrcan American discourses from the United States and the affirmation of blackness associated with them was a mass phenomenon in Brazil, Panama, and Caribbean states such as Jamaica and Trinidad, in Colombia, it represented a marginal phenomenon without a significant following among blacks. Here, the Black Power movement was ignored or openly denounced by both white elites and blacks as "inverted racism" or "separatism" because of its inherent challenge to the official image of the harmonious "mestizo nation" (Mosquera Rosero-Labbé, Laó-Montes, and Garavito).

Similar to other Afro-Latin American experiences, Colombia's black community was largely isolated from transnational Afro-diasporic exchange processes until the late 1970s. Despite the impact of the African American freedom struggle on the discourse of individual Afro-Colombian intellectuals and socio-political leaders, who struggled to consolidate a national movement of ethnic and racial assertion, these influences did not manifest themselves in the development of a mass movement comparable to North American Black Power. In this sense, no massive popular movements advocating the Afro-Colombian cause emerged, but rather individual demonstrations or small groups of intellectuals who did produce relevant works, but mostly without reaching the large masses. In Colombia, most black political struggles took place within the mainstream of politics and traditional political parties, including the left. The black political leaderships were linked to the established parties – the Liberal Party in particular–, since the local circumstances made it impossible to found independent black parties. Due to persistent endemic aspects such as economic backwardness, social fragmentation, and other factors that characterize Afro-Colombian social history until today, the production and dissemination system that shaped the cultural and political development of African Americans in the United States never occurred in our country.

Hemispheric Dialogues: Black America and Afro-Colombia in the Civil Rights/Black Power era

Despite these adverse conditions for diasporic dialogue between black America and Afro-Colombia, the influence of U.S. African American cultural and social movements was evident among Afro-Colombian intellectuals since the 1940s. Writer Manuel Zapata Olivella was a key figure in the dissemination of knowledge about international black freedom struggles in Colombia. Born in 1920 on the Caribbean coast of Colombia, Zapata Olivella is considered, along with Nicolás Guillén from Cuba, the most important writer of Afro-Latin America in the twentieth century. Despite his impressive oeuvre, which includes a large number of essays and novels on the social realities of Afro-Colombians, and his contributions to the emergence of an Afro-diasporic perspective on Latin America, Zapata Olivella's works have not been included in the canon of the Latin American literary boom dominated by names such as Carlos Fuentes, Mario Vargas Llosa, Gabriel García Márquez, and Julio Cortázar. From 1946 to 1947, Zapata lived in Harlem as an illegal immigrant and was hosted there by none other than poet and writer Langston Hughes, laying the foundation for a close friendship during which both learned much about the realities of other Afro-diasporic communities outside their respective countries of origin (Prescott). While in the United States, Zapata Olivella gained experiences about African American struggles against racism and the global dimensions of the African diaspora, which were of particular importance to his literary and political activities in the decades that followed. Personal acquaintances with influential Afro-diasporic luminaries like Hughes, Abdias do Nascimento, Aimé Césaire, Nicolás Guillén, and Édouard Glissant had a formative influence on his ideological and artistic direction. In 1977, Zapata Olivella organized and chaired the *Primer Congreso de la Cultura Negra de las Américas* in Cali, which was an important milestone on the road to black hemispheric networking as it gathered influential Afro-diasporic organizations, artists, and activists from the Caribbean, North and Latin America (Valero, *Los Negros*). In his novel *Changó, el gran putas* (1983), Zapata incorporates all these influences by adopting a hemispheric perspective on the history of the African diaspora from enslavement to the liberation movements of the 1960s. Putting icons of slave resistance such as Benkos Biohó from Colombia, Zumbi dos Palmares from Brazil, Toussaint L'Ouverture from Haiti, Sojourner Truth, Harriet Tubman, and Nat Turner from the United States in dialogue with 1960s and 1970s black revolutionaries such as Malcolm X, Angela Davis, and the Black Panthers, Zapata Olivella's *Changó* not only illustrates the transgenerational continuum of the black radical tradition but also represents the first Spanish language novel which emphasizes the transnational connections of freedom struggles in the African diaspora and the outstanding role of the Civil Rights-Black Power era within those movements.

Although the specific conditions in Colombia prevented the emergence of a local version of the Black Power comparable to the Black Rio movement in Brazil (see the essay of Carlos Alberto Medeiros in this volume), its influence was nevertheless felt. The black and diasporic aesthetic proclaimed by the Black Arts Movement was heard on the radio and diffused through records, was seen on television and in movies, it appeared on the covers of magazines and in books, and was advertised with one of the most famous slogans of the twentieth century: "Black is beautiful." Even the black revolution's heroes – considered true antiheroes by the establishment's propaganda machine – were part of the popular iconography. The display of what constituted a real cultural revolution fostered and inspired local leaders and activists in Colombia, who had an utmost respect for the great sacrifice that actors such as the black Panthers made as the revolution's avant-garde. This new cultural and political attitude of black assertiveness, which I consider to be the most relevant influence of the Black Power era on Afro-Colombian individuals and organizations, contributed to the creation and reassertion of a novel ethnic and racial cultural identity and became evident in the trends that led to the emergence of Afro-Colombian organizations in the 1970s. And, of course, this attitude, of course, did not result solely from the black movement in its unique American expression, but also drew from the global pan-African movement and its successive schools of thought since the 1920s, including Garveyism, the concept of *négritude* as conceptualized by Aimé Césaire and Léopold Sédar Senghor, the ideas of Frantz Fanon, Afro-Caribbean and Afro-Latin American movements such as Brazil's *movimento negro*, processes of decolonization in Africa and the struggle against apartheid in South Africa.

Coinciding with the demise of Black Power in the United States and paralleled by similar developments in other Latin American countries, the mid-to-late 1970s witnessed a surge in black political activism in Colombia. The Black Power shock wave of the late 1960s and early 1970s was reflected in a new vigor of organizations that launched initiatives that are still considered historic milestones of the Afro-Colombian movement. The formation of an anti-racist *movimiento social afro-colombiano* and the construction of an Afro-diasporic identity discourse in Colombia was the result of the commitment of a small circle of Afro-Colombian activists and intellectuals and inspirations from abroad. According to a local black activist, the international trade in the port city of Buenaventura on the Pacific coast facilitated direct contact with the Black Power movement:

> In the late 1960s, some influence from blacks in the United States arrived in Buenaventura. When Luther King died, discussion groups were organized here and some were linked to this discourse. There were contacts with black Americans who came to the port. At the time of Malcolm X and the Black Panthers, there was a group here called *Black Power* inspired by Stokely Carmichael's idea. (Wabgou et al. 91, translation mine)

Indicative of the significant impact of Black Power on Colombia's Pacific Coast, Buenaventura also witnessed the emergence of groups such as *Panteras Negras* [Black Panthers] and *Musulmanes Negros* [Black Muslims] in the late 1960s and early 1970s (117).

In 1975, Valentín Moreno Salazar, a lawyer from the department of Chocó on the Pacific Coast was a key figure in the organization of the *Primer Encuentro de la Población Negra de Colombia* [First Encounter of Colombia's Black Population] in Cali which gathered local black leaders and activists from across the country to discuss the realities and struggles of Afrodescendants in Colombia. The Cali meeting was followed by the foundation of *Movimiento de Negritudes y Mestizaje de Colombia* by Moreno Salazar, a political and cultural organization which endorsed Dr. Juan Zapata Olivella (the brother of Manuel Zapata Olivella) when he was nominated to run as the first Afro-Colombian presidential candidate for the 1978 national elections (Moreno). The *Primer Encuentro* at Cali also initiated a series of regional and national conferences in Tumaco (1975), Quibdo (1976), and Cartagena (1977), as well as *Congreso Nacional de Negros* in Bogotá (1975) and *Congreso de Negritudes* in Medellín (1977) which were of pivotal importance for the emergence of a broad Afro-Colombian social movement in the years and decades that followed (Wabgou et al. 99–130). The presence of renowned Pan-African activists and intellectuals from all over the Americas and Africa, including the Nigerian writer, playwright, poet, and future Nobel laureate Wole Soyinka at the mentioned 1977 *Primer Congreso de la Cultura Negra de las Américas* in Cali was a milestone in the internationalization of Colombia's black movement that benefitted from chair Manuel Zapata Olivella's extensive personal network of black intellectuals and activists.

Encouraged by the success of these conferences, political associations and committees emerged in several parts of the country. The seeds of a black social movement were sown by mainly Afro-Colombian students from the Pacific region who, in the urban context of university cities such as Bogotá and Pereira, gained access to literature on the transnational black movements of the time and began to organize themselves on the basis of these influences. Such was the case for the student group SOWETO, founded in 1975, out of which the still existing *Movimiento Nacional Cimarrón* emerged in 1982. These groups drew extensively on information they received from the African American freedom struggle, anti-colonial liberation movements in the Third World, and resistance against apartheid in South Africa. Juan de Dios Mosquera, the founder of SOWETO and *Cimarrón*, confirmed the concept of *cimarronismo* as these movements' development was based on a combination of local traditions of slave resistance as manifested in the *palenques* (maroon communities) with the methods, strategies, and political thought of Malcolm X, whose role as the central inspirational figure of black radicals in the 1960s and 1970s was not limited to the United States but extended throughout the hemisphere (Wabgou et al., 112).

Presencia Negra and *Revista Negritud:* culture and media as tools of black resistance

The promotion of black culture was a key factor of early Afro-Colombian social movements. Many of the most important Afro-Colombian artists and cultural spokesmen were very involved in the launch and development of various organizations that aimed to assert the particular and specific value of the African influence in Colombian culture and to consolidate identity sources for Afro-Colombian individuals and communities. In this regard, famous personalities of the local scene had a remarkable role in the strengthening of the appreciation of cultural issues among new organizations. For instance, the intellectual Aquiles Escalante and the choreographer Delia Zapata Olivella (the sister of Manuel Zapata Olivella) led the IV Commission of Material and Artistic Creativity at the *Primer Congreso de la Cultura Negra de las Américas* in 1976, which identified several axes of African contributions in the fields of Colombian music, dance, painting, sculpture, architecture, language, literature, crafts and technology.

Even though the development of media as a strategic element in the contemporary context was not included among the axes analyzed by the Commission, the first attempts to achieve mass circulation and national influence by the Afro movement emerged in this period, decisively advanced by an energetic sociologist and activist from Chocó by the name of Amir Smith Córdoba. As a leader of *Movimiento Cultura Negra* and founder of *Centro para la Investigación de la Cultura Negro* [CIDCUN/ Center for Research and Development of Black Culture], he launched the newspaper *Presencia Negra* in 1976 and the magazine *Revista Negritud* in 1979. Illustrating the role model function of African American politics and culture in Amir Smith Córdoba's articulation of an Afro-Colombian counter-discourse, there was an article on protagonists of the U.S. black freedom struggle such as Harriet Tubman, Frederick Douglass, Richard Wright, and Langston Hughes in the first number of *Presencia Negra* (Valero and Ramos 161). These publications, printed in Bogotá, circulated until the 1980s and had to overcome great financial and even technical difficulties to keep a sustained production and to guarantee an effective circulation, in particular concerning the proper functioning of a medium with nationwide circulation. Against all odds, these publications made a difference in regard to the more established press media, due firstly to their emphasis on the development of a new kind of journalism, and secondly – and perhaps most importantly – to their nature as unveiled black editorial productions, especially in the political sense.

Presencia Negra and *Revista Negritud* resembled other Afro publications that emerged in the United States in that they were aimed at an intellectual readership and oriented towards a highly specialized intellectual expression in the production of knowledge (such as *Crisis* magazine, edited by W.E.B. DuBois). Smith Córdoba believed in the imperative need to increase black literature that promoted the high purposes of researching and disseminating the true meaning of the black contribution in building the country. *Negritud* and *Presencia Negra*, as well as other publications edited by Smith Córdoba under the imprint of CIDCUN, such as *Cultura negra y avasallamiento cultural* (1980) and *Visión sociocultural del negro en Colombia* (1986) had a great impact due to their novelty and their direct approach to local issues, as well as the information they provided about events of the diaspora, with a special focus on the assertion of the Afro identity. Such achievements far outweighed their problems in terms of technical execution, design, and editing.

The aforementioned publications are true classics of Afro journalism, not only because of what they meant to avid readers of contemporary black Colombian history, but also due to their pioneering attitude and the ideas they instilled into their audience's imagination, as they gathered, for the first time, important and diverse Afro-Colombian voices. All these efforts, however, failed to crystallize a strong development of the cultural and artistic production at the local level, that could express, reflect, and enhance the substance of the Afro movement as a unified endeavor. Their precariousness and dependence on insecure sources of funding perhaps prevented the successful integration of artists and creatives that allowed the development of a strong movement. The combination of politics and culture that shaped the creation of media products such as those established by Smith Córdoba, in a certain way, share the same style, approach, and editorial line with the iconic newspaper *The Black Panther,* founded in April 1967 as part of a communication strategy that aimed to "inform, educate and organize the people and promote the 10 Points-Program" (Jennings n. pag.) of the Black Panther Party. However, the fundamental difference between *Presencia Negra, Revista Negritud* and *The Black Panther* newspaper was the impressive qualitative leap achieved by the latter. *The Black Panther* began as an amateur publication of just four simple pages, but very soon it turned into a true weekly newspaper that printed three hundred thousand copies and featured the young graphic artist Emory Douglas, who provided an influential and now legendary identity through a dynamic visual style directly related to popular culture. In the Colombian case, editor Amir Smith Córdoba's mid-1970s call to unpublished Afro writers to submit their texts for publication in his newspaper and magazine did not include, not explicitly at least, artists and graphic designers that could have brought forward the consolidation of a professional but also creative journalistic project.

Conclusion

Looking at the most popular Afro-Colombian cultural products of the period, which conformed to the rhetoric of the established culture industry, one finds that this artistic production seems to follow a certain course: it reflected the cultural climate in vogue, but remained tangential, at best, in regard to the ongoing vibrant social movement. A completely different situation occurred in the United States, where the artistic movement, even if closely tied to the dynamics of industrial production, was the direct reflection of the African American socio-political drive and acted as first-rate illustrator, organizer, and anchor. That is, the artistic expressions represented the powerful public and popular voice of the Black movement. Nonetheless, this does not mean that the Afro-Colombian cultural production was irrelevant or halted, or that some important artists did not exert a relevant activism in the Black movement's promotion, but rather that the cultural and artistic production was overshadowed and entire fields never developed into autonomous platforms for the expression of the momentum and the spirit of the times. In Colombia, Afro-cultural expressions have mostly been viewed as ethnic assertions. Hence, their mere staging becomes, in itself, a type of declaration. The Afro-Colombian culture, built on the solid foundation of its social experience "in the fiery furnace of slavery" (Hayes 21) just like black culture in the United States, influences with undeniable force its inner circles; outwardly, however, it suffers from the "invisibility syndrome" that the writer Ralph Ellison noted in his novel *The Invisible Man* among African Americans. The persistence of these complex factors shapes the intercultural relations between Afro-Colombians and other groups of Colombian society, particularly those established on the basis of their economic, political, and cultural power.

Artistic creations are very seldom understood as an important political capital that serves to the formation of discourses. Apparently, it is assumed that the development of specific languages is not needed in the artistic creation. This factor contributes significantly to the characteristic exile of Afro-Colombian culture, in a context where there are still no effective mechanisms to control its cultural products outside the institutional framework that allows for the production of invigorating ideas and relevant exhibitions. Such an assessment must certainly include important exceptions that are considered among the highest contributions of artistic conception and creation not only in Afro-Colombian but also in Colombian history. This approach is likely to be broadly discussed, in a conversation that, as an Afro-Colombian artist and cultural critic, I would like to start.

Works cited

Ellison, Ralph. *Invisible Man.* New York: Random House, 1952. Print.

Hayes, Diana L. "Movin'on up a Little Higher – Resolving the Tensions between Academic and Pastoral Approaches to Black and Womanist Theologies." *Walk Together Children: Black and Womanist Theologies, Church and Theological Education.* Ed. Dwight N. Hopkins and Linda E. Thomas. Eugene: Cascade Books, 2010. 13–25. Print

Jeffries, Judson. *Huey P. Newton: The Radical Theorist.* Jackson: UP of Mississippi. 2002. Print.

Jennings, Billy. "Remembering the Black Panther Party Newspaper." N.d. Web. https://summerof.love/remembering-the-black-panther-party-newspaper/.

Locke, Alain. "The New Negro". *The New Negro: An Interpretation.* Ed. Alain Locke. New York: Atheneum, 1925. 1–16. Print.

Moreno Salazar, Valentín. *Negritudes.* Cali: Editores XYZ, 1995. Print.

Mosquera Rosero-Labbé, Claudia, Agustín Laó-Montes, and César Rodriguez Garavito, eds. *Debates sobre ciudadanía y políticas raciales en las Américas Negras*. Bogotá: Universidad Nacional de Colombia, 2010. Print.

Prescott, Laurence E. "Brother to Brother: The Friendship and Literary Correspondence of Manuel Zapata Olivella and Langston Hughes." *Afro-Hispanic Review* 25.1 (2006): 87–103. Print.

Smith Córdoba, Amir. *Cultura negra y avasallamiento cultural.* Bogotá: Centro para la Investigación de la Cultura Negra, 1980. Print.

———. *Visión sociocultural del negro en Colombia.* Bogotá: Centro para la Investigación de la Cultura Negra, 1986. Print.

Valero, Silvia. *"Los negros se toman la palabra" – Primer Congreso de la Cultura negra de las Américas: Debates al interior de las comisiones y plenarias.* Bogotá: Editorial Pontificia Universidad Javeriana, 2020. Print.

Valero, Silvia, and Erick Ramos. "Amir Smith Córdoba y la revista Negritud (1976). Contrapuntos por el lugar del negro en la historia." *Memorias* 42 (2020): 146–170. Print.

Wabgou, Maguemati, Jaime Arocha, Juan Alberto Carabalí, and Aiden José Salgado. *Movimiento Social Afrocolombiano, Negro, Raizal y Palenquero: El largo camino hacia la construcción de espacios y alianzas estratégicas para la incidencia política en Colombia.* Bogotá: Universidad Nacional de Colombia, 2012. Print.

Zapata Olivella, Manuel. *Changó, el gran Putas.* Bogotá: Biblioteca de Literatura Afrocolombiana, 2010. Print.

The Quilombo Movement in Brazil: Becoming Invisible, Becoming Visible, Becoming Multivocal

CARLA GUERRÓN MONTERO

> When the deported marooned through the forests, leaving the plantation, the footprints they followed did not imply neither abandonment of themselves nor desperation, but also not pride or swelling of the person … the footprint traverses through the land, which will never become territory again. (Glissant 23)[1]

In December 2013, the United Nations General Assembly proclaimed the years between 2015 and 2024 the International Decade for People of African Descent, with the theme "Recognition, Justice, and Development." While such proclamations by multilateral organizations are often merely symbolic, this one promotes awareness of the enduring history of resistance to oppression by peoples of African descent worldwide and their quest for recognition and sovereignty. In the Americas, peoples of African descent banded together in collective societies outside the colonial plantation system during slavery, forming emblematic sites of both resistance and cultural creation. These societies are known as maroon towns in the English-speaking world, *palenques* in Spanish-speaking Latin America, and *quilombos* in Brazil. They played essential roles as pre- and post-emancipation political models for determining land ownership, constitutional rights, cultural heritage questions, and the formation of ethnic identities.

This chapter traces the history of the rise of the quilombo movement and its connections with the *movimento negro* [Black movement] in Brazil. The importance of quilombos in Brazilian history cannot be overstated. Quilombos have been a constant force from colonial and imperial times through independence, the republican period, and under the current Federal Constitution of 1988, where quilombos were granted (at least under the law) the ability to apply for ownership rights to their territory and protection for their cultural practices. Thus, understanding the rise of the quilombo movement is essential not only because it sustained continuity through a long history of slavery and emancipation (Gomes, *Mocambos e Quilombos*) but also because it represents a foundational component of the Brazilian nation-state.

I propose that *quilombagem,* a movement against oppression fostered by quilombolas (the inhabitants of quilombos), started in parallel with the institution of slavery in 1530 and that it was manifested tangibly in the formation of independent communities outside the plantation system, alongside *bandoleirismo* [brigandage, banditry], and insurrections (Moura). Quilombagem, in fact, preceded the liberal abolitionist move-

---

1 All translations from Portuguese and Spanish to English are mine.

ment that started in the mid-1860s. Wherever there were passive and active acts of resistance against the slavery system, there was the expression of the quilombo movement as a direct challenge to the state and in a quest for social change. The rich celebration calendar, cultural practices, and oral history of quilombos represent instrumental aspects of this movement. Moreover, in the twenty-first century, the term quilombo has experienced a resemantization process that has reached Afro-Brazilians beyond the confinements of quilombo territories (Arruti; Reis and Gomes; O'Dwyer).

I also argue that the quilombo movement had significant effects on the formation and development of the Black power movement in Brazil. While the officially organized modern quilombo movement started in the 1990s and was influenced by the Brazilian Black movement, collective efforts against oppression and for sovereignty have been constant in the lives of quilombolas since the early days of slavery. I explore these issues in this chapter and propose that quilombos moved from becoming invisible to becoming visible to finally becoming multivocal. That is, the quilombola movement formed a unified voice that stressed its linkages with the African diaspora while at the same time opening up to a multiplicity of voices from within – women, youth, rural and urban quilombolas, quilombolas of different religions, and with different political views. This chapter is informed by archival and ethnographic research conducted in the state of Rio de Janeiro since 2015.

The beginning of the resistance: becoming invisible

The quest to end slavery through *quilombagem* appeared simultaneous to slavery. The most visible form of resistance was the formation of independent societies known as quilombos. Historically, communities of escaped enslaved peoples have been referred to as both quilombos and mocambos. The term *mocambo* was more frequently used until the 1700s in Brazil, when it became common to designate settlements or hiding places of escaped enslaved peoples as quilombos (Vansina 457). These societies were primarily composed of peoples of African descent, but they also included white, indigenous, and racially mixed peoples. While independent in many ways, quilombos were by no means isolated. They maintained considerable ties to plantations and nearby towns through trading and interaction. In addition, while most quilombos were located in the rural areas, there were many established in urban and suburban areas (Reis and Gomes). This pattern remains present until today.

The Portuguese Crown was the first to recognize the existence of quilombos. The most famous quilombo in academic and popular contexts in Brazil is the Quilombo dos Palmares, often referred to as the Republic of Palmares. Palmares developed in today's northeastern state of Alagoas from 1605 until it was suppressed in 1694. Because of Palmares' size and level of organization, its leaders were able to negotiate with the state; however, this ability was exceptional and uncharacteristic of the relationship of quilombos with the state (Carneiro; Ennes; Gomes, *A Hidra*; Péret).

The origins of the term *quilombo* can be found in the Kimbundu language, which is the second most commonly spoken Bantu language in Angola. In Kimbundu, the word *kilombo* means both a specific region in Angola and war and courage (Leite, "The Brazilian Quilombo" 1227). According to Vansina (1996), the word *quilombo* entered the Portuguese vocabulary in Angola around 1615, whereas the term *mocambo* was already in common use in the sixteenth century (453–454). From a legal perspective, quilombos were present during both colonial (1500–1815) and imperial (1822–1889) times, evident in that the law consistently criminalized and penalized rebellion and escape attempts by enslaved peoples throughout those periods. By 1722, there was legislation that punished people of African descent who formed quilombos (Guimarães, *A Negação* 131). In 1740, as a response to a consultation from Portugal, the *Conselho Ultramarino* [Overseas Council] developed an institutionalized definition of the term for use in its colonies. The council defined quilombos as "all places of habitation of black people, more than five, in a partly unpopulated location, that do not have homes erected or pillars" (Cunha and Albano 159).

After the abolition of slavery in 1888, quilombo communities became, in many ways, socially invisible. Their existence did not fit into the national conception outside of a system of enslavement. As Afro-Brazilian militant and intellectual Abdías do Nascimento aptly put it, Afro-Brazilians became "citizens" after 1888, but they also became "unwelcome niggers," and this was "an even more monstrous and cruel crime" than slavery had been (Nascimento, *O Quilombismo* 63). While local and national governments continued to consider new ways to control these rural communities, the laws of the Republic evidenced the disappearance of quilombos from official sources (Andrews). Instead, policymakers continued to look for effective ways to build a modern society within the constraints of what they assumed to be social and material backwardness and low levels of education, health, and material welfare. Meanwhile, quilombolas persisted, living their lives under varied circumstances, interacting with their neighbors, and strengthening their communities (Cunha and Albano 159).

For Brazilian society at large, quilombos remained relevant primarily as mythical spaces – as "revered and inspirational representatives of a model of black resistance" (Treece 168). The reference I make to quilombos "becoming invisible" is also connected to the lack of written records about them. Portugal and its colonies gave primacy to the written word, but documents about quilombos are, at best, sparse. Taylor (2015) proposes that Western thought creates a hard-to-surmount dichotomy between performing and archiving. The act of performing a dance or narrating a story is not considered as valid as writing *about* it. But at quilombos, performing has always been a vital act of keeping their heritage alive – literally *not archiving* it. Through the act of performing, quilombos strengthen and express their multiple voices (Vilas).

For these reasons, quilombos remained essentially "invisible" for decades. In fact, quilombolas did not even think of themselves as quilombo members until relatively recently, when categories such as *comunidades negras rurais* [Black rural communities] in the center, south and southeastern regions of the country and *terras de preto* [lands of Blacks] in the north and northeastern regions gave way to the current widely recognized category *comunidade remanescente de quilombo* [quilombo remnant community]. I detail this process later in the chapter.

Becoming visible: activism and the Brazilian Black movement

It took the rise of the Brazilian Black movement in the twentieth century to open up democratic processes for quilombos, which the movement achieved by expanding its political reach beyond its urban origins to speak to the ethnic demands of Black populations considered traditional (Rodrigues et al. 218). At the same time, the quilombo project exemplified a progressive and antiracist approach amid Brazil's long periods of dictatorship. The Black movement took the focus on resistance as a collective project from quilombo ideals; thus, the term quilombo became a synonym for Black resistance. To place this collaborative project in context, a summary of the development of the Brazilian Black movement is necessary.

Black movements date back to the nineteenth century, during the colonial period, and the abolitionist movement. The first expressions of an Afro-Brazilian movement originated in the eighteenth century with *irmandades*, Black Catholic brotherhoods and sisterhoods. Organized around the devotion to Catholic saints, these associations resulted from social strategies common to enslaved peoples and produced social networks that expanded ethnic identities and inter-ethnic alliances (Reis). The Brazilian abolitionist movement that started in the late nineteenth century was not the exclusive purview of the white elite (Andrews). Peoples of African descent contributed in fundamental ways to this movement. As Andrews argues, "the radical abolitionism of the 1880s sparked a massive response among a slave population which over time had displayed considerable sensitivity to, and canniness in exploiting, changes in public and official attitudes toward slavery" (150). There was a significant group of Black intellectuals from the middle classes who had been born free and who worked through the press and in politics to combat slavery as a means to delineate what it really meant to be a free Afro-Brazilian citizen. This fact contradicts the assumption that peoples of African descent were disorganized and uninterested in politics. The opposite is, in fact, true. Peoples of African descent were especially visible in the cultural and political life of prominent cities such as Rio de Janeiro and São Paulo and turned out to be instrumental actors in the abolitionist movement (Magalhães Pinto; Needell).

At the beginning of the twentieth century, Black activists organized their common causes in associations, clubs, and the press. Black newspapers, which functioned during the 1800s and early 1900s (including *Clarim da Alvorada* [1924–1932], *O Getulino* [1923–1926], and *Progresso* [1928–1931]) (Butler, "Up from Slavery"), advocated racial equality and political ideals stemming from the pan-African press, such as Marcus Garvey's *Negro World* [1918–1933].[2] One of the most prominent associa-

2 Black social clubs, craft guilds, and mutual aid societies were also important means by which peoples of African descent expressed their political views. A detailed analysis of them, however, lies outside the scope of the present chapter.

tions during this period was the *Centro Cívico Palmares* [Palmares Civic Center], founded in 1926 by Major António Carlos of Minas Gerais in São Paulo. The center was the first Afro-Brazilian organization to coalescence around a platform of integration and equality for all Black peoples. It started with approximately twenty members, mostly young men who had already participated in other Black organizations and wrote for other Black newspapers. The center ultimately grew to have between 100 and 150 members.[3] It offered secondary school courses that enabled many young and old students to continue their education; it also organized a theater group and ran a medical clinic (Butler, *Freedoms Given*). According to Butler, the center was the first organization focused on Black racial pride that "combined social services, recreational activities, and protests in a way that no earlier groups had attempted" (106). The center lasted only about three years; it lost popularity due to leadership and financial problems. Its model, however, was closely followed by the most active Black political organization in Brazil during the 1930s, the *Frente Negra Brasileira* [Brazilian Black Front], FNB. Moreover, the work carried out by the *Centro Cívico Palmares* during the 1920s – the public campaigns and activities that brought visibility to the Afro-Brazilian movement – demonstrates Black peoples' preparedness to organize politically.

At about the same time, the overturn of the Old Republic (1889–1930) and the establishment of the Second Republic (1930–1964) stimulated Black activists in São Paulo to form the FNB in 1931 (Andrews). This movement proposed that the poverty and neglect endured by peoples of African descent in Brazil were due to their moral weakness, lack of education, and so-called archaic customs (Guimarães, "Democracia Racial"). It was further suggested that Afro-Brazilians needed to abandon their "backward culture" by emulating European practices and lifestyles. Simultaneously, the movement embraced a xenophobic approach enveloped in nationalistic rhetoric. The *Frente* became a political party in 1936. But due to the repression experienced during the *Estado Novo* [New State] led by Getúlio Vargas (1937–1945),[4] this organization became extinct in 1937 (Domingues).

Some of the ideas of the FNB were shared by the *Teatro Experimental do Negro* (TEN). Co-founded in 1944 in Rio de Janeiro by scholar, artist, activist, politician, and poet Abdias do Nascimento, and by poet, painter, actor, filmmaker, and militant Solano Trindade, the TEN had an ambiguous vision. On the one hand, it aimed to overcome the assumed retrograde African culture that plagued Afro-Brazilians, much like the FNB. This presumed backwardness was believed to be cultural and not biological, and thus "temporal, reversible, and possible of being overcome" (Rodrigues et al.

3 Members of the *Centro Cívico Palmares* include some of the future leaders of the *Frente Negra Brasileira*, Arlindo and Isaltino Veiga dos Santos and Alberto Orlando and Vicente Ferreira.

4 Getulio Vargas was a lawyer and politician who served as Brazil's interim president (1930–1934), its constitutional president (1934–1937), and, ultimately, a dictator (1937–1945). He was later democratically elected as president in 1951 and served in that office until his death in 1954.

215). But, on the other hand, it aimed to promote a Black "African" ethos, particularly in the form of arts (Guimarães, "Democracia Racial").

Nascimento was the first Afro-Brazilian member of Congress (in 1983) to center his working platform on civil rights for peoples of African descent, including a series of affirmative action legislation proposals.[5] He put forward the notion of *quilombismo* to refer to the "entire complex of African social phenomena, of Afro-Brazilian *praxis*" (Nascimento, "An Afro-Brazilian" 152; emphasis in the original). It referred to the collective efforts of associations of peoples of African descent not only in quilombos, assumed to be illegal, but also in associations deemed "legal," such as brotherhoods, clubs, *terreiros* (houses of worship of the Afro-Brazilian religion), *tendas*, *afoxés*, samba schools, *gafieiras*, gremios, and *confrarias*. In the words of Nascimento (152), these "were and are Quilombos legalized by ruling society." By this time, Quilombismo reaffirmed the necessity for all Afro-Brazilians to win back their identity, relating it to the spirit of resistance of the ancient quilombos.

One of the projects connected to the TEN was the *Jornal Quilombo*, founded in 1948 by Nascimento. This magazine was published for two years, during which it focused on informing the public about the plight of peoples of African descent and the organizations that worked to improve their lives. It also aimed to make public discrimination cases against Afro-Brazilians (Nascimento, "Rio Grande" 6). The TEN further organized several highly timely events, including the *Conferencia Nacional do Negro* [National Conference of Black People], scheduled on May 13, 1949, in preparation for the *1ro. Congresso Nacional do Negro Brasileiro* [1st National Congress of Brazilian Blacks], expected in 1950 (Nascimento, "Conferência" n. pag.). The conference included sessions where the Quilombo dos Palmares, the Muslim revolt of the Malês in Salvador da Bahia (1835), maroon escape practices, and quilombos' "folkloric survivals" were discussed (n. pag.).

As noted previously, these organizations were given the right to express themselves more freely during the period known as the Second Republic (1930–1964), after the return to democracy in 1945. However, their mission was not overwhelmingly popular. While white Brazilian intellectuals and politicians congratulated themselves for living in what they considered a racial democracy that did not exhibit the institutional racism that afflicted the United States (Guimarães, "Democracia Racial"), organizations such as FNB and TEN were highly critical of the ways the social sciences exoticized Black peoples and how white intellectuals denied the existence of racial discrimination. Consequently, they proposed that abolishing slavery in Brazil *for the second time* was one of their main objectives.

The Second Republic was overthrown in 1964 by a military government that lasted twenty-one years. During this period, the influence of the U.S. Black Power movement, which was in full bloom, resonated across the hemisphere. In Brazil, the

5 Do Nascimento also created the *Museu de Arte Negra* [Museum of Black Art, MAN] in 1950. He was elected a member of Congress in 1983, and of the senate for the periods 1991–1992 and 1997–1999.

Black Power movement was a catalyst for the emergence of other Black movements such as the Black Rio movement in the mid-1970s (Alberto), institutions such as the *Instituto de Pesquisa e Cultura Negra* [Black Culture and Research Institute], IPCN, founded in Rio de Janeiro in 1975, and print media such as the newspapers *Jornegro*, *Árvore das Palavras* and *Cadernos Negros* in São Paulo, and *Sinba* in Rio de Janeiro, all founded in the mid-1970s.

The political liberalization or *abertura* of 1974, led by Ernesto Geidel, aided in the public emergence of social movements that had been suppressed for emphasizing in their discourses Black self-affirmation and the need to rescue the ethnic and cultural identity of Afro-descendants, as well as women's and students' groups (Gohn). As Kenny (2011) notes, "new social actors began to reconfigure the cultural, social and economic rights of the 'excluded' (Blacks, Indigenous peoples, riverine dwellers, gypsies, rubber tappers, gays and lesbians, religious groups)" (94–95). Quite significantly, these rights were understood as intersectional. For instance, during the *Congresso das Mulheres Brasileiras* [Congress of Brazilian Women] in July 1975, Black female leaders presented the *Manifesto das Mulheres Negras* [Manifesto of Black Women], calling for the recognition of racial divisions within the Brazilian women's movement.

In this context, the concept of quilombo once again became a synonym for resistance in the political discourses of the Black movement. Thus, the ideal of the quilombo expanded to serve as a cultural reaction to colonialism, reaffirming Afro-Brazilian heritage and the search for a uniquely Brazilian model for reinforcing national ethnic identities. The resulting quilombo movement proposed a progressive and democratic vision of resistance. For instance, the *Grêmio Recreativo de Arte Negra Escola de Samba Quilombo* [Quilombo Recreational Guild of Black Art and Samba School], founded by singer-songwriter Antônio Candeia Filho in Rio de Janeiro, took its inspiration from the great historical example of Black resistance evidenced in quilombos. While Brazil's military dictatorship was at its peak, organizations such as this one "proposed a progressive, democratic vision of resistance as a collective creative project, which placed black aesthetic and philosophical traditions at its core while inclusively cutting across racial color lines" (Treece 166). Another example of the power of the quilombo ideal comes from the official name and celebration date of the National Day of Black Consciousness. A day of Black consciousness was celebrated by Black movements since the 1960s, initially on May 13, to commemorate the official end of slavery in 1888 (Cunha and Albano 159). However, in 1971 the *Grupo Palmares* from Porto Alegre (Rio Grande do Sul) selected November 20, 1971, the estimated date of the assassination of Palmares' last leader, Zumbi, to commemorate the struggles of peoples of African descent (Souza 114). The purpose behind this move was to break away from the presumption that the abolition of slavery effectively ended the violence exerted by the state against peoples of African descent.

Consequently, since 1971, November 20 has been reserved to commemorate Black consciousness by numerous cities and several states. In 2003, it officially made its way into the national school calendar. And, in 2011, the date was legally adopted as

Dia Nacional de Zumbi e da Consciência Negra [National Day of Zumbi and Black Consciousness].

Interestingly, and despite the tremendous weight of Quilombo dos Palmares and Zumbi as symbols of resistance and freedom, Black movements have also worked toward moving away from an excessive focus on the connection between quilombos and Quilombo dos Palmares. Alternatively, they have called for the need to problematize Palmares. The problem with using Palmares as a prototype, they have argued, is that it dramatically limits the very definition of quilombo, restricting it to communities composed of outlaws who either committed a crime against the slavery system under colonial law or who escaped to freedom through armed resistance. As Mary Lorena Kenny notes, some Black movement leaders recognized that "it was misguided to evaluate contemporary rural black communities according to concepts based on quilombos of 300 years ago (communities of 'resistance' exhibiting unchanged cultural content), such as Palmares" (Kenny 95).

In the 1970s, partly due to an exchange of ideas with African American activists and an understanding that the reality of racial relations in the United States was not altogether different from the one in Brazil, Afro-Brazilians and progressive whites allied to raise awareness of these issues. At this moment, a new phase of the Black movement in Brazil was born, the *movimento negro contemporâneo* [contemporary Black movement], or Black 70s Movement. The movement had two main objectives: first, to denounce the myth of "racial democracy" in Brazil and, second, to assert positive Black diasporic identities (Medeiros, this volume). An excellent example of such a radical shift in approach by the Brazilian Black movement is the *Movimento Unido Contra a Discriminação Racial* [United Movement Against Racial Discrimination], MUCDR, founded on June 18, 1978, as a response to the country's opening [*abertura*] four years earlier. The MNU was renamed *Movimento Negro Unificado*, MNU [Black Unified Movement] in 1979 (Covin). The MNU broke away from the integrationist position of previous organizations to denounce racial inequality unabashedly. It emphasized self-affirmation and a true renaissance of Africa-derived Black culture, evidencing a new level of maturity for the movement.

Right from the start, the MNU rejected both racism and the idea of racial democracy and called for quilombismo as a positive identifying element for peoples of African descent. Influenced by Lusophone anticolonial liberation movements, the MNU centered its approach on the consolidation of ethnic rights of Black peoples, critiquing their marginal integration into society and the racism they encountered regularly. Some of the early successes of MNU include the acquisition of permits for the functioning of candomblé and the implementation of multicultural school curricula. Likewise, MNU contributed to the expansion of the ethnic rights of quilombolas at the legal level, and – after years of concerted efforts, as I will discuss in the next section – it contributed to the collective efforts of several civil society sectors to secure a kind of reparations policy for quilombos.

At the time, there was no consolidation of a quilombola movement around ethnicity or culture. Quilombolas' identities were tied almost exclusively to peasant and rural worker struggles. Self-identifying as a quilombola was secondary to self-identifying as a Black rural peasant who demanded agrarian reform. Even though there was coordination between the rural Black communities and the urban Black mobilizations (Souza 115–116), it was the Brazilian Black movement that carried out the struggle around ethnicity because the connection between territory and cultural identities had not been put to the forefront. Therefore, a type of ventriloquism emerged.

Historian Andrés Guerrero (2018) used the term ventriloquism to refer to the way colonial scribes transformed indigenous peoples into citizens by virtue of granting them a voice and, more broadly, by "making an indigenous person talk" ("El Proceso" 382). In other words, it refers to a situation where a dominant group speaks for a subjugated group. Here, I borrow the term to refer to how the Black movement in Brazil spoke for quilombolas until they could have their voices and speak for themselves. While Martínez Novo (2018) notes that ventriloquism in the case of communities of color refers to the use of post-racial and racial democracy theories, I believe the term applies to the quilombo case.[6] As the CONAQ (2020) expresses it: "In the period of post-abolition, the black population was excluded from several fundamental rights, and the fight for quilombola rights was added to the fight for rights of the black population in general, becoming a strong banner for organized black movements during the twentieth and twenty-first century" (n. pag.).

In the 1980s, the MNU experienced a process of atomization and decentralization. By 1988, the MNU was divided into several autonomous entities, a factor that decreased its influence because of the multiple dimensions of the Afro-Brazilian struggle that it tackled. Nonetheless, this juridical consolidation process opened up space to debate the concept of *comunidades remanescentes de quilombo* and other related concepts such as territoriality, identity, self-determination, and juridical protection.

As this brief history confirms, the Black movements that developed from the 1930s to the 1980s were instrumental in developing new political, cultural, and juridical guidelines for quilombos. The next section discusses how quilombos "became visible" once again after Brazil returned to democracy.

Becoming visible: the legal process

When the brutal dictatorship that had plagued Brazil for twenty-one years ended in 1985, Black and women's movements played crucial roles in the reconceptualization of democracy and citizenship to fully include minority and ethnic populations (Leite, "Humanidades"). One essential aspect of this reconceptualization had to do with quilombos which, as noted in the previous section, were viewed by these movements as

6 It should be noted that the Ecuadorian indigenous movement incorporated Afro-Ecuadorian peoples in their struggle (Guerrero, "El Proceso" 379).

historical symbols of a new, self-reflective Brazilian society that they hoped would finally materialize. Organizations such as the MNU and the *União dos Negros pela Igualdade* [Union of Black Peoples for Equality], UNEGRO, were at the center of the efforts to propose an antiracist struggle where gender, race, and class intersected (Rodrigues et al. 215).

The MNU used the vast expansion of the Black movement throughout the nation and mobilized to influence the writing of the new constitution prepared by the National Constitutive Assembly in 1988, marking the centenary of the abolition of slavery. Quilombos were thus of great symbolic relevance at this moment in Brazilian history. In preparation for this pivotal moment, the MNU organized the *Convenção Nacional do Negro* [National Black Convention], CNN, in Brasilia in 1986. At the convention, members of the Black and women's movements worked alongside quilombolas and the *Subcomissão dos Negros, Populações Indígenas, Pessoas Deficientes e Minorias* [Sub-commission for Black Populations, Indigenous Populations, Disabled Persons, and Minorities] to influence the writing of the new constitution.

However, quilombos were relevant not only symbolically but also as active participants. Quilombola leaders organized numerous meetings and mobilized what were then called "Black rural communities" throughout the country. Particularly dynamic were the movements in the states of Maranhão and Pará. In Maranhão, with the support of the *Centro de Cultura Negra Maranhão* [Center for Black Culture of Maranhão], forty-six communities and workers' unions participated in their first meeting. The second and third meetings took place in 1988 and 1989. Similar meetings were organized in Pará in 1988 and 1989, where the *Centro de Estudo e Defesa do Negro do Pará* [Center for the Study and Defense of Black People in Pará, CEDENPA] participated (Souza 116–117). As anthropologist Ilka Boaventura Leite (2004) observes, "relaunched by militants and intellectual peoples of African descent, the quilombola issue became a political event gradually, by becoming visible and interacting with a variety of progressive sectors that had a voice in the Constitutive Assembly" (*O Legado* 19).

Quilombo communities, organizations of the Black urban movement, peasant organizations, researchers, and members of the Parliament worked together to include "the quilombola issue" in the unfolding Constitution of 1988. Ultimately, these groups claimed a crucial political victory with the preparation and approval of Article No. 68 of the *Atos e Disposições Constitucionais Transitórias* [Transitory Constitutional Acts and Provisions, ADCT]. Article 68 established the following: "To the quilombo remnant communities that are occupying lands, they are recognized as their definite property; the State has the responsibility to issue their respective titles" (Senado Federal 162). Two additional articles, Articles 215 and 216, complemented Article 68. Article 215 protected popular, indigenous, and Afro-Brazilian cultural manifestations, while Article 216 recognized that the cultural heritage of Brazil includes material as well as immaterial permanent assets.

Article 68 guaranteed the right of property of the quilombo residual communities in urban or rural areas. Later baptized *terra de quilombo* [quilombo lands], the Article was a tremendous accomplishment for the Black movement because it represented the conquest of the political space of difference through legislative means. The Article clearly demonstrates the interface between the Black urban movement and the quilombo movement, which was still part of the Black movement (Rodrigues et al. 215). Some scholars argue that this Article was a form of reparation for centuries of violent exclusion of lack populations from Brazilian society. In sum, the constitution consecrated the rights of quilombolas to participate actively in Brazil's political and juridical construction.

One of the most interesting aspects of this process is that the victory of Art. 68 *did not* represent semantic unanimity because, for most members of the Constitutive Assembly, this Article merely consolidated the rights of "archaic quilombos" to have access to land. The understanding of the idea of quilombismo was absent from the article.[7] Thus, the consensus was that very few actual communities would fall into the juridical category of "*comunidade remanescente de quilombo*" who could claim a legal right to the territory where they lived. Quilombos were viewed purely as fossilized sites of memory, as spaces with mere artistic, historical, archeological, and ecological value.

As a whole, Articles 68, 215, and 216 effectively establish that quilombos are part of the cultural heritage of Brazilian society. They officially recognize the contributions of peoples of African descent to the nation's heritage (Kenny 94–95). With these articles, a category that had once been regarded under the law as transgressive and criminal became a category representing political, cultural, and economic rights (Souza) – a measure of the extent of reparations. The Federal Constitution of 1988, in effect, acknowledges the existence of a pluriethnic Brazilian state and guarantees its ethnic differences. However, the constitution did not solve the question of identifying actual quilombos. The responsibility of conferring legal status to quilombo territories was given to the *Instituto Nacional de Colonização e Reforma Agrária* [National Institute of Colonization and Agrarian Reform], INCRA. INCRA was charged with the recognition of quilombos as such, based on the *Relatórios Técnicos de Identificação e Delimitação* [Technical Reports of Identification and Delimitation], RTIDS, and of the concession of collective territory property titles. Since 2003, the process has been twofold: the *Fundação Cultural Palmares* [Palmares Cultural Foundation], FCP, an entity that belongs to the Ministry of Citizenship, is responsible for certifying quilombo communities using criteria of self-attribution (Cunha and Albano 161). After certification, quilombo communities must turn to INCRA to approve a collective land title.

In sum, with the Federal Constitution of 1988, Brazil achieved a degree of self-determination when its main protagonists were oppressed populations such as women, quilombolas, and indigenous peoples. The vitality that resulted from the development

7 The expression "traditionally occupied lands" was included in the article, but mainly because the expression "immemorial lands" did not get any traction, as it narrowly referred to assumed "autoctonous lands" with "natural" and unequivocal rights (Rodrigues et al.).

of this constitution had long-term repercussions. First and foremost, it strengthened the self-realization that brought renewed organizational energy to the Black movement. It also ignited the desire among quilombolas to speak for themselves and fight to implement the hard-fought rights that stemmed from this constitution. However, the triumph of this constitution also provided a framework for violent new disputes for rights because quilombolas challenged the dominant conception of capitalist property that was part of the juridical order. In the next section, I will discuss how this struggle continued.

Becoming quilombola, becoming multivocal

What could be termed the "quilombo heritage" became relevant for rural communities composed of Black peoples due to a confluence of social, economic, and political processes. These processes were part of broader trends that took place throughout Latin America in the 1980s and 1990s, such as the Afro-Colombian *raizal* and *palenquero* movements (Wabgou et al.) or the Francisco Congo movement in Peru (Minardi).

The process of organization, decision-making, and reflection required to obtain legal victories at the federal level strengthened quilombolas' internal organizations, following which ventriloquism was no longer necessary. The result was the rise of a formal, visible quilombola movement that specifically addressed and defended quilombola rights, with characteristics different from those of the urban Black movement to which it had been subsumed. It should be stressed, however, that this movement was not altogether new. It had already been present in the 1970s and 1980s in the form of mobilizations for the protection of quilombo territory in response to the state's agricultural development policies and its takeover of quilombolas' land. It was also present in the preparation of Article 68 of the Constitution of 1988.

Furthermore, it was present at the local, regional, and state levels through quilombo organizations. These were all precursors to the national quilombo movement. Therefore, in some instances, the national movement informed the creation of quilombo organizations. Still, in other cases, it was the other way around: these organizations were crucial for developing the national movement. More importantly, had there not been decisive organization on the part of quilombolas at the local, regional, and state levels, there would not have been a quilombo movement today (cf. Brandão Costa, qtd. in Bowen 135).

In November 1995, the *I Encontro Nacional das Comunidades Negras Rurais Quilombolas* [1st National Meeting of Black Rural Quilombola Communities] convened in Brasília. The *Comissão Nacional Provisória das Comunidades Rurais Negras Quilombolas* [National Temporary Commission of Black Rural Quilombola Communities] was created as a result of this convention. The national commission developed public policies at the federal level for quilombos. Here, the experience of individual states such as Maranhão, Bahia, Pará, São Paulo, Goiás, and Rio de Janeiro was essential in setting up an organization that had both social and political impact

(CONAQ). It put the concept of resistance at the center of its platform, understood not only as a historical process but also as an operational necessity. The commission incorporated local and state quilombo organizations and associations, federations, coordinating teams, and local commissions (Souza 157).

In May 1996, at the first national meeting in Bom Jesus da Lapa (Bahia), this temporary commission became the *Coordenação Nacional de Articulação das Comunidades Negras Rurais Quilombolas* [National Coordination of Quilombola Black Rural Communities, CONAQ]. This was the first moment at which quilombolas became multivocal. Today, CONAQ is the national organizing body for quilombola rights. CONAQ gathers quilombola organizations at the regional and state level and has representatives in 23 out of 26 states (Souza 158; cf. CONAQ).

A second moment of becoming multivocal for the quilombo movement took place four years later, in 2000, during the *II Encontro Nacional das Comunidades Negras Rurais Quilombolas* [II National Meeting of Black Rural Quilombola Communities] that convened in Salvador da Bahia. Until then, the national representation of the quilombo movement had both quilombola representatives and representatives from the Black urban movement. However, during this second national meeting, quilombola leaders assumed full representation of the quilombo movement through CONAQ (Souza 158). For instance, they decided that only quilombolas could vote on coordination-related issues during their meetings.

Official recognition of the struggles of the quilombola movement came in 2003. Under the leadership of President Lula da Silva, and in collaboration with anthropologists and other "cultural experts" as well as CONAQ, the federal government modified the definition of quilombo from a rigid, static interpretation to a more fluid one. Decree No. 4.887 of November 20, 2003, establishes that: "Quilombo remnant communities, for purposes of this Decree, are considered ethno-racial groups, *according to criteria of self-attribution*, with their historical trajectory, with specific territorial relations, with a presumption of black ancestry related to resistance to a suffered historical oppression" (Diário Oficial [da] República Federativa do Brasil 2003; emphasis added). This decree radically transformed the criteria that had been in place since 1988, which stated that the validity of quilombos' legitimacy claims required historical or archaeological evidence backed up by "cultural experts." As many scholars and activists have noted, the demand for material proofs disqualified *a priori* many potential plaintiffs, placing them as "usurpers of the history of their ancestors" (Salaini and Fagundes Jardim 196). In the words of Kenny, self-attribution "radically shifted the notion of quilombolas from a historical artifact (descendants of fugitive slaves), to a political group (oppressed minorities defending their territory) and resulted in a significant increase in groups mobilizing to be federally recognized by the FCP" (Kenny 97). A second encouragement followed this decree for quilombolas to speak up: the federal government's creation of the *Programa Brasil Quilombola* [Brazil Quilombola Program] in 2004. The program's objective was to coordinate governmental actions to support remaining quilombo communities at the local and inter-institutional levels through projects connected to land rights, health, essential services, and employment, among others (Cunha and Albano 162).

The third moment of multivocality is related to the quilombola movement that brought its causes to the international arena. For instance, the quilombola movement has been present at the World Social Forum since 2003 and the World Conference to Combat Racism, Racial Discrimination, Xenophobia, and Related Intolerance in Durban in 2001. In addition, in 2007, CONAQ representatives were present at the OEA and discussed cases of violation of collective rights by the Brazilian state. These engagements opened up the possibility of dialogues about how peoples of African descent and indigenous peoples have responded to neocolonial oppression.

Conclusions: from *quilombagem* to *quilombismo* to *aquilombar-se*

With the formation of the CONAQ, the quilombola movement received recognition as one of the most important agents of the Black movement today. Moreover, quilombos became, as Leite (2015) has proposed, a metaphor for Afro-Brazilian identity ("The Brazilian Quilombo" 1226). During the 1960s and 1970s, the Brazilian Black movement, however restricted, could speak for quilombolas. At the time, and as detailed in this chapter, quilombolas did not define themselves as such, but as Black peasants or *caiçaras negros* and, later, *negros camponeses*. Thus, a kind of ventriloquism continued to take place for quite some years. Today, those former *caiçaras negros* and *negros camponeses* self-identify as quilombolas and have established essential means to speak for themselves and cooperate with other marginalized populations. Yet, the message conveyed by CONAQ is that the struggle continues and that resistance remains a call to action for Brazilian quilombolas.

And the struggle indeed continues. The *Secretaria Especial de Políticas de Promoção da Igualdade Racial* [Special Secretary for Racial Equality Promotion Policies, SEPPIR] and INCRA both estimate that there are 2,847certified quilombo communities in Brazil, 1,533 open processes at INCRA, and 154 titled quilombos, out of which 80% have been regularized by state governments (CONAQ). Thus, less than 7% of quilombos have received collective ownership of their territories. These numbers demonstrate that the actual implementation of the Constitution of 1988 is slow-paced, at best.

While CONAQ and its members consider themselves part of the Brazilian Black movement, they also see differences between their struggles and those of Afro-Brazilians who are not quilombolas – particularly those who live in urban areas. There is a small number of urban quilombos throughout Brazil, but most quilombos are rural, and CONAQ emphasizes quilombolas' attachment to territory and nature as essential. According to Josilene Brandão Costa, a quilombola activist and member of CONAQ, there is a spirit of solidarity and common cause among quilombos:

> Being close to the land and nature gives us a special sensitivity and compassion that urban black people are losing. These features impact the different ways we organize our

> communities. In the quilombos, we are stronger and more united in our struggles for our rights than the urban black communities .... The Black Movement and the quilombo movement have the same African roots. We are the consequence of the same social process and suffer from the same social problem: racism. But we have different institutional forms. (Brandão Costa qtd. in Bowen 135)

In effect, CONAQ continues the struggle for the right to collective land ownership. As is stated in their official website,

> the notion of communal land, as quilombola land is conceived, puts in crisis the model of society based on private property as the only form of access to the land, instituted since the Law of Lands (1850). Thus, the state needs to rethink its agrarian structure by recognizing its interethnic character concerning territorial occupation. (CONAQ)

The CONAQ is also concerned with implementing sustainable development projects and public policy to support its constituents. It also works on quality quilombola education, giving prominence and autonomy to quilombola women, providing opportunities to quilombola youth to stay in their territories, and protecting natural resources and the environment (CONAQ).

The movement calls for the notion of *aquilombar-se* as essential. Aquilombar-se refers to guaranteeing the rights of quilombolas on multiple fronts, including the coordination of associations and federations. Aquilombar-se further refers to the fact that "the struggle continues not for the right to survive but for the right to exist in all its grandeur" (CONAQ). In this light, the quilombola movement demonstrates a move from *quilombagem*, a noun, passing through *quilombismo*, a reference to the collective, to its most active version, *aquilombar-se*, a verb, a process – the act of becoming quilombola or taking on quilombola identity and causes. The notion of aquilombar-se was already present during colonial times and referred to a group of people coming together to protect themselves in a quilombo. Contemporary quilombolas use the same term to refer to the act of effectively becoming quilombolas, recognizing the long history of resistance and the need to continue the fight for quilombola rights. Peoples of African descent have also used it to refer to learning about quilombo history as part of their heritage and thus actively becoming aware of the struggles of all Afro-Brazilians (Abramowicz and Gomes). The term has further been adopted by the Afro-Brazilian Black feminist movement to refer to the act of gaining strength from their ancestors to come together to fight for their rights – "aquilombar o feminismo" (Novais and Jucá n. pag.).

Resistance brings with it the concept of existence – an existence that exemplifies what the Martinican writer and philosopher Édouard Glissant (2006) called "circular nomadism," the right to invoke more than one root and more than one culture as legitimate. Aquilombar-se refers to the right of quilombolas to resist and thus to exist, independently, in their collective territories and with their practices as full-fledged Brazilian citizens. As the present chapter proposes, the quilombo movement has come full circle to proffer inspiration and wisdom to the Brazilian Black movement, and in the process, to continue strengthening its multivocality.

Works cited

Abramowicz, Anete, and Nilma Lino Gomes, eds. *Educação e Raça: Perspectivas Políticas, Pedagógicas e Estéticas*. Coleção Cultura Negra e Identidades. São Paulo: Autêntica Editores, 2017. Print.

Alberto, Paulina. "When Rio was Black: Soul Music, National Culture, and the Politics of Racial Comparison in 1970s Brazil." *Hispanic American Historical Review* 89.1 (2009): 3–39. Print.

Anderson, Nelson Robert. "The Quilombo of Palmares: A New Overview of a Maroon State in Seventeenth-Century Brazil." *Journal of Latin American Studies* 28.3 (1996): 545–566. Print.

Andrade, Lúcia Mendonça Morato. *Terra de Quilombo: Herança e Direito*. São Paulo: Comissão Pró-Índio de São Paulo, 2005. Print.

Andrews, George Reid. "Black Political Protest in São Paulo, 1888–1988." *Journal of Latin American Studies* 24.1 (1992): 147–171. Print.

Arruti, José Maurício. "Quilombos." *Raça: Novas Perspectivas Antropólogicas*. Ed. Osmundo Araújo Pinho and Livio Sansone. Salvador: EDUFBA, 2008. 315–350. Print.

Bowen, Merle L. "The Struggle for Black Land Rights in Brazil: An Insider's View on Quilombos and the Quilombo Land Movement." *African Diaspora in Brazil: History, Culture, and Politics*. Ed. Fassil Dimissie. London / New York: Routledge, 2014. 133–154. Print.

Butler, Kim D. "Up from Slavery: Afro-Brazilian Activism in São Paulo, 1888–1938." *The Americas* 49.2 (1992): 179–206. Print.

———. *Freedoms Given, Freedoms Won: Afro-Brazilians in Post-Abolition, São Paulo and Salvador*. New Brunswick, NJ: Rutgers UP, 1998. Print.

Carneiro, Edison. *O Quilombo dos Palmares*. 2nd ed. São Paulo: Companhia Editora Nacional, 1958. Print.

CONAQ (Coordenação Nacional de Articulação das Comunidades Negras Rurais Quilombolas). "Nossa História." CONAQ. 2020. Web. http://conaq.org.br/nossa-historia/.

Covin, David. *The Unified Black Movement in Brazil, 1978–2002*. Jefferson, NC / London: McFarland, 2006. Print.

Cunha, Felipe Gibson, and Sebastião Guilherme Albano. "Identidades Quilombolas: Políticas, Dispositivos e Etnogêneses." *Latinoamérica: Revista de Estudios Latinoamericanos* 64 (2017): 153–184. Print.

Domingues, Petrônio. "Movimento Negro Brasileiro: História, Tendências e Dilemas Contemporâneos." *Dimensões* 21 (2008): 101–124. Print.

Ennes, Ernesto. "As Guerras Nos Palmares: Subsídios Para a Sua História." *Brasiliana*. 1938. N. pag. Print.

Federal, Senado. *Constituição da República Federativa do Brasil*. Brasilia: Secretaria de Editoração e Publicações, 2016. Print.

Glissant, Édouard. *Tratado del Todo-Mundo* [Traité du Toute-Monde]. Translated by María Teresa Gallego Urrutia. Barcelona: Editorial El Cobre, 2006. Print.

Gomes, Flávio dos Santos. *Mocambos e Quilombos: Uma História do Campesinato Negro no Brasil*. São Paulo: Claro Enigma, 2015. Print.

———. *A Hidra e os Pântanos: Mocambos, Quilombos e Comunidades de Fugitivos no Brasil (Séculos XVII–XIX)*. São Paulo: Polis, 2005. Print.

Guerrero, Andrés. "El Proceso de Identificación: Sentido Común Ciudadano, Ventriloquía y Transescritura. Del Tributo de Indios a la Administración de Poblaciones en el Ecuador del Siglo XIX." *Antología del Pensamiento Crítico Ecuatoriano Contemporáneo*. Ed. Gioconda Herrera Mosquera. Buenos Aires: CLACSO, 2018. 343–388. Print.

Guimarães, Antônio Sérgio Alfredo. "Democracia Racial: O Ideal, o Pacto e o Mito." *Estudios Sociológicos* XX (2001): 147–162. Print.

Guimarães, Carlos Mago. *A Negação da Ordem Escravista: Quilombos em Minas Gerais no Século XVII*. São Paulo: Ícon, 1988. Print.

Kenny, Mary Lorena. "Making Heritage in Brazilian Quilombos." *Antípoda: Revista de Antropología y Arqueología* 12 (2011): 91–111. Print.

Leite, Ilka Boaventura. "The Brazilian Quilombo: Race, Community and Land in Space and Time." *The Journal of Peasant Studies* 42 (2015): 1225–1240. Print.

———. "Humanidades Insurgentes: Conflitos e Criminalização Dos Quilombos." *Nova Cartografia Social: Territórios Quilombolas e Conflitos*. Manaus: Projeto Nova Cartografia Social da Amazônia/UEA Edições, 2010. 18–40. Print.

Magalhães Pinto, Ana Flávia. *Escritos De Liberdade: Literatos Negros, Racismo e Cidadania no Brasil Oitocentista*. Campinas: Editora Unicamp, 2019 Print.

Martínez Novo, Carmen. "Ventriloquism, Racism and the Politics of Decoloniality in Ecuador." *Cultural Studies* 32.3 (2018): 389–413. Print.

Minardi, Giovanna. "La Presencia Negra en el Perú." *África, Iberoamérica, y Europa: Intercambios Culturales desde una Perspectiva Multidisciplinar*. Ed. Diego Melo Carrasco. Madrid: Editorial Dykinson, S. L., 2021. 127–136. Print.

Moura, Clovis. *História do Negro Brasileiro*. São Paulo: Ática, 1989. Print.

Nascimento, Abdias. *O Quilombismo: Documentos de uma Militância Pan-Africanista*. Petrópolis: Vozes, 1980. Print.

———. "An Afro-Brazilian Political Alternative." *Journal of Black Studies* 11.2 (1980): 141–178. Print.

———. "Conferência Nacional do Negro." *Jornal Quilombo* 1 (9 May 1949): 5–6. Print.

———. "Rio Grande do Sul: União dos Homens de Cor." *Jornal Quilombo* 3 (9 Dec. 1948): N. pag. Print.

Needell, Jeffrey D. *The Sacred Cause: The Abolitionist Movement, Afro-Brazilian Mobilization, and Imperial Politics in Rio De Janeiro*. Stanford, CA: Stanford UP, 2020. Print.

Novais, Maysa Carvalhal dos Reis, and Roberta Laena Costa Jucá. *Aquilombar of Feminismo*. International Seminar Fazendo Gênero 11 & 13th Women's Worlds Congress (Anais Eletrônicos), Florianópolis, 2017. N. pag. Print.

O'Dwyer, Eliane Cantarino, ed. *Quilombos: Identidade Étnica e Territorialidade*. Rio de Janeiro: FGV, 2002. Print.

Péret, Benjamin. *O Quilombo de Palmares: Crónica da "República dos Escravos."* Lisboa: Fenda Ed, 1998. Print.

Reis, João José. "Identidade e Diversidade Étnicas nas Irmandades Negras no Tempo da Escravidão." *Tempo* 2.3 (1996): 7–33. Print.

Reis, João José, and Flávio dos Santos Gomes, eds. *Liberdade Por um Fio: História dos Quilombos no Brasil*. São Paulo: Companhia das Letras, 1996. Print.

Rodrigues, Bruno de Oliveira, Tayra Fonseca Rezende, and Tiago de Garcia Nunes. "Movimento Negro e a Pauta Quilombola no Constituinte: Ação, Estratêgia e Repertório." *Revista Direito e Praxis* 10.1 (2019): 198–221. Print.

Salaini, Cristian, and Denise Fagundes Jardim. "Batalha Dos Papéis: Notas Sobre as Tensões entre Procedimentos Escritos e Memória na Regularização Fundiária de Terras de Quilombos no Brasil." *Universitas Humanística* 80 (2015): 189–212. Print.

Souza, Bárbara Oliveira. *Aquilombar-Se: Panorama Histórico, Identitário e Político do Movimento Quilombola Brasileiro*. Mestrado em Antropologia Social, Universidade de Brasília, 2008. Print.

Taylor, Diana. *El Archivo y el Repertorio: El Cuerpo y la Memoria Cultural en las Américas*. Santiago de Chile, Chile: Ediciones Universidad Alberto Hurtado, 2015. Print.

Treece, David. "Candeia, o Projeto Quilombo e a Militância Antirracista Nos Anos 1970." *Revista do Instituto de Estudos Brasileiros* 70 (2018): 166–188. Print.

Vansina, Jan. "Quilombos in São Tomé, or in Search of Original Sources." *History in Africa* 23 (1996): 453–459. Print.

Vilas, Paula Cristina. "A Voz do Quilombo: Na Senda das Vocalidades Afro-Brasileiras." *Horizontes Antropológicos* 11.24 (2005): 185–197. Print.

Wabgou, Maguemati, Jaime Arocha Rodríguez, Alden José Salgado Cassiani, and Juan Alberto Carabalí Ospina. *Movimiento Social Afro-Colombiano, Negro, Raizal y Palenque: El Largo Camino Hacia la Construcción de Espacios Comunes y Alianzas Estratégicas Para la Incidencia Política en Colombia*. Bogotá: Universidad Nacional de Colombia, 2012. Print.

Soul Music and Sisterhood as Expressions of Black Power

KENSEDEOBONG BLESSED OKOSUN

This chapter will explore soul music and Sisterhood as expressions of Black Feminism in the Black Power era. It intends to highlight the operation of Sisterhood outside the Black Power movement. It is apparent that the concept is not original, but as Audre Lorde has suggested "there are [only] new ways of making it felt" (Lorde 39). Sisterhood developed new strands within the prism of soul music (and body politics, fashion, and beauty) in the 1960s that coincided with the emergence of the feminist movement and the heydays of the Black Power movement. As Susan McClary argues, music as a vulnerable element of culture absorbs prevalent societal dynamics which can be weaponized for political purposes (McClary 117). It mirrors the socio-political paradigms that mark a society. This chapter engages with a demonstration of Black female artist's contextualization of Sisterhood within the framework of soul music. Black female artists have been sonically assertive in their solidarity with fellow sisters and the overall elevation of the black community. Musical Sisterhood can be traced to the blues repertoire of Bessie Smith in the early twentieth century where she counseled and admonished women, while simultaneously addressing black subjectivity and social conditions.

As Ashley D. Farmer indicates, the roots of the Black Power movement are traceable to "the intellectualism and activism of postwar women radicals" that flourished under the political tutelage of Marcus Garvey's Universal Negro Improvement Association in the 1920s and 1930s. Known for its core tenets, which included a mass return to Africa, segregation, and self-determinism, the disintegration of the movement after the Great Depression led to a massive flow of Black women into the United Communist Party (Farmer 20–21). The party framed Black emancipation around the template of the working class, which comprised Black women, and the new affiliation resonated significantly due to its adoption of "Garveyite Nationalist Frameworks" that fostered a political navigation of the triple oppressions militating against Black women, namely – racism, sexism, and capitalism (21). However, the male-dominant Black Power movement did not recognize Black women as major stakeholders. While some functioned in varying capacities within the movement, others operated as outsiders.

Black feminist theorists like Audre Lorde (2007 [1984]) and bell hooks (1984) identify Sisterhood as a germane component of the quest for political solidarity amongst women and a relevant tool in the agitation against sexism. In this view, the social empowerment of women is predicated on their ability to encourage and promote each other, an attribute which "is not pathological but redemptive" (Lorde 111). According to hooks, suspicion, comparativeness, competitiveness, and defensiveness are some of the sexist externalizations by women: "It is sexism that leads women to feel threatened by one another without cause .... Sexism teaches women woman-hating, and both consciously and unconsciously we act out this hatred in our daily contact with one another" (hooks, *Feminist Theory* 47).

Sexist oppression marks the reality of women and should, by default, prompt solidarity. But as hooks observes, a social indoctrination has facilitated absoluteness in compliance to societal dictates. Women are socialized to self-devalue and seek existential legitimacy through relationships with men. They are taught that female bonding disparages their reality. "We are taught that women are 'natural' enemies, that solidarity will never exist between us because we cannot, should not, and do not bond with one another" (hooks, *Feminist Theory* 43). hooks demonstrates that the negligence of female identification corrodes an inherently enriching support system.

Within the context of the feminist movement, both theorists attribute the debilitation of Sisterhood to a historical disconnect between women of the most diverse backgrounds and the inconsideration of the intersectionality which defined their unique experiences. The marginalization of difference, a fundamental tool for the achievement of peaceful coexistence, impeded the understanding of the collective struggles that challenge women of all ethnicities (Lorde 118; 123). Solidarity is enhanced through the affirmation of diversity, and hooks notes that the multiplicity of women's experiences translated to dissimilar needs, and no one-dimensional principle could veritably address the political necessities of all (hooks, *Feminist Theory* 58).

Furthermore, she stresses that the attainment of societal transformation occurs through the unlearning of sexist values, the acceptance of difference in all ramifications and a reinvention of the female consciousness. In her conclusion,

> [w]omen do not need to eradicate difference to feel solidarity. We do not need to share common oppression to fight equally to end oppression. We do not need anti-male sentiments to bond us together, so great is the wealth of experience, culture, and ideas we have to share with one another. We can be sisters united by shared interests and beliefs, united in our appreciation for diversity, united in our struggle to end sexist oppression, united in political solidarity. (hooks, *Feminist Theory* 65)

In essence, for hooks, Sisterhood should be driven, not by man-hating, but by a desire to harness the uniqueness of experiences that diversity presents. Her suggestion implies that even though political solidarity amongst women can be read as excluding men, it inevitably benefits the collective. Within the Black community, Lourde is right in her observation that Sisterhood is not a novelty because a long history of uninhibited intra-racial bonding amidst socio-historical deterrents has existed (48). Afro-diasporic women intellectuals like Ida B. Wells from the U.S., Amy Jacques Garvey from Jamaica, Lélia Gonzalez from Brazil, to name a few, played a prominent role in mobilizing Black women seeking social change. Their indispensability is undeniable in the quest for Black Nationalism, because "any serious history student of Black activism knew that Black women were regularly driving forces" (Kendi 365).

As already hinted, Black female singers have deployed music to mirror their personal and social experiences. In his demonstration of the saliency of Black Music across the social history of African Americans, Amiri Baraka writes in his seminal work, *Blues People* that:

> The most expressive Negro music of any given period will be an exact reflection of what the Negro himself is. It will be a portrait of the Negro in America at that particular time. Who he thinks he is, what he thinks America or the world to be, given the circumstances, prejudices, and delights of that particular America. Negro music and Negro life in America were always the result of a reaction to, and an adaptation of, whatever America Negroes were given or could secure for themselves. (Baraka 137)

Clearly, Black music ebulliently mirrors the social circumstance and evolution of the Black subject. Linked to the task at hand, Black female singers in the Black Power or "Soul Power" era contested the Black masculinist thought which shaped the movement. They musically expressed Sisterhood through the voicing of the Black female experience, by means of music and public statements which involved rhetoric and fashion. In view of the political volatility of the 1960s and the parochial gendering of the Black Power movement, Robin Morgan's characterization of voicing as insurgency (Morgan 4), can be adjudged in this context, as significant and fundamental in the demolition of constructed social barriers.

It is common knowledge that the Black male leadership, Black Nationalist movements, and fundamentalist Christian rhetoric contributed to the invalidation of the Black female. In her deliberation on self-esteem in the black community, bell hooks notes in *Rock My Soul*: *Black People and Self Esteem* (2003) that the Black male leadership's insular perception of gender egalitarianism (which has been an age-long contention) in the quest for racial elevation took a new dimension at the dawn of the twentieth century. Marcus Garvey, for instance, weaponized his platform for the propagation of sexist thoughts. This patriarchal structure became the template for subsequent movements like the Black Power movement (hooks, *Rock My Soul* 5). Accordingly, the pathology of patriarchal socialization undergirded the black collective thought process. Consequently, Black Sisterhood can be interpreted as the Black woman's solitary attempt towards self-redemption.

Against this backdrop, this chapter examines the intersection of gender, music, and identity politics through a historicization of the soul sound of the 1960s. It discusses the significance of soul music to black identity politics, and the Black Power movement. It weaves the narratives and anecdotes that constituted Black masculinist and feminist thoughts and illustrates Black female artists' resistance through Sisterhood. Moreover, the chapter delivers a close reading of song lyrics of selected soul singers and explores their musical engagement with Black feminism and Sisterhood. The selected Black female artists are chosen based on their musical virtuosity and fortitude to challenge established norms and to chart new frontiers.

Soul music, soul power

Soul music scholars agree that the genre emerged in the early 1960s. It was a cross-pollination of early rhythm and blues elements (blues and big band swing), and Black gospel music elements (the piano, call and response structure, and girl-chorus). It facilitated a sonic synergy between the sacred and secular perception of culture which had been reinvented by modernism. Sacredness had defined every facet of the African worldview, and Lawrence Levine's account of the Negro Spirituals (which included work songs, freedom songs, field holler, etc.) show a ubiquitous presence in the field, home, and church (Levine 332). "Travelers in the Old South and slaves themselves reported that music about god and the Bible was sung during work time, play time, and rest time as well as on Sundays at praise meetings" (Gates Jr and McKay 5).

In the 1960s, soul music was omnipresent in the black cultural and political spaces. As Nelson George observes, Ray Charles's new creation sired off-springs and proselytized converts. His sanctification of the hitherto 'devilish and iniquitous' landscape of rhythm and blues opened the floodgate for gospel's best voices to navigate the secular terrain:

> By breaking down the division between the pulpit and bandstand, recharging blues concerns with transcendental fervor, unashamedly linking the spiritual and the sexual, Charles made pleasure (physical satisfaction) and joy (divine enlightenment) seem the same thing. By doing so he brought the realities of the Saturday night sinner and Sunday-morning worshipper-so often one and the same-into a raucous harmony. (George 70)

Singers like Aretha Franklin, Sam Cooke, and Jackie Robinson switched musical borders, and became the "archetypes of the ubiquitous sacred – secular dichotomy in African American music" (Burnim 79).

That soul music became the embodiment of black identity politics was unsurprising, in view of the semantic shift which occurred in the meaning of rhythm and blues. R&B was a cover term for Black popular music in the early twentieth century (and in contemporary times). According to legend, Alan Freed, a Radio Disc Jockey, engineered the shift from R&B to "rock n roll" with the objective of deethnicization, creation of consumptive accessibility, and capitalistic exploitation of a potential white market in Jim Crow America.

The shift marked the commencement of an aesthetic alteration and whitening process. According to George, Chuck Berry became rock'n'roll's pioneer electric guitarist and so the instrument relegated R&B's saxophone to the background (George 68). Little Richard's sonic style remained unaffected, although his fan base gradually morphed from blacks to juvenile whites. But music miscegenation engendered co-optation, appropriation, and, ultimately, professional, and economic debilitation of the black artist. The whitening process enabled the entrance of new white acts and further propelled a white group-identification which militated against black artistic progression. As George notes, the final stage of the whitening process transmuted "rock'n'roll" to rock, which became the definitive white boys' music and a conduit for the musical articulation of white cultural experience. This development was deemed repugnant by black audiences. R&B, by contrast, embodied a musical and extra musical resonance which stimulated black self awareness and ethnic solidarity (George 93). Consequently, its transformation to soul music, afforded the black community a culturally reflexive music style with inherent socio-political currency.

The designation "Soul" qualified distinctive beliefs which framed black cultural experience and reflected for Black Americans, as Tanisha C. Ford notes,

> [t]he cultural manifestations of the feelings, thoughts, and emotions of a black person's inner being, a spirit that had survived the Middle Passage, slavery, and Jim Crow, as well as apartheid. Soul provided a cultural language through which people of African descent could speak about the horrors of slavery and colonialism while also serving as a source of cultural pride and political solidarity. (Ford 6)

Soul music was sonically affiliated with the movement and utilized for socio-political gatherings. Fred Hampton, chairman of the Chicago chapter of the Black Panther Party, who was assassinated by police forces in 1969, often used the Supremes' "Someday We'll Be Together" as a rally song (Sullivan 71). "Soul" was synonymic with black; as such, the phrase "Black Power" was interchanged with "Soul Power" for two reasons: the depiction of power as a collective objective and the legitimization of an individual's group-identification (9). During the revolts of 1964, 1965, and 1967 in Harlem, Watts, Detroit, and Newark, respectively, signs that read "soul brother," anomalous to the biblical blood of the lamb marked on the doors of Israelite homes in Exodus, were displayed on windows by Black entrepreneurs to avert pillaging by African American youth (Maultsby 278). The term's utilitarianism flowed into a plethora of Black cultural productions like arts, music, fashion, cuisine, etc., and was also exploited by mainstream corporate organizations for profit.

Black Power and Black masculinity

The Black Power movement was an outgrowth of the Civil Rights Movement and had, on its left wing, the Black Panther Party. The slogan "Black Power" encapsulated the disillusionment, forbearance, and fatigue associated with Martin Luther King's nonviolence philosophy. It signified righteous indignation, ignited a sense of urgency, and charted a new direction. It was a communal call to be agents in the cause of social change and Black liberation. Although the movement's emergence is connected to Stokely Carmichael, it bears reiterating that Black women have been indispensable in the agitation for Black Nationalism.

Paul Gilroy has observed that amidst the rhetoric and agitation for Black Nationalism undergirding Black American social movements, the recognition and acknowledgement of the "family relations that sustain the race," in essence, Black women, were marginalized (Gilroy 98). Despite the oppressions that challenged Black women, the Black Power movement sidelined their voices. "Black nationalism became the vehicle to push black patriarchal values" (hooks, *Rock My Soul* 5). "In the late 1960s, assertions of Black male pride remained at the center of calls for Black power that were implicitly and explicitly gendered male" (Feldstein 1367). Clearly, the attainment of racial elevation, in their myopic perception, was premised on the perpetual subjugation of Black women. The justification for this Black masculinist thought is gauged through the Black Panther spokesman Eldridge Cleaver's delineation of Black women as a racial threat and the status quo's weapon of Black male emasculation (hooks, *Rock My Soul* 7). Furthermore, the Black woman was regarded as "the downfall of the black man in that she is "evil," "hard to get along with," "domineering," "suspicious," and "narrow minded" (Lincoln 107). This thought process undermined the achievements of Black women, previously embraced as progressive for the collective and many male Black Power advocates began to regard the liberation of Black women as a "covert attack on black males" (hooks, *Rock My Soul* 7).

The paucity of evidence of Black women's interpretations of, and contributions to, the discourse on Black Power and its entire framework disallows a holistic assessment of the inner operations within the Black Power movement. As Ashley Farmer observes, while notable figures like Angela Davis, Assata Shakur, and Elaine Brown revealed through writings the malignant sexism within the movement, there was solidarity amongst the Black women collective which added value to the operation (Farmer 6). Although, Farmer challenges the notion of sexism in her inquiry of Black women's reinvention of gender and racial divisions during the era, her view is ambivalent. On the one hand, she considers the collective perception of the Black Power movement as a misogynist organization as mythical. She argues that "black women's formulations of womanhood were important sites of Black Power expression" which impacted "ideological and organizational trajectories" (6). They "left a record of direct and copious engagement with Black Power discourses, symbolism, and politics expressed through their ideas about their rights and roles" (10) and often contested the roles assigned to them by men. But on the other hand, their contestations were insufficient to overturn black patriarchy (10). This only implies that the movement positioned women on the periphery, sacrificed gender egalitarianism and collective progression – a view further attested to by the Combahee River Collective standpoint in 1977 – for a power-interest which was often reflected in the music.

Misogynistic thoughts were conspicuous in the music of soul icon James Brown. Mr. Dynamite celebrated his racial pride through songs like "Say it Loud, I'm Black and I'm Proud," fostered black consciousness in "I Don't want Nobody to Give Me Nothing," and imparted inspiration in "Get Up, Get Into It, Get Involved," etc. But "It's a Man's Man's Man's World" (1966) could be read as the sonic emblem of black patriarchy. The song highlights "man's" inventions. The repetition of the noun "man" alludes to a masculinized trinity at the helm of control, but the lyrics fail to convey "man's" identity or identities. It veils the "man's" grammatical number and race(s). The song presents a gender hierarchy which considers "a woman or a girl" as an afterthought.

E. Taylor Atkins (2015) has argued that historical antecedents like the lynching and emasculation of Black men in America fore-grounded the assertion of black manhood through the suppression of Black women. As such, Brown's song was "a response to the Women's Liberation Movement of the 1960s and 1970s as a misogynistic backlash, an effort to re-establish a male-dominated order in which women were primarily and fundamentally objects for male titillation and sexual conquest" (Atkins 338). Meanwhile, many male (and female) soul artists like Stevie Wonder, Marvin Gaye, and others were initially unidentified with sonic identity politics due to Motown's founder Berry Gordy's apolitical position and capitalistic cross-over objective, which involved ensuring the cultivation of his artists in the art of assimilation, in order to blur racial borders. But, as Matti Steinitz has shown, groups like Curtis Mayfield & the Impressions were trendsetters through their expressed musical solidarity with the cause of Black liberation. They promoted consciousness awakening songs like "Keep on Pushing" and "People Get Ready" at a time when it was unfashionable, whereas most soul artists would keep their lyrics strictly apolitical in fear of alienating white audiences. It was James Brown who would prove that message songs could also ensure economic success with the release of his Black Power anthem "(Say it loud) I'm Black and I'm Proud" in 1968 (Steinitz 90).

James Brown's importance as a highly influential leader of Black America was validated on April 5, 1968, the day after MLK's assassination, when he was billed to perform in Boston. His televised concert succeeded in preventing possible riots in that city. It is probably that he had assumed that these mesmerizing accomplishments were bound to get translated into racial equality. But Nelson George has stated that within the music industry, "Say It Loud …" strained Brown's relationship with whites (George 103). Sullivan states that the song, expectedly, resonated with the Black community, but lacked a mainstream appeal due to its perceived subversiveness which was further accentuated by its adoption by the Student Nonviolent Coordinating Committee (SNCC) and other Black Power groups. Brown, she notes, believed that the development robbed him of his white audience (Sullivan 95). As such, one would assert that the song's presumed economic success was the result of Black patronage. Secondly, the notion that Black entertainers feared alienating white audiences is partly correct, as attested to by Motown, but it also warrants holistic attention. The era was marked by cases of state suppression and many entertainers such as Nina Simone, John Lennon, Jimi Hendrix, and others were kept under state surveillance. Many artists were underpromoted like jazz artist Eugene McDaniel whose *Headless Heroes of the Apocalypse* (1971) promoted black pride. According to Sullivan, after the release of the aforementioned album, Spiro Agnew, Nixon's Vice President, purportedly called Atlantic Records to demand a termination of McDaniel's career (Sullivan 118). She asserts that "Entertainers without huge bases but with … spiritual, philosophical, or ideological grounding … were among the artists officially marked dangerous…. Without high-powered management on their side, they started to drift from consumer consciousness" (118). The censorship and repression of music activism perpetrated by the

Nixon Government and the Federal Bureau of Intelligence led by Edgar Hoover have also been addressed by Mark Anthony Neal in his book, *What the Music Said* (1999). The above narratives reveal the identity politics surrounding music during the era. Clearly, one could posit that if most soul artists adopted an apolitical stance in the years prior to 1968, it was informed by the need for self-preservation due to the times' highly volatile political atmosphere.

Black Sisterhood: Nina Simone and Aretha Franklin

The 'evil' black woman may have been marginalized within the movement, but she remained undeterred in her quest for social justice through music, outside the movement. Mark Anthony Neal accentuates the significance of Black female singers when he notes that: "Historically, black women's willingness to articulate the rich diversity of human emotions within black popular culture, particularly given the lack of accessible language to articulate such emotions, has served to broaden the limits of black popular expression" (Neal 74–75). Nina Simone and Aretha Franklin typified this expressionism.

Eunice Kathleen Waymon, later known as Nina Simone, was born to a church minister mother; endowed with a musical gift evident at age four, she was encouraged to sing and play the piano alongside the choir at her mother's church (Sullivan 32). She would work as an accompanist at an Atlantic City Piano bar after she was denied admission to the Curtis Institute of Music, Philadelphia. With her newfound path, she renamed herself to avert the communal shaming, as was the norm, that might have ridden her family due to her abandonment of 'holy' music for the 'devil's music' (32). The internationally acclaimed music virtuoso's close affiliation with the *crème de la crème* of the literary and artistic scene like James Baldwin, Langston Hughes, Amiri Baraka, Dick Gregory, and others, who actively campaigned for equity and equality, expanded her consciousness about the political terrain (17).

Here, it should be pointed out that Simone's overall perception was significantly sharpened by a Sisterhood that comprised Black female artists such as jazz vocalist Abbey Lincoln, the South African, exiled singer Miriam Makeba, and playwright Lorraine Hansberry who she called "her more politically informed friend" (Feldstein 1376). "Simone made relationships between women central to the very idea of black pride" (1375–1376). Hansberry's political impartation fostered Simone's participation in the quest for Black Power, and in her words, helped her "to think about myself as a black person in a country run by white people and a woman in a world run by men" (1375).

She understood active black participation to be ammunition for social change (Sullivan 33). Her interest in the composition of protest songs was ignited after Abbey Lincoln had been denounced by critics for consistently including messages of dissent in collaborations with jazz drummer and later husband, Max Roach such as their album *We Insist. Freedom Now Suite* (1960). Lincoln thematized race relations and the sluggishness that characterized the pursuit of change (Feldstein 1361). Simone's music would equally mirror the combustibility of the era and featured as a soundtrack at the SNCC meetings. Her contralto and "vocal eccentricity" conveyed panache to Black Power (Brooks, "Planet Earth(a)" 114).

The concurrence of the murder of NAACP Secretary, Medgar Evers in Mississippi and the murder of four girls in the basement of a church in Alabama in 1963 incited Simone's musical indictment of southern racism in "Mississippi Goddam." It was "delivered like a satirical show tune by a woman on fire" (Sullivan 27). "Mississippi Goddam" expressed indignation and disillusionment with race relations and solidarity disseminated through MLK's integration principle. And when she declared, "Me and my people are just about due," Simone unofficially became a force of reckoning in the terrain of Black activism. The musical polemic was banned from media broadcast. As Feldstein notes, "the principal objection raised by most critics to the Mississippi song was apparently not so much its militant lyrics, but the fact that an entertainer, and a woman entertainer at that, had dared to put them to music" (Feldstein 1368).

Another less militant, but culturally affirming song was "To Be Young, Gifted and Black" (1969). It was a message song to motivate and uplift young black Americans, written in memory of Lorraine Hansberry who had transitioned in 1965 at the age of 34. The playwright-activist addressed social issues like racism and gay rights in her works, which included *A Raisin in the Sun* (1959). And was the embodiment of youthfulness, intellect, and self-acceptance in her blackness. "To Be Young, Gifted and Black" inspired racial pride, self-value, and was a psychological therapy to the issues of Black self-esteem, one of the Black Power movement's goals. The movement's promotion of black aesthetics and "call for self-acceptance laid the foundation for a psychological revolution" (hooks, *Rock My Soul* 42–43).

Self-acceptance was externalized through the incorporation of natural and African-inspired beauty and fashion statements during the Black Power era like Afrocentric hairstyles (Afros and cornrows), Afrocentric jewellery, and African attires (dashikis and African printed fabrics). This body politics was critical and symbolic to both black liberation and women's liberation across the globe. Fashion became a mode of activism as Black women exercised their body autonomy. The "soul style," according to Tanisha C. Ford, fostered a reaesthecization of the black body as a measure of "rebuilding their psyches and healing emotional and physical wounds" (Ford 7). Miriam Makeba, the U.S.-exiled South African anti-apartheid singer, who had married Stokely Carmichael was a representation of naturalness read as "pro-black and anti-imperialist" (18). Her meeting with Simone in 1961 offered the latter a sense of connectedness in the celebration of blackness. Both women, in conjunction with Odetta Holmes and Abbey Lincoln, centralized and celebrated black aesthetics such as natural hair in their public appearances, contributing to the popularization of the Afro which would become a global symbol of black radicalism against the system through the iconic appearance of Angela Davis in the early 1970s. These women's collective expression of blackness

> subverted expectations of what a respectable black woman's body should look like, they also gave a generation a new set of terms and tools for asserting themselves. In a world where black women's bodies were often objectified and used as placeholders in a variety of competing ideologies – whether as symbols of "primitive" black sexuality or as keepers of black respectability. (Ford 14)

Furthermore, Simone prioritized black female politics in "Four Women" (1966), where she politicized black women's body aesthetics. Feldstein has argued that "Simone offered a vision of black cultural nationalism … that insisted on female power – well before the apparent ascendance of black power or second-wave feminism…" (Feldstein 1367). The song highlights the complexities of black self-esteem and black female tropes, while reflecting the historical legacy of Black women's trans-generational traumatization.

The four women Aunt Sarah, Saffronia, Sweet Thing, and Peaches tell their stories of disenfranchisement within a society that glorifies fair skin, blue eyes, and straight blond hair as beauty standards. Aunt Sarah is the unambiguous Black woman with "black skin," "woolly hair," long arms, and a strong back. Her physical aesthetics epitomize the mule and strong worker. Saffronia is the tragic but privileged mulatto who navigates the dual racial poles with ease. Sweet Thing has "tan" skin and is endowed with fine hair and inviting hips. She represents the sexualized Black woman whose beauty and sexuality are commodified. Finally, Peaches fits the embittered and angry Black woman trope with a tough and aggressive attitude, incensed by the memory of her ancestral legacy and the concomitant traumatization emanating there from.

Abbey Lincoln's 1966 article, "Who Will Revere The Black Woman" validates Simone's lyricism. It chronicles the in-depth dehumanization of Black women who have been made "the scape-goat for what white America has made of the "Negro personality" (Lincoln 107). Considering this socio-cultural history, Simone shows solidarity with Black women through an honest and contextualized representation of them as products of a racialized society which employs shaming strategies like stereotypes while suppressing the origins of the social problem. Ironically, the claim that "Four Women" disparaged Black women prompted the song's ban from airplay by Black radio stations (Sullivan 61).

Despite the cultural castigation which encumbered Black women, Aretha Franklin demanded "Respect" from a society that gave the Black woman none. The Queen of Soul began her career as a child, singing the gospel at the New Bethel Baptist Church, Detroit, where her father Reverend Clarence Lavaughn Franklin pastored. The embryonic phase of her professional career at Columbia Records was unremarkable. However, her transfer to Atlantic Records in 1966 marked the advent of a more fulfilling and acclaimed career that spanned over five decades. Although Franklin stated that "I don't make it a practice to put my politics into my music or social commentary" (qtd. in Lordi 181), her 1967 release "Respect" had immense political significance and became an anthem of protest because, as Steinitz alludes, the paucity of message songs during the early phase of the political era meant that activists could encode social meaning into personal songs (Steinitz 90). And "Respect" was one such song. Originally performed by Otis Redding, Franklin's revision of the lyrics and rhythm enriched its appeal as an "anthem of black power, more specifically of black female power" (Lordi 199). The song intersected Black Nationalism and feminism. It enabled a Black male – Black female dialogue in the context of the answer back pattern, which became an established rap staple in the 1980s. Basically, as Cheryl L. Keyes has pointed out, "one rap is posed as a response or answer to a previous release." The trend evolved as musical battle between the sexes (Keyes 312–313). Franklin's response to Redding symbolized the Black female's indignation and confrontation of sexism, and lopsided Black male expectations, which exploited her with an indifference that ignored their shared reality. Her voicing of Black women's experience in relationships mirrored the "hatred of black womanhood [which] is ever present in this culture and gathering added momentum" (hooks, *Salvation* 107).

Daphne A. Brooks's eulogy following the decease of Franklin in 2018 underscores her essence to Black women. She writes:

> She dared to voice and make public the nuanced, emotionally heterogeneous interiority of black womanhood, becoming a conduit for articulating the beauty and sensuousness, the rage and the despair, the sadness as well as the joy of black life transuded through African American female musicianship. She turned the "vocal run" itself into a thousand miles of freedom. (Brooks, "Drenched" n. pag.)

Franklin's voice also functioned as a beacon of hope to Black women not only sonically but through the issuance of bold public statements. In a demonstration of Sisterhood to Angela Y. Davis, member of the Black Panther and gender activist, who was jailed on trumped up charges in 1970, Franklin offered to pay the bail which ranged between \$100,000–\$250,000 to obtain Davis's freedom. In a statement originally extracted from a *Jet* Magazine article, dated December 3rd, 1970, she stated:

> Angela Davis must go free. Black people will be free. I've been locked up (for disturbing the peace in Detroit) and I know you got to disturb the peace when you can't get no peace. Jail is hell to be in. I'm going to see her free if there is any justice in our courts, not because I believe in communism, but because she's a Black woman and she wants freedom for Black people. I have the money; I got it from Black people – they've made me financially able to have it – and I want to use it in ways that will help our people. (qtd. in Merelli n. pag.)

By 1970, Franklin had developed a political inclination. Her comment signals the power inherent in active political participation, a ripened consciousness and personal commitment to the black political struggle. Davis symbolized the shackled Black woman and Franklin's comment transported the desire for the liberation of Black people and the Black female, in particular. We do not observe a castigation of Davis for her radicalized political belief but a solidarity which honored and respected the sovereignty of the Black woman to choose her affiliation and make her decision. With black economic autonomy at the core of Black Power, Franklin's reference to her financial gains, attributed to the support of her community and pledge to support her kindred, emblematized the objective of self-sufficiency without recourse to external handouts.

In the field of poetry, Franklin's solidarity would be reciprocated by ace poet and key player in the Black Power-inspired Black Arts Movement, Nikki Giovanni. She canvassed for the cultural protection of Aretha Franklin and the maintenance of her nascent legacy, at the time. She sensitized the Black community on the multifarious responsibilities (mother, wife, public figure, leader) shouldered by the Black female artist. Emily J. Lordi's critique of Giovanni's eulogy, "Poem for Aretha" reveals the latter as a self-ordained foot soldier with the self-initiative to truncate the tragic pattern which had shortened the lives of Bessie Smith, Dinah Washington, and Billie Holliday. The poem reflects Franklin's challenges within the domestic and social domains, as well as the high expectations and inconsideration of her humanity which devalued her essence. As Lordi writes, "Giovanni asks black readers to … take responsibility for female singers' survival … She seeks to save Franklin from 'the way we are killing her' before it is too late" (Lordi 185). Giovanni's observation, one may add, redirects attention to the Black female artists who lacked a support system to shield them from the fiery darts of social critique and expectations. Giovanni reminds us of the chequered careers and tragic lives of Whitney Houston and Phyllis Hyman (both of whom died prematurely), and the nomadic Nina Simone, Donna Summer, Tina Turner, Chaka Khan, and Jody Watley of Shalamar (whose search for respite led to a self-exile in Europe). Franklin was seldom conversational, but Giovanni became her voice. It would not be erroneous to argue, therefore, that this Sisterhood was efficacious in averting at least some foreseen and unforeseen tragedies.

The above-mentioned musical-literary dichotomy evokes the solidarity shared between Bessie Smith and Zora Neale Hurston during the Harlem Renaissance era. In sum, both women were committed to the promotion of the "African American aesthetic" and resisted the assimilation tenets of the Harlem Renaissance patriarchs through their persistent promotion of folk culture (Davis 155). As alluded to earlier, Smith prioritized the Black female community and framed the harshly dehumanizing Black cultural experiences in her music. And Hurston fictionalized those elements in her writing (154–155).

Turning back to Franklin, her political solidarity can also be read within the context of her musical citation of other female artists. In my view, musical reinterpretation reflects the following: An inter-genre stylistic variation, a commemoration of a deceased or the reintroduction of an older artist to a younger audience, and veneration of the original artist. When examined within the context of Sisterhood and Black Power, the third factor encapsulates Franklin's interpretation of Nina Simone's "To Be Young, Gifted and Black." Although her version is reconstructed, it marks her entrance into the political terrain and an externalized recognition of the Black cause, as earlier stated. Her choice of this anthem reflects identification with Simone's message and activism because on the cover of the album *Young, Gifted and Black* (1972) which features the song, Franklin emulates the Afrocentrism and soul style of Simone. Both women represented the untameable and unsuppressed soul power unleashed at a time when repression ruled their environment. Neal has argued that Franklin and Simone's music was the similitude of musical foremothers like Rainey, Smith, Washington, and

Holiday. Their collective voices were characterized by "black rage and militancy, with nuanced demands for human respect and human decency" (Neal 74).

Conclusion

This essay has attempted to demonstrate the significance of soul music to black identity and Black Nationalism. It has further studied the contextualization of Sisterhood within its framework during the Black Power era. While Sisterhood was customary for Nina Simone, it was merely symbolic and selective for Franklin. She had a reputation for competitiveness in her personal relationships with her two sisters, Erma and Carolyn, and in her professional relationships with singers Dionne Warwick, Natalie Cole, etc. (cf. King). Nonetheless, if she was highly esteemed and aggrandized, she had earned the crown.

Feminist Black Power discourse continued into the 1970s, with singers like Mavis Staples, Valerie Simpson, Roberta Flack, Marlena Shaw, Linda Jones, and Esther Phillips, who deployed their voices to broadly mass mediate "racial and gender-based suffering" while extolling the resiliency of Black women in surpassing manifold oppressions (Neal 75). Finally, it should be stressed that Black female singers from the U.S., such as those portrayed in this chapter, have played the significant role of beacons of Black female empowerment in the Americas, when compared to their more subjugated peers in other Afro-diasporic musical forms such as Salsa or Reggae.

Works cited

Atkins, E. Taylor. "The Funky Divas Talk Back: Dialogues about Black Feminism, Masculinity, and Soul Power in the Music of James Brown." *Popular Music and Society* 38.3 (2015): 337–354. Web. https://www.tandfonline.com/doi/full/10.1080/03007766.2014.929321.

Baraka, Amiri (Leroi Jones). *Blues People*. New York: Harper Perennial, 2002. Print.

Brooks, Daphne A. "Planet Earth(a): Sonic Cosmopolitanism and Black Feminist Theory." *Cornbread and Cuchifritos: Ethnic Identity Politics, Transnationalization, and Transculturation in American Urban Popular Music*. Ed. Wilfried Raussert and Michelle Habell-Pallán. Trier: WVT / Tempe, AZ: Bilingual, 2011. 111–125. Print.

———. "Drenched in Glory: How Aretha Gave Voice to Embattled Black Women – and Transformed a Nation." *The Guardian* (17 Aug. 2018): n. pag. Print.

Burnim, Mellonee V. "Crossing Musical Borders: Agency and Process in the Gospel Music Industry." *Issues in African American Music: Power, Gender, Race, Representation*. Ed. Portia K. Maultsby and Mellonee V. Burnim. New York: Routledge, 2017. 79–89. Print.

Davis, Angela Y. *Blues Legacies and Black Feminism: Gertrude "Ma" Rainey, Bessie Smith, and Billie Holiday*. New York: Vintage, 1998. Print.

Farmer, Ashley D. *Remaking Black Power: How Black Women Transformed an Era*. Chapel Hill: U of North Carolina P, 2017. Print.

Feldstein, Ruth. "'I Don't Trust You Anymore': Nina Simone, Culture, and Black Activism in the 1960s." *The Journal of American History* 91.4 (Mar. 2005): 1349–1379.

Ford, Tanisha C. *Liberated Threads: Black Women, Style, and the Global Politics of Soul.* Chapel Hill: U of North Carolina P, 2015. Print.

Gates Jr, Henry Louis, and Nellie Y. Mckay. *The Norton Anthology of African American Literature*. New York: W.W. Norton & Company, 1997. Print.

George, Nelson. *The Death of Rhythm and Blues*. New York: Pantheon, 1988. Print.

Gilroy, Paul. *The Black Atlantic*. London: Verso, 1999. Print.

hooks, bell. *Feminist Theory: From the Margin to the Center.* Boston: South End Press, 1984. Print.

———. *Salvation: Black People and Love*. New York: Harper Perennial, 2001. Print.

———. *Rock My Soul: Black People and Self-Esteem*. New York: Washington Square Press, 2003. Print.

Kendi, Ibram X. *Stamped From the Beginning*. London: Penguin Random House, 2016. Print.

Keyes, Cheryl L. "'Ain't Nuthin' but a She Thang': Women in Hip Hop." *Issues in African American Music: Power, Gender, Race, Representation.* Ed. Portia K. Maultsby and Mellonee V. Burnim. New York: Routledge, 2017. 306–328. Print.

King, Jason. "How Aretha Franklin Earned Her Crown as the Queen of Soul." *Pitchfork.* 16 Aug. 2018. Web. https://pitchfork.com/artists/6279-aretha-franklin/.

Levine, Lawrence W. "The Antebellum Period." *Issues in African American Music: Power, Gender, Race, Representation*. Ed. Portia K. Maultsby and Mellonee V. Burnim. New York: Routledge, 2017. 331–342. Print.

Lincoln, Abbey. "Who Will Revere the Black Woman?" *SOS – Calling All Black People: A Black Arts Movement Reader*. Ed. John H. Bracey, Jr., Sonia Sanchez, and James Smethurst. Amherst / Boston: U of Massachusetts P, 2014. Print.

Lorde, Audre. *Sister Outsider*. Berkeley: Crossing Press, 2007. Print.

Lordi, Emily J. *Black Resonance: Iconic Women Singers and African American Literature.* New Brunswick: Rutgers UP, 2013. Print.

Maultsby, Portia K. "Soul." *African American Music: An Introduction.* Ed. Mellonee V. Burnim and Portia K. Maultsby. New York: Routledge, 2015. 277–298. Print.

McClary, Susan. "Introduction: A Material Girl in Bluebeard's Castle." *Music and Identity Politics*. Ed. Ian Biddle. Farnham: Ashgate, 2012. 93–132. Print.

Merelli, Annalisa. "When Aretha Franklin Offered to Post Bail for Angela Davis." *Quartz.* 16 Aug. 2018. Web. https://qz.com/quartzy/1356841.

Morgan, Robin. *Sisterhood is Global*. New York: Anchor Books, 1984. Print.

Neal, Mark Anthony. *What the Music Said: Black Popular Music and Black Public Culture.* New York: Routledge, 1999. Print.

Steinitz, Matti. "'Calling Out Around the World' – How Soul Music Transnationalized the African American Freedom Struggle in the Black Power Era (1965–1975)." *Sonic Politics: Music and Social Movements in the Americas*. Ed. Olaf Kaltmeier and Wilfried Raussert. New York: Routledge, 2019. 88–106. Print.

Sullivan, Denise. *Keep on Pushing: Black Power Music from Blues to Hip-Hop*. Chicago: Lawrence Hill Books, 2011. Print.

Discography

Brown, James. "It's a Man's Man's Man's World." King Records, 1966.
———. "(Say It Loud) I'm Black and I'm Proud." King Records, 1968.
———. "I Don't Want Nobody To Give Me Nothing." King Records, 1969.
———. "Get Up, Get Into It, Get Involved." King Records, 1970.
Franklin, Aretha. "Respect." Atlantic Records, 1967.
———. "To Be Young, Gifted and Black." Atlantic, 1972.
Mayfield, Curtis & The Impressions. "Keep On Pushing." ABC Paramount, 1964.
———. "People Get Ready." ABC Paramount, 1965.
McDaniel, Eugene. *Headless Heroes of the Apocalypse.* Atlantic Records, 1971.
Roach, Max, and Abbey Lincoln. *We Insist. Freedom Now Suite.* Candid Records, 1960.
Simone, Nina. "Mississippi Goddam." Philips Records, 1964.
———. "Four Women." Philips Records, 1966.
———. "To Be Young, Gifted and Black." RCA Victor, 1969.

Black Rio: Music, Politics, and Black Identity

CARLOS ALBERTO MEDEIROS

It was early 1974 when, in a rehearsal of Mangueira Samba School, I was introduced to engineer and "disc-jóquei" Asfilófio de Oliveira Filho, aka Dom Filó, who invited me to a party he was producing on Sunday nights at Renascença Clube, a "historically black" social club located in Andaraí, in Rio de Janeiro's predominantly Afro-Brazilian Zona Norte. It was the *Noite do Shaft* [Shaft Night], which, I would find later, was one of the most important of the numerous soul parties that gathered hundreds of thousands of Rio's black youth to the sound of Aretha Franklin, Marvin Gaye, Diana Ross, Curtis Mayfield, The Four Tops, The Temptations, and the idol supreme, James Brown. It was surprising for me to see the club's ballroom taken by a true ocean of Afros, something especially important for me, as one of the first to wear that style in Rio de Janeiro – which probably also means in all of Brazil –, arousing reactions that varied from admiration to despise. Actually, the experience of exclusively black parties was nothing new to me, as they were simply the rule in Rio Grande do Sul, my mother's land, a state characterized by the presence of German and Italian immigrants, and their descendants, in which racial segregation was very common in what I call non-public spaces of conviviality. Even in the favelas, or slums, all parties were segregated, something that generally surprises Brazilians from other regions, accustomed to associate segregation to the United States and to see our country as a unity, neglecting its major cultural, social, and regional differences – a problem that generally affects studies about social relations in Brazil.

Dom Filó's *Noite do Shaft* was a case of love at first sight. I fell in love with that party – and with soul parties, in general. While I had experienced the black social clubs of Porto Alegre like the Floresta Aurora (founded in 1872, 16 years before the abolition of slavery), the Marcílio Dias or the Satélite Prontidão as bunkers where blacks protected themselves of racist jokes and nicknames, Rio's *bailes black* or *bailes soul*, as they were called, distinguished themselves by a specific feature I had not seen anywhere else. They were like temples to praise blackness, synthesized by James Brown in "Say it Loud, I'm Black and I'm Proud," at which young blacks had perhaps their first chance to meet with the possibility of recognizing their own beauty. At *Noite do Shaft*, slides were exhibited with photos taken from African American magazines like *Ebony* and *Essence*, showing black women, men, and families with Afro styles, along with subtitles stimulating self-esteem, the importance of studying and forging black unity. Aside from that, groups were formed in areas that were more distant from the sound systems to discuss race relations in Brazil and beyond, including cases of discrimination, films, books, and articles about that topic. I was taking part in one of those groups when someone informed us that the next Saturday there would be a debate on the abolition of slavery at the Centro de Estudos Afro-Asiáticos, at Candido Mendes University. I went to the meeting and became an activist of Brazil's black movement [*movimento negro*]. Years later, reading *Lideranças Negras* by anthropologist Márcia Contins, to which I had contributed with an interview I found out that my case was far from being unique: many black militants came to activism through soul parties.

As a frequent guest at these parties and as close friend of some of their organizers, especially Dom Filó, I started to be a link between the *movimento negro* and the *bailes black*. At a time when one did not feel any danger in circulating through the night in Rio, even in its peripheral areas, I used to go to different parties in different neighborhoods, which gave me a perception of the dimension of the phenomenon that would be known as Black Rio. Alarmed by the impact of soul music on Afro-Brazilian youth, the security forces of the military dictatorship put pressure on some organizers like Dom Filó, who was forced to do night *car rides* in which they were questioned, with an emphasis on the "external sources" of the money with which they allegedly financed the parties. According to reports from these agencies, there was a suspicion that African Americans from the U.S., namely the Black Panthers or the musician Quincy Jones, had contributed millions of dollars for the dissemination of soul in Brazil and, of course, the anti-White racist ideology supposedly popularized through that genre.

On July 17th, 1976, the *Caderno B*, a cultural supplement of *Jornal do Brasil*, one of the most important Brazilian newspapers at that time, published a four page story about a phenomenon that was taking place in the peripheral areas of the North and West Zones of the city of Rio de Janeiro. Written by a journalist named Lena Frias, under the title of "Black Rio: o orgulho (importado) de ser negro no Brasil" ["Black Rio: the (imported) pride of being black in Brazil"], the text was about the subculture associated with *bailes black* which were attended every weekend by hundreds of thousands of black youngsters celebrating the sound of soul music, a genre associated to African American culture and to the assertion of blackness.

Although the first *bailes black* emerged in the early 1970s, the fact that they were taking place in peripheral areas had made them invisible to the intellectual and political elites, symbolically concentrated in the city's wealthy Zona Sul. The story – which is an example of the influences of journalism on history, since it was after its publication that one started to talk about "Black Rio," "Black São Paulo," "Black Belo Horizonte," "Black Bahia" – aroused reactions of curiosity and sympathy, but mainly of rejection and fear – both on the left and right poles of the political spectrum.

To the Brazilian right and the rulers of the military dictatorship that had taken control of the country in 1964, Black Rio represented the arrival of divisive ideas associated to radical African American organizations, such as the Black Panthers, and thus a threat to national security. As for the left, and also for their acolytes in the world of samba, who saw soul music as a competitor, it was only and purely another abominable expression of American imperialism, aimed at undermining the sacrosanct national culture (Alberto).

In our view, this phenomenon must be understood in the context of the identity movements that emerged in this new phase of the globalization process that began in the mid-1960s, defined as "liquid modernity" by Zygmunt Bauman and intrinsically linked to the advancements in the area of telecommunications. Born, according to most students of American musical culture, in the early 1960s, after a fusion of earlier black genres such as jazz, blues, R & B, and gospel, soul became a great vehicle for the national and international dissemination of the stances of the black movement, sometimes expressed in the lyrics of the songs, but, more broadly, in the gestures, clothing, and hairstyles of singers and musicians.

It must be highlighted that the early 1960s to the mid-1970s constituted a particularly effervescent period of recent history in which the foundations of Western societies were radically questioned. Attacks not only came from uprisings in peripheral areas against established forms of domination such as the struggles which finally put an end to the European colonization of the African Continent, but also from within the very core of the system. These movements were led by blacks, indigenous people, women, homosexuals, and other historically discriminated groups, not to mention those which challenged traditional moral and aesthetic values, such as the hippies and other manifestations of the so-called counterculture. New forms of communication allowed and stimulated the exchange among people and groups who, from the perception of similarities, real or imagined, began to unite under common flags. That is the case of the emerging new black identity, which was based on the common struggles of Africans and African Americans and a revalorization of the history and culture of Africa and the African Diaspora, and also the black phenotype as manifested in the popular slogan "Black Is Beautiful."

In Brazil, in spite of the dominance of an authoritarian regime (and/or in reaction to it), these ideas coming from abroad had a considerable impact, opening sectors of the elites to new interpretations of Brazilian reality itself. One of the areas where this effect was felt was the debate on the issue of race. Up to then, the idea of Brazilian racial exceptionality, condensed in the myth of "racial democracy," was widely hegemonic. To sustain this nationalist ideology, the alleged absence of race-based discrimination in Brazilian society was contrasted with the information that arrived here about the reality of race relations in the U.S., characterized by segregation and racial hatred. When African Americans made significant progress in their quest to change these realities in the Civil Rights/Black Power era, their achievements certainly helped Afro-Brazilians, along with progressive Whites, change their perception on the issue of race in Brazil. That's when a new phase of the Brazilian *movimento negro*, also referred to as the Contemporary Black Movement took its beginning. The two main points in its agenda consisted in denouncing the myth of "racial democracy" as a farce, and forging a positive black identity, based on affirming the history and culture of Africa and the African Diaspora and celebrating the black phenotype. Soul parties, with the promotion of an Afro aesthetics, contributed significantly to that process.

Soul in Brazil

In "The Funky Diaspora: the diffusion of soul and funk music across the Caribbean and Latin America" (2007), Thomas Fawcett presents "black music" (to use a more generic term) as "a transnational and multilingual phenomenon that disseminated across Latin America, the Caribbean and beyond. Soul and funk were copied and reinvented in a wide array of Latin American and Caribbean countries including Brazil, Panama, Jamaica, Belize, Peru and the Bahamas" (Fawcett 2).

The repercussion of soul music in Brazil is another example of the reciprocal, though asymmetrical, exchange between this country and the U.S. in the area of popular music. The sonic exchange between both countries did not start with rock'n roll or bossa nova, but had its beginnings in the first decades of the twentieth century, when jazz was adopted by influential and renowned Brazilian musicians, as shown by musical critics José Lino Grünewald (1970) and Tárik de Souza (1988), among others. In the 1920s, Ary Barroso and Benedito Lacerda, famous musicians and composers, played in jazz bands. Pixinguinha, considered to be the pioneer of samba, was heavily influenced by jazz music as manifested in the repertoire of his Oito Batutas band which included fox-trots, shimmies, and ragtimes and the use of instruments such as saxophones, clarinets, and trumpets (Souza et al.). During World War II, when Brazil became an important ally in the efforts of the United States to dominate the South Atlantic, Walt Disney created Zé Carioca, a character that, in the film *Saludo amigos*, welcomes Donald Duck to the sound of "Aquarela do Brasil," a famous Brazilian song of the time. Originated in the late 1950s, bossa nova is perhaps the most poignant example of those reciprocal influences: born out of the incorporation of jazz elements into samba by Brazilian musicians, it came to have a great repercussion in the U.S., influencing, in turn, American composers and interpreters.

We can identify the diffusion of soul music in Brazil in different environments which converged sometimes. One of them was music production, with composers and interpreters dedicated to the genre or at least temporarily influenced by it. Singers and bands which stood out on the Brazilian soul scene were Tim Maia, Toni Tornado, Cassiano, Carlos Dafé, and Gerson King Combo, Banda Black Rio, and União Black. The influence of soul could also be felt in the music of Ivan Lins, Jorge Ben, Roberto Carlos, and Bebeto. Here, it is important to emphasize the role played by music festivals, events with great popular appeal in which the most influential composers and singers of the time participated, and through which Brazilian soul music was first introduced to a larger audience. Of great importance, in that sense, was the 5th International Song Festival [V Festival Internacional da Canção], produced in 1970 by Globo Television Network, in which the genre was represented by artists like Dom Salvador and Grupo Abolição ("Abolição 1869–1980"), Ivan Lins ("O amor é meu país"), and, most of all, Toni Tornado and Trio Ternura with their winning theme "BR3." In 1971, Tornado, who had spent several years as an immigrant in 1960s Harlem, caused a national scandal when he entered the stage at the 6th edition of the Festival Internacional da Canção, wearing an Afro, and raising his fist for a Black Power salute while singing a song titled "Black Is Beautiful" – a defiant act of black assertiveness for which he was arrested by the military police right after his show. The impact of soul music in Brazil can also be traced in the soundtracks of successful soap operas of the time, like *Sol de verão*, *Loco-motivas*, *O astro*, *Pecado capital*, *Louco amor*, *Dancing days*, *Cavalo de aço*, *Vale tudo*, and others which featured songs interpreted by the likes of Janet Jackson, Candi Staton, The Commodores, Billy Paul, Cameo, Marvin Gaye, Timmy Thomas, Gladys Knight and the Pips, Stevie Wonder, Whitney Houston, Natalie Cole, Chaka Khan, Rick James, and Billy Preston.

While festivals and soap operas contributed significantly to the emergence of Brazilian soul music, their influence does not seem to have been decisive in what would become known as the Movimento Black Rio. In this youth movement, clothing, hairstyles, and the attitudes represented by icons of soul music were at least as important as the music itself. So-called "blaxploitation movies" as *Shaft*, *Cleopatra Jones*, *Trouble man*, and *Black Belt Jones* – action movies with beautiful, intelligent, and courageous black men and women as their central characters – became important manifestations of black pride and soul culture. Those movies, along with soul video clips occasionally exhibited on TV, were instrumental in popularizing the new African American aesthetic in Brazil. One of the main symbols of this aesthetic was the Afro or natural hairstyle, significantly called in Brazil the *cabelo black power* [black power hair]. In the early 1970s, *bailes black* emerged as spaces where these positive black images were celebrated.

At that time, much more than now, foreign music, particularly Anglo American music, prevailed in radio shows and, as a consequence, in the hit parades – something that stimulated Brazilian singers and bands to sing in English and to adopt aliases in that language (like Steve McClean, Michael Sullivan, Light Reflections, Mark Davis [Fábio Jr.], and the most successful of all, Morris Albert [Maurício Alberto], whose "Feelings" was recorded, among others, by Barbara Streisand, Shirley Bassey, Andy Williams, Ella Fitzgerald, and Nina Simone. Thus, it did not come as a surprise that parties promoted by pioneering DJs as Big Boy and Ademir Lemos who played rock, pop, and, occasionally, soul, were extremely successful among young people. Big Boy and Ademir were the hosts of *Baile da Pesada*, a weekly dance party at Canecão, one of Rio's main nightclubs of the time. As anthropologist Hermano Vianna describes them, these parties "attracted five thousand dancers from all neighborhoods of the city, both from South and North Zones. The musical schedule also tended to eclecticism: Ademir played pop, rock, but did not hide his preference for soul music as interpreted by James Brown, Wilson Pickett, and Kool and the Gang" (Vianna, *O mundo* 42). With the "gentrification" of Canecão, Vianna goes on, "the *Baile da Pesada* was moved to peripheral neighborhoods, each week at a different one .... The *Bailes da Pesada* were also promoted in other cities, getting to Brasília in 74" (43).

The first sound systems [*equipes de som*] devoted only to soul were created by black youngsters who used to attend Big Boy's parties, where they could, at certain moments, exhibit their elaborate soul steps, but who wanted to settle a space, in which soul would be played exclusively. There is a dispute between different *equipes* like

Black Power, Uma Mente numa Boa, Soul Grand Prix, Revolução da Mente, and Alma Negra about who started the movement. The evidences point to Oséas Moura dos Santos, aka Mr. Funky Santos, who started to promote soul parties in the early 1970s at Astória, a social club at Tijuca which is closed by now. He explains the motivation and the success of the parties:

> In this meeting here everybody feels together because they are in their environment. People have not deliberately created a difference. Unintentionally, the thing created itself. Nowadays blacks are connected to this Afro thing. In the old days, blacks straightened their hair. Now blacks try hard to be like black Americans, our brothers from the other side, now what I mean? So it becomes as you are seeing, each one dances his own way. (Frias 4–6, translation mine)

This view of the parties as spaces of affirmation of black pride is reinforced by Dom Filó, the leader of the *Soul Grand Prix* sound system and the creator of *Noite do Shaft*, which took place on Sundays at Renascença in Rio's Zona Norte:

> We chose a name, Shaft Night, based on the film directed by Gordon Parks with music composed by Isaac Hayes, who had just won the Oscar for best original score. As we could show pieces of the film through slides, with the charismatic detective John Shaft (main character and a symbol of blackness hero), that's when the idea got a final touch. … It was the ace in the hole for the event, because we mixed images from the movie with photos of the partygoers. It had an almost pyrotechnical effect, made the audience shake and see themselves with self pride. (Sebadelhe and Peixoto 62, translation mine)

The testimonies of Mr. Funky Santos and Dom Filó clearly express the main quality which really attracted black youngsters to those parties: the celebration of black identity in spaces where they did not feel insulted, get called by racist nicknames or depreciated as they used to be in the various environments in which there was – and, we can say, still is – a prevalence of internalized and naturalized mechanisms that impose and reinforce the privileges of whiteness, even if there was not an explicit segregation based on skin color.

Although there was no formal connection between the new organizations of the *movimento negro* and the promoters of the soul parties, there was a link between them for two reasons: the fact that there was a significant number of activists who also participated in the soul scene and also that the parties were big and well attended spaces of construction and affirmation of a positive black identity, something conspicuously absent in the parties and ceremonies structured around samba and other forms of expression of Afro-Brazilian culture, but one of the main points in the agenda of the new movement.

Samba vs Soul, or how to create a nonexistent rivalry

Among the arguments presented by the opponents of Black Rio on the right and the left poles of the political spectrum was the idea that soul fans were guilty of treason against Brazilian cultural traditions, particularly samba. Soul aficionados were denounced as divisionists, interested in undermining the presumed "Brazilian racial harmony," to which cultural expressions of African origin served as main symbols. It's actually a vision that started to be implemented in the 1930s by the Estado Novo, a protofascist dictatorship led by Getúlio Vargas, influenced by the ideas of sociologist Gilberto Freyre which aimed at articulating an ideology of Brazilian nationality by designating a specific, disguisedly inferior, place for blacks, Native Americans, and *mestiços* in it. Thus, the state not only stopped the formerly common open persecution of these expressions, but started to make use of them, particularly of samba, as fundamental labels of our nationality (Vianna, *O mistério*; Fernandes).

Samba has historically represented an expression of Afro-Brazilian cultural resistance and over decades its practitioners were subjected to police persecution and social degrading. Curiously, the genre passed through a gradual process of co-optation by the state, and also by the middle class, which, transformed it into a tool for the diffusion of official propaganda. Significantly, the Samba School Union of Rio de Janeiro delegated the right to organize carnival parades, including the criteria and the jurors in charge of evaluating them, to the City Hall in the mid-1930s. Thus, oriented by the state, samba schools began to privilege plots which praised "brasilidade," or Brazilian patriotism, with an emphasis on its supposedly characteristic miscegenation (Vianna, *O mistério*). After the mid-1950s, a process of invasion and appropriation of Rio de Janeiro samba schools by the white middle class took place which resulted not only in the alteration of the structure of *samba-enredos* [plot sambas], which became shorter and more pleasant to these new audiences, but also of the clothes used in the parades which stopped representing the specific colors of the schools. Getting to the very power structures, there were no more black samba school presidents; so-called *carnavalescos* were introduced who were responsible for supervising all aspects of the schools for the parades, generally people with an academic degree in arts – and all of them white. It's a complex process, in which a multiplicity of factors come to play, as Kiffer and Ferreira show us:

> Interpreted, nowadays, as an expression of purity as well as of the almost atavistic relationship between samba schools and "Africanity," the incorporation of "black" themes and aesthetics by samba schools in the end of the 1950s can be seen as the product of an intensive dialogue among diverse and often conflicting interests that include actors so diverse as, for example, groups dressed as "Africans" in parties, plastic artists with college degrees, Hollywood movies, decoration of carnival ballrooms, interests of Brazilian intellectuals and, of course, the members of samba schools. (Kiffer and Ferreira 69, translation mine)

While samba was widely regarded as an obstacle to the development and integration of blacks, even in Afro-Brazilian publications such as *A Voz da Raça* [The Voice of Race], newspaper of the Frente Negra Brasileira [Black Brazilian Front] still in the 1930s, the genre was resignified as one of the main symbols of Brazilian national culture and became the label of a new aesthetic. Decades later, the Brazilian Black movement, as opposed to its predecessors, took samba as a paramount symbol of resistance of Afro-Brazilian culture, of affirmation, and pride of belonging to the black race.

> The official agenda, until a long time after the 1930s, did not accept assertions that linked samba to blacks only; not even in a tangential way this subject would be present in the creations and/or statements of those involved with the creation of samba.
>
> Only in the 1970s, more exactly in its second half, did this link that now seems to be perpetual acquired a dominant feature in intellectual debates. From "mestiço brasileiro" of uncertain color, good samba, the "true" and "authentic" one, came to present just one color, a well-defined one. (Fernandes 137)

In this context, the lyrics of the samba song "Sou mais samba" [I'm more samba] by Candeia in which he not only expresses his contempt for the Movimento Black Rio, but also rejects Africanity as a fundamental aspect of samba's genealogy, are curious to say the least:

> Eu não sou africano, eu não/Nem norte-americano!/Ao som da viola e pandeiro/sou mais o samba brasileiro!
> [I am not African, not me/ Nor Afro-American/ To the sound of viola and tamborine/I am more Brazilian samba]

But there were other forces interested in exploiting this artificial conflict, which never reflected on the samba or soul parties. In his personal testimony, Dom Filó reveals the confession by Candeia that he had written the specific song by request of RCA recording company, interested in promoting a competition that would draw the attentions of potential consumers from both sides, since it produced samba and soul records.

Deliriums, fantasies, and intellectual dishonesty

The attitudes of Brazilian elites toward the soul phenomenon are revealed in the reports by intelligence agents responsible for surveilling the soul parties. In the beginning, they saw what they were told they would see, producing exaggerated, distorted, and even ridiculous reports, according to which, for example, "a group of black youngsters with high intellectual level is being created in Rio, which intends to generate a climate of hostility between whites and blacks … led by a black American who controls the money that seems to arrive from outside, possibly from the United States." One of their "goals" would be "kidnapping the children of white industrial entrepreneurs."[1]

In another document, produced by CISA (Centro de Informações de Segurança da Aeronáutica, or Air Force Security Information Center), the agents' fantasies led them to identify among the new black cultural organizations that were "mushrooming" in Rio de Janeiro and São Paulo a segment, perceived as "radical," whose members "get inspiration from the Black Panthers from the United States and *worship IDI AMIN DADA*" (emphasis added). And soul parties could not be absent from the delirious plot: "The radicals are promoting a recruitment campaign among the Soul Club habitues. Up to the moment, it has not been possible to determine if the Soul Music Bands are involved" (AMA_ACE_2671/82).

1 Report n. 17/75B, Ministry of the Army, I Army, February 7th 1975.

A deeper study of these documents, with their evident exaggerations and contradictions, would help to reveal important aspects of these agencies' *modus operandi*, and how supposedly "subversive" people were jeopardized by inaccurate and dishonest reports of police agents, frequently resulting from the simple necessity of "showing work." Anyway, Dom Filó, Paulão Black Power, and other sound system leaders were informally interrogated during long *car rides* into the night in which intelligence agents unsuccessfully tried to confirm their suspicions about political goals and external financing of the movement. But their main resource was the espionage on the parties. Eventually, those undercover agents, who were black, young and adequately styled for their task, started to perceive that the parties were not dangerous: there were no fights nor drug consumption, much less racist or even political messages.

Brazil's antiimperialist left did not even bother to go to the parties, since they *already knew* what was going on. To many of us, who had a direct experience with *bailes black,* it couldn't have been more disappointing to see so-called "alternative" periodicals such as *O Pasquim* and *Movimento*, which opposed the military dictatorship, expressing their negative vision on a phenomenon that they simply did not know. In "Carta aberta ao Black-Rio" [Open letter to Black Rio], music journalist Roberto M. Moura, described our movement as

> an insidious neocolonialist advertising campaign, aimed only at creating a subject to consume the surplus of an outside production. (…) It is clear that this social cluster is not thinking; it's being thought. From the outside in. If suddenly comes an order stimulating them to wear some other kind of clothing, they will take off the jacket and weird shoes. (Moura 2)

Here we see reflected one of the core tenets of the Brazilian left in the cultural arena at that time: the Gramscian category of the national-popular that was aimed at identification with the working class was coupled with an anti-imperialist discourse which considered U.S. interference as their main enemy (Kiffer and Ferreira). Under that perspective, adopted by the then influential Center for Popular Culture, leftists interpreted the soul music wave as manifestation of a cultural invasion which used and manipulated the black youth, homogenized as poor, uneducated, and alienated. As can be observed repeatedly in Brazilian history, once more there was a convergence of left and right in the rejection of anything that posed a serious challenge to the Brazilian racial status quo.

Conclusion

Even if not explicitly political, the Movimento Black Rio was extremely important when it came to the construction of a black identity that was opposed to the widely established stereotypes sustained by the racially dominant group. Soul parties had a significant impact on the consciousness of most of the activists who became involved in Brazil's *movimento negro* in the late 1970s and early 1980s. In the same way, anthropologist Antônio Risério, in *Carnaval ijexá*, reveals that the origins of *blocos afro*, the Afro carnival groups from Salvador, Bahia, are also to be found in *bailes black* where young Afro-Brazilians had the idea of creating these cultural organizations, centered around carnival, aiming at the racism openly expressed by traditional (white) carnival groups in Salvador de Bahia (Risério).

The demise of Black Rio in the late 1970s was related to three main factors, two of them external and one internal. Externally, the musical scene in the U.S., the origin of the genre, started to change when the affirmation of blackness ceased to be a key topic of many composers and interpreters and disco music emerged. Simultaneously, soul parties in Brazil were subjected to an insidious smear campaign led by Globo Network comedy shows, in which black comedians like Grande Otelo, Muçum and Tião Macalé helped to transform soul party goers in laughingstock. However, up to these days the genre is periodically celebrated in parties promoted in different points of Rio de Janeiro, from Downtown and Santa Teresa to the famous Padre Miguel boardwalk. And in Belo Horizonte, a weekly soul music event called *BH Soul* attracts younger and older generations of dancers every Saturday in a central part of the city.[2]

In the last few years, we are seeing a sort of revival of the 1970s in Brazil, with numerous blacks, specially the youngsters, adopting an Afro aesthetics that includes clothing, hairstyles, and turbans, often associated to the celebration of black identity and ancestry. Movements such as *Empoderamento Cresco* [Kinky Empowerment] and events such as the Marches of Black Women, aside from revealing a healthful women's protagonism, are examples that the identitary stands, of which Movimento Black Rio was a vehicle, were not buried 40 years ago.

Works cited

Alberto, Paulina. "When Rio Was Black: Soul Music, National Culture, and the Politics of Racial Comparison in 1970s Brazil." *Hispanic American Historical Review* 89.1 (2009): 3–39. Print.

Bauman, Zygmunt. *Identidade*. Rio de Janeiro: Jorge Zahar Editor, 2005. Print.

Contins, Marcia. *Lideranças negras*. São Paulo: Aeroplano, 2005. Print.

Fawcett, Thomas. "The Funky Diaspora: The Diffusion of Soul and Funk Music Across the Caribbean and Latin America." *Comunicação apresentada à XXVII Conferência Anual de Estudantes da AEIELA (ILLASA)*, 1–3 de fevereiro, 2007. N. pag. Print.

Fernandes, Dmitri Cerboncini. "A negra essencialização do samba." *Luso-Brazilian Review* 51.1 (2014): 132–56. Print.

Frias, Lena. "Black Rio: o orgulho (importado) de ser negro no Brasil." *Jornal do Brasil* (7 Jul. 1976): 1–5. Print.

Grünewald, José Lino. *História da música popular brasileira*. Ary Barroso. V. 5. São Paulo: Abril Cultural, 1970. Print.

2 https://www.youtube.com/watch?v=BgYLeszZjWY.

Kiffer, Danielle, and Ferreira, Felipe. "Isto faz um bem!: as escolas de samba, a Coca-Cola e a 'invasão da classe média' no carnaval carioca dos anos 50." *Textos Escolhidos de Cultura e Arte Populares* 12.2 (Nov. 2015): 55–72. Print.

Kove, Mikel. *Blaxploitation films*. Harpenden: Pocket Essentials, 2001. Print.

Moura, Roberto M. "Carta aberta ao Black-Rio." *O Pasquim* (Sep. 1977): 2–8. Print.

Risério, Antônio. *Carnaval ijexá*. Salvador: Corrupio, 1982. Print.

Sebadelhe, José Octávio, and Luiz Felipe de Lima Peixoto. *1976 – Movimento Black Rio*. Rio de Janeiro: José Olympio, 2016. Print.

Souza, Tarik de, Ary Vasconcellos, Roberto Muggiatti, Roberto M. Moura, Luís Carlos Mansur, and João Máxim. *Brasil musical: viagem pelos sons e ritmos populares*. Rio de Janeiro: Art Bureau, 1988. Print.

Vianna, Hermano. *O mistério do samba*. Rio de Janeiro: Jorge Zahar, 1995. Print.

———. *O mundo funk carioca*. Rio de Janeiro: Jorge Zahar, 1988. Print.

Names of the *equipes*

Soul Grand Prix, Black Power, Jet Black, Dynamic Soul, Santos Brasilian Soul, Vip's, Uma Mente Numa Boa, Furacão 2000, Boot Power, Equipe Modelo, Cash Box, Modulo Magnético, Sorac, Black King, Scorpio, Black Panter, Hollywood, Revolução da Mente, Tropa Bagunça, Rick, Arte Negra, Alma Negra, A Cóva, Geração Black, Petrus, Truta Soul, Atabaque, Cap Som, Jay Top, Mancha Negra, Soul Brown, A Torre, Mercado Soul, Prelúdio, Enigma Soul, Fênix, Apoluison, Soul Lazer, My Soul, Mancha Negra, Solid State, Celula Negra, J. B. Santos, Music Box, Pop Rio, Olho Negro, Cranius, África Soul, Virgiaure, Afrosoul, A Máquina, Grupo Brown, Black Angola, Geração Black, Black Children, A Mancha, Black Soul, Horus, Black Flower.

Afro-Knowledge, Sonic Aesthetics, and the Musical Practices of 'Latin Beats'

Ángel G. Quintero-Rivera

This paper sets to examine the meaning of the basic revolutionary features of Afro-Latin music emerging during the Black Power struggles, in terms of world vision, and human-nature interchange. I will try to show how these musical aesthetic practices respond to and develop an alternative epistemology to basic postulates of capitalist Western modernity. These ways of elaborating musical expressions had been evolving for centuries, in the creative interplay between European and African musical traditions within very complex and unequal colonization processes through which the Black Power struggles of the 1960s and 1970s acquired an evident transformative character. The implicit socio-political meanings emerged as part of a movement that intertwined Black American claims to U.S. nation building with migrant Latino struggles.

Early 1950s witnessed the first massive emigration of Puerto Ricans to the United States. This population, racially mixed and varied was nonetheless considered "colored" in the United States. Militant protest groups of second and third generation Puerto Rican migrants formed part of the Black Power struggles. In fact, the Young Lords Party in Chicago and New York was, to a great extent, inspired by the Black Panthers: a youth movement initially constituted around street gang ideology of barrio territoriality that was rapidly developing a wider social scope.

Justice

Against the backdrop of the late 1960s Black Power struggles, Eddie Palmieri, a New York musician of Puerto Rican parents, a figure of fundamental importance in the formation of *salsa* and Latin jazz and a recipient of many Grammy awards, released a long play record (LP) with the title *Justicia* [Justice] in 1969. In contrast to what was then prevalent in popular music – Latin or Anglo and, effectively, in several other venues –, this LP is not just a compilation of songs. Palmieri proceeds in this record to create a discourse over the length of the entire record. This begins with one of his own compositions, the one that gives the LP its title. In it, as the work opens, Palmieri reveals one of the defining characteristics of the "way of making music" that was going to be called *salsa* ("sauce," because of its complex commingling of elements). In this sense, salsa is a spontaneous combination of different Caribbean musical rhythms and forms, evocative of various geographies – within the Caribbean world – and, above all, of different times in its complex history. *Salsa* contains in it a history that is marked by ruptures and constant reconstitutions that can never be squeezed into the systematization of the "modern West's" notions of linear progress and which results of the oblique paths it has been compelled to follow against the force of the most powerful colonial metropolises: first Spain, England, France, and the Netherlands, later the United States, and the then Soviet Union. In "Justicia"'s polyform and polyrhythmic combinations, the *guaracha* is, nonetheless, predominant. This is quite significant, for this genre was one of the first clearly urban musical popular forms in the Caribbean, at a time when the Caribbean world was still overwhelmingly rural. In what Willie Colón later called a "legal alien," and from within the community of Puerto Rican immigrants in the great runaway's village of the contemporary Caribbean's marooning, New York (the most urban of possible worlds), Palmieri musically initiates his discourse-opus evoking perhaps the oldest of popular urban forms from his region of origin. On a base of polyrhythmic combinations in which the *guaracha* predominates, the lyric optimistically demands justice for "boricuas y niches" [Puerto Ricans and blacks]:

Justice will come, justice they'll see	(future tense)
in the world, those suffering discrimination	(present tense)
With the singing of the Tangó	(projected past tense)
Hey, it's justice I demand!	(present tense)
… if we had no tyranny	(past-present conditional)
we would all of us be brothers,	(future conditional)
have sweet peace and harmony,	
everybody happy be,	
just wait and see. (Palmieri, *Justicia*)[1]	(certainty in the future)

Beyond the interplay of different tenses, it is interesting to note his attempt to eliminate the distinctions between concepts (which at first glance may appear abstract) and concrete realities.

Like all the compositions on this LP, "Justicia" incorporates extraordinary instrumental improvisations, better known as jam sessions, that are inspired by the best tradition of jazz with its long history of mutual exchange and cross-fertilization with Afro-Caribbean Latin music (Acosta, *Descarga cubana*) – a connection between African American and Afro-Caribbean musical traditions that grew stronger in the age of Black Power. It is significant to note that the jam session trumpet solos [descargas] in "Justicia" should allude to the best-known social protest bolero of Puerto Rico's most celebrated popular pre-salsa composer, Rafael Hernández's "Puerto Rican Lament." It is particularly true because the latter was known throughout Latin America as *El jibarito* and was written while its mulatto author was living as an immigrant worker in New York in 1929, that is, at the height of the Great Depression (Quintero, *¡Salsa, sabor y control!* ch. 5). In effect, "Justicia" intermixes time spheres in utopian aesthetics practices.

1 Translation of Palmieri's lyrics by Roberto Márquez.

While the chorus repeats, in a tone of uncertain longing, "Oh, when will we see justice come?" the soloist reaffirms the certainty of the yearned for the materialization of the utopia:

> My man, you'll see,
> I'll make you dance guaracha
> when that day finally comes,
> everything'll be just fine.
> Justice will come to us all! .... (Palmieri, *Justicia*)

The LP then continues to merge traditional "Latin" Caribbean music, newer sounds that would later be known as Latin Jazz, with music from black working-class neighborhoods, blending an enormous heterogeneity of forms, tempos, and rhythms.

Advancing the central thesis of his musical discourse, Palmieri incorporates chords from the song "Somewhere" from Leonard Bernstein's and Stephen Sondheim's *West Side Story*[2] between one composition and another (or sometimes after two songs).

After two songs on traditional Latin forms and a second interlude, the LP takes an obvious turn toward the novel in a piece that includes avant-garde references to the first centuries of the creation of Caribbean societies titled "My Spiritual Indian." The composition is an entirely instrumental jam session [descarga]. The only vocal utterance appears at the end, "India, te bendigo india"[3] [Indian woman, I bless you, Indian maid].

The piece evokes (significantly, in the feminine) the maroon encounter between Amerindian women and escaped black slaves with an interesting combination of scales identified with indigenous music and Afro-Caribbean rhythms. The original harmonies and instrumental improvisations give us a pioneering composition of what has been defined as Latin Jazz.

The second side of the record opens with "Everything is Everything," a song in English based essentially on urban music from America's black ghettos, which again elaborates on the theme of justice with which the other side had begun in Spanish. Dialogues between Latin-Caribbean musicians and Afro-American counterparts had a long tradition, as it is evident in the origins of jazz (what Jelly Roll Morton referred to as the "Latin Tinge"[4]). But, in the era of the Black Power struggles these sonic black-Latino interactions intensified as was manifested in the emergence of pre-salsa genres such as Latin soul and Latin boogaloo (Steinitz). Its Latin identity character turned Newyorican salsa in the 1970s and onwards into an almost exclusively Spanish language expression, but at the peak of the late 1960s Black Power movement it was very much part of those dialogues and included songs in English. In the LP *Justicia*, Palmieri composes in Spanish all the songs that are identified as salsas mainly because

2 Broadway Play 1957; Film – with 10 Oscar awards – 1961.

3 In fact, in a recording of a live performance in the famous American prison at Sing Sing the song is presented as "My Spiritual Woman" (Palmieri, *Recorded Live)*.

4 Cf. Ortíz; Roberts (*The Latin Tinge*; *Latin Jazz*).

of their Afro-Latin Caribbean foundations. As it deals with African American music, "Everything is Everything" is written in English (the only other song in English on this LP is "Somewhere," originally sung as a duet – in *West Side Story* – by a male descendent of European migrants and a female descendent of Puerto Ricans). It is from the barrio sound of the ghetto, enriched by jazz, soul, and funk (which basically emerged from there also), that Palmieri gave a Black Power "Third World" ("subaltern discourse's") amplitude to Puerto Rican calls for social justice and to his utopia of a new solidary way of life:

> Everything is everything about justice,
> so they tell me.
> But why, why, why
> do I see so much injustice …
> But tell a black man
> or an Indian or a Mexican …
> and the three of them will look at you …
> and tell [you]:
> everything is *not* everything about justice. (Palmieri, *Justicia*)

In a period permeated with uncertainties, Palmieri attempts to rescue the beauty of "The Simple Truth" that Puerto Rico's greatest female poet was wont to stress when she migrated to New York decades before (Burgos 1). This does not eliminate the uncertainties, but does add nuance to them with a few basic unquestionable truths:

> The idea of justice is so simple,
> That it's incredible to see;
> if the whole World would see
> how simple and beautiful it would be
> trouble-free,
> it would eliminate wars,
> eliminate all forms of divide …
> it's so simple, it's so groovy:
> I want to be your brother,
> I want to speculate *on* justice,
> speculate *for* justice. (Palmieri, *Justicia*)

After another interlude, the band launches into a long jazzy jam session full of complex be-bop polyrhythms of the most avant-garde jazz of the time on "Verdict on Judge Street," also composed by Palmieri. *Justicia*, with its quite noteworthy title, concludes with a version of Leonard Bernstein's "Somewhere" from his celebrated modern romantic maroon utopia *West Side Story*. The song, which gives voice to the most general and at the same time the most concrete of utopias – the longing for a place and a time to live – is transformed with jazz modulations and a pronounced Puerto Rican accent by Palmieri:

> Somewhere a place for us …
> Someday, a time for us …
> … open-aired
> … with time to spare

hold my hand and we
are halfway there…
Someday, somewhere
We'll find
A new way of living …. (Palmieri, *Justicia*)

Someday, somewhere

The late 1960s were a time of important youth struggles. In Latin America, these were strongly linked artistically with the new genre of protest songs also known as *nueva trova* that developed poetic lyrics for revolutionary social change. However, in some communities of significant Afro-diasporic presence, the youth struggles intermingled with the transnational impact of the Black Power movement. As a result, the "new song" movement incorporated their new lyrics, giving rise to transformations in the Afro-aesthetics of musical practices that came to represent alternatives to Western values and worldviews. It is no coincidence that in the same years, the musical world experienced the emergence of soul-influenced music, such as reggae in Jamaica, the *Tropicalia* movement in Brazil, and the *Newyorican*-Hispanic Caribbean salsa. I have written extensively on the latter (Quintero, *Cuerpo y cultura*) and will only resume some of its basic characteristics in terms of their contribution to Black Power struggles.

In a documentary film interview (García), Palmieri describes salsa music's endeavor by underlining the importance of rhythmic elaboration that is rhythm as a terrain of artistic complexity. This challenges the Western colonial distinction between civilization and barbarism, where rhythm is considered to be a part of human primitive "instincts." Palmieri also emphasizes the dialogue between the different players as a fundamental element of music elaboration: not only to follow a score of an ever-present composer, but the way players enrich the composition through multiple dialogic improvisations. Last, he stresses the somatic impact of aesthetic sound development, breaking the mind-body distinction with an ecological view of body as a terrain of culture in the dancing arts.

As Wilfried Raussert asserts,

> [many] African rhythms call forth a dance movement which is bound to a certain place. Kinetic energy in European dances tend to lead to a forward movement, in African dances it translates a polycentric movement on the spot. … Diverse body centers within the African dance performance create kinetic transformations; several physical movements take place simultaneously. Furthermore, the body movements can be seen as an expression of a polyrhythmic feeling since they are not necessarily coincidental with the rhythms played by drums or marked by hand clappings. (6)

With reference to jazz, Raussert continues: "The present emerges from a simultaneous experience of past and future, the experience of the vanishing and rising beat" (7).

There are at least three basic epistemological principles related to Black Power struggles in these aesthetic practices within Palmieri's description. At the higher education level, Black Power questioned a holistic singular interpretation of history and civilization values. Student, academic, and community struggles emerged for the establishment and recognition of Black Studies and Area Studies Programs (Puerto Rican Studies, for example). These programs objected to the canon of Western history as History (with capital H), negating the belief that History was the logical development of a set of basic principles. Such assertions meant not only an impugnation of white (usually male) Western bias, but more profoundly a refutation of a monistic form of knowledge: a pyramidal logical deductive procedure of understanding as an unfolding of a basic certitude or "law" (e.g., the Newtonian law of gravity in Physics). Similarly, Black and Area Studies incorporated many processes and their multiple interrelations in time and space (in geography and history) into academic analysis. It did not mean that Western knowledge was intrinsically false, but that it was partial and incomplete.

Simplifying for the sake of argument in this short essay a very rich and complex history, the centered monism of Western epistemology represented in music the dominant role of melody (or more generally, tonality), where other spheres of music, like textures and rhythm, become subsidiary to this. Faced with this monism, Afro-Latin musical practices stress the importance of dialogues between various sonorous spheres each with its possible autonomous development. This did not mean the substitution of the dominant role of melody by rhythm, as the importance of rhythmic elaboration may make one suspect, but the displacement of a pyramidal procedure by a dialogic one, where the aesthetic elaboration of both rhythm and melody developed in their constant dialogic intermingling. In fact, as a symbolically "mulatto" artistic expression, Afro-Latin music is capable of recognizing the very rich and important melodic development of Western music while at the same time articulating a critique of its ideological assumption that it represents *the* most developed (and thus civilized) sonorous achievement.

Challenging hierarchical procedures, musical practices based on dialogue open possibilities of numerous democratic endeavors, which can be seen related to civil rights and the extension of citizenship. Palmieri mentions the dialogues between the various musicians of an ensemble, which usually means also dialogues between melody, harmony, rhythm, and textures as represented by different instruments. But, within the dialogic *Weltanschauung* (epistemology, feelings, and world view), Afro-Latin musical practices enriched its aesthetic elaborations through many more dialogic relationships. Let us start with the relationship between composition and improvisation (e.g., de Carvalho and Segato). Composition refers to an individual creator who, previous to the sonorous experience, has thought and elaborated the musical ideas that they organize in a score of dramatic rounded musical form with introduction – development – climax – and conclusion evident to the ear. It means a great development for music elaboration, but it gradually concentrated on the composer the creative expression. Afro-Latin musical practices combined composition with the multiple dialogues between the musicians, reminiscences of open-ended musical communal gatherings. "Mulatto" Afro-Latin salsa music combines the rounded and open-ended musical forms. Usually, the song starts with the composition, it moves to an open-ended improvisation section, first in the lyrics (*soneo*) and then in the instrumental expression (*descargas*), returning to the composition for the conclusion.

Second, in the open-ended soneo, the back-up singers repeat a chorus line that summarizes the composition, i.e., the basic lyrical idea of the individual composer, while the lead singer improvises in dialogue with the chorus line. The individual creation becomes social, while the singer – member of the collective ensemble – manifests its individuality, but only in dialogue with the composition now turned into a social voice. Shattering boundaries between communality and individuality is a basic principle also of the instrumental open-ended section or descargas (similar to jam sessions in jazz). A first instrument begins to manifest its creative virtuosity in dialogue with the composition. Then a second instrument starts its improvisation dialogue with both the composer and the player before him; then a third, and so on. Individual virtuosities are not individual manifestations, but expressions of individuality in a collective endeavor; in other words, they are meaningful only within a chain of communication in their dialogues. Improvisation turns into an expression of reciprocity (character of community) confronting the theory of possessive individualism of Hobbes, Locke, etc. as the basis for the political organization of bourgeois society (MacPherson). The importance of community in Black Power struggles through neighborhood pride in modern Western societies' segregated ghettos found musical expression on dialogic reciprocity. Community neighborhood pride in black affirmation struggles had numerous manifestations worthy of further research, from the very problematic youth street gangs of some of its early history in the U.S. to carnival *comparsas* in many other Caribbean and Latin American countries.

Dialogues in salsa are not limited to those between composer and musicians (the producers) but also take place between them and the supposed consumers, that is, the dancers. It is important to bear in mind that even the most musically complex salsas remain dancing music, because they symbolically represent the dialogues between the times of the sonorous expressions and the space of the dancing elaborations. Salsa is also a couple dance, and corporal dialogues unfold along different compositions. It represents a recognition of the importance of body communication in Black history, where slave-owners tried to hinder verbal communication in many different ways (Moreno Fraginals; Quintero, *Cuerpo y cultura*). In addition, in contrast to the centered monism of Western "structure of feeling" (to use Raymond William's concept 1983), which structured dance movements in terms of the spinal column, Afro dance developed dialogues between different body parts, which Western eyes would consider chaos, because of their frequently decentered character (Gottschild; some examples in Radano and Bohlman). The important role of dance in Afro-Latin music breaks the distinction between culture and nature (Descoda) and between materiality and spirituality, as the body participates in the aesthetic elaboration practices (e.g., Thompson, *Flash of the Spirit*; *Tango*). In this respect, Black Power and youth insurrection intermingled again.

The centered monism of Western *Weltanschauung* manifested itself in dance movements from and to the spinal-cord of the dancing body. As Afro-American dancer and choreographer Gottschild observes:

> Africanist dance idioms show a democratic equality of body parts. The spine is just one of many possible movement centers; it rarely remains static. … movements may simultaneously originate from more than one focal point (the head and the pelvis, for example) …. The component and auxiliary parts of the torso – shoulders, chest, rib cage, waist, pelvis – can be independently moved or articulated in different directions (forward, backward, sideward, or in circles) and in different rhythm. (8–9)

The centered monism of the Western structure of feeling in music was further challenged by Afro-Latin sonorous elaboration through some harmonic and melodic practices. What came to be known in jazz as the "blue note" produces a harmonic effect of inconclusiveness (minor seventh), which shades the rounded musical form with an open-ended character, open to different possible imaginative turnings (Lipsitz, *Dangerous Crossroads* 4). This relates to a different conception of time and memory, to which we will return promptly. Another way in which Afro-Latin music expresses a decentered character melodically is through a common use of what is called slide in jazz (*glissando* and *portalamento*), meaning to move from one note to the next (higher or lower) with all possible gradations or fractions of tone. In contrast to Western diatonic scale, microtonality allows playing with what in Western terms would be considered imprecision. Lipsitz describes these sounds as "not pure tones" (Lipsitz, *Time Passages* 110); Zoila Gómez and Victoria Eli refer to those as on-purpose utilization of *timbres borrosos e imprecisos* [blurred and imprecise tones] (Gómez and Eli 70). The slide is manifested especially in singers and in the trombone. It is no coincidence that the trombone is one of the most important instruments in salsa; it imprinted its rough urban Newyorican character to salsa.

Finally, I would like to relate Black Power struggles towards a reconceptualization of history and future to Afro-Latin musical emphasis on the aesthetic elaboration of rhythmic complexity. Western teleology of modernity often implied a linear conception of time as progress, and, through retrospective determinism, history as the unfolding of civilizing processes towards it. By the emergence of salsa, Black and Area Studies, as the so-called Literature of the Boom with its magical realism in Latin America (Rincón) and *dependentista* sociology (Quijano), demonstrated that the Americas had experience (and were experiencing) multiple time frames, indeed a simultaneity of different epochs, a variety of tempos and processes (de Carvalho). Western meters (2/4, 3/4 or 4/4 …), which gradually subordinated rhythm to them beginning in the seventeenth and eighteenth centuries (Acosta, *Música* 236; 237), felt short of representing this lived complexity, and Afro-Latin "mulatto" music turned to the African notion of time-lines for the metric structuring of the evolvement of compositions. Time-lines in Afro-Latin musical expressions are referred to as claves. The most common is clave 3–2:

Another example among many is the rumba Columbia clave as transcribed in 6/8 by American salsa musicians (Gerard and Sheller 69):

The heterogeneity of times had more affinity with meters formed by non-equivalent units whose syncopation fostered more complex rhythmic elaborations than traditional Western meters which objectivated time. Numerous psychological studies have shown that humans experience time in complex ways. The objectivated meters would consider this a subjective "error." However, considering subjectivity not as a misrepresentation of an external "reality" but as reality of experience in itself, opens a field for a wider artistic elaboration of time present in the evident rhythmic complexity of Afro-Latin musical genres. The women struggles' slogan of "the personal as political" intermixes with these Black Power struggles to work aesthetically with the complexity of subjectivity in time through rhythm.

Among the most significant repercussions of Black Power were its linkages with youth, feminine, and ethnic struggles present in Afro-Latin aesthetic musical practices developing and aspiring a different place and time in our world.

Someday, somewhere.

Works cited

Acosta, Leonardo. *Descarga cubana: el jazz en Cuba 1900-1950*. La Habana: Ed. Unión, 2000. Print.

———. *Música y descolonización*. La Habana: Arte y Literatura, 1982. Print.

Burgos, Julia de. *Canción de la verdad sencilla*. San Juan: Imp. Baldrich, 1939. Print.

de Carvalho, José Jorge. "Globalization, Traditions, and Simultaneity of Presences." *Cultural Pluralism, Identity, and Globalization*. Ed. Luíz Eduardo Soares. Río de Janeiro: UNESCO–ISSC–EDUCAM, 1996. 414–456. Print.

———, and Rita Segato. *Sistemas abertos e territórios fechados: para uma nova compreensão das entrelaces entre música e identidades sócias*. Brasília: U. de Brasília, Serie Antropologia 164, 1994. Print.

Descoda, Phelippe. *Beyond Nature and Culture*. Chicago: U of Chicago P, 2014. Print.

García, Ana María. *Cocolos y Rockeros*. Film documental. S. J.: Pandora Films, 1992.

Gerard, Charley, and Marty Sheller. *¡Salsa! The Rhythm of Latin Music*. Crown Point, IN: White Cliffs Media Company, 1989. Print.

Gómez García, Zoila, and Victoria Eli Rodríguez. *Música latinoamericana y caribeña*. La Habana: Pueblo y Educación, 1995. Print.

Gottschild, Brenda Dixon. *Digging the Africanist Presence in American Performance, Dance, and Other Contexts*. Westport, CT: Praeger, 1998. Print.

Lipsitz, George. *Dangerous Crossroads, Popular Music, Postmodernism, and the Poetics of Place*. London: Verso, 1994. Print.

———. *Time Passages, Collective Memory, and American Popular Culture*. Minneapolis: U of Minnesota P, 1990. Print.

MacPherson, Crawford Brough. *The Political Theory of Possessive Individualism, Hobbes to Locke*. London: Oxford UP, 1962. Print.

Moreno Fraginals, Manuel, ed. *África en América Latina*. México: Siglo XXI, 1977. Print.

Ortíz, Fernando, ed. "La influencia afrocubana en el jazz norteamericano." *Etnia y Sociedad*. La Habana: Editorial de Ciencias Sociales, 1993. 245–251. Print.

Palmieri, Eddie. *Recorded Live at Sing Sing II*. LP, s.l.: Tico, CLP1321, c.1973.

———. *Justicia*. New York: Tico Records [Disco LP#1188], 1969.

Quijano, Aníbal. "Modernidad, identidad y utopía en América Latina." *Imágenes desconocidas. La modernidad en la encrucijada postmoderna*. Ed. Fernando Calderón. Buenos Aires: CLACSO, 1988. 17–24. Print.

Quintero Rivera, Ángel G. *¡Salsa, sabor y control!, Sociología de la música "tropical."* México: Siglo XXI, 1998. Print.

———. *Cuerpo y cultura. Las músicas "mulatas" y la subversión del baile*. Madrid: Iberoamericana / Frankfurt a.M.: Vervuert, 2009. Print.

Radano, Ronald, and Philip V. Bohlman, eds. *Music and the Racial Imagination*. Chicago: U of Chicago P, 2000. Print.

Raussert, Wilfried. *Negotiating Temporal Differences. Blues, Jazz, and Narrativity in African American Culture*. Heidelberg: Winter, 2000. Print.

Rincón, Carlos. *La no simultaneidad de lo simultáneo, postmodernidad, globalización y cultura en América Latina*. Bogotá: Universidad Nacional de Colombia, 1995. Print.

Roberts, John Storms. *The Latin Tinge*. New York: Oxford UP, 1979. Print.

———. *Latin Jazz: The First of the Fusions 1880's to Today*. New York: Editorial Macmillan, 1999. Print.

Steinitz, Matti. "We got Latin Soul! Transbarrio Dialogues and Afro-Latin Identity Formation in New York's Puerto Rican Community during the Age of Black Power (1966–1972)." *Human Rights in the Americas*. Ed. Luz Kirschner, Maria Herrera Sobek, and Francisco Lomeli. New York / London: Routledge, 2021. 243–262. Print.

Thompson, Robert Farris. *Flash of the Spirit: African Art and Afro-American Philosophy*. New York: Random House, 1983. Print.

———. *Tango: The Art History of Love*. New York: Pantheon, 2005. Print.

Williams, Raymond. *Culture and Society*. New York: Columbia UP, 1983. [First edition in London, 1958]. Print.

Dancehall Culture and Elements of Black Power

LISA TOMLINSON

Introduction

Black Power movement (BPM) spans many artistic expressions where cultural workers have used their work to assert racial pride. More significantly, Black Power movements have supported the development of Black cultural productions such as art, film, literature, and music. Through these various artistic mediums, Black cultural workers have (re)created space to assert cultural identity, exert cultural resistance, and form a shared diasporic history that includes the Black Atlantic and Africa. Like Pan-Africanism and Garveyism, the Black Power movement which originated in the United States has maintained a consistent dialogue within the African diaspora both politically and culturally. Culturally, the message of the U.S. Black Power spilled over into various sounds of Caribbean music to express racial pride and encourage economic empowerment for Black people. Jamaican popular music such as reggae became the mouthpiece in the Caribbean to follow in the footstep of America's Black Power to continue the project of Black liberation. My paper, however, focuses on Jamaican dancehall music as one of the many cultural expressions that has served as a vehicle to assert a form of Black nationalism that is found in cultural and literary movements such as the Harlem Renaissance and Black Arts Movement, all resonance of a Black Power ethos. Despite heavy criticism of dancehall music's preoccupation with materialism, sex, and violence, dancehall culture has represented a site of contestation against (neo)colonial and imperial powers. Like other cultural expressions framed in Black Power ideologies, dancehall culture has also offered an alternative vision for Black Jamaican working-class social reality, Black consciousness, and political protest that speaks to the emancipation of Black people globally. The chapter engages in a content analysis of relevant songs of dancehall artists from Jamaica to demonstrate how the genre can in many ways fit within a Black Power discourse. The chapter also provides a brief overview of Black Power in the Caribbean and Jamaican popular music as forms of resistance and Black Power.

Black Power in the Caribbean

In the present chapter, the term Black Power is used to cover a wide time frame, starting from the Haitian Revolution as CLR James points to (Jackson 149). Therefore, my understanding of "Black Power" is not limited to the 1960s and 1970s but encompasses all expressions of Black resistance from the Haitian Revolution up to the present. The start date of Black Power discourse is not entirely different from what has been historically constructed as Black Power of the 1970s. As such, the assertion of Black Power has maintained similar characteristics over time while also manifesting differences. Racial pride, economic/political empowerment, the valorization of African-oriented cultures, and the creation of cultural institutions are some of the salient features that have remained relevant to the global assertion of Black Power's political figures, cultural workers, and grassroot activists. At the same time, however, Black Power was also deployed in the context of the Caribbean against the new local ruling elite who were viewed as a conduit for neo-colonial foreign domination (Martin 252). This contrasted with the U.S. Black Power movement, which aimed to challenge "the traditional denial of human rights to African Americans" (252). The U.S. binary construction of race that informed the Black Power struggle is also worth noting in that the "Caribbean conception of Black Power were formed in Black majority and multiethnic societies, where not all problems could reduce to a conflict between 'black' and 'white'" (Quinn 18). For instance, in pluralist societies like Trinidad and Guyana, any conceptions of Black Power had to contend with the challenge of a historic divide between their dominant African and Indian populations (18).

The Haitian Revolution has been celebrated and marked as the most exemplifying historical event relating to Black Power in the Caribbean. This revolution established Haiti as the first Black republic in the Americas. A significant political development, the revolution occurred even though the French engaged in extortionary and predatory actions that compromised Haiti's experience of independence and the British and U.S. governments refused to recognize the country's status as an independent nation. It is within this context of Haiti's struggle for freedom as the first Black republic that I embark on a brief discussion of Black Power in the Caribbean.

William R. Lux in his seminal article "Black Power in the Caribbean" points out that "in the nineteen century slave revolts were the focal points of black assertion" (Lux 212). Similarly, C.L.R. James recognizes that the significance of Black assertion which the Haitian Revolution opened up in the Caribbean, became a means to shift toward a Black Power movement (Jackson 149). James saw the Revolution as an example of the potential of the Black masses in the Americas to transform society and to better their social conditions and as the exercise "of the power of white elites and its power structure to suppress revolutionary zeal and action" (149). At the height of the Black Power movement in 1969, James wrote that "1789 was a landmark in the history of Negro revolt in the West Indies. The only successful Negro revolt, the only successful slave revolt, had its root in the French Revolution, and without the French Revolution its success would have been impossible" (149). James, therefore, characterizes the events in Haiti as part of the struggle for African emancipation worldwide as well as an essential element of global revolutionary history. As such, Black Power is linked to this significant event in Caribbean history "as the latest stage in the region's long struggle for meaningful independence and black liberation" (Quinn 4).

Without a doubt, the Haitian Revolution can be defined as an historical event that set the stage for Black liberation in the New World as well as the initiator of the Black Power movements that have echoed across national borders, offering examples and ideologies that have been since greeted by political leaders and cultural workers across the Black Atlantic. Frantz Fanon and Marcus Garvey, for example, took on strands of a Black Power movement in their quest to challenge imperial powers. Marcus Garvey promoted his ideas of "radical pride and nationalist organization" (Lux 200) and the "Back to Africa" movement in Harlem. In his effort to estrange and liberate himself from a French assimilation colonial identity, Fanon began writing about his experiences in Martinique as a colonial subject and he later joined the armed struggle in Algeria to help fight for its independence. Thus, Africa for many Caribbean Black Power figures in the early part of the twentieth century acted as the central focus while "Black Power and its Africanness became the driving force behind the Caribbean's search for its identity" (208).

During the twentieth century, the meaning of "Africa" as the main root of Black identification in the Americas shifted. Black Power as an intellectual and cultural movement in more contemporary periods "changed in emphasis from a wistful longing to return to Africa to an asserted claim on the New World retaining those desired aspects of African culture" (Lux 210). Except for Rastafarian (an extension of BPM), the sixties and mid-seventies witnessed another phase of the Black Power movement that was not solely preoccupied with Africa as the motherland. So, "while Kwame Nkrumah and other African leaders are admired, the black man looks to Mother Barbados, Haiti, Guyana, Trinidad-Tobago, Jamaica, and so forth" (210). This shift in the outlook toward Africa as no longer the "homeland" to return to meant that, for many Black Caribbean intellectuals and cultural workers, the continent became the spiritual or symbolic source of Black identity, thus supporting the way in which African Caribbean people adapted Africa to the environments they were living in. Additionally, the rise of the Black Power movement in the 1960s in the United States reignited the philosophical teachings of Garvey that highlighted Black self-hate in the region. The movement attacked the practices of Black people's attempt to strengthen their hair, bleach the skin, and deny the existence of Black culture (Hickling 38). Even though the Black Power movement in the Caribbean has often been overlooked or overshadowed because of an emphasis being placed on the United States, England, or Canada, the Caribbean would not only become a significant place for the development of Black consciousness but also a fertile ground for the growth of Black Power activities.

Additionally, in his essay, Lux further discusses how in the quest to culturally break from European domination, African Caribbean people used Black Power ideologically to assert an African Caribbean identity, which was refashioned and expressed through religion at its core. As Fernando Ortiz has documented, religion persists through Black societies, rites, initiations, dances, and the like (Ortíz). For instance, African-centered religions such as African Cuban Santería is practiced by Cuban immigrants across the United States, especially in Miami. While Ortiz's observation was made many decades ago, this presence of African-oriented spirituality is also the same for Vodoun practiced outside of Haiti by Haitian immigrants in New York. Lux sees this cultural retention as a form of Black Power and an identification with Africa. As he notes, "[i]n summary, the Caribbean world of displaced people is emerging from the purview of European cultural imperialism and Black Power as the vehicle for reaching back intellectually and emotionally (through religion) to Mother Africa for a cultural identity" (Lux 212). Moreover, Quinn draws parallels to radical African syncretic religious movements such as Ethiopianism and Rastafari as embodying multiple streams of Caribbean Black Power (Quinn 17).

As he further highlights the influence of Black Power, Lux points to the agendas of political and economic development that have been articulated by Marcus Garvey and other adherents of this political tendency. In this way, he also expounds on the major Black Power movements, such as the Rodney Rebellion in Kingston, Jamaica, October 16, 1968, that have existed throughout the Caribbean region and that have strived to gain economic independence from its colonizers. The banning of Guyanese university lecturer and Black Power activist Walter Rodney by the Jamaican government of Hugh Shearer fueled the social disturbances. Walter Rodney was expelled from Jamaica by the government out of fear that his "interaction with the leading figures at the grass-roots could lead to the emergence of a radical political ideology taking hold among them and that instability would ensue if such a political movement became an oppositional force threatening the political system of independent Jamaica that was barely six years old" (Lewis, "Walter Rodney" 7). The possible link between the intellectuals and the grassroot population became a source of concern among the leaders of the ruling Jamaica Labor Party. To date, there has been no concrete evidence of Rodney attempting to overthrow the Jamaican government (7). Rodney was actively involved in the Black Power movement, and he was highly critical of the class oppression of African people in many Caribbean nations. Rodney's socialist politics intertwined with a Black Power message aimed at raising the political and cultural consciousness of the Black Jamaican working class. The rebellion was soon suppressed by the police, following the killing of two persons (7). Rodney's political idea of BP eventually spread and influenced other Caribbean countries. On April 21, 1969, Port of Spain, Trinidad also experienced a mini political uprising when members of the island's army participated in a mutiny, forcing Prime Minister Eric Williams to declare a state of emergency. The protest left four dead, caused extensive destruction of property by fire, and resulted in considerable apprehension (Lux 213). Other Black Power activities in the Caribbean included riots and bombings in islands such as Grenada, Bermuda, and Curacao.

William Lux also hints at the different ways that various Caribbean governments had responded to the Black Power movement in the post-independence years: Forbes Burnham in Guyana managed to stay ahead of the movement by assuming a quasi-leadership role. Black-controlled government in Jamaica is headed by Black Prime Minister Hugh Shearer who is opposed to accommodation with Black Power advocates, even keeping agitators off the island (214). After gaining independence from

Great Britain, the first Prime Minister of Grenada, Eric Gairy, suppressed growing Black Power sentiment among the opposition, but was toppled in March 1979 through a bloodless coup by the New Jewel Movement, an organization led by Maurice Bishop which combined Marxism-Leninism with Black Power ideologies. Bishop established a People's Revolutionary Government (PRG) with close ties to Cuba, Nicaragua, and other socialist-leaning countries from the region – an experiment that was ended with the execution of Bishop by rival military forces and the invasion of the United States in 1983 (Simba).

Lux's cultural, political, and economic position on the emergence and assertion of Black Power has no doubt been voiced wholesale in the creative work of the Caribbean cultural workers. He identifies Haiti as the precursor to using African-inspired art "for the Caribbean search of African identification" and the "first of the predominantly black areas to produce black literature" (Lux 209). As a result, Lux contends that Haiti again took the lead in a cultural development seeped in "Africanness, whereas the other areas were still under European or white control" (209). In "Literary Black Power in the Caribbean," Rita Keresztesi notes how some Caribbean literary writers in the 1970s critically and directly engaged Black Power themes in their work. She mentions writers such as Earl Lovelace, V.S Naipaul and his novels *The Return of Eva Peron* and *Guerrillas* along with Kamau Brathwaite whose work she maintains "recuperate the African content of Black Power as a constructive element to spiritual, cultural, intellectual and psychological survival after the trauma of slavery and forced diaspora" (Keresztesi 111).

Even though Lux nudges toward the literature of Haitian writer Carolian Ardouin as the first forms of resistance and advocacy of African Caribbean people, I argue that Black musical expression is another early channel of Black Power protest. Moving from his political and economic discussion of BPM and the Caribbean's struggle for political and economic control, Lux himself gives us an example of the lyrics of calypsonian Lord Valentino response to the riots in Trinidad: "We were marching for Unity/Black power and black dignity, Dr Williams/No, we don't want no revolution" (213). Also, the musical ingenuity in the diverse forms of Caribbean music such as calypso and reggae and the conscious lyrics provoked revolutionary Black Power tropes provoking bans and restrictions from television and radio stations (Lewis, "Black Power" 630). Clearly, in his discussion of Black Power ideology in the Caribbean, Lux and others alike are aware of how the impact of expressions of Black counterdiscourse such as religion and literature functioned alongside the work of political activists to spearhead BPM in the Caribbean region.

Jamaican popular music and Black Power

Using music to express Black Power ideas or raise class consciousness is not uncommon in Caribbean history. As far back as African work songs, Caribbean popular music has always been used to voice resistance against colonial dominance and racial oppression. It was through the work songs that the traditions of political protest became viable not only to be used as forms of entertainment or humor but also to covertly critique the colonial system and to raise black consciousness among its population. As such, work songs "recounted hardships, recorded aspirations for freedom and expressed both covert and overt opposition to [the black working class'] their situation" (Tomlinson 6). Also, work songs served to articulate African Jamaican identity and to keep alive collective memory (7), thus embracing a Black Power articulation of Black racial pride. As an example, Harry Belafonte's mento song, "Banana Boat Song (Day O)," took on a traditional work song aesthetic to raise class consciousness and to highlight the exploitation of African Jamaican workers on the banana plantations. In the song's first two stanzas, we hear a Black laborer's request for wages. The laborer had tirelessly toiled all night picking bananas for the pittance of an income:

> Day-o, day-o
> Daylight come and me wan' go home
> Day, me say day, me say day, me say day
> Me say day, me say day-o
> Daylight come and me wan' go home
>
> Work all night on a drink of rum
> Daylight come and me wan' go home
> Stack banana 'til de mornin' come
> Daylight come and me wan' go home. (Harry Belafonte, "Banana Boat Song")

Work songs like Belafonte's Banana Boat Song, therefore, can be traced back to one of the earliest forms of social resistance and Black consciousness in the Americas which later evolved into various styles of Black Atlantic music such as mento, calypso, ska, and reggae. All these varied sounds expressed Black Power ideas and resistance in the same way African-oriented religion spoke to the consciousness of the people as Lux reports.

Additionally, soul music in the 1950s to early 1960s had an influence on Jamaican music and inspired Black Power messages. When Jamaica was coming out of the outmoded Calypso era and still a British colony, African American sounds intersected and added a new form to the Black Jamaican working-class cultural tradition (Fared 66–67). Jamaican popular musicians managed to indigenize their own brand of music which contained Black Power ideas that helped to raise race consciousness among Jamaica's people. The diasporic flow of Black music created a cultural bond between Blacks in the Americas despite their geographical displacement and their distance from one another. For instance, some of the most popular rhythm and blues songs became staples in Jamaican dance halls of the late 1950s and early 1960s. Commercially, rhythm and blues hits helped to maintain the business of dancehall promoters by appealing to large crowds who attended dancing venues regularly to listen to their favorite R&B songs. Roscoe Gordon's slow-tempo R&B songs "No More Dogging" and "Going Home Tomorrow" also influenced the beat of a number of Jamaican tunes, including Theophilus Beckford's "Easy Snappin" and Laurel Aitken's "Boogie In My Bones" (Chang and Cheng 23–24). The rise of Black consciousness through the Americas maintained the cultural conversation or link between African Americans and Black people in the Caribbean. As Jamaicans continued to listen to U.S. soul music, there emerged a greater development of Jamaican indigenous sounds and themes that would inform the music genres rock steady and reggae. While the earlier genres of Jamaican popular music incorporated elements of social protest, racial pride, and repatriation (King 28; Hylton 26), reggae represented a musical form that came to be recognized as the voice of the people. Its lyrical content was symbolically tied to Black Power for its overt criticism of slavery, colonialism, and neo-colonialism, advocacy of Pan-Africanist politics and call for Black unification and self-love. Bob Andy and Marcia Griffith's cover version of vocalist Nina Simone's "Young, Gifted and Black" and Big Youth's sample of R&B singer Borris Gardiner's 1974 "Every Nigger is a Star" challenged notions of Black inferiority that had been established under white supremacy. Instead, following the Black Power discourse, which promoted popular slogans such as "Black is Beautiful," they celebrated Blackness. Both songs had a distinctive reggae vibration. More revolutionary Black Power-oriented reggae tunes came from artists such as Peter Tosh, Bob Marley, and Burning Spear whose lyrics explicitly attacked white supremacist structures of oppression and encouraged Black political empowerment. The decade of a visible Black Power philosophy heard in Jamaican popular music did not end entirely in the 1980s. However, this period ushered in another genre of Jamaican popular music, namely, the dancehall. This genre was perceived as lacking the level of political consciousness of reggae music in the 1960s and 1970s and early 1980s, and yet, it continued to articulate Black consciousness and resistance in a more disputed way.

Dancehall music: a jus' reality

Like reggae music, dancehall emerged from the marginalized youth culture of Kingston's ghettos. Unlike its predecessor reggae, dancehall music represented a problematic site in the way that it articulated its message. For instance, dancehall music has been criticized for its violent gun lyrics, promotion of criminal behavior, and anti-gay content. Paradoxically, dancehall perpetuates the exclusion of the LGBTQ community as it seeks recognition for an undervalued, Black, working-class masculinity. Dancehall's anti-gay issue came to international attention with the controversy surrounding the release of Buju Banton's "Boom Bye" – a song that explicitly advocates violence against gay men. The message of dancehall music also consists of lyrics that is referred to as "slackness," in the Jamaican language, translated as lewd sexual lyrics. It is the slackness and gun violence of the dancehall that frequently stands in direct opposition to the music from the so-called 'golden age' of reggae in the 1970s.

Paradoxically, the genesis of this overtly sexual dimension and eroticism of dancehall can be traced back directly to the long established, localized musical tradition of mento. Like many genres of Jamaican popular music, and despite the sexual content that was associated with its sounds, Mento carried forms of resistance and consciousness as demonstrated in Harry Belafonte's "Song of a Banana Man." Hence, in his book *Aint' no Black in the Union Jack*, Paul Gilroy argues that dancehall moved away from its political and historical roots toward "slackness: crude and often insulting wordplay pronouncing sexuality and sexual antagonism" (Gilroy 188). What Gilroy overlooks in his analysis of dancehall is that similar to reggae, dancehall music has been used as a commentary against issues such as slavery, colonialism, neo-colonialism, state repression, and urban poverty. Notwithstanding Gilroy's observation that dancehall is politically conservative, I concur with Carolyn Cooper (1993) as she suggests that dancehall as a "political subversion" should be seen as resistance in the dancehall space in spite of dancehall culture being male-dominated, homophobic, and misogynist. Similarly, Angelique Nixon points out how reggae-dancehall artists like Damian Marley and Tanya Stephens's negotiation between dancehall and roots reggae speak to their common origins in Jamaican culture, Rastafarian, Black Nationalism, and African diasporic history (Nixon 199). In contrast to Marley, Nixon ties Timothy Chin's notion of a "Decolonized Caribbean discourse" to Stephens's engagement with Black resistance. She works with Chin's "Decolonised Caribbean Discourse," stating that the discourse "makes the critique of homophobic and sexist ideologies an integral component" (196) of Caribbean cultural expression. Although Stephens, Marley, and a few other conscious artists are the exception to the tendency of dancehall entertainers' consistency as organic intellectuals, we must be careful not to create divisive dichotomy between the two genres and recognize that dancehall and reggae are consistently speaking to each other and are connected in complex ways (192). Cooper and Nixon's position allows us to explore the complexities within dancehall culture and to gain a better understanding of the music's role in raising social and political consciousness.

One of the most outstanding differences between these two forms of musical articulation lies in how the dancehall deejay's worldviews depart from those of conventional reggae artists. Reggae artists have traditionally expressed admiration for a united Africa with Ethiopia serving as the core in Rastafarian faith and reggae music. This philosophical position is not to overlook the fact that there are still some dancehall artists who draw on Rastafarian aesthetics and a roots reggae tradition in their attempt to express Black unification globally as well as to express Black Power or consciousness. In this way, I borrow from Angelique Nixon's concept of "hybrid space" that she describes as a "current manifestation of roots reggae dancehall" which "asserts a consciousness that evokes a liberatory view of history and forges resistance" (Nixon 192). She adds that "this kind of resistance posits a Black-centered consciousness within the Caribbean context that is not a simple rehashing of the past but an interrogation of history into the present (192). Nixon draws on the lyrics of Damion Junior Gong and Tanya Stephens to demonstrate how the two artists create this "hybrid space." I will, however, analyze the lyrics of dancehall associated artists Sizzla, Buju Banton, and Bounty Killer to contextualize Nixon's notion of "hybrid space."

Sizzla's entry onto the dancehall scene began as a youngster doing conscious lyrics that were not tied to the Rastafari faith (Bernard). Sizzla's debut album included hardcore dancehall songs and Black conscious songs such as "Mother of Nations." After his conversion to the Rastafarian faith, his follow-up albums such as *Black Woman and Child* and *Praise Ye Jah* were released in 1997. According to Bernard, Sizzla was popular among Jamaican youths because he was able to lyrically address current social, economic, and political issues of the time (Bernard). Within this context, because of his ability to relate to urban issues that challenged state power while simultaneously speaking to Rastafari religiosity and Black Power, ideas of racial pride, and the self determination of Black people, Sizzla can be located within the "hybrid space" that Nixon describes.

In the song "Black Woman and Child," he honors Black women and their offspring before gaining wealth:

> Black woman and child, yeh yeah
> For you I really have so much love for
> Dollars bills and coins will fade away
> They could never make I so proud. (Sizzla, "Black Woman and Child")

Although Sizzla's praise for Black women can be interpreted as superficial and chauvinistic, one cannot ignore the way he attempts to centralize their worth and value above worldly riches. This adoration for Black women is contrary to society's negative representation of Black women.

In the introduction of the song, Sizzla takes a strong Black cultural nationalist position as he declares love for his race and he embraces his skin color as representation of civilization. Sizzla's love for his race and his identification of the Black race as the creator of civilization represents a Black consciousness discourse that counteracts the white supremacist notion of Black people's racial and cultural inferiority.

> What, The Black nation? I love It …
> From the day me born, me did done know say my color a the first I no
> lost … so how you expect I fi research?
> Rasta food … fi the youths. ("Black Woman and Child")

Sizzla's use of the Rastafarian ethos to articulate love for his race ties back to Lux's assertion that religion is a critical site for the expression of Black Power and African identification.

In a similar way, dancehall deejay Buju Banton's musical persona can also fall within a hybrid space. Unlike Sizzla, Buju Banton began his music career by performing what would be considered traditional dancehall songs. In the mid-1990s, Banton transitioned to the Rastafarian faith where his lyrical content also began to reflect the faith. Even though he took on the symbolic dreadlocked hairstyle, he remained popular among dancehall fans and maintained some of the dancehall aesthetics. His lyrical sound also shifted back and forth between reggae and dancehall dealing with spirituality, social and political issues as well as love. His seminal Rastafarian influence album *Til Shiloh* was a blend of conscious roots lyrics with a hard-hitting dancehall aggression, themes that are not commonly present in militantly expressed reggae songs. However, it was the Black consciousness expressed throughout the album that became the focal point. In one of his popular Pan-African songs, "Til I'm Laid to Rest" for instance, Buju Banton incites a revolt against the despairing economic conditions of Black people, the exploitation of the poor, before suggesting repatriation to Africa as the final solution:

> I'm laid to rest, yes
> Always be depressed
> There's no life in the West uh
> I know the East is the best, yes
> Propaganda dem spread
> Tongues will haffi confess. (Buju Banton, "Til I'm laid to Rest")

Banton also nods to Black Nationalist Marcus Garvey's demand for Black unification when he chants: "What could a bad so bout di East/ Everybody wants a piece/ Africa fi Africans/ Marcus Mosiah speak/Unification." Marcus Garvey is also a key figure in the Rastafarian culture as he is seen as a prophet and his message of Black economic empowerment fits within the Black Power model. In "How the World A Run," from his earlier dancehall album, Buju Banton bemoans the unequal distribution of wealth between the rich and the poor. He goes as far as highlighting how dogs are afforded a higher standard of living than the Black working class is:

> Let us see a betta day for our grandchildren
> Ah wi look inna wi heart and see wey wi can mend
> Where food is concern, there is a problem
> Woman cyan find food fi give di children
> While the rich man have di chicken back and feed di dog dem. ("How the World A Run")

Significantly, Buju Banton's album *Til Shiloh* had an impact on dancehall music culture. Reminding us that dancehall patrons had not forgotten the message that roots reggae expounded with the use of roots culture, it harkened back to Black Power movement and its resistance to race and class oppression. This observation is not to say that dancehall artists abandoned hardcore erotic and violent lyrics altogether, but that Banton's Rastafarian-inspired album opened the path to a new movement in dancehall that would see others like Buju not only embrace the Rastafarian spirituality, but also espouse social or culturally conscious themes that often fell in line with Black Power and Black nationalist ideology. Capleton was one such dancehall artist that took this route. Buju Banton's follow-up albums *Inner Heights* continued to offer Rastafarian spirituality and African consciousness. The song "African Pride," for instance, engages multiple elements of Black Power messages. The chorus begins with naming random African countries and calls for African pride in the midst of Africa's struggle for liberation:

> (Ethiopia) Africans with African pride
> (Somalia) Fighting to attain our rights
> Want no more shedding of blood
> For our nation to move forward
> (Mozambique) Africans with African pride

(Zambia) Fighting to attain our rights
Want no more shedding of blood
For dis nation to move forward. ("African Pride")

What is more, the second verse encourages African unification:

What make we can't all unite
Put each man difference aside
Why can't we just come together
Cease from tribal wars and fight...
A source of collective insight. ("African Pride")

Another verse underscores Black self-sufficiency and economic empowerment:

Self help with inner motivation
Teach I to be self sufficient
Don't want to depend on no one
For attainment of my bread
Oh these words
Oh my calling
Children crying white squall tears
Hunger rampant harvest plenty. ("African Pride")

In addition, Nixon's concept of "hybrid space" can be applied to what I will label as more "hardcore dancehall," comprising of artists in the 1990s who were not self-identified Rastafarian. Yet, their lyrics expressed Black Power and class consciousness themes and generally articulated lyrics on social and economic concerns affecting the urban and rural poor that would otherwise be referred to as "reality tune." Bounty Killer is a hardcore dancehall artist who operates within such hybrid spaces. Unlike some of the other artists (such as Shaba Ranks) who occasionally deejayed reality songs in response to criticism of the music itself, Bounty Killer is consistent in operating on a conscious political level. Aside from the "bad" guy persona that he performs, much of Bounty Killer's lyrics include social commentary, with the result that he has elected himself as the "Poor People Governor." Bounty Killer's lyrics signal an awareness of class and race politics. Furthermore, contrary to Sizzla, Bounty Killer's Black Power songs deal less with the past, the glorification of Africa or a desire to return to Africa. Instead, Bounty Killer's lyrics speak to Nixon's assertion of a hybrid space interrogating the present. Therefore, his music "produces and reproduces cultural identities that can speak of resistance while challenging new oppression" (Nixon 192). As an Example, one of his popular songs called "Fed up" engages with the current suffering and frustration of the working class in Jamaica. In the song, Bounty Killer holds the politicians accountable for their ongoing corruption and neglect of the slums, expressing concern for poor Black lives that are taken daily due to gun violence that has to do with poverty and soaring rates of youth unemployment.

Well, this one reaching out to all the leaders, and the media,
Well this is Rodney Price aka Bounty Killer,
The leader for Poor People Government
Well poor people fed up to how yuh system sheg up

Yuh issue gun fi wi pickney bus
Poor people fed up to how yuh system sheg up
Well everyday the ghetto youths dead up. (Bounty Killer, "Fed up")

All the themes with which Bounty Killer engages resonate with Caribbean Black Power. Indeed, his music highlights the concerns and the value of Black lives, it interrogates the neo-colonialism as a structure that forces Black Jamaicans into poverty, explicitly denouncing the role third world government play in *downpressing* Black people and how they are not qualitatively different from the *downpression* of imperial nations.[1]

While one may argue that some of Bounty Killer's songs pandered to the lifestyle and outlook of the predatory and community-destabilizing lumpen element (personal communication), other songs such as "Look into my eyes" can be read as a political protest against society. Similar to Richard Wright's controversial protagonist Bigger Thomas in the protest novel *Native Son*, Bounty Killer represents his character in the song "Look into my eyes" as a victim of environmental determinism. Therefore, like Bigger's character, Bounty's unnamed speaker tragically embodies the menacing criminal that only a hostile impoverished environment such as Kingston's ghetto can breed:

Look into my eyes, tell me what you see?
Can you feel my pain? am I your enemy?
Give us a better way, things are really bad,
The only friend I know is this gun I have.
Listen to my voice, this is not a threat
Now you see the nine are you worried yet?
You've been talking 'bout' you want the war to cease
But when you show us hope, we will show you peace. (Bounty Killer, "Look into my Eyes")

"Look into my Eyes" is also an attempt to put the oppressive system on trial for its neglect of the suffering poor who are at times forced to turn to criminal activities for survival. A close analysis of the lyrical content also highlights Bounty Killer's commitment to culturally conscious production because rather than the lyrics "being a glorification of the 9mm gun and bad man style, the song instead is a desperate plea on behalf of the poor for help to find an alternative life" (Imani 263).

In his song entitled "Black Power," he deejays about Black empowerment and self-determination through gaining wealth from gold, diamonds, and pearls that colonial powers extracted in Africa, echoing Marcus Garvey's economic philosophy for Africans. His vision of Black ownership also reads as a capitalistic enterprise wherein Bounty Killer interprets Black Power as gaining material wealth, for instance "ghetto people owning a Benz." Bounty Killer's articulation of Black wealth is perhaps also in line with the 1960s interpretation of Black Power as economic nationalism and Black

---

1 Downpressing is the Rastafarian alternative expression for oppression. This altering of words comes from Rastafarian play on words removes all the power that negative words like oppression have. In other words, oppression is changed to depression because oppression keeps one down instead of lifting one up.

capitalism, promoted by soul singer James Brown, who was an icon of working-class Black success in the United States of America.[2] At the same time, however, while Bounty Killer advocates Black empowerment and self-determination, he excludes Black gay Jamaican men. The anti-gay sentiment is on display where Bounty Killer, Buju Banton, and Sizzla's Black Power lyrical content reads similar and is one of the factors that reveals the complexity of the genre. This homophobic exclusion is also not surprising given the fact that historically Black Power in its fight against white supremacy has been rooted in anti-gay sentiments (Green and Payne 557). Black feminist poet Cheryl Clarke in her essay "The Failure to Transform: Homophobia in the Black Community" indicates that "it is ironic that the Black Power movement could transform the consciousness of an entire generation of people regarding self-determination and, at the same time, fail so miserably in understanding the sexual politics of the movement and of black people across the board" (Clarke 199). Hence, the dancehall deejays anti-gay sentiments point to the social conservativism that Gilroy describes in the genre. This further exemplifies the continuity of masculinist liberation ideologies (patriarchy, misogyny, and homophobia) that guided the Black Power movement in the 1960s. Steve Estes recounts how the notion of ideal manhood "espoused by Eldridge Cleaver and other Black Power leaders had serious negative implications for men who did not fit into the model and also women, who surprisingly, had difficulty achieving ideals of manhood in any form" (Estes 162). Estes concludes that "Homophobia became a tool wielded by movement participants during the Black Power" era despite the instrumental role gay men played in the struggle (162).

Conclusion

In proposing to view dancehall as a representation of Black Power and resistance in the Americas, I do recognize that the genre supports patriarchy and homophobia. Even though it is liberatory in its celebration of Blackness and provides an alternative vision for working class Black people, dancehall culture expresses a troubling "contradiction with an ideology of Black consciousness and resistance that is also anti-gay and sexist" (Nixon 195). It is this contradiction and gap within dancehall culture that needs to be challenged by archiving the voices of women and people of all sexual orientation or sexualities into its Black Power discourse. Nixon points to Tanya Stephens as a woman deejay who through her feminist sensibility has attempted to insert Black women into a Black consciousness framework. She argues that many of Stephens's songs "assert a strong cultural identity and sexual subjectivity for black women while rooted in consciousness empowering lyrics that celebrate sexuality" (195). Tanya Stephens has also been quite vocal against anti-gay lyrics in this music. In an interview, she refers to anti-gay rhetoric as "stupidness," asserting that "this [anti-gay] point of view does not

2 Before his performance at Madison Square, Garden, New York, Brown announced that "James Brown is totally committed to Black Power, the kind that is achieved not through the muzzle of a riffle but through education and economic leverage" (Werner 17).

represent the wider Jamaica" (Dreisinger n. pag.). The efforts to widen the popular discourse of Black Power in dancehall, however, still fall shorts in including LGBT community into the discourse of Black liberation.

I also recognize that not many dancehall artists neatly fit into Nixon's 'hybrid space.' Likewise, I acknowledge that two progressive songs in the catalogue of major dancehall artists cannot transform them into politically conscious artists. What needs to be highlighted is the fact that dancehall like any other Black musical genre has engaged Black consciousness and, in many ways, continues to shape discourses around it. Despite its contradictions, we must be cautious also in not diminishing the music's contestatory and emancipatory potential as a platform of social protest and Black assertiveness.

Works cited

Bernard, Allan. "A Focus on Sizzla Kolonji: A Leading Influence on A New Generation of Rastafari Youth." *Rastafari in the New Millennium: A Rastafari Reader*. Ed. Michael Barnett. New York: Syracuse University, 2014. 277–288. Print.

Chang, Kevin O'Brien, and Wayne Cheng. *Reggae Routes: The Story of Jamaican Music*. Philadelphia: Temple UP, 1998. Print.

Cheney, Charise. "'We men ain't we': Mas(k)ulinity and the Gendered Politics of Black Nationalism." *Time Longer Than Rope: A Century of African American Activism, 1850–1950*. Ed. Adam Green and Payne Charles. New York: New York UP, 2003. 536–563. Print.

Clarke, Cheryl. "The Failure to Transform: Homophobia in the Black Community." *Home Girls: A Black Feminist Anthology*. Ed. Barbara Smith. New Brunswick: Rutgers UP, 1983. 190–201. Print.

Cooper, Carolyn. *Noises in the Blood: Orality, Gender, and the "Vulgar" Body of Jamaican Popular Culture*. London: MacMillan, 1993. Print

Dreisinger, Baz. "Activists Take on Culture's Anti-Gay Lyrics." *Los Angeles Times*. 18 Sep. 2004. Web. www.latimes.com/archives/la-xpm-2004-sep-18-et-dreisinger18-story.html.

Estes, Steve. *I am a Man!: Race, Manhood, and the Civil Rights Movement*. Chapel Hill / London: U of North Carolina P, 2005. Print.

Fared, Grant. "Wailin' Soul: Reggae's Debt to Black American Music." *Black Power, Politics, and Pleasure*. Ed. Richard C. Green. New York: New York UP, 1998. 56–75. Print.

Gilroy, Paul. *There Ain't No Black in the Union Jack. The Cultural Politics of Race and Nation*. Chicago: U of Chicago P, 1991.

Hickling, Frederick W. "Psychopathology of the Jamaican People." *Perspectives in Caribbean Psychology*. Ed. Frederick W. Hickling, Brigitte K. Matthies, Kai Morgan, and Roger C. Gibson. Kingston, Jamaica: CARIMENSA, University of the West Indies, 2008. 32–69. Print.

Hylton, Patrick. "The Politics of Caribbean Music." *Black Scholar* 7.1 (Sep. 1975): 23–29. Print.

Imani, Tafari-Ama. *Blood, Bullets, and Bodies: Sexual Politics Below Jamaican Poverty*. Burscough, Lancashire: Beaten Track Publishing, 2006. Print.

Jackson, Maurice. "No Man Could Hinder Him: Remembering Toussaint Louverture and the Haitian Revolution in History and Culture of African American People." *African Americans and the Haitian Revolution: Selected Essays and Historical Documents*. Ed. Maurice Jackson and Jacqueline Beacon. New York: Routledge, 2010. 140–152. Print.

Keresztesi, Rita. "Literary Black Power in the Caribbean." Conference paper quoted in Jerome Tellucksingh, *Civil Rights in America and the Caribbean, 1950s–2010s*. Cham: Palgrave Macmillan Press, 2017. 111. Print.

King, Stephen. *Reggae Rastafarian and the Rhetoric of Social Control*. Mississippi: University of Mississippi, 2002. Print.

Lewis, Rupert. "Walter Rodney: 1968 Revisited." *Social and Economic Studies* 48.1: *New Currents in Caribbean Thought* (Sep. 1994): 7–22. Print.

———. "Black Power in the Caribbean." *The Oxford Handbook of Caribbean Constitutions*. Ed. Richard Albert, Derek O'Brien, and Se-shauna Wheatle. Oxford: Oxford UP, 2020. 606–630. Print.

Lux, William R. "Black Power in the Caribbean." *Journal of Black Studies* 3.2 (1972): 212. Print.

Martin, Tony. "African And Indian Consciousness." *General History of the Caribbean: Volume 1. The Caribbean in the Twentieth Century*. Ed. Pieter C. Emmer, Bridget Breton, and Barry W. Higman. New York: Palgrave Macmillian Publishers, 2003. 224–281. Print.

Nixon, Angelique. "Blackness, Resistance and Consciousness in Dancehall Culture." *Black Renaissance* 9.2-3 (2009): 191–199. Print.

Ortíz, Fernando. *Los negros brujos*. Madrid: Librería de Fernando Fe, 1906. Print.

Quinn, Kate. "Introduction: The New Perspective of Black Power Movement." *Black Power in the Caribbean*. Ed. Kate Quinn. Gainesville: U of Florida P, 2014. 18. Print.

Simba, Malik. "Maurice Bishop (1944–1983)." 2009. Web. https://www.blackpast.org/global-african-history/bishop-maurice-1944–1983/.

Tomlinson, Lisa. *The African-Jamaican Aesthetic: Cultural Retention and Transformation Across Borders*. Leiden: Brill / Rodopi, 2017. Print.

Werner, Craig Hansen. *A Change is Gonna Come, Race & the Soul of America*. Ann Arbor: U of Michigan P, 2006. Print.

Discography

Belafonte, Harry. "Banana Boat Song (Day' O)." Track 1 on *Calypso*. RCA Victor, 1956.

Bounty Killer. "Fed up." Track 1 on *My Xperience*. TVT Records, 1996.

———. "Look into my Eyes." Track 16 on *5th Element*. 1999.

Buju Banton. "African Pride." Track 5 on *Inna Heights*. Penthouse / VP Records, 1997.

———. "Til I'm laid to Rest." Track 4 on *Til Siloh*. Loose Canon / Island original release, 1995.

———. "How the World A Run." Track 12 on *Mr Mention*. Penthouse, 1992.

Sizzla. "Black Woman and Child." Track 4 on *Black Woman & Child*. VP Records, 1997.

Contributors

Alberto Abreu Arcia, based in Matanzas, Cuba, is an activist, novelist, essayist, and cultural critic who writes on topics such as race, identity, and LGBT issues. He is a member of the Cuban chapter of the regional black civil rights organization *Articulación Regional Afrodescendiente de América Latina y el Caribe* (ARAAC). He runs the blog *Afromodernidades*. His most recent book, published in 2017, is entitled *Por una Cuba negra: literatura, raza y modernidad en el siglo XIX.*

George Reid Andrews is Distinguished Professor at the University of Pittsburgh where he has taught Latin American history since 1981. He is the author of several books on Afro-Latin American history, such as *Afro-Latin America: Black Lives, 1600–2000* (2016), *Blackness in the White Nation: A History of Afro-Uruguay* (2010), and *Blacks and Whites in São Paulo, Brazil, 1888–1988* (1991). Two of his recent publications are *Afro-Latin American Studies: An Introduction* (2018), co-edited with Alejandro de la Fuente, and *Voices of the Race: Black Newspapers in Latin America, 1870–1960* (2022), co-authored with Paulina Alberto and Jesse Hoffnung-Garskof.

Valeria L. Carbone is Associate Professor at the Chair of History of the United States of America at *Facultad de Filosofía y Letras* (Universidad de Buenos Aires) and researcher at *Instituto Interdisciplinario de Estudios de América Latina* (INDEAL). She is chief editor of the journal *Huellas de Estados Unidos: Estudios, perspectivas y debates desde América Latina*. Dr. Carbone has authored *Una historia del movimiento negro estadounidense en la era pos derechos civiles (1968-1988*) (2020) and co-edited *Anatomía de un Imperio: Estados Unidos y América Latina* with Mariana Mastrángelo (2019). Her current research revolves around the influence of Black Power in Latin America, and radical (Afro-)Latin-American movements in the United States.

Afua Cooper is a Jamaican-born Canadian historian, writer, and dub poet. She is an associate professor of sociology at Dalhousie University where she works as the founding chair of the Black Canadian Studies Association. Afua Cooper has served as the Poet Laureate of Halifax Regional Municipality for the term 2018–2020. Her twelve books range across such genres as history, poetry, fiction, and children's literature and deal with enslavement and emancipation in 18th- and 19th-century Canada, Black women and diaspora, social justice, inequality, and decolonization. Her publications include *The Hanging of Angelique: The Untold Story of Canadian Slavery and the Burning of Old Montreal* (2006) and *Black Matters* (2020), co-created with Wilfried Raussert.

Carlos Alberto Medeiros earned his PhD in history at the Universidade Federal do Rio de Janeiro (UFRJ). He is a journalist, black movement activist, and scholar of comparative race relations with a focus on Brazil and the United States. In the 1970s, he participated in the Black Rio movement and became involved in the anti-racist struggle, including in his role as president of the historical *Instituto de Pesquisa das Culturas Negras* (IPCN). He is the author of *Na Lei e na Raça. Legislação e Relações Raciais, Brasil-Estados Unidos* (2004) and *Racismo, preconceito e intolerancia* (2015), which he has co-authored together with Jacques d'Adesky and Edson Borges. He has translated works of Zygmunt Bauman, Slavoj Žižek, Frantz Fanon, Martin Luther King, and many others into Portuguese. Currently, he presents the weekly Afro-Brazilian program *Cultne na TV*, produced by Asfilofio Filó Filho.

Carla Guerrón Montero is a cultural and applied anthropologist trained in the United States and Latin America. Specializing in the anthropology of tourism, the anthropology of food, and the African diaspora, Dr. Guerrón Montero is a Professor of Anthropology at the University of Delaware, with joint appointments in Africana Studies, Latin American and Iberian Studies, and Women and Gender Studies. Her most recent publications include the historical ethnography *From Temporary Migrants to Permanent Attractions: Tourism, Cultural Heritage, and Afro-Antillean Identities in Panama* (2020) and the co-edited volume *Why the World Needs Anthropologists* (2021).

John Munro is lecturer in U.S. history at the University of Birmingham. He is the author of *The Anticolonial Front: The African American Freedom Struggle and Global Decolonization 1945–1960* (2017) and *Imperialism: A Syllabus* with Radhika Natarajan (Public Books, 2021).

Jeffrey O.G. Ogbar is Professor of History at the University of Connecticut, and the founding Director of the Center for the Study of Popular Music. His research interests include the 20th-century United States with a focus on African American history, more specifically social justice movements, black nationalism, and U.S. popular culture. He is the author or editor of several books, including *Black Power: Radical Politics and African American Identity* (2004), *Hip-Hop Revolution: The Culture and Politics of Rap* (2009), *Harlem Renaissance: Politics, Arts, Letters* (2010), and *Keywords in African American Studies* with Erica R. Edwards and Roderick A. Ferguson (2018).

Kensedeobong Blessed Okosun is currently a doctoral student at Bielefeld University, Germany. Following her BA from the University of Abuja, Nigeria, she had a stint as News Reporter at NTA Abuja, Channel 5. Her research interests include the evolution of Rhythm and Blues in the 1990s, spirituality and the songs of *Earth, Wind and Fire*, American female musicianship, and the significance of the anti-sexist male and sisterhood in the quest for gender egalitarianism.

Portia Owusu earned her PhD at SOAS, University of London. Currently, she is an Assistant Professor of English at Texas A&M University, where she teaches and researches topics in African American, African, and diaspora literature. Her research interests include history/historiography, memory, cultural philosophy, and contemporary narratives of slavery. She has published on these topics in several articles as well as in her book, *Spectres from the Past: Slavery and the Politics of "History" in West African and African-American Literature* (2019). Her current project is on death and mourning in Africa and the diaspora.

Ángel Perea Escobar is a Bogotá-based interdisciplinary artist and cultural critic specializing in Afro-American art and culture and the African Diaspora. As a musicologist, professor, and lecturer, he focuses on the social history of Afro-American music and culture. He has worked as a cultural investigative journalist, director, and producer of radio programs on Afro-American music and culture. Furthermore, he has worked as a playwright and screenwriter, creative director, and producer of cultural events, film festivals, and exhibitions. He is the founding director of A.P.E. Prods Creative Agency for research and production of cultural contents.

Ángel G. Quintero-Rivera is Research Project Director and Professor at the Social Science Research Center of the University of Puerto Rico (CIS-UPR). He has published extensively on the historical sociology of Caribbean societies, mainly Puerto Rico. His research has centered on the sociology of culture: music, popular festivities, urban relations, and social movements. His book *¡Salsa, sabor y control!* (1998) was awarded the Casa de las Americas prize in Cuba in 1998, and the Ibero-American Prize from the Latin American Studies Association (LASA) in 2000. His *Cuerpo y cultura, las músicas "mulatas" y la subversión del baile* (2009) received the Frantz Fanon Award from the Association of Caribbean Philosophy for its contribution to Caribbean thought.

Wilfried Raussert is Professor of North American Literatures and Cultures and Inter-American Studies at Bielefeld University, Germany. He is Director of the International Association of Inter-American Studies and member of the steering committee of CALAS. He is co-founder of the Black Americas Network and principal researcher in the Canadian government funded project A Black People's History of Canada. Among his recent publications are the edited *The Routledge Handbook of the Culture and Media in the Americas*, the monograph *'What's Going On': How Music Shapes the Social* (2020), and the award-winning *Black Matters* (2020) with Afua Cooper. He is award winning photographer with a series of international exhibits and has released music albums in 2019 and 2021.

Matti Steinitz is a researcher at the Center for InterAmerican Studies at Bielefeld University with a focus on Afro-diasporic movements and cultures and practices of hemispheric black transnationalism between the Caribbean, North, and Latin America. As a co-founder and coordinator of the Black Americas Network he has organized the international conferences *Entangled Black Americas* (2017), *Black Power: Movements, Cultures, and Resistance in the Black Americas* (2018), and *#hiphophavanaberlin: Urban counter-cultures and social movements in the Black Atlantic* (2022). His dissertation thesis, *Hemispheric Soulscapes: Soul Music and the Rise of Black Power between Spanish Harlem, Rio and Panama*, is forthcoming in 2022. He is a 2018 alumnus of the Mark Claster Mamolen Dissertation Workshop at the Afro-Latin American Research Institute (Harvard University) and also works as a DJ and journalist.

Lisa Tomlinson is a lecturer in film and Caribbean Cultural Studies at the Institute of Caribbean Studies at the University of the West Indies, Mona Campus. She is a Research Fellow with The Dancehall Archive and Research Initiative and specializes in literary criticism and cultural studies of the Caribbean and Black diaspora, Black popular culture, film, and visual culture. She is the author of *The African-Jamaican Aesthetic: Cultural Retention and Transformation across Borders* (2017) and the biography of *Una Marson* (2019).

INTER-AMERICAN STUDIES
Cultures – Societies – History

ESTUDIOS INTERAMERICANOS
Culturas – Sociedades – Historia

This interdisciplinary series examines national and transnational issues in the cultures, societies, and histories of the Americas. It creates a forum for a critical academic dialogue between North and South, promoting an inter-American paradigm that shifts the scholarly focus from methodological nationalism to the wider context of the Western Hemisphere.

Vol. 1
Raab, Josef, Sebastian Thies, and Daniela Noll-Opitz, eds. *Screening the Americas: Narration of Nation in Documentary Film / Proyectando las Américas: Narración de la nación en el cine documental.* 2011. 472 pp.

WVT Wissenschaftlicher Verlag Trier	ISBN 978-3-86821-331-7	€ 29,50
Bilingual Press / Editorial Bilingüe	ISBN 978-1-931010-83-2	$ 29.50

Vol. 2
Raussert, Wilfried, and Michelle Habell-Pallán, eds. *Cornbread and Cuchifritos: Ethnic Identity Politics, Transnationalization, and Transculturation in American Urban Popular Music.* 2011. 292 pp.

WVT Wissenschaftlicher Verlag Trier	ISBN 978-3-86821-265-5	€ 29,50
Bilingual Press / Editorial Bilingüe	ISBN 978- 1-931010-80-1	$ 29.50

Vol. 3
Butler, Martin, Jens Martin Gurr, and Olaf Kaltmeier, eds. *EthniCities: Metropolitan Cultures and Ethnic Identities in the Americas.* 2011. 268 pp.

WVT Wissenschaftlicher Verlag Trier	ISBN 978-3-86821-310-2	€ 29,50
Bilingual Press / Editorial Bilingüe	ISBN 978-1-931010-81-8	$ 29.50

Vol. 4
Gurr, Jens Martin, and Wilfried Raussert, eds. *Cityscapes in the Americas and Beyond: Representations of Urban Complexity in Literature and Film.* 2011. 300 pp.

WVT Wissenschaftlicher Verlag Trier	ISBN 978-3-86821-324-9	€ 29,50
Bilingual Press / Editorial Bilingüe	ISBN 978-1-931010-82-5	$ 29.50

Vol. 5
Kirschner, Luz Angélica, ed. *Expanding* Latinidad*: An Inter-American Perspective*. 2012. 292 pp.

WVT Wissenschaftlicher Verlag Trier	ISBN 978-3-86821-309-6	€ 29,50
Bilingual Press / Editorial Bilingüe	ISBN 978-1-931010-84-9	$ 29.50

Vol. 6
Raussert, Wilfried, and Graciela Martínez-Zalce, eds. *(Re)Discovering 'America': Road Movies and Other Travel Narratives in North America / (Re)Descubriendo 'América': Road movie y otras narrativas de viaje en América del Norte*. 2012. 252 pp.

WVT Wissenschaftlicher Verlag Trier	ISBN 978-3-86821-384-3	€ 29,50
Bilingual Press / Editorial Bilingüe	ISBN 978-1-931010-91-7	$ 29.50

Vol. 7
Kaltmeier, Olaf, ed. *Transnational Americas: Envisioning Inter-American Area Studies in Globalization Processes*. 2013. 278 pp.

WVT Wissenschaftlicher Verlag Trier	ISBN 978-3-86821-415-4	€ 29,50
Bilingual Press / Editorial Bilingüe	ISBN 978-1-931010-92-4	$ 29.50

Vol. 8
Raab, Josef, and Alexander Greiffenstern, eds. *Interculturalism in North America: Canada, the United States, Mexico, and Beyond*. 2013. 312 pp.

WVT Wissenschaftlicher Verlag Trier	ISBN 978-3-86821-460-4	€ 29,50
Bilingual Press / Editorial Bilingüe	ISBN 978-1-931010-99-3	$ 29.50

Vol. 9
Raab, Josef, ed. *New World Colors: Ethnicity, Belonging, and Difference in the Americas*. 2014. 418 pp.

WVT Wissenschaftlicher Verlag Trier	ISBN 978-3-86821-461-1	€ 29,50
Bilingual Press / Editorial Bilingüe	ISBN 978-1-939743-00-8	$ 39.50

Vol. 10
Roth, Julia. *Occidental Readings, Decolonial Practices: A Selection on Gender, Genre, and Coloniality in the Americas*. 2014. 284 pp.

WVT Wissenschaftlicher Verlag Trier	ISBN 978-3-86821-446-8	€ 26,50
Bilingual Press / Editorial Bilingüe	ISBN 978-1-939743-07-7	$ 32.50

Vol. 11
Thies, Sebastian, Gabriele Pisarz-Ramirez, and Luzelena Gutiérrez de Velasco, eds. *Of Fatherlands and Motherlands: Gender and Nation in the Americas / De Patrias y Matrias: Género y nación en las Américas*. 2015. 344 pp.

WVT Wissenschaftlicher Verlag Trier	ISBN 978-3-86821-528-1	€ 29,50
Bilingual Press / Editorial Bilingüe	ISBN 978-1-939743-08-4	$ 39.50

Vol. 12

Fuchs, Rebecca. *Caribbeanness as a Global Phenomenon: Junot Díaz, Edwidge Danticat, and Cristina García*. 2014. 298 pp.

WVT Wissenschaftlicher Verlag Trier	ISBN 978-3-86821-533-5	€ 26,50
Bilingual Press / Editorial Bilingüe	ISBN 978-1-939743-09-1	$ 32.50

Vol. 13

Andres, Julia. *¡Cuéntame algo! – Chicana Narrative Beyond the Borderlands*. 2015. 202 pp.

WVT Wissenschaftlicher Verlag Trier	ISBN 978-3-86821-569-4	€ 25,00
Bilingual Press / Editorial Bilingüe	ISBN 978-1-939743-11-4	$ 28.50

Vol. 14

Hertlein, Saskia. *Tales of Transformation: Emerging Adulthood, Migration, and Ethnicity in Contemporary American Literature*. 2014. 228 pp.

WVT Wissenschaftlicher Verlag Trier	ISBN 978-3-86821-570-0	€ 25,00
Bilingual Press / Editorial Bilingüe	ISBN 978-1-939743-10-7	$ 31.50

Vol. 15

Raab, Josef, and Saskia Hertlein, eds. *Spaces – Communities – Discourses: Charting Identity and Belonging in the Americas*. 2016. 382 pp.

WVT Wissenschaftlicher Verlag Trier	ISBN 978-3-86821-590-8	€ 29,50
Bilingual Press / Editorial Bilingüe	ISBN 978-1-939743-13-8	$ 39.50

Vol. 16

Mehring, Frank, ed. *The Mexico Diary: Winold Reiss between Vogue Mexico and Harlem Renaissance. An Illustrated Trilingual Edition with Commentary and Musical Interpretation* (includes color plates and audio CD). 2016. 244 pp.

WVT Wissenschaftlicher Verlag Trier	ISBN 978-3-86821-594-6	€ 29,50
Bilingual Press / Editorial Bilingüe	ISBN 978-1-939743-14-5	$ 39.50

Vol. 17

Raussert, Wilfried, Brian Rozema, Yolanda Campos, and Marius Littschwager, eds. *Key Tropes in Inter-American Studies: Perspectives from the* forum for inter-american research (fiar). 2015. 374 pp.

WVT Wissenschaftlicher Verlag Trier	ISBN 978-3-86821-627-1	€ 29,50
Bilingual Press / Editorial Bilingüe	ISBN 978-1-939743-16-9	$ 39.50

Vol. 18

Mörtl, Heidrun, Josef Raab, and Olaf Kaltmeier, eds. *De/Colonization in the Americas: Continuity and Change / De/Colonización en las Américas: Cambios y continuidades*. 2021. 362 pp.

WVT Wissenschaftlicher Verlag Trier	ISBN 978-3-86821-670-7	€ 39,50
UNO University of New Orleans Press	ISBN 978-1-60801-226-8	$ 43.50

Vol. 19

Rehm, Lukas, Jochen Kemner, and Olaf Kaltmeier, eds. *Politics of Entanglement in the Americas: Connecting Transnational Flows and Local Perspectives*. 2017. 226 pp.

WVT Wissenschaftlicher Verlag Trier	ISBN 978-3-86821-675-2	€ 27,50
Bilingual Press / Editorial Bilingüe	ISBN 978-1-939743-17-6	$ 32.50

Vol. 20

Britt Arredondo, Christopher. *Imperial Idiocy: A Reflection on Forced Displacement in the Americas*. 2017. 194 pp.

WVT Wissenschaftlicher Verlag Trier	ISBN 978-3-86821-706-3	€ 26,50
Bilingual Press / Editorial Bilingüe	ISBN 978-1-939743-20-6	$ 30.00

Vol. 21

Schemien, Alexia. *Of Virgins, Curanderas, and Wrestler Saints: Un/Doing Religion in Contemporary Mexican American Literature*. 2018. 218 pp.

WVT Wissenschaftlicher Verlag Trier	ISBN 978-3-86821-724-7	€ 27,50
Bilingual Press / Editorial Bilingüe	ISBN 978-1-939743-22-0	$ 32.50

Vol. 22

Fulger, Maria Diana. *The Cuban Post-Socialist Exotic: Contemporary U.S. American Travel Narratives about Cuba.* 2020. 266 pp.

WVT Wissenschaftlicher Verlag Trier	ISBN 978-3-86821-769-8	€ 32,50
Bilingual Press / Editorial Bilingüe	ISBN 978-1-939743-27-5	$ 36.00

Vol. 23

Raussert, Wilfried, and Olaf Kaltmeier, eds. *InterAmerican Perspectives in the 21st Century. Festschrift in Honor of Josef Raab.* 2021. 320 pp.

WVT Wissenschaftlicher Verlag Trier	ISBN 978-3-86821-803-9	€ 32,50
UNO University of New Orleans Press	ISBN 978-1-60801-211-4	$ 36.00

Vol. 24

Kaltmeier, Olaf, Mirko Petersen, Wilfried Raussert, and Julia Roth, eds. *Cherishing the Past, Envisioning the Future. Entangled Practises of Heritage and Utopia in the Americas.* 2021. 176 pp.

WVT Wissenschaftlicher Verlag Trier	ISBN 978-3-86821-804-6	€ 23,50
UNO University of New Orleans Press	ISBN 978-1-60801-206-0	$ 27.50

Vol. 25

Raussert, Wilfried, and Matthi Steinitz, eds. *Black Power in Hemispheric Perspective. Movements and Cultures of Resistance in the Black Americas.* 2022. 292 pp.

WVT Wissenschaftlicher Verlag Trier	ISBN 978-3-86821-959-3	€ 35,00
UNO University of New Orleans Press	ISBN 978-1-60801-229-9	$ 37.50

Vol. 26
Raussert, Wilfried. *'What's Going On': How Music Shapes the Social.* 2021. 224 pp.
WVT Wissenschaftlicher Verlag Trier ISBN 978-3-86821-811-4 € 28,50
UNO University of New Orleans Press ISBN 978-1-60801-199-5 $ 34.00

Vol. 27
Frank-Job, Barbara. *Immigration as a Process: Temporality Concepts in Blogs of Latin American Immigrants to Québec.* 2021. 138 pp.
WVT Wissenschaftlicher Verlag Trier ISBN 978-3-86821-820-6 € 20,00
UNO University of New Orleans Press ISBN 978-1-60801-215-2 $ 24.00

Vol. 28
Roth, Julia. *Can Feminism Trump Populism? Right-Wing Trends and Intersectional Contestations in the Americas.* 2021. 168 pp.
WVT Wissenschaftlicher Verlag Trier ISBN 978-3-86821-821-3 € 23,00
UNO University of New Orleans Press ISBN 978-1-60801-205-3 $ 26.00

Vol. 30
Buitrago Valencia, Clara. *Missionaries: Migrants or Expatriates? Guatemalan Pentecostal Leaders in Los Angeles.* 2021. 236 pp.
WVT Wissenschaftlicher Verlag Trier ISBN 978-3-86821-818-3 € 28,50
UNO University of New Orleans Press ISBN 978-1-60801-210-7 $ 34.50

Vol. 31
Schwabe, Nicole. *De-Centering History Education: Creating Knowledge of Global Entanglements.* 2021. 92 pp.
WVT Wissenschaftlicher Verlag Trier ISBN 978-3-86821-828-2 € 18,00
UNO University of New Orleans Press ISBN 978-1-60801-214-5 $ 21.00

Vol. 32
Manke, Albert. *Coping with Discrimination and Exclusion. Experiences of Free Chinese Migrants in the Americas in a Transregional and Diachronic Perspective.* 2021. 162 pp.
WVT Wissenschaftlicher Verlag Trier ISBN 978-3-86821-829-9 € 23,00
UNO University of New Orleans Press ISBN 978-1-60801-207-7 $ 27.00

Vol. 33
Rohland, Eleonora. *Entangled Histories and the Environment? Socio-Environmental Transformations in the Caribbean, 1492-1800.* 2021. 92 pp.
WVT Wissenschaftlicher Verlag Trier ISBN 978-3-86821-833-6 € 18,00
UNO University of New Orleans Press ISBN 978-1-60801-208-4 $ 21.00

Vol. 34
Kaltmeier, Olaf. *National Parks from North to South. An Entangled History of Conservation and Colonization in Argentina.* 2021. 208 pp.

WVT Wissenschaftlicher Verlag Trier	ISBN 978-3-86821-834-3	€ 27,50
UNO University of New Orleans Press	ISBN 978-1-60801-204-6	$ 32.50

Vol. 35
Raussert, Wilfried. *Off the Grid. Art Practices and Public Space.* 2021. 232 pp.

WVT Wissenschaftlicher Verlag Trier	ISBN 978-3-86821-835-0	€ 29,50
UNO University of New Orleans Press	ISBN 978-1-60801-213-8	$ 34.50

Vol. 36
Ravasio, Paola. *This Train Is Not Bound for Glory. A Study of Literary Trainscapes.* 2021. 114 pp.

WVT Wissenschaftlicher Verlag Trier	ISBN 978-3-86821-836-7	€ 18,00
UNO University of New Orleans Press	ISBN 978-1-60801-216-9	$ 21.00

Vol. 37
Schäfer, Heinrich Wilhelm. *Protestant 'Sects' and the Spirit of (Anti-)Imperialism. Religious Entanglements in the Americas.* 2021. 242 pp.

WVT Wissenschaftlicher Verlag Trier	ISBN 978-3-86821-855-8	€ 29,50
UNO University of New Orleans Press	ISBN 978-1-60801-209-1	$ 34.50

Vol. 39
Stefan, Madalina. *Espacio nómada en el ensayo autobiográfico del* Accented Cinema. 2021. 228 pp.

WVT Wissenschaftlicher Verlag Trier	ISBN 978-3-86821-894-7	€ 34,50
UNO University of New Orleans Press	ISBN 978-1-60801-232-9	$ 38.00